Practice

by Simon Fischer

250

step-by-step

practice

methods

for the violin

LONDON · FRANKFURT · LEIPZIG · NEW YORK

Peters Edition Limited
10–12 Baches Street
London
N1 6DN

First published 2004
© 2004 by Hinrichsen Edition, Peters Edition Limited London
2nd impression, 2006

ISBN 1 84367 008 9

A catalogue record for this book is available from the British Library

Music-setting and typesetting by Musonix
Photographs by Simon Farrell

Cover: Juan Gris, *Violin and Glass*
Courtesy of the Fogg Art Museum, Harvard University Art Museum
Gift of Mr and Mrs Joseph Pulitzer, Jr
Photo © 2004 President and Fellows of Harvard College

Text design by c eye, London

Printed in Great Britain by Caligraving Limited, Thetford, Norfolk
Set in Adobe Systems Frutiger and Monotype Plantin

Copyright Acknowledgements

Bartók: Roumanian Folk Dances (arr. Székely)
© Copyright 1926 by Universal Edition and for the USA by Boosey & Hawkes, Inc. Copyright renewed 1953 by Boosey & Hawkes, Inc. New York. Reprinted by permission.

Bloch: Nigun
© Copyright 1924, 1940 by Carl Fischer, Inc. Copyright renewed. International Copyright Secured. All Rights Reserved. Reproduced by permission.

Elgar: Chanson de Matin
© Copyright 1899 Novello & Company Limited. Reproduced by permission.

Elgar: Sonata in E minor, op. 82
© Copyright 1919 Novello and Company Limited. Reproduced by permission.

Falla: Danse espagnole (arr. Kreisler)
Reproduced by permission of Editions Max Eschig, Paris / United Music Publishers Limited.

Glazunov: Violin Concerto
Reproduced by permission of M. P. Belaieff Musikverlag, Frankfurt.

Granados: Danse espagnole (arr. Kreisler)
© Copyright 1915 by Carl Fischer Inc., New York. Copyright renewed 1945. Reproduced by permission. All Rights Reserved.

Hubay: Bolero, op. 51 no. 3
© Copyright 1894 Bosworth & Company Limited. All Rights Reserved. Reproduced by permission.

Kreisler: Caprice Viennois, op. 2
© Copyright 1910 B. Schotts Soehne, Mainz & Carl Fischer Inc., New York. Copyright renewed 1938. Reproduced by permission of Schott for the world (excluding North America) and Carl Fischer Inc. for North America. All Rights Reserved.

Kreisler: Praeludium and Allegro
© Copyright 1910 Schott Musik International, Mainz & Carl Fischer, Inc., New York. Copyright renewed 1938. Reproduced by permission of Schott for the world (excluding North America) and Carl Fischer Inc. for North America. All Rights Reserved.

Kreisler: Sicilienne
© Copyright 1997 Schott Musik International, Mainz & Carl Fischer Inc., New York. Reproduced by permission of Schott for the world (excluding North America) and Carl Fischer Inc. for North America. All Rights Reserved.

Kreisler: Rigaudon
© Copyright 1997 Schott Musik International, Mainz & Carl Fischer Inc., New York. Reproduced by permission of Schott for the world (excluding North America) and Carl Fischer Inc. for North America. All Rights Reserved.

Kreisler: Variations on a theme of Corelli
© Copyright 1910 B. Schotts Soehne, Mainz. Copyright renewed 1938. Reproduced by permission.

Messiaen: Thème et variations
© Copyright by Alphonse Leduc, Paris. Reproduced by permission.

Moffat: Intrada
© Copyright 1921 by Schott & Co, London. Reproduced by permission.

Prokofiev: Cinq Melodies, op. 35 No 2
© Copyright 1921 by Hawkes & Son (London) Ltd. Reprinted by permission of Boosey & Hawkes Music Publishers Limited.

Prokofiev: Violin Sonata in D, op. 94 bis
© Copyright by Boosey & Hawkes Music Publishers Ltd. Reprinted by permission of Boosey & Hawkes Music Publishers Limited.

Prokofiev: Violin Concerto no. 2 in G minor, op. 63
© Copyright 1937 by Hawkes & Son (London) Ltd. Reprinted by permission of Boosey & Hawkes Music Publishers Limited.

Ravel: Tzigane
Reproduced by permission of Editions Durand S.A., Paris / United Music Publishers Limited.

Sibelius: Violin Concerto in D minor, op. 47
© Copyright 1905 by Robert Lienau, Berlin. Reproduced by permission.

Vaughan Williams: The Lark Ascending
© Copyright 1925 by Oxford University Press. Reproduced by permission.

Contents

Introduction

The music examples in *Practice*, drawn from the standard solo violin repertoire, illustrate typical musical and technical demands that arise during the normal course of playing.

What are the practice methods for?

Some of the practice methods are ways of improving tone, intonation, shifting, vibrato, relaxation, and so on. Some are ways of finding out what the problems actually are. Often we know that something is not quite right, but we do not know what it is or why; or we can get a piece only so far and then we feel stuck, and do not know what to do next to improve it.

Some of the practice methods are ways of trying to cause yourself problems, so that afterwards what you actually have to do feels easier. Some methods build and improve technique at the same time as making a specific passage easier to play, so that each time you practise them your technique grows or strengthens. Then all other passages of that type take less time to learn because they feel easier to play in the first place.

Making fast progress

Whatever stage you are at in learning a piece, the fastest progress comes from being able to look at a phrase or passage from many different angles. Then it is much easier to isolate whatever changes need to be made, either musical or technical. The more ways you have of taking a passage apart and putting it back together again, the better. *Practice* contains a large repertoire of widely varied methods, and you can quickly move from one to another, improving the phrase or passage with each new approach.

How long do they take?

Most of the practice methods should end up as something that you do for a matter of seconds, even if they take half a page to describe in words, and five minutes to do for the first time if the idea is new to you. For example, once you know how to lighten shifts by repeating them up and down very quickly (*'Trilling' shifts*, page 183), it becomes something that you do without thinking about it, as part of the normal flow of practice.

Working on a short phrase of separate-bow sixteenth-notes (semiquavers), you might check the intonation by relating each note, one at a time, to other notes or fingers (*Testing, relating, comparing,* page 207); you might play the passage with slurs instead of separate bows to make sure that the left-hand fingers are even (*Using slurs*, page 119); you might work on clarity, co-ordination and purity of tone by playing only the first note, then the first two notes, then the first three notes, etc. (*Adding one note at a time*, page 21).

Then you might improve the tone by playing the phrase at different distances from the bridge (*Playing a phrase on each soundpoint*, page 48); then you might decide to work on the bow strokes by playing the passage on open strings, without the left hand (*Bowing on open strings, fingering on adjacent strings*, page 61); and so on.

Once you are familiar with the five practice methods outlined above, you might use all of them within the space of just a few minutes. In other words, they become integrated and merged into a general, seamless, intuitive approach to practice.

Some methods take longer to do, and can use up an entire practice session. An advanced player may spend a whole day practising, say, the last movement of the Tchaikovsky Concerto in rhythms and accents (*Rhythm practice*, page 36; *Accent practice*, page 43).

One thing improving another

One practice method often improves another at the same time. After practising a passage using rhythms, accent practice feels easier to control. After practising in rhythms and accents, you are then starting at a much higher level when you go on to practise the same passage in other ways, e.g. by beginning slowly then gradually speeding up with the metronome (*Speeding up with the metronome*, page 2).

Combining practice methods

The different practice methods also become integrated when you use several at the same time. Speeding up with the metronome is good to apply to rhythm or accent practice. At the same time as tuning a double-stop passage by playing only one line at a time (*Playing one string at a time while fingering both strings*, page 225), you could also be placing the fingers with extra lightness (*Building up from **pp***, page 234), or practising in rhythms, or practising without the thumb on the neck of the violin (*Lightening the thumb*, page 230). At the same time as improving the tone by making deep, rounded accents with the bow (*Deepening the tone: pulsing*, page 54), you could be playing without vibrato (*Vibrato not as a substitute for tone*, page 133), or practising string crossings by playing them as a double stop (*Crossing early*, page 102).

Doing one thing at a time

Equally, the most effective practice often consists of doing one thing at a time, rather than trying to fix everything all at once. The different methods and approaches presented in *Practice* make it easy to take just one feature of playing and focus on it exclusively.

You may decide to work through your entire concerto looking only for chances to use more bow (*Using enough bow: exaggeration*, page 117); or concentrate only on keeping the bow near enough to the bridge (*Point of contact*, page 57); or check that you really are balancing the weight of the bow at every opportunity, rather than gripping it (*Balancing with the fourth finger*, page 255). You may decide to check intonation by going through the whole piece, thinking only about tuning the open-string notes to the open strings, and tuning all the sharps and flats to the natural directly above or below (*Uniform intonation*, page 207). You might focus on shifting, practising all the intermediate notes (*Intermediate notes*, page 160), so that afterwards – even if you forget about 'shifting' altogether, and just concentrate on the music – you have a feeling of great technical security because of the foundation work you have done.

Improving your playing overall

Part 7 (Freedom and ease) looks at ways to make playing feel easy and effortless. The ideal, achieved by many string players, is that the arms, hands and fingers remain free from any tension or strain, so that by the end of playing a symphony or a concerto they feel as light, balanced and free as they did at the beginning. The practice methods explore how to add thousands of moments of release to every phrase and passage, and to base technique on everyday principles of proportions and mechanics. There are also a few key exercises, for releasing the back and neck, to use as a part of daily practice.

Part 8 (Further essentials) touches on more general areas. *Memory* (page 292) outlines various ways to strengthen playing from memory, and how to make these a routine part of practice. The key principles of *Mental rehearsal* (page 290), which form the foundation of everything that we do on the violin, musical as well as technical, are included here.

Part 8 also includes *Technical basics* (page 297), a brief summary of some important points of technique.

Enjoying making music

The more ways you have of practising, the more you can combine them to find new, unique, personal practice routines and methods. Approached in this way, practising is an endlessly creative process. It is always stimulating, interesting and rewarding; you get fast, wide-ranging results in the shortest possible time, and achieve the ultimate aim: to be able to make music without anything getting in the way.

The great Russian violinist Nathan Milstein was once asked what he thought about while he was playing. 'Nothing, really,' he replied, 'I am just trying not to spoil the music!'

Acknowledgements

Preliminary drafts of *Practice* were shown to a number of teachers, players and students, and I am grateful for the many helpful comments I received. Particular thanks to Enrico Alvares, Raymond Fischer, Guido de Groote, Kyra Humphreys, Peter Lale, and Shirley Turner, for checking in detail through several versions of the manuscript. Shirley's help was also invaluable in choosing the photographs. Thanks also to Ian Baird, Walter Carrington, Alice Colby, Dorothy DeLay, Emanuel Hurwitz, Yfrah Neaman, Maciej Rakowski, Liz Watson, and many others, whose suggestions and encouragement for the project are gratefully acknowledged.

Thanks also to Tim McNally, of Thames Information Systems Ltd, for keeping my computer and software up-to-date and functioning.

Finally, I am very grateful to Jennifer King who modelled for the photographs.

Jennifer King marking the start of one of the photo sessions

Fast passages

part **1**

Tempo

Practising very slowly

The legendary teacher Ivan Galamian was once asked which practice method, out of all the different ways of practising, would he consider to be the very best if he could choose only one. He replied: 'Playing through at half speed, because it gives you time to think.'[1]

The benefit that comes from playing through under tempo, with the luxury of plenty of time to plan, measure and control the playing, is that when you speed up again there is still a feeling of having plenty of time.

Exactly how slowly depends on the type of piece or passage. If it is only moderately difficult, a little under tempo may be enough. If it is of great complexity and difficulty, a quarter the tempo or even slower may be appropriate. You do not have to keep to one tempo. Play some passages more slowly than others; play some notes more slowly than others within the same passage or phrase.

As well as phrases or passages, practise bigger sections under tempo as well – even whole movements at a time.

[1] See also *Playing under tempo, exaggerating expression*, page 296; *Some other ways to use playing-through practice*, no. 5, page 305.

Example 1

Beethoven: Sonata in F, op. 24 ('Spring'), *mov. 3, b. 18*

(1) Play very slowly, using a long stroke on the string.

(2) Play very slowly, using *spiccato*.

Example 2

Tchaikovsky: Concerto in D, op. 35, *mov. 1, b. 111*

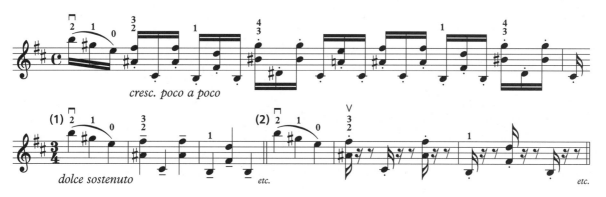

- Practise as in Example 1.

2

Practising at performance tempo

Slow practice is a quick way to learn because it gives you time to think. Another way is to play a phrase or passage over and over again *at performance tempo*.

'You cannot run before you can walk' may be true, but practising a passage at the speed you want to end up at can be one of the fastest ways to learn it.

- Practise the phrase or passage at performance tempo, even if you are in the early stages of learning it, and even if it is a struggle to get through it.

- Listen and note what happens, and decide what to do differently next time, and then repeat.

3

Speeding up with the metronome

Gradually speeding up from a slow tempo to a fast one, using a metronome, is an easy and effective way to build individual phrases or complete passages. You can also use it for playing through entire movements.

- The four main factors of playing are **pitch**, **sound**, **rhythm** and **physical ease**. Practise at each speed until:

    1 Every finger falls easily in tune

    2 Every note is clean

    3 Every note is rhythmically exact

    4 The passage feels physically comfortable and easy to play

- Then increase the metronome to the next speed – practise it again until in tune, clean, in time, and feeling easy – increase the metronome to the next speed, and so on. The ideal is to continue speeding up until you can play a passage faster than you need to play it in performance.[1]

Some different ways to speed up with the metronome:

1 Start at a slow, comfortable tempo, and speed up in such small steps that you do not notice the difference. The metronome speeds could be as follows:

♪ = 80, 84, 88, 92, 96, etc., then:

♩ = 60, 63, 66, 69, 72, etc., then:

𝅗𝅥 = 60, 63, 66, 69, 72, etc.

2 10 steps forward, 5 steps back: increase by 10, then decrease by 5, then increase by 10, etc.

♩ = 60, 70, 65, 75, 70, etc.

3 Start at a medium tempo. Then increase by, say, 5 if you play it very well; decrease by 5 if there is any improvement you could make in pitch–sound–rhythm–ease.

4 Alternate slow and fast while gradually increasing the tempo:

♪ = 80 ♩ = 80   ♪ = 84 ♩ = 84   ♪ = 88 ♩ = 88   ♪ = 92 ♩ = 92   ♪ = 96 ♩ = 96, etc.

[1] As well as practising at the speed he wanted to play at, the Russian violinist Nathan Milstein always made a point of practising the fast movements of a concerto ten points on the metronome faster than he wished to play them, and the slow movements ten points slower. After all, suppose the conductor took the orchestra much faster or slower, in any particular passage, than Milstein had expected: Milstein wanted to make sure that he would be able to play well whatever happened.

Examples

Pugnani-Kreisler: Praeludium and Allegro, *Allegro, b. 5*

Vieuxtemps: Concerto no. 5 in A minor, op. 37, *mov. 1, b. 109*

A suitable starting tempo for these examples might be ♪ = 80. If you cannot play the passage 'perfectly' at any particular tempo, it does not necessarily mean that you should not go on to the next tempo. It may be better to continue speeding up, so that when you return to a slower tempo it then feels much easier at that speed than it did originally, and you can now play it better anyway.

Fast runs: controlling the speed

Strengthen rhythmic control in fast runs by practising speeding up and slowing down. The more evenly you can make each *accelerando* or *ritardando*, the more under control the passage is. Use the following patterns:

- Slow–fast–slow

  Fast–slow–fast

  Fast–slow

  Slow–fast

See also Exercise 31, page 67.

Example 1   Bruch: Concerto no. 1 in G minor, op. 26, *mov. 1, b. 10*

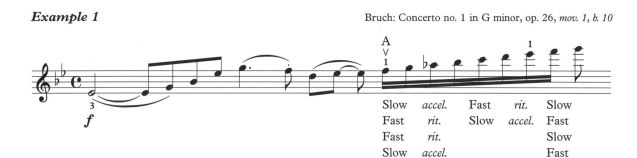

Slow	*accel.*	Fast	*rit.*	Slow
Fast	*rit.*	Slow	*accel.*	Fast
Fast	*rit.*			Slow
Slow	*accel.*			Fast

Example 2   Bruch: Scottish Fantasy, op. 46, *mov. 1 b. 37*

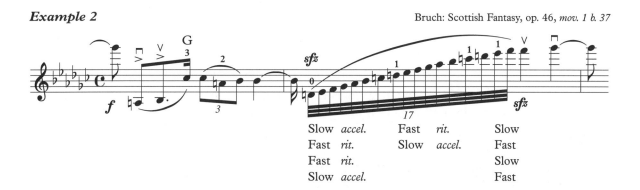

Slow	*accel.*	Fast	*rit.*	Slow
Fast	*rit.*	Slow	*accel.*	Fast
Fast	*rit.*			Slow
Slow	*accel.*			Fast

Example 3   Sarasate: Zigeunerweisen, op. 20 no. 1, *b. 40*

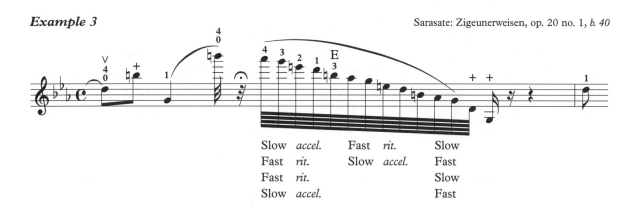

Slow	*accel.*	Fast	*rit.*	Slow
Fast	*rit.*	Slow	*accel.*	Fast
Fast	*rit.*			Slow
Slow	*accel.*			Fast

Example 4   Chausson: Poème, op. 25, *b. 151*

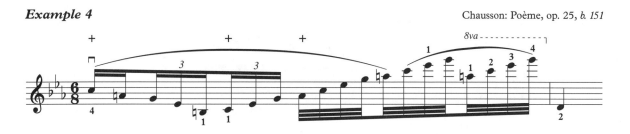

This practice method can also be used where the note values are not all the same.

- Start at any of the points marked '+', playing the speed variations from there to the end of the bar.

Keeping the fingers near to the string is good not only for fast passages, but as a general rule throughout most playing. The easiest finger action comes when the fingers 'hover' above the strings, ready to fall directly onto their notes (Fig. 1a). Lifting and dropping the finger then uses far less energy than when it moves several centimetres above and/or away from the string (Fig. 1b).

The fingers can be likened to helicopters, or vertical take-off planes, which hover above the landing-pad before landing, as opposed to ordinary aircraft which approach the runway from afar.

Fig. 1

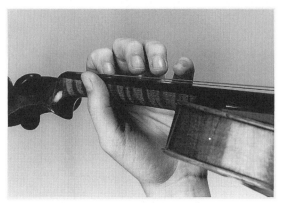

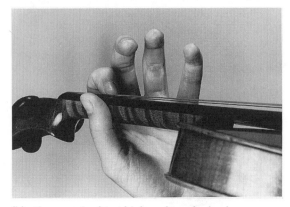

(a) **Fingers ready to fall onto their notes**

(b) **Fingers raised too high and too far back**

5 Holding down the fourth finger

Depending on the shape of the phrase, it is sometimes possible to hold the fourth finger down on an adjacent string while playing the other fingers. This may feel awkward, and you may have to play slowly, but holding down the fourth finger stops the others from lifting too far from the string. Afterwards, playing normally without holding down the fourth finger, it will feel much easier to keep the fingers close to the string.

- Playing on the E string, hold the fourth down on the A. On the G string, hold the fourth down on the D.

- On the middle strings, you can hold the fourth finger down on an upper or lower string, but the greatest benefit comes from holding it down on the lower string.

Example 1
Bériot: Scène de Ballet, op. 100, b. 70

- Play double stops, or hold the fourth finger down silently and play only the upper line:

Example 2
Sarasate: Zigeunerweisen, op. 20 no. 1, b. 13

Example 3
Schumann: Sonata in A minor, op. 105, mov. 2, b. 8

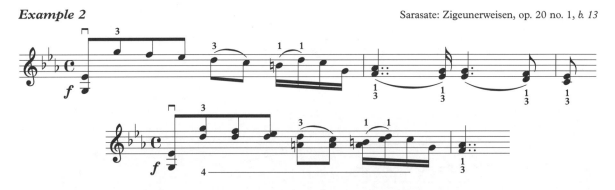

In this example the held-down finger is written as an x-note:

Practising extra-close to the string

6

- Practising by exaggeration, play with such low fingers that they barely clear the strings at all when they lift. This should cause many impurities in the tone, but afterwards lifting the fingers only a little further will seem very easy and natural.

Example 1   Mendelssohn: Concerto in E minor, op. 64, *mov. 3, b. 81*

- Begin at a slow tempo with very low fingers. Gradually increase the tempo without lifting any higher:

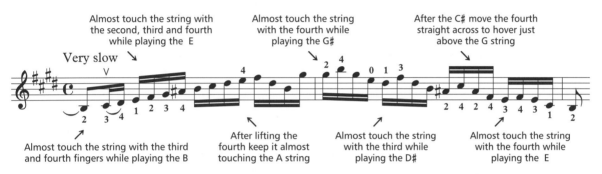

Example 2   Mozart: Concerto no. 5 in A, K219, *mov. 1, b. 49*

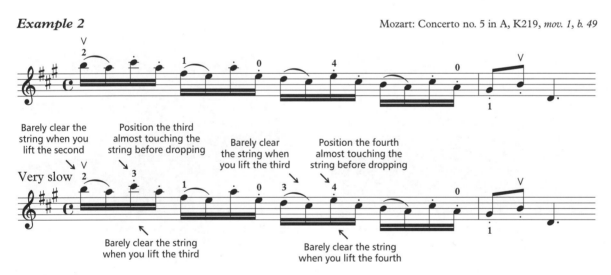

Example 3   Brahms: Sonata no. 1 in G, op. 78, *mov. 1, b. 3*

- Apply the same method to slow passages for the smoothest *legato*:

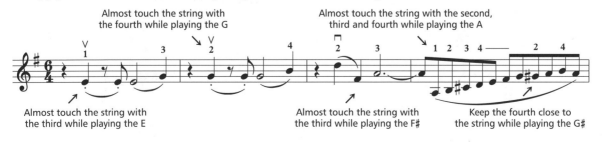

7

Staying close after a shift

Be particularly careful to keep the fingers close to the string after an ascending shift (Fig. 2a), rather than raising them upwards and outwards from the string (Fig. 2b).

- During the shift arrange the fingers into their correct spacing for the notes that immediately follow the shift.

- Arrive on the shifted-to note with the other fingers already hovering above their notes.

Example 1   Rode: Concerto no. 7 in A minor, op. 9, *mov. 1, b. 98*

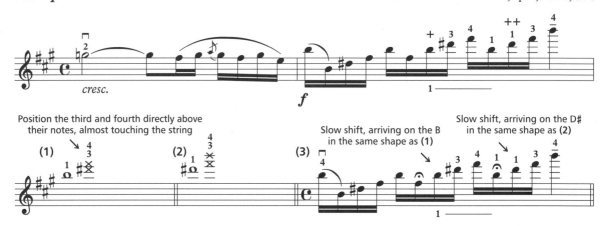

(1) Pause on the first finger B (marked '+' in the example above). During the pause, arrange the third and fourth fingers so that they are just above the string over their respective notes (Fig. 2a).

(2) Do the same while pausing on the D♯ ('++'). Positioning the third and fourth fingers just above the string, aim 'low' with the third finger to avoid its being pulled up too high by the following extended fourth finger.[1]

[1] See *Extensions: notes before and after*, page 206

(3) Pause on the note before the shift. Shift slowly to the B or D♯, changing the shape of the fingers during the shift so that you arrive in the same shape as (1).

Fig. 2

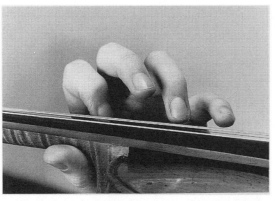

(a) **The fingers are ready just above their respective notes**

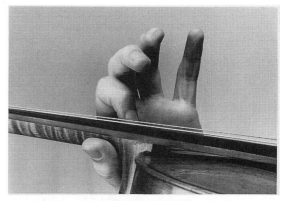

(b) **The fingers have too far to travel to reach the string**

Example 2   Sarasate: Carmen Fantasy, op. 25, *Introduction, b. 49*

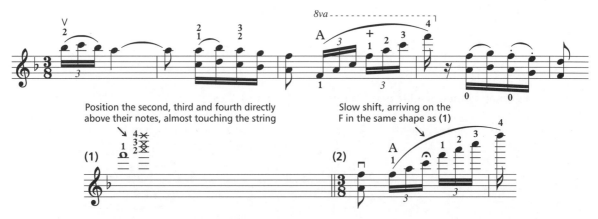

- Practise as in Example 1.

Fast fingers

'Fast fingers' is one of the most important elements of technique. It refers to the speed of dropping or raising fingers, not the speed of the passage. You can use fast fingers in slow passages.

The faster the finger drops onto the string or raises from it, the *later* the dropping or raising must begin.

The later the finger drops or raises, the *longer* the time between each finger action.

The longer the time between each action, the *slower* the passage feels.

- Play through any moderate-to-fast phrase, passage or section at a very slow tempo, while dropping and lifting the fingers very fast.

- Wait until the last possible moment before moving each finger – keep the finger still for so long that waiting just another instant would cause the note to be late; then lift or drop extremely fast.

Example 1   Vivaldi: Concerto in G minor, op. 12 no. 1, *mov. 1, b. 41*

- Play very slowly, sustaining the tone **_f_** so that the string vibrates widely. The wider the string swings from side to side, the faster the finger must drop and lift.

- Listen to the 'ping' as the fingers drop onto, or lift from, the string.[1]

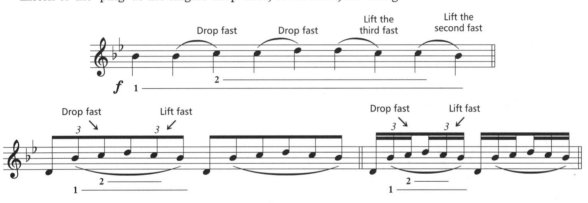

Example 2   Mozart: Concerto no. 4 in D, K218, *mov. 1, b. 47*

- Practise as in Example 1:

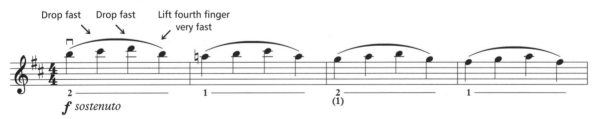

- Use fast *spiccato* or *sautillé* as a further practice method to gain the feeling of moving the fingers fast, at the last possible moment. The fingers have to lift and drop very fast to co-ordinate with the bow:

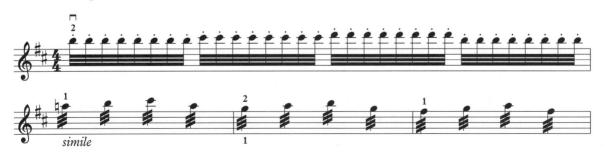

[1] Producing a 'ping' with the left fingers, while not used in *dolce* or legato passages, is also one of the keys to clarity, articulation and precision.

There are two things necessary to produce a ping:

1 Play with a ringing tone (**_mp_** to **_ff_**), the string vibrating widely and evenly.

2 Lift and drop the fingers very fast. They need to be fast (rather than heavy) so that the string changes from one length to another as quickly as possible. See *Placing fingers gently*, page 240.

Example 3

Mendelssohn: Concerto in E minor, op. 64, *mov. 1, b. 14*

When practising 'slow tempo fast fingers' place prepared fingers on the string as normal, without undue speed or impact. Fingers played with separate bows should be 'placed' fast rather than 'dropped' fast.[1]

- Play very slowly, sustaining the tone f.
- Lift and drop the fingers with exaggerated speed, listening to the 'ping' with each drop and lift-off when playing slurred notes. Begin the movement towards or away from the string at the last possible moment, a fraction of a second before the bow moves.
- Raise, drop or place all the other fingers very fast.

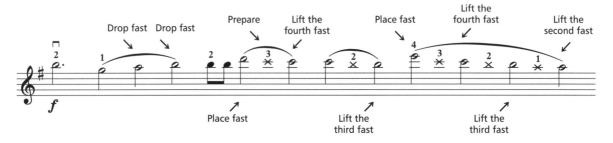

- Fast *spiccato* or *sautillé*:

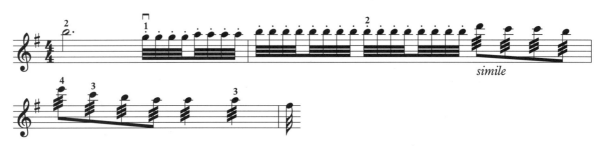

Example 4

Handel: Sonata in D, op. 1 no. 13, *mov. 2, b. 30*

- Place the fingers marked '+' on the string gently.
- Raise or place all the other fingers very fast, at the last possible moment.

- Fast *spiccato* or *sautillé*:

etc.

Example 5

Chausson: Poème, op. 25, b. 177

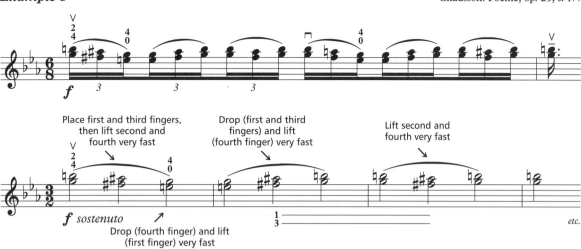

Place first and third fingers, then lift second and fourth very fast

Drop (first and third fingers) and lift (fourth finger) very fast

Lift second and fourth very fast

f sostenuto

Drop (fourth finger) and lift (first finger) very fast

etc.

- Fast *spiccato* or *sautillé*:

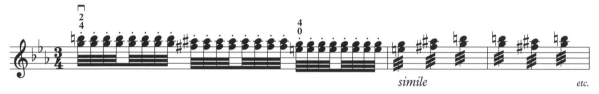

simile   *etc.*

Example 6

Wieniawski: Polonaise brillante, op. 21, b. 155

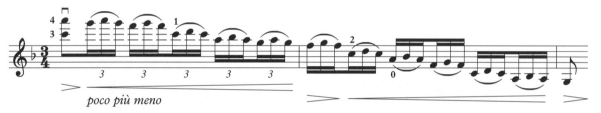

poco più meno

The dropping action should generally be fast (unless playing a specific *dolce*), but because the lift-off action is pulling against a resistance it should feel *faster* to equalize the two actions of lifting and dropping.

- While pausing on each lower note, touch the string and lift off again as quickly as if touching something very hot:

Drop and lift the fourth finger very fast

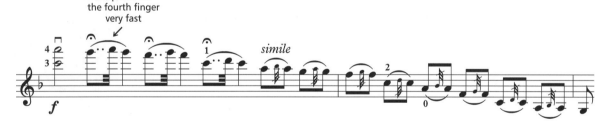

simile

- Then play the passage as written, feeling the same fast drop and lift-off.

Example 7

Sarasate: Zigeunerweisen, op. 20 no. 1, b. 7

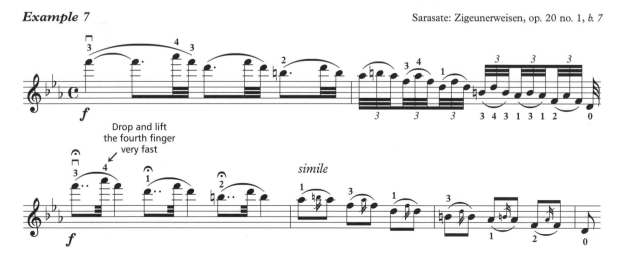

Drop and lift the fourth finger very fast

simile

Example 8   Vivaldi: Summer (The Four Seasons), op. 8 no. 2, *mov. 3, b. 48*

Fast lift-off, at the last possible moment, is often helpful in building good co-ordination:

- Play at a very slow tempo. At each '+' lift the preceding finger off the string with exaggerated speed, at the last possible moment before the bow moves.

  Pull the finger back from the base joint so quickly that you almost cannot see it move – one moment the finger is on the string, the next moment it is exaggeratedly far away from the string.

Move each finger 'back', i.e. a movement to the right, rather than 'up'. Keep the shape of the finger the same when lifted from the string as it was when on the string. See Figs. 3a and 3b.

Fig. 3

(a) **The finger exaggeratedly pulled back for practice purposes**

(b) **Do not allow the finger to straighten like this as it lifts off the string**

Example 9   Fauré: Sonata in A, op. 13, *mov. 3, b. 4*

It is often most helpful to practise separate-bow passages first with slurs.

- Play at a very slow tempo with fast fingers, listening to the 'ping' with every lift-off:

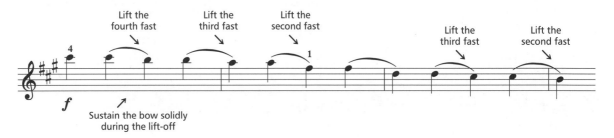

Blocks

Playing slurred notes at a slow tempo, you can raise and drop each finger as an individually directed action. As the playing gets faster, at some point a speed limit is reached making it more difficult to direct each finger individually.

To play faster, raise or drop groups of fingers together, in a fan-like shape (Fig. 4). The fingers all move at the same time in one single action, but they touch or leave the string one after another. In most cases you need a combination of individual finger actions and blocks; in the very fastest playing you can use blocks almost exclusively.

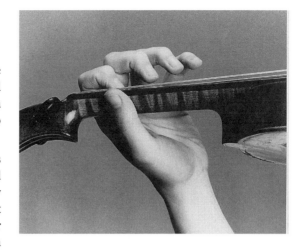

9

Fig. 4

The fingers ready to drop together as one action

Example 1

Paganini: Concerto no. 1 in D, op. 6, *mov. 1, b. 298*

Ascending

- First clarify the tone–semitone pattern of the fingers by dropping them onto the string together. This is like playing a double or triple stop on one string, so that the upper finger is the only one you actually sound, the lower fingers on the string remaining silent. Drop the fingers together as one action.

- Begin slowly, and gradually speed up:

- Then, before dropping the fingers, 'hover' the fingers above the string. Arrange the tips so that the lowest finger is closest to the string, the highest finger furthest from the string (Fig. 4).

- Drop them together as before, one action bringing both or all the fingers towards the string at the same time. Because the lower finger starts off nearer the string than the upper finger, it contacts the string an instant before the upper finger and the two notes sound very fast:

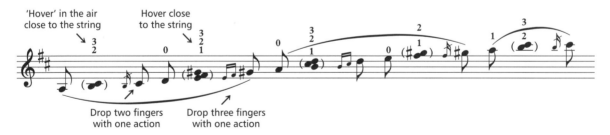

Descending

- Before lifting the fingers, arrange them all on the string in their correct tone–semitone patterns.

- Lift the fingers off the string together as one action.

- Lift the fingers at a slight angle so that the upper fingers leave the string a fraction before the lower fingers.

Example 2   Tchaikovsky: Concerto in D, op. 35, *mov. 1, b. 99*

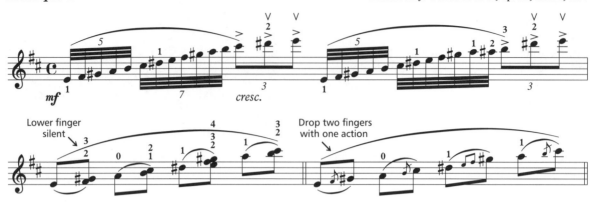

Example 3   Vivaldi: Autumn (The Four Seasons), op. 8 no. 3, *mov. 1, b. 41*

● Arrange the fingers on the string, in tune, before lifting them all off at once with one action:

Example 4   J. S. Bach: Concerto no. 2 in E, BWV1042 *mov. 1, b. 12*

Example 5   J. S. Bach: Concerto no. 2 in E, BWV1042 *mov. 3, b. 113*

Example 6 Wieniawski: Polonaise brillante, op. 21, *b. 21*

It is often helpful, and sometimes necessary, to stop the bow on the string before placing the next block or finger.

- At each '///' stop the bow on the string; place the next fingers; then continue:

Example 7 Wieniawski: Scherzo-Tarantelle, op. 16, *b. 40*

Example 8 Chausson: Poème, op. 25, *b. 176*

10 Co-ordination

Good co-ordination means that the finger completely stops the string before the bow moves, i.e. the left fingers lead and the bow follows.

When co-ordination is not good it means that the finger is a fraction of a second late, fully stopping the string only after the bow has already begun to move. Because the finger is not stopping the string completely, the note begins with 'fuzz' and lacks clarity.

- Improve co-ordination by placing the fingers a fraction of a second too early, before the bow has finished playing the previous note. This is called 'overlapping'.

After practising overlapping for only a short time, when you play the passage again normally, you will notice a dramatic improvement in co-ordination.[1]

[1] See also *Co-ordination: overlapping with the previous bow*, page 179

Example 1   Pugnani-Kreisler: Praeludium and Allegro, *Allegro, b. 3*

- Play the same length of stroke, and in the same part of the bow, as in the passage itself. Keep the bow firmly sustained in the string.

- Begin with a clear, solid extra note caused by dropping the finger 'too early':

Very smooth, sustained slurs

- Then gradually shorten the extra note until it is only a fraction of a second early – the same degree early as the finger would be late if the co-ordination were poor:

Example 2   Mozart: Concerto no. 3 in G, K216, *mov. 1, b. 106*

This method of placing the fingers slightly too early works just as well with mixed bowings of slurred and separate notes.

- Begin slowly, and gradually speed up to as fast a tempo as possible:

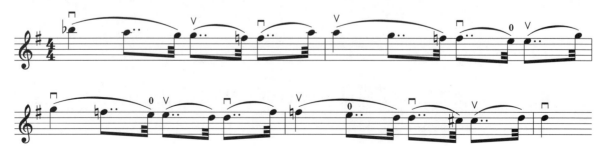

Example 3

Mendelssohn: Concerto in E minor, op. 64, *mov. 3, b. 53*

Example 4

Wieniawski: Concerto no. 2 in D minor, op. 22, *mov. 1, b. 86*

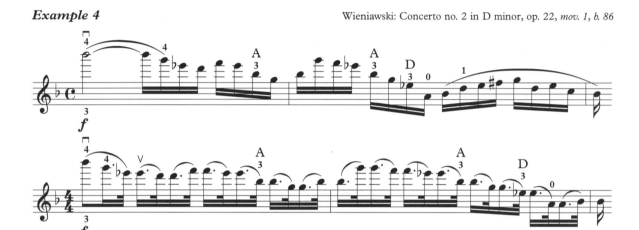

Example 5

J. S. Bach: Concerto no. 2 in E, BWV1042, *mov. 1, b. 53*

Example 6

Vivaldi: Concerto in G minor, op. 12 no. 1, *mov. 1, b. 7*

Overlapping is a general cure-all for poor co-ordination, and is equally effective when the passage is not so fast.

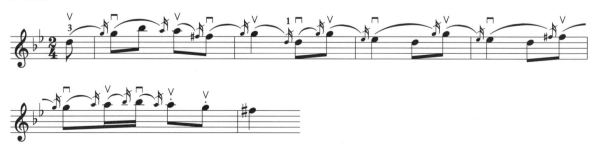

11 Loops

Play groups of notes forwards and backwards, making 'loops' that are played round and round in a circle. An extremely powerful method, this is one of the quickest ways to gain control and fluency.

There can be three notes in a loop or as many as seven or more. For example, playing in groups of five notes:

- Play the first five notes in their correct order and then play backwards, in reverse order, to the beginning again. In other words play notes 1–2–3–4–5, followed by 4–3–2.

- Repeat continuously, learning how to play the loop in tune, with an even tone, even rhythm, and with ease.

- Then do the same beginning on the second note of the passage, and so on to the end.

Example 1
Tchaikovsky: Three pieces, op. 42, *Meditation*, b. 53

- Three notes forward, one note back:

Repeat many times

simile

[1] See 'Trilling' shifts, page 183

- Because the loops both ascend and descend, 'trilling' the shifts is a particularly appropriate and effective exercise to do at the same time:[1]

ppp *Repeat many times*

- Four notes forward, two notes back:

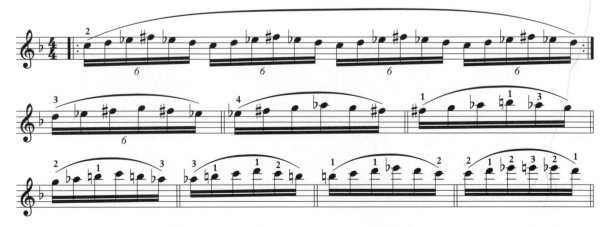

- Five notes forward, three notes back:

Example 2

Pugnani-Kreisler: Praeludium and Allegro, *Allegro, b. 101*

Practising separate-bow passages in loops, use long slurs as well as separate bows.[1]

[1] See *Using slurs,* page 119.

- Three notes forward, one note back:

- Four notes forward, two notes back:

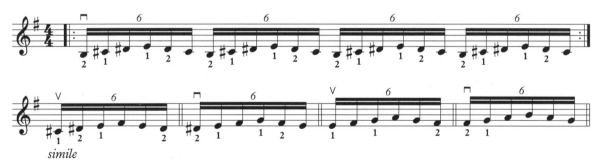

- Five notes forward, three notes back:

Example 3

Lalo: Symphonie espagnole, op. 21, *mov. 1, b. 37*

- Miss out any groups of notes that do not need loop practice, i.e. playing the loop feels so easy that there is no point in practising it. In this example any group which does not include a shift has been omitted.

- Three notes forward, one note back:

Repeat many times

simile

- Four notes forward, two notes back:

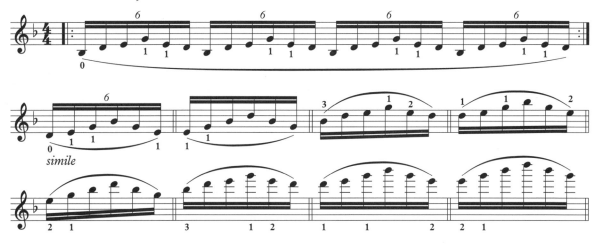

simile

- Five notes forward, three notes back:

simile

- 'Trill' the shifts:

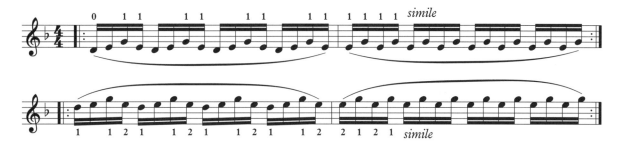

Example 4

Beethoven: Concerto in D, op. 61, *mov. 3, b. 137*

Practising in loops can also be helpful for learning bowing patterns.

- Five notes forward, three notes back:

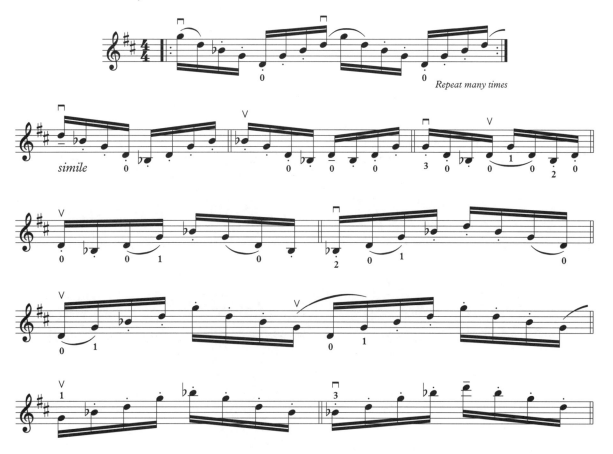

- Practise loops in rhythms and accents, for example:[1]

[1]See *Rhythm practice*, page 36; *Accent practice*, page 43

Example 5

Tchaikovsky: Concerto in D, op. 35, *mov. 3, b. 114*

- Three notes forward, one note back. First play all slurred, and then play the separate or mixed bowings:

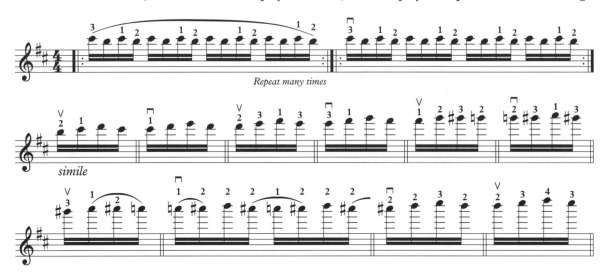

Repeat many times

simile

- Four notes forward, two notes back:

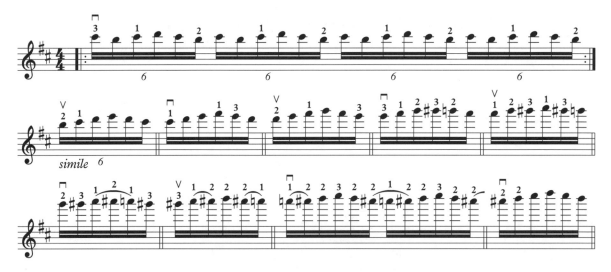

simile

- Five notes forward, three notes back:

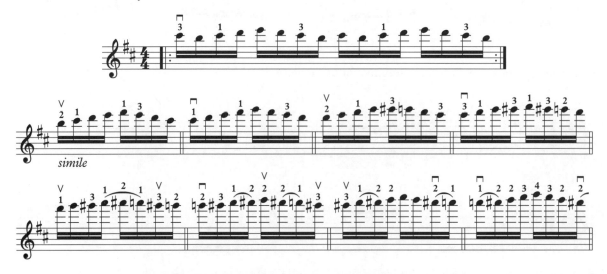

simile

Adding one note at a time

Adding one note at a time gives you the opportunity to consider each note individually. As well as being very good for building passages up technically, it is also helpful for quick memorization.

- In each of the following examples, use the same amount of bow (in the same place in the bow) as in the passage itself.

- Play with musical feeling, rather than only mechanically.

Example 1   Bruch: Concerto no. 1 in G minor, op. 26, *mov. 1, b. 152*

- Working up from the beginning, accent and lengthen each final note:

- Working down from the end:

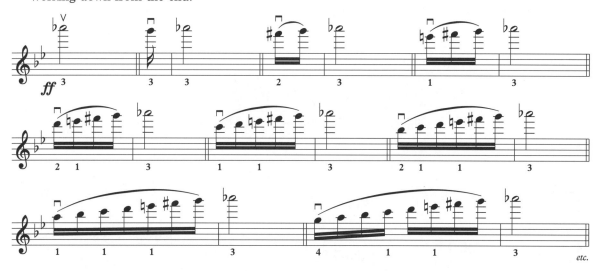

- You can also use other notes as points to work up to, or to work down from:

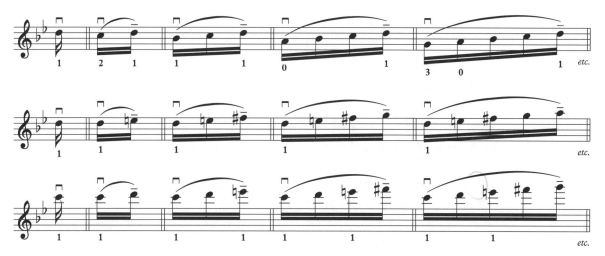

Example 2

Beethoven: Romanze in F, op. 50, *b. 28*

● Working down from the beginning, accent each final note:

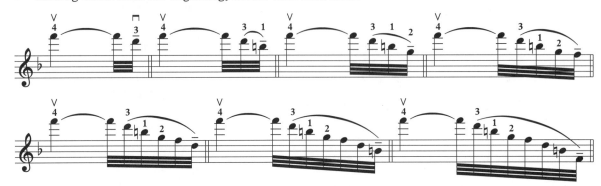

● Working up from the end:

● Working up from after the shift:

Example 3

Dvořák: Romance, op. 11, *b. 81*

Remember to use the same stroke, in the same part of the bow, as when playing the passage normally. In this case, the notes marked with dots are played with barely separated, short *détaché* strokes on the string.

● Working up from the beginning of the last phrase (marked '+' above), accent each final note:

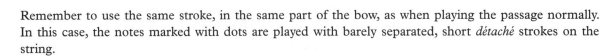

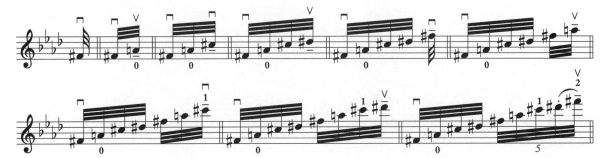

- Working down from the end:

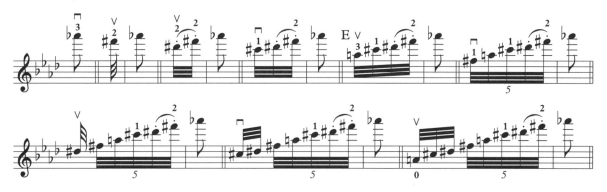

Example 4   Bloch: Nigun (no. 2 from 'Baal Shem'), b. 35

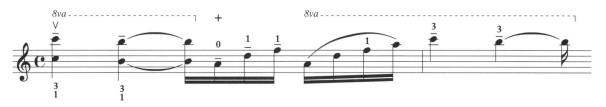

- Working up from the beginning (marked '+' above), accent each final note:

- Working down from the end:

Example 5   Chausson: Poème, op. 25, b. 298

- Working up from the beginning, accent each final note:

- Working down from the end:

13 Groups

Playing at slower speeds you can direct each note with an individual mental command. As the playing gets faster, at some point you reach a speed limit where it is impossible to direct each action individually.

To play faster, combine groups of notes into one unit, with all the notes in that unit played together under one mental command. The number of notes, or the type of note-pattern, depends on the specific passage. In general, the faster the passage, the larger the group of notes seemingly under one command.[1]

Slow speeds: One note = one unit = one mental command

Fast speeds: Two or more notes = one unit = one mental command

- Practise in beat groups, with a short pause between each.
- Feel each group of notes as 'one action', made with one mental command.
- Gradually speed up using a metronome. Begin at a moderate speed and increase to as fast a tempo as possible.

[1] The examples shown are all of fast passages, but the same principle of playing two or more notes with 'one command' naturally applies throughout almost all playing, and is one of the single most important aspects of technique and music making. It is like speaking fluently in phrases and sentences, with stresses on particular syllables or words, as opposed to pronouncing each syllable or word one at a time.

Practising in groups is also a great aid to memorization.

Example 1   Sarasate: Zigeunerweisen, op. 20 no. 1, b. 72

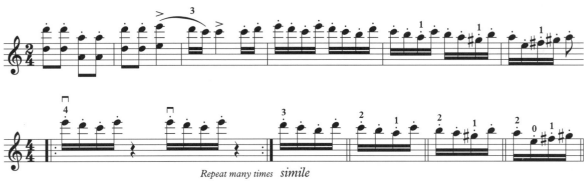

Repeat many times *simile*

- Repeat each group many times so that the actions of playing the individual notes merge into one. Finally, instead of many individual actions, it feels as if one single action plays all the notes of the group together.

Example 2   Vivaldi: Winter (The Four Seasons), op. 8 no. 4, *mov. 1, b. 26*

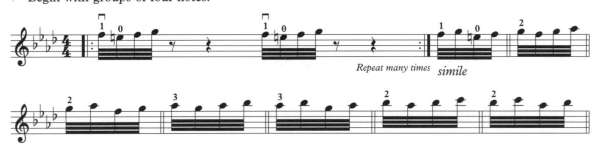

- Begin with groups of four notes:

Repeat many times *simile*

- Then build groups of eight notes, all of which can be played as 'one action', under one mental command:

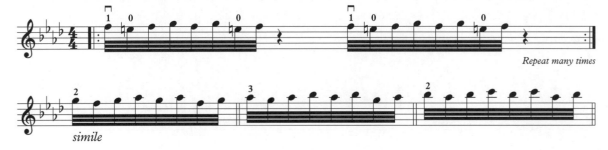

Repeat many times

simile

Example 3

Paganini: Moto perpetuo, op. 11, *b. 1*

Carry on over to the first note of the next group to build greater continuity.

- First play in groups of four notes, adding the first note of the next group.

- Repeat each group until the notes merge into one action:

- Then play in groups of eight notes, adding the first note of the next group:

Example 4

Wieniawski: Scherzo-Tarantelle, op. 16, *b. 12*

- First play groups of three notes, adding the first note of the next group. Repeat each group until the notes merge into one action.

- Then play groups of six notes, adding the first note of the next group.

Example 5

Mozart: Concerto no. 4 in D, K218, *mov. 1, b. 78*

- Practising with accents is a simple way to get the feeling of groups of notes played under one mental command. In this example aim for only four 'commands' rather than as many as sixteen:

- Then repeat without accents, but with the same feeling of each group of notes needing only one command.

Example 6

Mozart: Concerto no. 5 in A, K219, *mov. 1, b. 108*

- Otherwise playing in tempo, pause slightly between each group:

- In a typical Mozart pattern like this (two slurred, two separate), the third and fourth notes of each beat are like an up-beat to the next slurred notes. Therefore you could also practise the groups as follows:

Example 7

Vieuxtemps: Concerto no. 5 in A minor, op. 37, *mov. 1, b. 111*

In staccato runs it is especially important to reduce the number of 'commands' by thinking in bigger groups, i.e. one command for four notes instead of four commands. Then there is a feeling of the staccato 'playing itself', yet with you remaining in control of it. This is also a good way to break the run down into smaller sections for more concentrated practice on each part of the run.

- Play each group in the same part of the bow as it would be in the run.
- Practise in groups of four notes, adding the first note of the next group:

- Then put the run together, adding one group at a time. Work up from the beginning of the run:

- Also work down from the end of the run in groups of four:

Clarity

Every note in a fast passage must be clear. Clarity is more important than sheer speed, since fast passages usually sound more brilliant when played a fraction more slowly – but with every note clear – than when played a little faster but with some of the notes not clear.

Drop-outs

14

Notes that 'drop out' are notes which, in a group of notes that should be even, are played shorter and/or more quietly than the surrounding notes. The most common notes to drop out are:

1 The note before or after a change of position (Examples 1, 3, 8)

2 The note before or after a change of string (Examples 2, 4, 5, 9, 10)

3 The note before or after a change of bow (Examples 3, 4, 5, 7)

4 Prepared fingers[1] (Examples 6, 8)

5 Fingers lifted too early[2] (Examples 11, 12)

- Equalize notes that drop out by playing them *longer* and *louder* than the surrounding notes.[3]

[1] See *Placing fingers gently*, page 240

[2] See *Lifting off at the last possible moment*, page 286

[3] As with any purely technical practice method it is worth remembering that (1) if you know exactly what you want musically without overlooking a single note, and (2) if you *listen*, then such a thing as a note dropping out will occur less often in the first place.

Nevertheless, some notes need more technical strengthening than others.

Example 1   Bloch: Nigun (no. 2 from 'Baal Shem'), *b. 22*

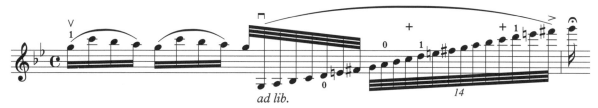

- Suppose you notice that you cannot really hear the notes before the shifts (marked '+' above), i.e. the scale comes out as follows (x-notes = the note barely sounding):

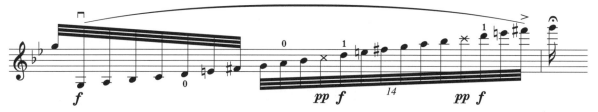

- Practise by performing the opposite; play the drop-outs longer and louder. Play the other notes up to tempo:

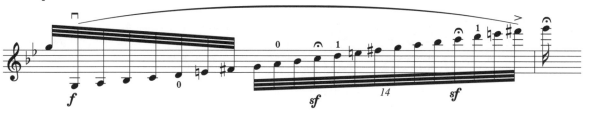

Example 2   Bruch: Concerto no. 1 in G minor, op. 26, *mov. 3, b. 27*

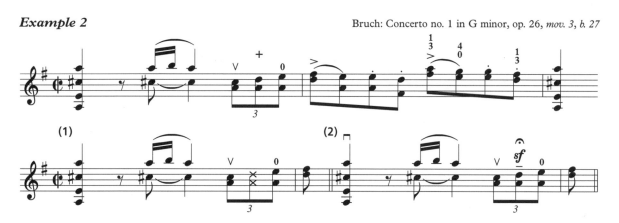

(1) The string crossing may make the middle note of the triplet weak, making the triplet come out as strong–weak–strong. The middle note may be weakened further if the third finger is not ready on the string in time before the bow. The x-notes represent the notes barely sounding.

(2) Practise playing the middle note longer and louder than the outer notes.

Example 3   Brahms: Sonata no. 3 in G minor, op. 108, *mov. 4, b. 9*

The notes before or after the shifts must be given their full musical value to avoid the passage coming out as follows (x-notes = the note barely sounding):

● Practise:

Example 4   Mendelssohn: Concerto in E minor, op. 64, *mov. 1, b. 105*

The third note of each triplet, since it occurs before a change of bow and wide string crossing, must be given its full musical value to avoid the passage coming out as follows:

● Practise:

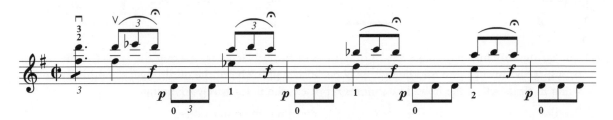

Example 5   Bériot: Concerto no. 9 in A minor, op. 104, *mov. 1, b. 62*

The second note of each triplet must be given its full musical value to avoid the passage coming out as follows:

● Practise:

Example 6   Vivaldi: Summer (The Four Seasons), op. 8 no. 2, *mov. 3, b. 116*

Except for the open strings, the second note of these slurs is a prepared finger. It will tend to drop out if the finger is not ready on the string before the higher finger lifts off.

● Practise:

● Also practise under one or two slurs:

Example 7   Vivaldi: Autumn (The Four Seasons), op. 8 no. 3, *mov. 1, b. 87*

The last note of a run should be played 'well' so that it becomes a platform on which the top note can sit.

(1) The note before a change of bow may easily drop out (x-note = the E barely sounding).

(2) Build the last note of the run by playing it extra-long and with extra tone.

Example 8

Paganini: La Campanella, op. 7, b. 105

(1) The double-stopped first finger (marked '+' in the Example) is both a prepared finger and the note before the shift. It may easily drop out completely if it is not ready on the string before the bow.

(2) Practise by accenting and sustaining the up-bow.

[1] See *Co-ordination*, page 14 **(3)** As well as pausing and accenting, put the finger down early.[1] Start slowly, and gradually speed up:

Example 9

Kreutzer: 42 Etudes ou caprices, No. 30, b. 11

(1) The B♮ (marked '+' in the example) is often lost altogether, partly because in this phrase the A string is an easily-missed middle string between the D and the E strings; partly because psychologically the player is looking ahead to gripping the E string with the bow to play the staccato fourth note.

(2) Practise by accenting and sustaining the A string.

Example 10

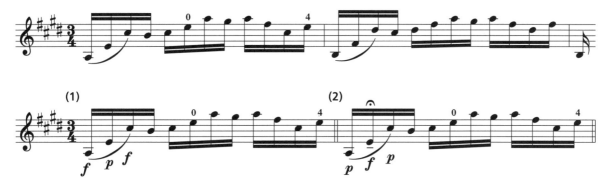

(1) The middle string of each slur must be given its full musical value to avoid the note dropping out.

(2) Sink the bow deeply into the middle string of the slur.

Example 11

Hubay: Bolero, op. 51 no. 3, *b. 49*

If the notes marked '+' are lifted too early:[1]

- Practise:

Example 12

Mozart: Concerto no. 4 in D, K218, *mov. 1, b. 59*

If the notes marked '+' are lifted too early:

- Practise:

[1] See also *Lifting off at the last possible moment*, page 286

15 Separate bows – staccato – accented legato

Use this three-step method to help every note in a slurred passage speak clearly and equally with the others:

1 **Separate bows.** Notice the clarity when you give each note a new bow. Later, each note should be as clear as this when you play with the slurs. Play expressively, rather than mechanically, as though the music were actually meant to be played with separate bows.

2 **Staccato.** Begin slowly, 'biting' the beginning of each note individually. Gradually speed up as far as you can, although it does not need to be very fast to be very effective.

For the purposes of this practice method use solid, on-the-string staccato, i.e. like a rapid series of tiny *martelé* strokes, not flying staccato (where the hair leaves the string after each note).

3 **Accented legato.** Slightly accent each note within an otherwise legato stroke.

Example 1 Bruch: Concerto no. 1 in G minor, op. 26, *mov. 2, b. 52*

1 Separate bows, on the string

2 Staccato

3 Accented legato

Example 2 J. S. Bach: Partita no. 3 in E, BWV1006, *Gavotte en Rondeau, b. 51*

- First play a separate bow on each note. Then play staccato, and then accented legato:

- Polish individual phrases:

Repeat each bar several times

Example 3   Brahms: Sonata no. 1 in G, op. 78, *mov. 3, b. 101*

- First play a separate bow on each note, either on the string or *spiccato*, and then as follows:

Example 4   Wieniawski: Concerto no. 2 in D minor, op. 22, *mov. 1, b. 115*

- First play a separate bow on each note, either on the string or *spiccato*, and then as follows:

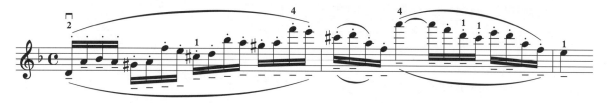

Example 5   Prokofiev: Concerto no. 2 in G minor, op. 63, *mov. 1, b. 241*

- First play a separate bow on each note, either on the string or *spiccato*, and then as follows:

16 Playing on open strings

This is a central practice method that immediately improves independence of the hands, legato bowing, and individual bowing patterns.

● Play the bowing pattern on open strings to focus on the bow without the distractions of the left hand.

Example 1

This is a well-known example of alternating clockwise and anticlockwise string crossings:

Example 2

Beethoven: Concerto in D, op. 61, *mov. 3, b. 75*

Practising on open strings is a quick way to get the feel of the unexpected string crossings in the second bar (marked '+' above):

Example 3

Prokofiev: Concerto no. 2 in G minor, op. 63, *mov. 1, b. 28*

Example 4

Beethoven: Sonata in C minor, op. 30 no. 2, *mov. 1, b. 55*

● Play on the string as well as *spiccato*:

Example 5

Pugnani-Kreisler: Praeludium and Allegro, *Allegro, b. 53*

Example 6

Brahms: Concerto in D, op. 77, *mov. 3, b. 37*

Example 7

Mozart: Sonata in E minor, K304, *mov. 1, b. 1*

- Practising on open strings is also helpful for slower passages, for example when working on the evenness and smoothness of the bow strokes:

espressivo

17 Rhythm practice

Practising in rhythms is a key practice method, and one of the fastest and easiest ways to improve many different types of medium-tempo to fast passage work. Use it on anything from short phrases to large sections at a time.

Everything in playing is a matter of 'command–response', i.e. a mental command followed by a physical response. Both the command and the response must be instantaneous: many mistakes are simply the result of there having been a delay in one or the other. When a passage is fluent it means that the mental picture is entirely clear and the fingers and bow respond at lightning speed. Then the hands and fingers seem to know on their own where they are going.

Rhythm practice works by setting the mind a series of timing and co-ordination problems to solve. In solving them the mental picture of the passage becomes clearer, and the physical response to each mental command becomes quicker.[1]

Rhythm practice is a thorough way to get rid of all drop-outs in one go.[2] It is also a quick way to memorize a phrase or a passage.

[1] 'What counts is not the strength of the muscles, but their responsiveness to the mental directive.

…The player has to present the mind-muscle unit with problems to solve, problems that proceed from the simple to the ever more complex. Any scale or passage that the player can perform with a great many different rhythms, accentuations and bowings is one that has been completely assimilated by the mind and muscles.'
Ivan Galamian: *Principles of Violin Playing and Teaching* (New Jersey, 1962), 5.

[2] See *Dropouts*, page 27

Basic rhythms

There are endless combinations and variations of rhythms you can use, but for normal practice purposes it is rarely necessary to go beyond the following simple two-note, three-note and four-note dotted patterns.

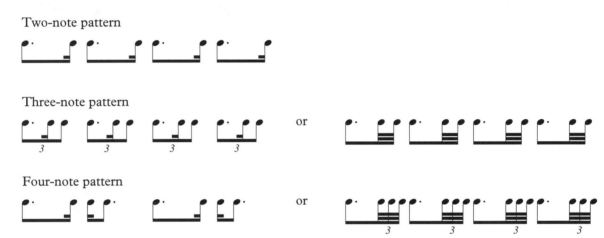

The goals of rhythm practice

The four main factors of playing are **pitch**, **sound**, **rhythm** and **physical ease**. Practise each rhythm variation until:

1 Every note is in tune

2 The tone of every note is pure

3 The rhythms are even and precise

4 The passage feels easy to play in that rhythm

Repeat the rhythm practice on many different occasions. Continue until you can play the passage in a particular rhythm pattern with each of these four key points excellent.

Timing of fingers

Rhythm practice is more effective when you move fingers at the last possible moment, rather than moving them slowly towards the string during the dotted note.

Bow stroke and place in the bow

Practise in the same part of the bow, using the same type of stroke, as you use for the passage normally.

If the passage uses a lifted stroke such as *spiccato*, practise it in rhythms using that stroke. Also practise it in rhythms using a solid stroke on the string.

If it is a separate-bow passage, the main rhythm work will normally be in separate bows; but also practise the passage in rhythms using slurs, with many notes in one bow. (See Example 3, page 38.)

Using the metronome

The goal is to be able to play a passage accurately and easily, in rhythms, without a metronome; but using one in the early stages of practice can save a lot of time. The essential thing is not to slow down or distort the rhythm in order to get round awkward groups of notes, and the metronome is a sure way to achieve this.

In Example 1 (this page) an average metronome speed for the two-note dotted rhythm might be ♩ = 110. In Example 2 (page 39) an average metronome speed might be ♩ = 100.

For very tight rhythmic control set the metronome twice as fast, i.e. in a passage that has four quarter-notes (crotchets) in a bar use the metronome in eighth-notes (quavers). Example 1 might then be played at ♪ = 220.

Combine rhythm practice with speeding-up practice.[1] Example 1 might then be played starting at ♩ = 60, and then 70, 80, 90, up to 160 or as far as possible.

[1] See *Speeding up with the metronome*, page 2

Two-note pattern

● Begin the two-note pattern on the first note of the passage, and then on the second note of the passage.

Example 1   Handel: Sonata in D, op. 1 no. 13, *mov. 2, b. 24*

♩♪ starting on the first note:

♩♪ starting on the second note. Either begin up-bow on the second note, or play the first note as an up-beat:

It is not necessary to practise the reverse of the basic dotted pairs – ♪♩· – since this is almost the same as playing ♩·♪ starting on the second note. (But see the four-note pattern on page 40.)

Example 2   Schubert: Sonata in A, op. posth. 162, *mov. 1, b. 20*

♩♪ starting on the first note:

♩♪ starting on the second note. Either begin on the second note, or play the first note as an up-beat:

Example 3   Tchaikovsky: Concerto in D, op. 35, *mov. 3, b. 53*

Before practising separate-bow passages in rhythms, it is often beneficial first to practise the rhythms slurred:

Three-note pattern

● Start three-note patterns on the first note, on the second note, and on the third note of the passage.

Example 1   Brahms: Sonata no. 3 in D minor, op. 108, *mov. 4, b. 107*

starting on the first note:

starting on the second note:

starting on the third note:

Example 2

J. S. Bach: Partita no. 3 in E, BWV1006, *Preludio, b. 36*

 starting on the first note:

 starting on the second note:

 starting on the third note:

Example 3

Bruch: Scottish Fantasy, op. 46, *mov. 3, b. 22*

 starting on the first note:

 starting on the second note:

 starting on the third note:

Example 4   Sibelius: Concerto in D minor, op. 47, *mov. 1, b. 246*

starting on the first note (marked '+' in the Example):

starting on the second note:

starting on the third note:

Four-note pattern

● Start four-note rhythm patterns on the first note, on the second note, on the third note, and on the fourth note of the passage.

Example 1   Beethoven: Concerto in D, op. 61, *mov. 1, b. 139*

starting on the first note: .

starting on the second note:

starting on the third note:

starting on the fourth note:

Example 2

J. S. Bach: Partita no. 2 in D minor, BWV1004, *Corrente, b. 7*

starting on the first note:

starting on the second note:

starting on the third note:

starting on the fourth note:

Example 3

Elgar: Sonata in E minor, op. 82, *mov. 2, b. 31*

starting on the first note:

Example 4

Fauré: Sonata in A, op. 13, *mov. 4, b. 205*

starting on the first note:

starting on the second note:

starting on the third note:

starting on the fourth note:

Accent practice

Like rhythm practice, practising with accents is one of the fastest ways to improve a passage and can be used as extensively.

18

- Use as little effort as possible to play the accents.[1]
- **Pitch, sound, rhythm, ease**: practise each accent pattern until every note is in tune, the tone of every note (including the accents) is pure, the rhythm is exact, and the accent pattern feels easy to play.
- Begin slowly, and gradually speed up to as fast a tempo as possible. (The faster the tempo, the less accent.)

Combine accent practice with speeding-up practice.[2] Accent practice is also a quick way to memorize a passage.

Basic accent patterns

- First play one accent in each group starting with the first note, and then the second, third and fourth:

- Then play two accents, on the first and second, second and third, third and fourth, and first and fourth notes:

- It may also be helpful to play accents on the first and third, and second and fourth notes:

- Create each accent not only by making the note louder than the surrounding notes, but also by making the surrounding notes quieter than the note you wish to emphasize. This avoids having to make too heavy an accent.[3]

Example 1   Mozart: Concerto no. 4 in D, K218, *mov. 1, b. 166*

The dotted notes in this passage may be played on the string, half-off, or completely off the string. Whichever stroke you eventually use, first practise the passage on the string with accents, and then off the string (with accents) if appropriate.

- Accent the first; second; third; fourth of each group:

[1] While playing each accent be alert to your hands, fingers, lower and upper arms, shoulders and neck. Make sure that you do as little as possible to make the accent – e.g. not pressing harder into the chin rest when you play a heavier bow stroke, or pressing the fingers of the accented notes harder than the non-accented ones. Make sure also that you are very relaxed *in between* accents. See *Localizing actions*, page 270.

[2] See *Speeding up with the metronome*, page 2

[3] The same applies to vibrato accents or extra vibrato expression: when you want the vibrato on a particular note to stand out, it is usually best to give less vibrato on the notes before and after – otherwise the extra vibrato that is needed to create the accent or expression can become excessive.

● Accent the first and second; second and third; third and fourth; first and fourth of each group:

● Accent the first and third; second and fourth of each group:

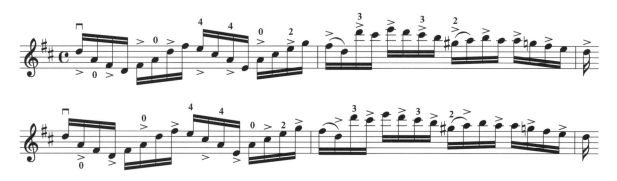

Example 2   Vivaldi: Spring (The Four Seasons), op. 8 no. 1, *mov. 1, b. 47*

● Accent the first; second; third:

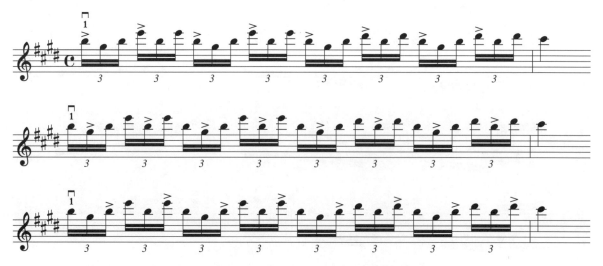

- Accent the first and second; second and third; first and third:

Example 3

J. S. Bach: Partita no. 2 in D minor, BWV1004, *Giga, b. 6*

- Accent the first; second; third notes of every group of three:

- Accent every other note starting on the first note, and starting on the second note:

- In groups of four, accent the first and second; second and third; third and fourth; first and fourth:

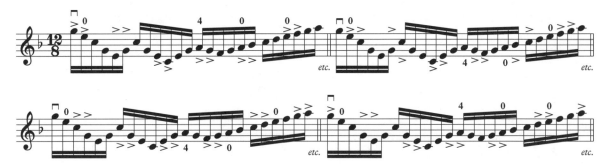

Example 4

Vaughan Williams: The Lark Ascending, *b. 3*

senza misura

● Keep the bow very evenly and smoothly sustained throughout:

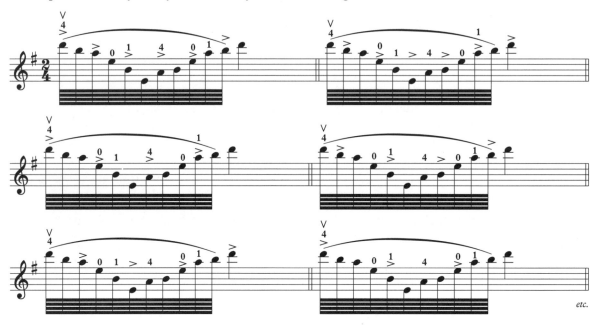

etc.

Example 5

Brahms: Concerto in D, op. 77, *mov. 1, b. 102*

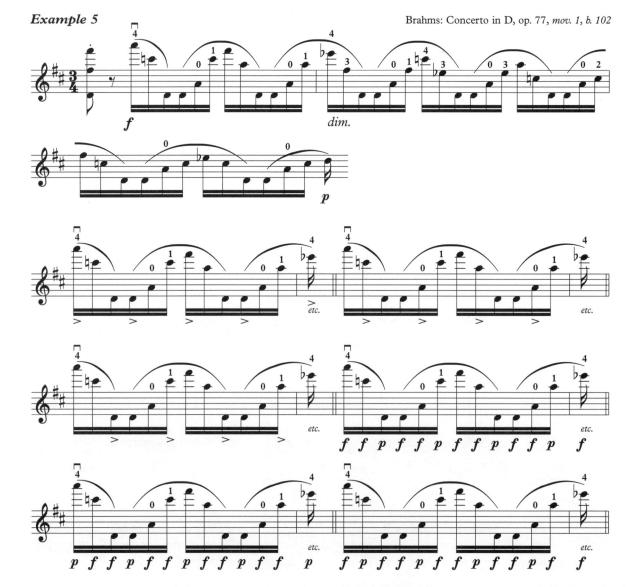

Tone

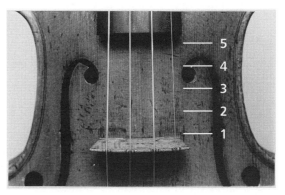

part **2**

Quality

Divide the area from the bridge to the fingerboard into five 'soundpoints' (Fig. 5):

1 Near the bridge

2 Between the bridge and the central point

3 At the central point

4 Between the central point and the fingerboard

5 At the fingerboard

Five soundpoints

Fig. 5

Near the bridge the string has a great deal of tension and feels hard under the bow. Playing in 1st position, the bow has to be very heavy and slow to engage the string. Near the fingerboard the string feels looser and softer. The bow has to be light and fast to avoid crushing the string.[1]

Every sound is the result of: (1) a particular speed of bow with (2) a particular amount of pressure. Both of these are dependent on (3) the tension of the string at that particular distance from the bridge.

At every distance from the bridge there is a certain amount of speed, combined with a certain amount of pressure, that produces the freest and, when wanted, the widest possible vibration of the string.

To get this 'widest possible vibration', tone production is based on speed of bow, not pressure. Unless darker, denser colours are required, speed of bow is always the first question, pressure the second question. Even when playing near the bridge, the flow of the bow and the distance from the bridge dictate the degree of pressure, not the other way round. The art of bowing is always one of 'stroking' the string, however heavily this must be done because of the 'hardness' of the string near the bridge, rather than of 'pressing' the string.

To avoid low-frequency, crushed or 'tearing' sounds, or to avoid flattening the pitch[2] of the notes:

● If the speed of bow does not change but you increase the pressure – move nearer the bridge

   If the speed of bow does not change but you move nearer the fingerboard – decrease pressure

● If the pressure does not change but you decrease the speed of bow – move nearer the bridge

   If the pressure does not change but you move nearer the fingerboard – increase the speed of bow

● If the soundpoint does not change but you decrease the speed of bow – decrease pressure

   If the soundpoint does not change but you increase the pressure – increase the speed of bow

To avoid high-frequency, squeaking (harmonic) sounds, or to avoid the tone losing its substance:

● If the speed of bow does not change but you decrease the pressure – move nearer the fingerboard

   If the speed of bow does not change but you move nearer the bridge – increase pressure

● If the pressure does not change but you increase the speed of bow – move nearer the fingerboard

   If the pressure does not change but you move nearer the bridge – decrease the speed of bow

● If the soundpoint does not change but you increase the speed of bow – increase pressure

   If the soundpoint does not change but you decrease the pressure – decrease the speed of bow

[1] An effective first step for elementary students is for them to press the string down with their index finger (i.e. without the bow), first on soundpoint 5 and then again on soundpoint 1. Gently pressing and releasing the string a few times makes its tension and elasticity immediately clear: looser and softer on soundpoint 5; tighter and harder on soundpoint 1.

The student should then play a few simple strokes on the same soundpoints, 'feeling' the string with the hair of the bow instead of with the index finger.

[2] See *Bow pressure and pitch*, page 60

19 Describing the sound

Describing tone is one of the fastest ways to improve tone production. The principles of tone production are simple, and almost entirely to do with proportions of speed, pressure, and soundpoint.

Scraping, tearing, crushed, lower-frequency sounds = too much pressure (or too slow).

Whistling, fizzing sounds of harmonics and high frequencies = too little pressure (or too fast).

When you describe tone in terms of proportions the description can be brief, and in most cases no more than six or seven words.

1   Play a bow stroke (a note, or a group of notes slurred), and listen closely to the sound.[1]

2   Describe the sound in terms of speed, pressure, soundpoint and evenness. For example:

'Too fast near the bridge (or too light)'

'Too heavy near the fingerboard (or too slow)'

'The right balance of speed, pressure and soundpoint until the middle of the bow; then the sound-point changed slightly and there was the crushed sound of too much pressure; then the speed, pressure and soundpoint were in balance again.'

'Good until just before changing bow when the bow speed suddenly increased, resulting in a slight whistling in the tone.'

3   Repeat the bow stroke, listen, describe, and so on. Continue until the stroke is exactly as desired and the tone is entirely free of blemish.

Describing sound in terms of speed, pressure and soundpoint quickly becomes both automatic and immediate. Having gone through the process of using words, you soon find yourself doing the same thing unconsciously, from moment to moment of playing.

[1] See also *Improving listening*, page 56

20 Playing a phrase on each soundpoint

Learning a phrase or passage on all five soundpoints, one soundpoint at a time, is one of the 'master methods' of practice on any string instrument. It instantly increases your sensitivity to the feel of the bow in the string so that you immediately gain the finest control. Practising on all five soundpoints is helpful whatever the soundpoint you will eventually use, and whatever the stroke.[2]

You can practise individual notes and phrases on each soundpoint one at a time, or you can play through entire pieces all on one soundpoint at a time. Work on soundpoints brings remarkably fast improvement in tone and control however it is used.

[2] See also *Soundpoint*, page 94

Example 1   Corelli (arr. Léonard): La Follia, op. 5 no. 12, b. 1

- Begin on **soundpoint 5**. Use fast, light strokes. Experiment with the proportions of speed and pressure, trying a little faster bow speed, a little slower, a little heavier, a little lighter, until you are sure that the string is vibrating as widely as possible during each note, with a ringing, resonant tone.

- Repeat on **soundpoint 4**. Although still fast and light, the strokes are now slightly slower and heavier than on soundpoint 5. By experimenting as before, find exactly the right speed and pressure to make the strings vibrate as widely and as evenly as possible on each note.

- Repeat on **soundpoint 3**. By now the bow pressure is significantly heavier than it was on soundpoint 5, and the speed of bow slower.

- Repeat on **soundpoint 2**. Now the weight of bow may be considerable, and the speed of bow much slower. Sink the bow heavily into the strings, feeling the different give of the hair and wood in different parts of the bow.[3]

[3] See also *Different qualities of the bow at heel and point*, page 69

- Repeat on **soundpoint 1** with as slow and heavy a bow as necessary. Note that it is often possible (and desirable) to play near the bridge with quite a light stroke.

- Having arrived on soundpoint 1, repeat again on soundpoints 2, 3 and 4, finally arriving back on 5.

In most cases it is possible to find proportions of speed, pressure and soundpoint that work, especially since you are always completely free to vary the tempo and the dynamics as much as necessary.

Example 2   Mozart: Concerto no. 2 in D, K211, *mov. 1, b. 22*

- On the E string you have to bow extremely lightly on soundpoint 5. If the string is simply too soft to play there, or the bow is scraping against the corner of the violin, squeeze the soundpoints closer together so that soundpoint 5 is a little closer to the bridge.

- Practise the first phrase:

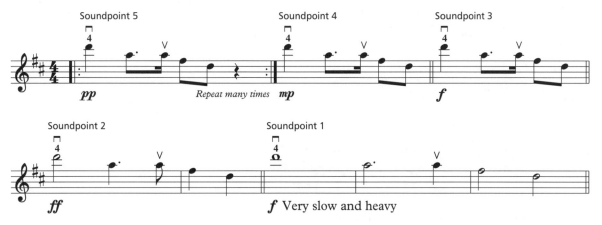

- Practise the next phrase in the same way:

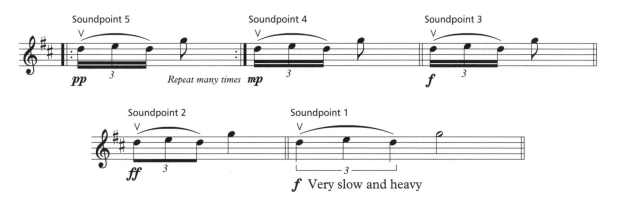

Example 3

J. S. Bach: Sonata no. 1 in G minor, BWV 1001, *Presto, b.1*

1 See *The higher the string, the nearer the bridge,* page 58

- In low positions the G string feels too hard near the bridge so you have to play very slowly and heavily, sometimes slowing the bow almost to a halt.[1] If a specific passage simply cannot be played there, or if there is little to be gained from doing so, then go only as far as soundpoint 2:

Example 4

Schubert: Sonatina in A minor, op. 137 no. 2, *mov. 4, b. 63*

2 See *Height and length,* page 93

Although the primary proportions to consider in *spiccato* are height and length,[2] in the moment that the hair is in contact with the string the usual proportions of speed, pressure and soundpoint apply.

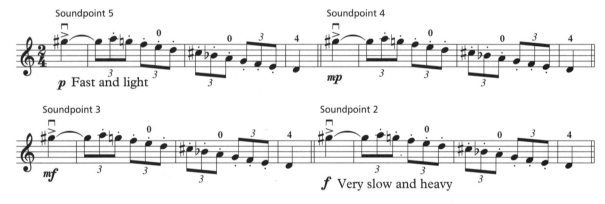

Example 5

Elgar: Chanson de Matin, *b. 30*

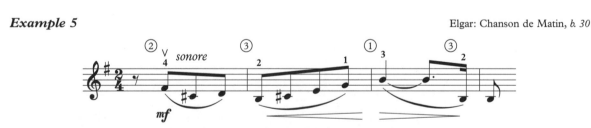

①②③ = approximate soundpoints which might be used in this passage.

- Play on each soundpoint, one at a time, to develop tone and 'feel', even when the soundpoint does not stay the same in the actual passage.

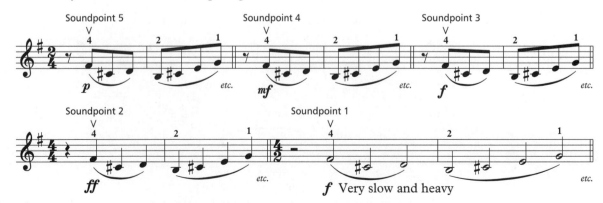

Example 6

Brahms: Sonata no. 3 in D minor, op. 108, *mov. 1, b. 1*

p sotto voce ma espressivo

- Practising on each soundpoint is good whatever the dynamic of the actual passage. This passage is probably best played somewhere around soundpoint 3–2. Even so, practise on all five soundpoints:

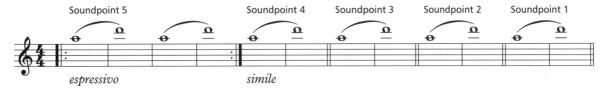

espressivo   *simile*

Example 7

Bruch: Concerto no. 1 in G minor, op. 26, *mov. 3, b. 237*

f espr.   *ff*

Practise high-position passages on each soundpoint from the fingerboard to the bridge, even though the short string-length means you should be near the bridge.[1] You simply have to play extremely lightly near the fingerboard to get proportions of speed, pressure and soundpoint that work.

Another approach is to begin nearer the bridge and squeeze the five soundpoints closer together. In this passage soundpoint 5 may have to be midway between the bridge and the fingerboard, i.e. the old soundpoint 3:

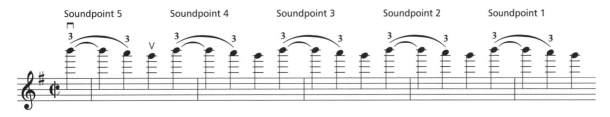

[1] See *The shorter the string, the nearer the bridge*, page 59

Example 8

Brahms: Concerto in D, op. 77, *mov. 3, b. 262*

f

- Take a rhythmic feature of a passage and repeat it on one note, on each soundpoint.
- Whatever the soundpoint you will use in the end (in this case beginning between 3 and 2 and ending up between 2 and 1) experiment with the speed and pressure on all five soundpoints to explore the whole range of the bow's depth of contact with the string.
- Use exactly the same type of stroke and length of bow as in the passage.
- On each soundpoint find the balance of speed and pressure that makes the string vibrate the widest.

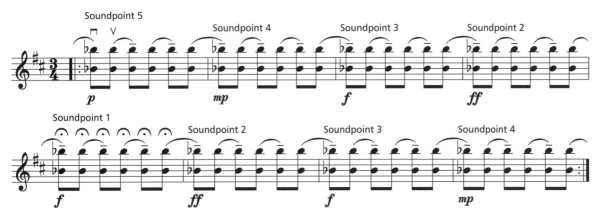

21 Building individual notes

- Practise selected notes on their own. Experiment with speed of bow, pressure and distance from the bridge until finding the desired tone quality.
- Then add vibrato.

Example 1   Sarasate: Playera, op. 23 no. 1, *b. 4*

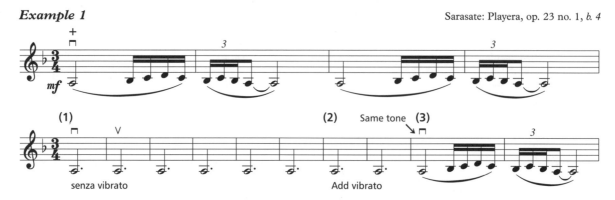

(1) Play without vibrato. Experiment with different distances from the bridge, with different bow speeds and pressures, to find exactly the desired tone.

Hear the music in your mind: during the third beat of the down-bow, imagine the sixteenth-notes (semiquavers) and 'feel' them in the contact of the bow and the string. During the first beat of the up-bow, imagine the triplet and the tied A.

(2) When you are completely satisfied with the tone quality and expressiveness throughout the whole length of the stroke, add vibrato without changing anything else: keep the speed–pressure–soundpoint design of the stroke exactly the same as before.

(3) Then without stopping, play straight in to the passage itself, finding exactly the same tone as before.

Example 2   Dvořák: Sonatina in G, op. 100, *mov. 1, b. 1*

- The strokes here are fast–slow, heavy–light, and slightly shortened.

(1) Play without vibrato. Experiment with different distances from the bridge, with different bow speeds and pressures, to find exactly the desired character, tone and type of stroke.

(2) Playing straight from (**1**) into (**2**) without stopping, add vibrato without changing anything else – keep the speed–pressure–soundpoint design of the stroke exactly the same as before. The vibrato should be fast–slow and wide–narrow because of the fast–slow and heavy–light bow stroke.[1]

[1] See *Vibrato accents,* page 89, 138

Example 3   Pugnani-Kreisler: Praeludium and Allegro, *Praeludium, b. 21*

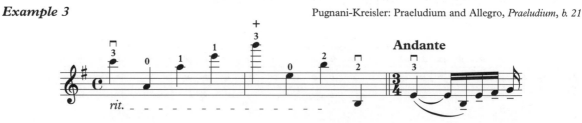

- Practise the top B on its own. Play whole bows close to the bridge. Play with the same intensity and attack as if you were in the middle of an exciting performance.
- First play without vibrato, experimenting with bow speed and pressure to find exactly the right combination to make the string vibrate the widest.
- Then add vibrato.

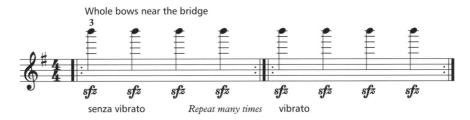

Example 4

Mozart: Sonata in E minor, K304, *mov. 2, b. 101*

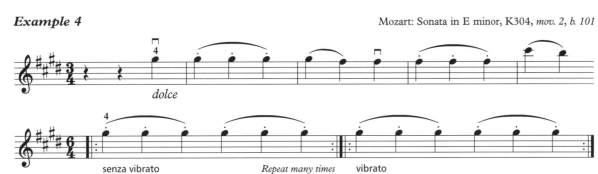

- Without vibrato play the three G♯'s many times while experimenting with the feel and tone on different soundpoints. Adjust the speed and pressure on each soundpoint until you find exactly the desired tone quality.

  The bow speed will be slightly fast–slow, the pressure slightly heavy–light, with a space between the strokes.

- Then add vibrato.

Example 5

Ysaÿe: Sonata, op. 27 no. 4, *mov. 1, b. 1*

- First, use the entire bow length. Play near the bridge, playing deeply into the elasticity of the wood of the bow, hair, and string. Adjust the speed and pressure until you find exactly the desired tone quality. Then add vibrato.

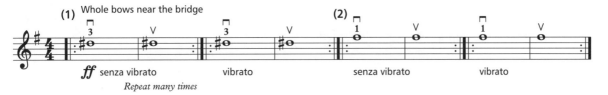

- Then using this tone as a model, practise the note in context with the right amount of bow, aiming to produce the same quality.

Example 6

Brahms: Scherzo (Sonatensatz), WoO2, *b. 1*

- Experiment at different distances from the bridge to find the ideal soundpoint:

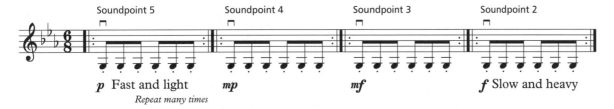

Example 7   Brahms: Concerto in D, op. 77, *mov. 3, b. 65*

The C (marked '+') needs to be played close to the bridge. Find how to make the string vibrate widely and freely on other soundpoints to sensitize the arm and hand to the feel of the bow in the string.

The string length of such a high note is too short to play near the fingerboard, but you could start at around soundpoint 3.

- At each soundpoint first play without vibrato. Find exactly the right amount of speed and pressure to make the string vibrate widely and freely.

- Then add vibrato without in any way changing the combination of soundpoint, speed and pressure.

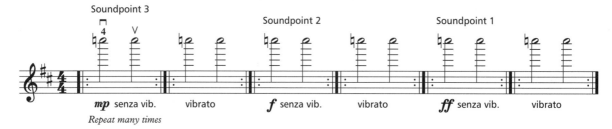

Example 8   Saint-Saëns: Concerto no. 3 in B minor, op. 61, *mov. 1, b. 28*

- Experiment at different distances from the bridge to find the ideal soundpoint:

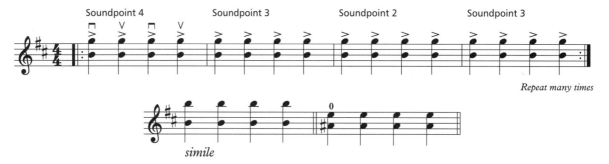

- Then find exactly the same tone and contact with the string when playing the double stop in context.

22 **Deepening the tone: pulsing**

Tone production is usually based on speed of bow, not pressure (as outlined on page 47). Nevertheless, when required the bow must sink deeply into the string for largeness and fullness of tone and to create great musical stature. As often as not, we need to play right down into the belly of the violin, as it were, rather than playing purely horizontally 'along the surface of the string'.

- Play smooth, deep accents within an unbroken legato stroke, making a throbbing or 'pulsing' effect.

   Begin each accent not with a sharp attack, but by sinking the bow deeply into the string. The tone of each pulse should be deep, rich and entirely free of scratch, scrape or bite.

   Play near enough to the bridge for the string to be able to take the weight of the bow. Experimenting with speed of bow and pressure, and feeling the give of the wood of the bow, hair and string, see how deeply into the string you can go without breaking the tone.

   Begin at a moderate tempo, later playing a little faster.

- Then play without the pulses. The point of the exercise is to keep the same depth of contact, through-out the whole length of the bow, as that which you had at the deepest point of each individual pulse.

Example 1

Glazunov: Concerto in A minor, op. 82, *mov. 1, b. 1*

dolce espressivo

- Each sixteenth-note (semiquaver) represents one smooth, rounded accent played deeply into the string:

espressivo

Example 2

Wieniawski: Concerto no. 2 in D minor, op. 22, *mov. 2, b. 1*

p semplice

- Do not release the bow too much between pulses, so that there is a feeling of deep *sostenuto* throughout.
- See how deeply you can bow into the string with each pulse – not because you want to play loudly in the end, but because you want to explore all the different feelings of the contact of the hair with the string.

espressivo

Example 3

Brahms: Sonata no. 3 in D minor, op. 108, *mov. 2, b. 1*

espress.

- Begin with two pulses on each sixteenth-note:

espressivo

- Playing slower than the usual tempo, repeat with four pulses on each sixteenth-note:

Example 4

Mozart, Concerto no. 5 in A, K219, *mov. 1, b. 46*

- Playing slowly, feel the hair sinking deeply into the string with each note:

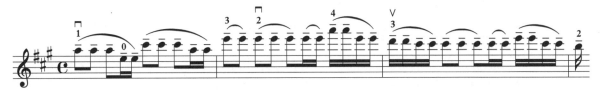

23

Improving listening

Listening is the single most important element of playing a musical instrument. If you do nothing else but improve your listening, so that you 'hang your ears on the sound' and are able to catch every sound that comes out of the instrument, this alone improves the overall standard of playing immediately and dramatically.[1]

[1] See also *Describing the sound*, page 48

One way of thinking about sound is that it gives you instant 'feedback' on what you are doing to the instrument. There is a difference between 'instant feedback' and 'delayed feedback':

> You are driving a car and you turn the steering wheel anti-clockwise. You can see the car turning to the left. The degree of turn is fed back to you so that you can adjust your movement of the steering wheel in order to obtain the effect you want. Your hand is on the tiller of a boat. You move the tiller one way ... but the boat is slow to respond so you push the tiller further over. Then the boat starts to turn and as it turns too much you push the tiller the other way. The boat swings wildly from side to side because you cannot adjust your movement of the tiller to give the right amount of turn. This is because there is a delay in the effect of your action being fed back to you. The same thing happens in a shower bath. You open the hot tap but the shower still seems cold, so you open the hot tap further. Suddenly the shower scalds you ... Because there is a delay in the feedback it is difficult to get the temperature right. [2]

[2] Edward de Bono: *Wordpower* (Penguin Books Ltd. 1979), page 99

'Listening' enables us to gain complete control because in effect we are using the instant feedback of the sound to adjust what we are doing from second to second of playing.

The question is, what do we listen to in the sound? The tone of a string instrument is made up of many different sounds. These include sympathetic vibrations, harmonics and overtones,[3] acoustic beats, vibrato 'throbs' or 'pulses',[4] extraneous sounds of too much or too little bow pressure or speed,[5] surface noise – as well as the sound of shifts, the 'ping' as fingers drop or lift,[6] bow changes, and so on. All of these sounds are clearly audible to the player even if many may not be apparent to the audience.

[3] See *Using the 'third tone' as a point of reference*, page 218

[4] See *Vibrato pulsing*, page 130

[5] See page 47

[6] See Example 1, page 7

- Improve listening by using some of these qualities of sound to 'hook' your attention on to: concentrate on one aspect of sound at a time while playing through a phrase or short passage.

Background resonance

Background resonance can be heard in the ringing-on of the tone after the bow is lifted from the string. This is most audible on open strings (but see margin note 2, page 140). You can also hear it *while* the bow is playing, the non-stop background resonance being clearly distinct from the principal sound.

- Listen to the ring carrying on during sustained notes, or between lifted strokes like *spiccato*; listen during changes of bow or string, and so on.

Sympathetic vibrations

Stopped A's, G's, D's and E's cause the open strings to vibrate in sympathy. Play first-finger A on the G string and see how the open A string vibrates. Notice how the tone has a tight, closed quality when the stopping finger is even slightly sharp or flat (even though the open string may still vibrate visibly). When the finger is right in the middle of the note, the open string vibrates the widest and the note has a broad, open quality.

- Stop and listen to every stopped G, D, A or E. Adjust the note (roll the finger very slightly above and below the note) to find the pitch that makes the open string vibrate the widest.

Surface noise

The sound of the hair's friction with the strings is another sound completely distinct from the principal sound. The closer to the bridge you play and the higher the left hand position, the louder the background surface noise.

- Play a few notes and listen to the surface noise. The more regular you can make it, i.e. the more even the volume and texture of the surface noise, the better the principal sound will be.

Acoustic beats

1 Play A on the D string in unison with the open A. Sustain both notes deeply in the string, one centimetre from the bridge, drawing the bow very evenly and balancing it equally on both strings.

2 Move the stopped A very slightly out of tune. Listen to the steady, rhythmic throb that this produces. The bigger the difference between the two notes, the faster the beat. When the two notes are exactly the same pitch, there is no beat.

3 Gradually move the finger lower on the D string, pausing on different pitches to hear the beat getting faster and faster. Continue until the finger reaches F♯. Even with the notes this wide apart, you can still hear them as a very fast beat.

A perfectly in-tune octave does not have a beat. An in-tune perfect fifth does have a beat, but while you are tuning the violin listen to the beat getting faster and slower as you move the pegs.

Instead of one player producing acoustic beats with an out-of-tune unison, two players can achieve the same effect playing one note each, even if they stand a large distance apart.

- Concentrate on one double stop at a time. Hear the two notes as an acoustic beat, rather than hearing only the two separate notes themselves.

Joins between strokes

The string stops vibrating for an instant when the bow changes direction (play separate bows on the open G and look at the string in the middle), so four quarter-notes (crotchets) played with separate bows will never sound like a whole-note (semibreve). You can sometimes create an illusion of one, unbroken sound at the bow change, depending on the acoustic you are playing in, especially if the note changes at the same time as the bow.

- Listen to each join from down-bow to up, or up-bow to down. If there is a space between the strokes, listen to the sound quality at the very end of one stroke, the silence in between, and the quality at the very beginning of the next stroke.

- If playing legato, try to create the illusion of a continuous tone through the bow change, resulting in a seamless connection. This depends very much on good co-ordination, since many impurities of tone at the bow change are due to the finger being late more than anything to do with the bow.[1]

Sound of shifting

- Listen to the sound of the finger moving lightly along the string. The instant feedback it provides means you always know exactly where you are and can easily arrive on the new note perfectly in tune.

[1] See *Co-ordination*, page 14

Point of contact

It is essential to avoid bowing too near the fingerboard too much of the time. Playing near the fingerboard is the place of least effort for the bow and strings so the bow automatically moves there, following the line of least resistance, unless you actively prevent it from doing so. Cellists need constantly to push in towards the bridge; violinists need constantly to pull in towards the bridge.

Nearer the bridge, the bow is able to sink more deeply into the string or to 'bite' the beginning of a note, allowing all kinds of accents and articulations that are impossible nearer the fingerboard where the string is much softer.[2]

Angle of strings to the floor

The neck and the body of the violin are joined at an angle. If the body is parallel to the floor the strings slope down away from the bridge (Fig. 6a). There is then a natural tendency for the bow to slide down towards the fingerboard. Note the sharp angle of the strings to the floor if the body of the violin itself slopes down (Fig. 6b).

To counteract this, hold the scroll higher so that the strings, not the body of the violin, are parallel with the floor (Fig. 6c). At times it helps keep the bow near the bridge if you raise the scroll even higher, so that the strings actually slope down towards the bridge (Fig. 6d).

- Play for extended periods with the scroll exaggeratedly high, or at least as shown in Fig. 6c.[3]

[2] No colours should be excluded, and playing only near the bridge is as undesirable as playing only near the fingerboard. But as well as possible weakness of tone or attack, if you habitually play too near the fingerboard there may also be an uncomfortable feeling of having always to hold back, since the bow cannot sink deeply into the string without the sound breaking.

Fig. 6

[3] Teachers of elementary students sometimes use a ping-pong ball to help children learn the feeling of keeping the violin in playing position. The strings must be level for the ball to stay in one place, without rolling backwards and forwards.

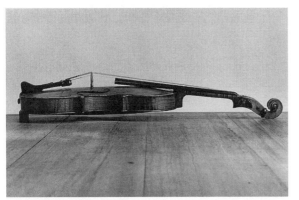

(a) Violin level with the floor: the strings slope down away from the bridge

(b) Note the sharp slope of the strings if the violin itself slopes down

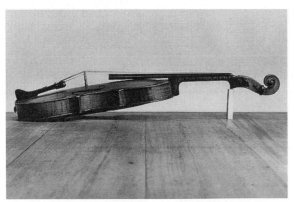

(c) The violin has to slope up for the strings to be level with the floor

(d) Raising the scroll makes the strings slope towards the bridge

25 The higher the string, the nearer the bridge

¹ See Fig. 5, page 47

Which soundpoint[1] to use depends not only on context and personal taste, but on the physical properties of the strings. In 1st position near the bridge the G string feels too hard under the bow. Near the fingerboard the E string feels too soft, unless the very lightest *flautando* is required.

Leaving aside musical considerations, the optimum places to bow the open strings are roughly as follows:

The same basic proportions then apply to stopped notes on each string.

● Practising by exaggeration, begin further from the bridge than normal, and gradually move in closer to the bridge than normal. Afterwards, the correct amount of change will feel entirely natural and automatic.

 ① ② ③ ④ ⑤ = soundpoints

Example 1   J. S. Bach: Concerto no. 1 in A minor, BWV1041, *mov. 1, b. 126*

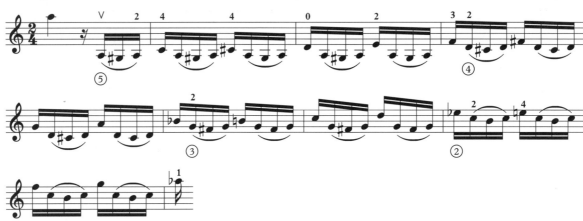

● Exaggerate the change of soundpoint by beginning far from the bridge. Gradually move closer to the bridge throughout the passage.

Example 2   Mozart: Concerto no. 5 in A, K219, *mov. 1, b. 44*

● Make the new colour on the top A by playing closer to the bridge.

Example 3   Kreutzer: Etudes ou caprices, No. 31, *b. 5*

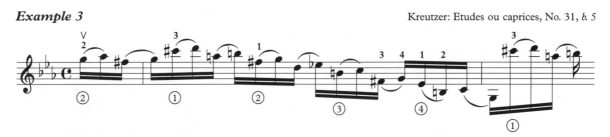

● After exaggerating the soundpoints the correct degree of movement will feel natural and automatic.

Example 4   Saint-Saëns: Concerto no. 3 in B minor, op. 61, *mov. 1, b. 43*

The shorter the string, the nearer the bridge

To keep the right proportions of bow speed, pressure and distance from the bridge, the bow should usually move closer to the bridge as the left hand plays higher up the fingerboard. Long shifts (i.e. big changes of string length from long to short) often require a visibly obvious movement of the bow towards the bridge.[1]

[1] See *Length of string and soundpoint*, page 297

The shorter the string length the less weight the string can take from the bow. Therefore, although the rule is that the nearer the bow is to the bridge the more weight it must inject into the string, when playing high notes the bow must play *lightly* near the bridge, even when playing f.

- Exaggerate the change of soundpoint by beginning nearer to the fingerboard, and moving closer to the bridge, than you need do ordinarily. Afterwards, the correct degree of movement will feel entirely natural and automatic.

① ② ③ ④ ⑤ = soundpoints

Example 1   Wieniawski: Légende, op. 17, *b. 144*

- Play the B♭ (marked '+') softly, very close to the bridge, with a pure tone. Gradually play more heavily:

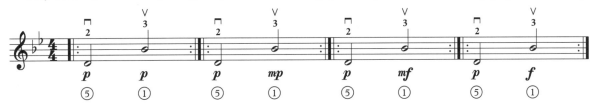

Example 2   Tchaikovsky: Three Pieces, op. 42, *Meditation, b. 77*

- Exaggerating the change of soundpoint, play the trill very lightly and close to the bridge.

Example 3   Sibelius: Concerto in D minor, op. 47, mov. 1, *b. 101*

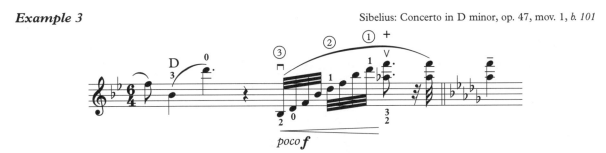

- Double stops can take more weight from the bow because it is shared between the two strings. Play the double stop marked '+' very deeply into the string, close to the bridge.

Example 4   Vieuxtemps: Concerto no. 5 in A minor, op. 37, *mov. 1, b. 87*

- Exaggerating the change of soundpoint, play the passage p. Repeat mf and f while keeping the tone pure.

27 ## Bow pressure and pitch

The left hand fingers are sometimes blamed for out of tune notes that are actually the fault of the bow. Too much bow pressure, too far from the bridge, 'bends' the pitch of a note flat.

1   The further from the bridge the softer the string, and the less weight it can take before the pitch wavers.

2   The higher the string the thinner it is, and the less weight it can take.

3   The shorter the string the less weight it can take.

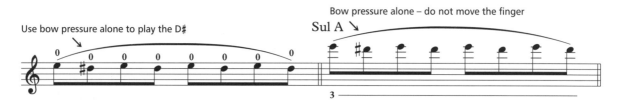

Alternate between an open E and a D♯ by using too much bow pressure. Bowing around soundpoint 3 or 4, keep the bow speed the same while increasing the pressure until the note changes pitch. The pitch of the note is easiest to 'bend' when playing in higher positions because of the short string length.

Example 1   Lalo: Symphonie espagnole, op. 21, *mov. 1, b. 120*

The G marked '+' can sound as an F♯ if played heavily on soundpoint 3, even if the left finger is in tune.

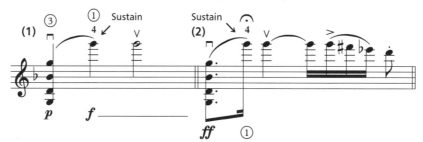

(1) Exaggerate by beginning *p* on soundpoint 3, and then move very close into the bridge.

(2) Otherwise playing up to tempo, pause on the top G, holding the bow deep in the string near the bridge.

Example 2

● At the top of a scale of thirds take particular care to play near enough to the bridge and to give the right amount of weight for each string. The A string is weaker than the E string; both strings are short; the more-sensitive A string is even shorter than the E.

Example 3   J. S. Bach: Partita no. 2 in D minor, BWV1004, *Sarabanda, b. 1*

● Even in first position, constantly remain alert to over-pressing or playing too near to the fingerboard.

Evenness

Bowing on open strings, fingering on adjacent strings

True independence means that the actions of one hand do not inadvertently influence the other. This three-step practice method immediately exposes and cures any disturbance to the bow stroke caused by the left hand.

1 Play a simple bow stroke on the open string. Do not yet make this stroke the same as the one you will use in the passage. Make a point of *not* thinking about the music: the aim is to remind yourself what a smooth, even, relaxed bow stroke feels like, unrelated to the music.

2 Continue bowing on the open string, but now while drawing the bow hear the music clearly in your mind. The bow stroke should now be the same as the one you will use in the actual passage, i.e. even, or fast–slow, heavy–light, crescendo, and so on. Listen closely to the tone to make sure there are no unwanted accents, or areas where the tone fades, or areas where the bow arm loses its smoothness or ease.

3 Repeat the same stroke on the open string, again hearing the music in your mind, but now finger the notes on a different string from the one you are bowing. Play with the same intensity of expression as when you are playing the music normally, and with vibrato, the only difference being that you are bowing on one string and fingering on another.

The bow stroke will become smoother and more flowing after the shortest amount of practising in this way, and a new resonance will come into the tone. Used on a regular basis this practice method transforms the overall playing. Applying it to notes, phrases or whole passages, use it frequently in every practice session.

Example 1

Bruch: Concerto no. 1 in G minor, op. 26, *mov. 3, b. 115*

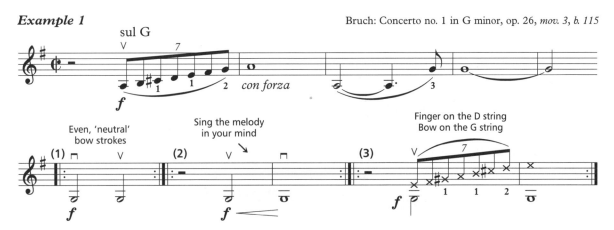

(1) Remind yourself of the feeling of an easy, smoothly flowing bow arm, playing with a rich, deep tone. Forget about the Bruch Concerto for the moment.

(2) Still without any fingers, play the bowing pattern while singing the melody in your mind. Play deeply into the string with full expression, staying near enough to the bridge to be able to do this without squashing the tone. (In this example, play around soundpoint 3 in the low positions, around soundpoint 2 in the high positions.)

(3) Still playing *espressivo* in the bow, silently finger the passage on the D string (shown as x-notes). Take care not to introduce any bumps or unevenness into the strokes.

Example 2

Brahms: Sonata no. 2 in A, op. 100, *mov. 1, b. 3*

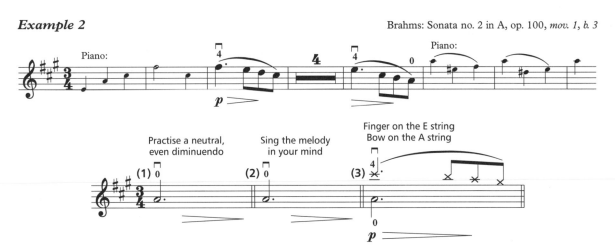

● Practise as in Example 1.

Example 3

Franck: Sonata in A, *mov. 2, b. 172*

- Silently finger on the D string while bowing the open E string:

- The exercise is equally effective if you bow on a different string from the one used in the passage, even though the feeling of playing the string is different. Silently finger on the E string while bowing the open A string:

Example 4

Paganini: 24 Caprices, op. 1, No. 17, *b. 9*

- Sustain the open D string evenly, and with deep sonority, while silently fingering the scale:

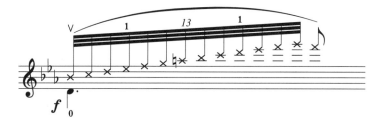

Example 5

Mozart: Concerto no. 4 in D, K218, *mov. 1, b. 68*

- Practise the slur. Silently finger on the A string while bowing the open E string.
- Vibrate the silent notes as normal, with an expressive feel in the fingers.

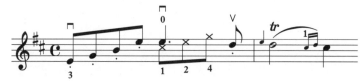

- Practise the trill. Silently finger on the E string while bowing the open A string:

Example 6   Moxart: Concerto no. 4 in D, K218, *mov. 1, cadenza (Joachim)*

- Sustain the open G string while fingering silently up to the top:

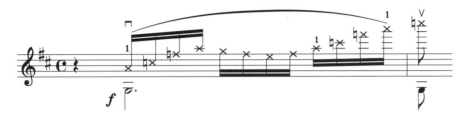

Example 7   Tchaikovsky: Concerto in D, op. 35, *mov. 1, cadenza*

- Sustain the open G string while fingering silently up to the top. (The first two notes will sound as written.)

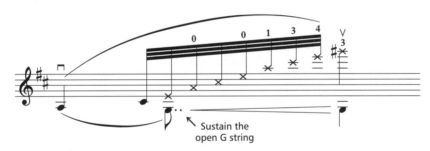

Example 8   Sibelius: Concerto in D minor, op. 47, *mov. 1, b. 41*

- Sustain the open G string while fingering the passage silently on the upper three strings:

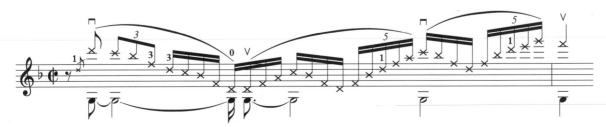

29 Equalizing ⊓ and V

Down-bows often have a tendency to come out more heavily than up-bows. This is partly because the lower half of the bow is heavier than the upper half; partly because of the feeling that down-bows go with gravity, and up-bows go against gravity; partly because at the heel the bow hand is directly above the string.

These factors may cause a heavy–light pattern in alternating down- and up-bows which spoils the musical line.

● Strengthen up-bows by giving them extra weight, or by using the down-bow as a model.

Example 1   Bruch: Concerto in G minor, op. 26, *mov. 1, b. 16*

Check the power and quality of up-bow attacks by using a down-bow attack as a model. Alternate between up-bow and down-bow until the up-bow attack is exactly the same as the down-bow.

● Make these two bars sound identical:

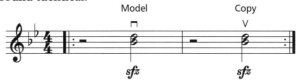

Example 2   Brahms: Sonata no. 2 in A, op. 100, *mov. 1, b. 31*

● To play the up-bows marked '+' attack the string hard, from the air, near the point. Practise as follows, making the second and fourth bars of each group sound identical.

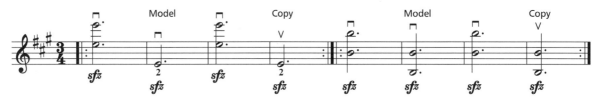

Example 3   Franck: Sonata in A, *mov. 2, b. 32*

● To gain greater evenness, practise with reversed (upside-down) bowing, alternating with the correct bowing until both bowings sound identical.

(1) There may be an inadvertent accent on the first and third beats.

(2) Alternate between reversed bowing and the correct bowing until they sound identical.

(3) Play the correct bowing with an extra accent on the second and fourth beats.

Example 4   J. S. Bach: Partita no. 2 in D minor, BWV1004, *Giga, b. 19*

(1) The down-bows may come out louder than the up-bows.

(2) The first note should not be too accented since it is the end of the preceding phrase. Begin a new colour on the lower A and crescendo through the dominant seventh to the G. The up-bow E (marked '+' in the Example) needs a lot of extra power for it not to sound too weak. Practise with an accent and a pause.

Example 5   Prokofiev: Sonata in D, op. 94 bis, *mov. 1, b. 42*

(1) The down-bows may come out louder than the up-bows.

(2) Alternate between reversed bowing and the correct bowing until they sound identical.

(3) Play the correct bowing with an extra accent on the up-bow eighth-notes (quavers).

Example 6   Mozart: Concerto no. 4 in D, K218, *mov. 1, b. 104*

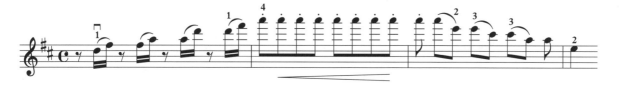

- As well as practising *spiccato* passages with reversed bowing, also practise with all down-bows, and all up-bows. Note the evenness of the strokes when they all go in the same direction, and use that evenness as a model for the correct bowing.

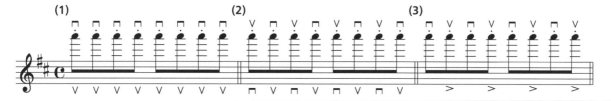

(1) Practise all down-bows, all up-bows. Note the evenness.

(2) Alternate between reversed bowing and the correct bowing until they sound identical.

(3) Play the correct bowing with an extra accent on the second and fourth eighth-notes of each group.

Example 7

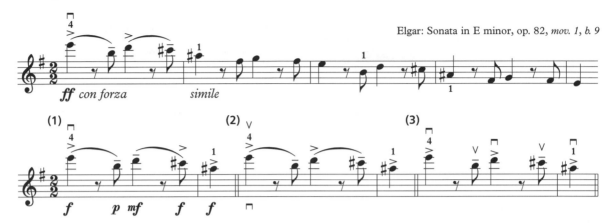

Elgar: Sonata in E minor, op. 82, *mov. 1, b. 9*

(1) The notes in the upper half of the bow should not come out weaker than those in the lower half.

(2) Alternate between reversed bowing and the correct bowing until they sound identical.

(3) Experiment with un-hooked, separate bows to use as a model of evenness for the correct bowing.

30 Stopping the finger while continuing with the bow

A good way to isolate the bow from the left hand, and to build up a phrase gradually, is to stop the fingers and continue with the bow on its own. Gradually add more notes one at a time until the whole phrase is complete.

Example 1

Mendelssohn: Concerto in E minor, op. 64, *mov. 1, b. 139*

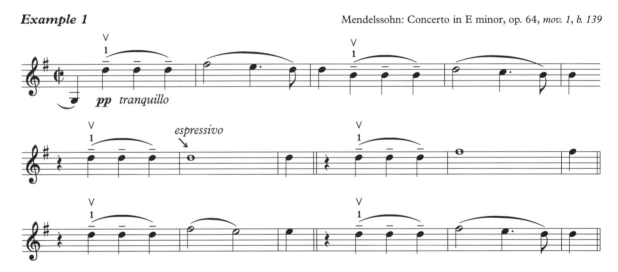

Example 2

Wieniawski: Concerto no. 2 in D minor, op. 22, *mov. 1, b. 108*

Tone exercise using dynamics

- Gain greater evenness and control of the bow by practising passages with crescendos and decrescendos.

  Afterwards you will notice that your right hand feels more sensitive and responsive to the constantly changing feelings of the hair–string contact in all parts of the bow.

- Use the following patterns:

p – *f* – *p*

f – *p* – *f*

f – *p*

p – *f*

See also Exercise 4, page 3.

Example 1
Sarasate: Zigeunerweisen, op. 20 no. 1, b. 4

Example 2
Mozart: Concerto no. 2 in D, K211, mov. 2, b. 9

Example 3
Beethoven: Concerto in D, op. 61, mov. 1, b. 174

32 **Building up from small amounts of bow**

The shorter the bow stroke, the easier it is to keep the bow speed and pressure even.

- Practise a stroke or phrase by beginning with a very small amount of bow and gradually increasing it to the desired length.

Example 1   Grieg: Sonata in C minor, op. 45, *mov. 1, b. 1*

1   Play through a stroke, phrase or passage in the middle of the bow, using only 5 centimetres of bow.

Apart from using so little bow, play as normally as possible: up to tempo and with full dynamics and expression. Feel how all the strokes, when confined within such a small amount of bow, are very concentrated and even.

2   Still in the middle of the bow, play through again with slightly more bow – perhaps 7 centimetres. Produce the same concentrated tone that you had before when you were using less bow.

3   Continue to repeat the phrase, adding a little more bow each time, until using more bow than you need to.

4   Then do the same in reverse. Starting with more bow than you will eventually use, with each play-through use a little less bow until again using only 5 centimetres in the middle of the bow.

Example 2   Brahms: Sonata no. 3 in D minor, op. 100, *mov. 1, b. 61*

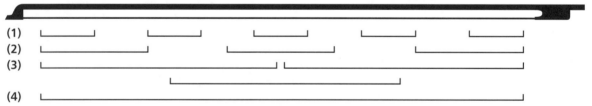

(1) Play the first bar, and the first note of the second bar, at the extreme heel using no more than 10 centimetres of bow.

- Sustain the sound solidly and evenly, sinking the hair of the bow deeply into the string.
- Still using no more than 10 centimetres, repeat higher and higher up the bow:
  - at the point-of-balance
  - in the middle
  - between the middle and the point
  - at the extreme point

(2) Start again at the extreme heel using 20 centimetres of bow. Repeat in the middle and at the point.

(3) Then use half the bow length, playing the phrase in the lower half, the middle and the upper half.

(4) Finally, use whole bows.

Throughout, keep the same feeling of contact with the string that you had when using the smallest amount of bow.

Sustaining **Different qualities of the bow at heel and point** 33

The bow has different qualities of give depending on where in the bow you play.

Sit the bow on the string a few centimetres away from the frog. Press the bow down as hard as you can. Notice how the hair of the bow gives but the wood remains rigid (Fig. 7a).

Do the same at the point. Rest the bow on the string a few centimetres from the tip and press down as hard as you can. Notice how the hair remains rigid but the wood of the bow (at the middle of the bow) bends easily (Fig. 7b).[1] Playing in the middle both the hair and the wood give equally.

[1] See *The give of the wood of the bow and the hair,* page 297

- Play short strokes in the lower half, the middle, and the upper half, feeling the different proportions of give in the hair and the wood.

- Find the same feelings in the bow in specific strokes or phrases.

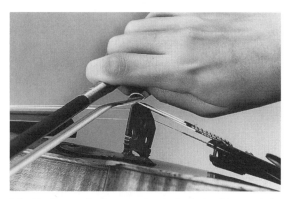

(a) **Playing at the extreme heel, the hair gives, and the wood of the bow is rigid**

(b) **Playing at the extreme point, the wood gives, and the hair is rigid**

Fig. 7

Example 1 Brahms: Hungarian Dance No. 1, *b. 1*

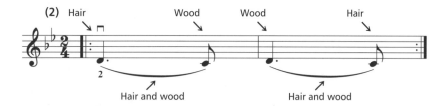

(1) Play a few notes near the heel. Playing quite heavily into the string, feel how the hair gives easily with every bow stroke but the wood remains rigid (Fig. 7a). Notice how your right hand and fingers respond to the bow and vice versa.

Repeat in the middle, feeling how both the hair and the wood have equal give and springiness.

Repeat in the upper half between the middle and the point. Feel how the hair is now much more rigid, especially near the point where it has no give at all (Fig. 7b). Feel how the wood (at the middle of the bow) gives easily with every bow stroke.

(2) Find the same feelings in the bow when playing the passage itself. Play slowly, exaggerating the give in the hair and the wood.

Example 2   Tchaikovsky: Concerto in D, op. 35, *mov. 1, b. 97*

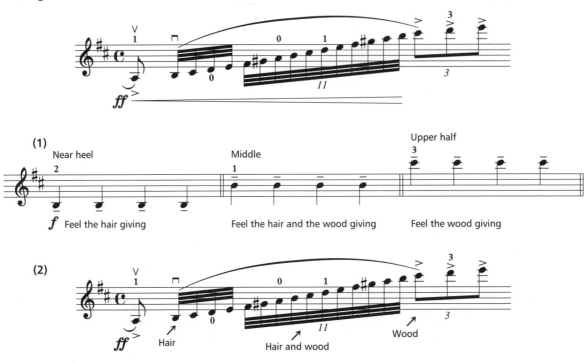

(1)

Near heel   Middle   Upper half

f Feel the hair giving   Feel the hair and the wood giving   Feel the wood giving

(2)

ff   Hair   Hair and wood   Wood

- Practise as in Example 1.

34 Pushing the wood of the bow down towards the hair

The more heavily the bow sinks into the string, the more the hair and the wood of the bow, and the string, want to spring back to their state of greatest relaxation. Bowing a string instrument is more a matter of playing with these forces of springiness *in* the hair and wood of the bow, than of holding and manipulating the physical bow itself.

Pushing the wood of the bow down towards the string is an extreme practice method which may sound harsh at first, but which can produce very fast results in broadening and deepening the tone.

- Place the bow on the string not too far from the bridge. Look at the middle of the bow. Without moving the bow along the string, push the wood at the middle of the bow down until it is almost touching the hair.

- Keep watching that distance between the hair and the wood, making sure that it remains exactly the same, while you bow up and down.

  Note that the middle of the bow is the only place the wood can come close to the hair. Keep your eye on the middle of the bow wherever in the bow you are playing – heel, middle or point.

- Play very, very slowly. Adjust the speed and pressure so that the sound remains as pure as possible.

Example 1

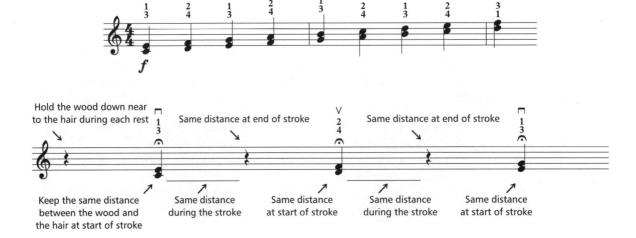

Hold the wood down near
to the hair during each rest   Same distance at end of stroke   Same distance at end of stroke

Keep the same distance   Same distance   Same distance   Same distance   Same distance
between the wood and   during the stroke   at start of stroke   during the stroke   at start of stroke
the hair at start of stroke

Example 2

Kreutzer: 42 Etudes ou caprices, No. 10, *b. 1*

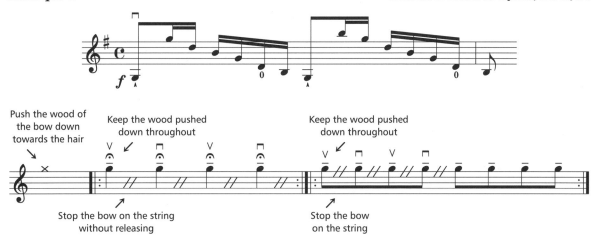

Push the wood of the bow down towards the hair

Keep the wood pushed down throughout

Keep the wood pushed down throughout

Stop the bow on the string without releasing

Stop the bow on the string

- Repeat using a note on the A string, and on the D and G strings.
- Then find the same feeling in the bow during the string crossings. While the bow is stationary on the string at the end of the bow stroke, pivot silently from one string to another while keeping the wood of the bow held down throughout:

Keep the wood pushed down throughout

Keep the wood pushed down while pivoting to the A string

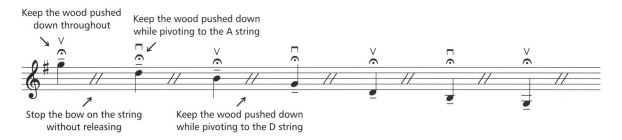

Stop the bow on the string without releasing

Keep the wood pushed down while pivoting to the D string

- Then find the same feeling in the bow when playing the passage normally: play deeply into the springiness of the stick.

Long, slow, sustained strokes: developing control

35

- To improve long, slow, sustained strokes, practise holding them for much longer than you need to. At the same time practise a few dynamic variations. Afterwards the long note in the passage will feel much easier to control.

Example

J. S. Bach: Concerto no. 1 in A minor, BWV1041, *mov. 2, b. 30*

- Using whole bows on each string, down-bow and up-bow, sustain the bow for as long as possible.
- Play near the bridge as slowly and as evenly as possible, at about ♪ = 40–60. The slower the better.

36

Balancing double stops: varying the weight

- Experiment with different degrees of weight on each string to find the best balance of the bow.

Example 1

Vivaldi: Autumn (The Four Seasons), op. 8 no. 3, *mov. 3, b. 30*

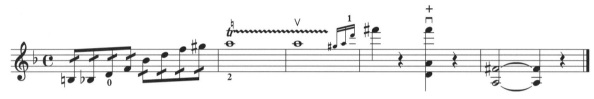

- Practise a phrase of double stops playing the lower string *f*, the upper string *p*.

- Staying *f* on the lower string, gradually play more and more loudly on the upper string until the tone is balanced evenly.

- Repeat the other way round. Keeping the upper string *f*, play the lower string gradually louder until both strings are equal.

Example 2

Franck: Sonata in A, *mov. 2, b. 225*

It is especially important to find the right balance of weight on the chord marked '+' because while the A is an open string, i.e. full length, the F♯ makes the E string less than half as long.

The bow must be much lighter on the E string in this chord than on the A string, because the shorter the length of string the less pressure it can take from the bow.[1]

- Practice as in Example 1:

Example 3

Bloch: Nigun (no. 2 from 'Baal Shem'), *b. 53*

The lower note of an octave is often played louder than the upper note.[2]

- Practise a phrase of octaves holding both fingers down but sounding only the lower note of each octave.

- Then begin to add the upper note. Begin with the lower note *f* and the upper note *ppp*.

- Keeping the lower note *f*, play the upper note gradually louder and louder until it is clear, though not as loud as the lower note.

[1] See *The shorter the string the nearer the bridge*, page 59; *Length of string and soundpoint*, page 297

[2] There are tonal advantages in playing the lower note of an octave louder than the upper note (special colours consisting of a solid body of sound with a 'sheen' on top). When first and second violins play in octaves, in a quartet or orchestra, the lower line often plays more loudly than the upper line.

There are also intonational advantages. If octaves are not exactly in tune they can be made to seem as if they are in tune if the lower note is played louder than the upper note.

Playing the lower note louder should not be confused with the fact that the hand position in playing octaves is based more on the *upper* finger.

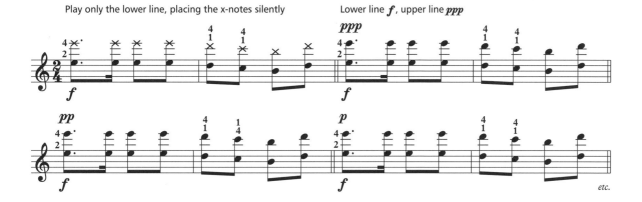

Play only the lower line, placing the x-notes silently

Lower line *f*, upper line *ppp*

Balancing double stops: tremolo

● Tremolo the bow across the strings as a quick practice method to balance the bow perfectly on each string.

Example 1

J. S. Bach: Partita no. 2 in D minor, BWV1004, *Ciaccona, b. 133*

● Find how to play the tremolo very fast and perfectly evenly, each note sounding clearly.

● Play the tremolo at the same dynamic, and at the same distance from the bridge, as the actual double stop.

Example 2

Rode: 24 Caprices, No. 4, *b. 1*

● Also practise in dotted rhythms, keeping the bow very close to both strings:

Example 3

Chausson: Poème, op. 25, *b. 73*

38 Avoiding an unintentional diminuendo

Since the bow does not automatically sink into the string, but wants always to release to its state of greatest relaxation, many unintentional diminuendos may occur unless you are careful to sustain the tone.

- If you notice that you are allowing the bow to make a musically unwanted diminuendo, practise by doing the opposite: play the phrase or passage with a crescendo. Afterwards, the normal sustaining will feel easier and automatic.

Example 1   Beethoven: Sonata in D, op. 12 no. 1, *mov. 1, b. 81*

- Practise with a crescendo to avoid a diminuendo before the *subito **p***:

Example 2   Mendelssohn: Concerto in E minor, op. 64, *mov. 1, b. 181*

- Play in the same part of the bow, using the same length of bow, as when playing the passage normally.

Example 3   Tchaikovsky: Concerto in D, op. 35, *mov. 1, b. 66*

Example 4   Brahms: Scherzo (Sonatensatz), WoO2, *b. 28*

In the bar marked '+' avoid an excessive diminuendo on the A♭ or E♭ so that the line is sustained, as an unbroken wave, through to the other side of the marked diminuendo.

- Playing up to tempo, practise with a long, sustained stroke on the A♭ and E♭, with full vibrato:

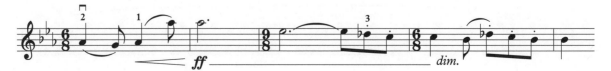

Example 5

Wieniawski: Polonaise brillante, op. 21, b. 76

Unless marked otherwise, it is especially important to crescendo to the top of a brilliant run:

Example 6

Bruch: Concerto no. 1 in G minor, op. 26, *mov. 3, b. 265*

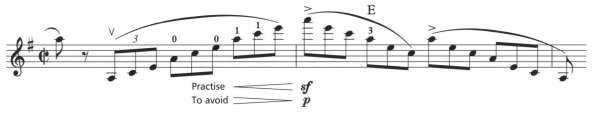

Example 7

J. S. Bach: Partita no. 3 in E, BWV1006, *Preludio, b. 49*

- Crescendo to the *subito p*; diminuendo to the *subito f* (avoiding an unwanted crescendo):

Example 8

Brahms: Sonata no. 1 in G, op. 78, *mov. 1, b. 24*

- On the up-bow attacks marked '+', avoid playing **fp** or **pfp**. Exaggerate playing full, equally sustained quarter-notes (crotchets) by playing the strokes longer, with a slower bow, deeper in the string, and nearer the bridge, than normal.

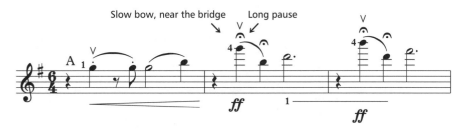

39 Angle of the bow to the bridge

1 See *Angle of the bow to the bridge*, page 302

Although the bow is usually parallel to the bridge you can move it closer to the bridge, or further away, by angling the bow slightly.[1] Angling the bow is useful either for sustaining the bow near the bridge or, by allowing the bow to drift to the fingerboard, for making a perfect diminuendo.

- Holding a long, sustained, f stroke near the bridge, bow slightly 'out' on the down-bow (Fig. 8a) and slightly 'in' on the up-bow (Fig. 8b) so that there is less chance of the bow wandering away from the bridge.

  Note that when the bow is 'out' the point of the bow points back, towards your left shoulder. The smallest amount of angling the bow is enough to hold a constant soundpoint.

- Bow 'in' towards the end of the down-bow to allow the bow to move to the fingerboard.

Fig. 8

(a) **The bow angled out**

(b) **The bow angled in**

Examples

Beethoven: Romanze in G, op. 40, *b. 56*

Messiaen: Thème et variations, *Fifth variation, b. 1*

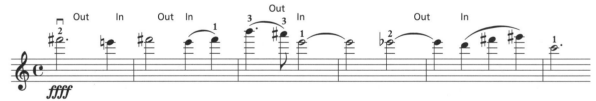

Bartók (arr. Székely): Roumanian Folk Dances, No. 4, *b. 19*

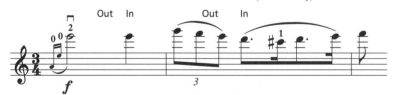

Chausson: Poème, op. 25, *b. 65*

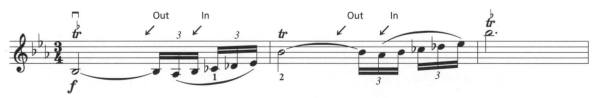

Rode: Concerto no. 7 in A minor, op. 9, *mov. 1, b. 80*

Key strokes

part **3**

Chords

Distance from the bridge

40

In four-string chords the bow often has to move towards the bridge during the chord. An alternative to moving towards the bridge is to play the upper strings more gently; but in a powerful chord, the bottom strings need to be played a little further from the bridge, and the top strings a little closer to the bridge.[1]

[1] See *The higher the string, the nearer the bridge*, page 58

- Practising by exaggeration, begin the chord near the fingerboard and end it near the bridge. Afterwards, a normal amount of pulling in to the bridge will feel natural and automatic.

Example 1

Franck: Sonata in A, *mov. 3, b. 4*

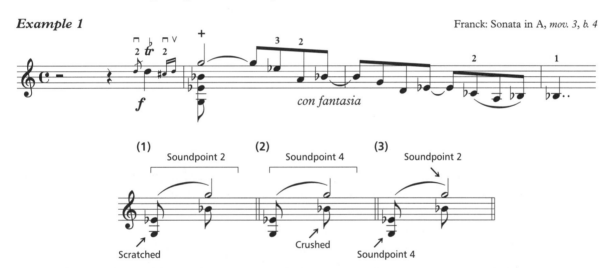

(1) If the four-string chord marked '+' is played on soundpoint 2, the bottom two strings may easily be scratched.[2]

[2] See Fig. 5, page 47

(2) If the chord is played on soundpoint 4, the upper two strings may easily be crushed.

(3) Practising by exaggeration, play the bottom strings on soundpoint 4, and the top strings on soundpoint 2.

Example 2

Bartók (arr. Székely): Roumanian Folk Dances, No. 1, *b. 12*

- Exaggerate the change of soundpoint as follows:

①②③④ = soundpoints

Example 3   J. S. Bach: Sonata no. 2 in A minor, BWV1003, *Fuga, b. 7*

The chords in the second bar are usually played as 'three–two' or 'three–two–one' chords (see page 84).

Nearer the bridge the curve of the four strings is more rounded and the strings have greater tension; it becomes more difficult to catch all three strings at once. Nearer the fingerboard the strings are flatter and softer under the bow; it is much easier to catch three strings at the same time, but the tone may easily be crushed.

The best soundpoint naturally depends on each particular chord, and whether it is on the lower three strings (i.e. further from the bridge), or on the upper three strings (nearer the bridge).

● Practise chords in the same way as *Playing a phrase on each soundpoint*, page 48: experiment with speed of bow, pressure and distance from the bridge until finding the desired tone quality.

②③④⑤ = soundpoints

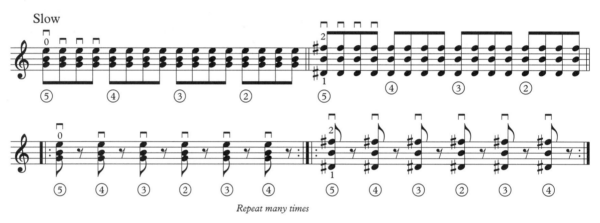

Repeat many times

41 Pivoting

Pivoting is the movement of the bow around the string. At the same time as playing on one string, the bow moves towards another (e.g. while playing on the A string the bow can move closer to the D or E strings).

When chords are split (e.g. playing the lower two strings of a three-string chord followed by the upper two strings), the bow pivots on the middle string to transfer from the lower to the upper pair of strings.

● Practise by first playing the pivot string as a full-length note between the bottom and top of the chord.

● Gradually shorten the note on the pivot string, binding the bottom and top of the chord together smoothly and seamlessly.

However you choose to play the chord, after you have practised the pivot strings in this way it will feel more secure.

Example   J. S. Bach: Partita no. 2 in D minor, BWV1004, *Ciaccona, b. 1*

Intonation

- Place all the fingers together as chords, but play only one line of the passage at a time – the lower notes, the middle notes, then the top notes.

- Continuing to put down all the fingers together as chords, play two strings together – first the lower two strings and then the upper two.

Example 1   Bruch: Concerto no. 1 in G minor, op. 26, *mov. 1, b. 34*

(1) Bow only the bottom string. The x-notes show the fingers playing silently on the other strings.

(2) Bow only the middle string.

(3) Bow only the top string.

(4) Bow only the lower two strings.

(5) Bow only the upper two strings.

Example 2   Paganini: Concerto no. 1 in D, op. 6, *mov. 1, b. 131*

- Practise as in Example 1.

Example 3   Sibelius: Concerto in D minor, op. 47, *mov. 1, b. 48*

- Practise broken three-string chords in the same way:

Example 4

Chausson: Poème, op. 25, *b. 87*

This practice method is also useful when the chords are not consecutive:

43 Bow balance and contact

In unaccompanied Bach the strings are often thought of as representing the voices in a choir, so that the open E–A–D–G strings are soprano, alto, tenor and bass respectively. To bring out an inner voice, after playing three strings together the bow continues to sustain the middle string (for example) alone.

Use the same approach to practise any chord sequence. This improves the balance and contact of the bow on the different strings, and also intonation.

● Play all three strings together and then sustain one string only, then pairs, and finally all three strings.

Example 1

Dont: 24 Etudes and Caprices, op. 35, No. 1, *b. 1*

Catch all three strings together

Each tie sounds like a half-note (minim)

(1) Play all three strings at once, using a few centimetres of bow, and then sustain only one string.

Place the bow on the middle string of the chord near the heel. Press the middle of the three strings down until you can see the bow hair contacting the outer strings of the chord.

Play as near to the bridge as possible. If the bow is too near the bridge it is difficult to catch all three strings at once; too near the fingerboard the tone may easily be crushed.

Do not allow any break in the sound during the tied notes, e.g. when sustaining the lower string, do not let the hair of the bow momentarily leave the lower string after playing the three strings together. Each tie should then sound like a half-note (minim).

(2) Play all three strings as before, using only a few centimetres of bow, and then sustain two strings.

(3) Finally, sustain all three strings at once.

In the four-string chords in the last bar, miss out the top note and then miss out the bottom note.

Example 2   Bruch: Scottish Fantasy, op. 46, *mov. 4, b. 11*

Isolating specific fingers

44

- Isolate specific fingers that may be awkward to place, and play only those fingers, the others remaining silently on the string.

Example 1   J. S. Bach: Sonata in G minor, BWV1001, *Fuga, b. 29*

- At the pair of chords marked '+' the first finger must quickly move from E on the D string to G on the E string. Play only the first finger, placing the others silently (shown as x-notes).

Example 2   Brahms: Concerto in D, op. 77, *mov. 1, b. 248*

At the chords marked '+' the first finger and fourth finger move in opposite directions.

(1) Place all the fingers but play only the fourth finger.

(2) Place all the fingers but play only the first finger.

45 Joining chords to each other

- Practise playing from the end of one chord to the beginning of the next.

Example 1   J. S. Bach: Partita no. 1 in B minor, BWV1002, *Sarabande, b. 1*

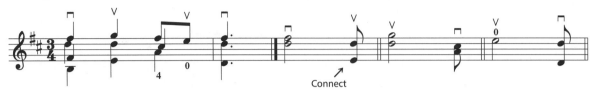

Example 2   Mozart: Concerto no. 3 in G, K216, *mov. 1 cadenza (Sam Franko)*

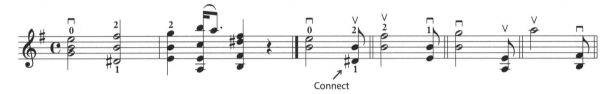

Example 3   J. S. Bach: Partita no. 2 in D minor, BWV1004, *Ciaccona, b. 127*

(1) Avoid accidentally catching the middle strings while crossing from the higher strings to the lower strings.

(2) Practise either lifting the bow slightly during the crossing, or stopping it on the string.

46 Splitting the chord: bow division

The lower strings of a split chord should usually be played with much less bow than the upper strings, e.g. when starting a chord at the heel, the top of the chord should normally begin at, or a little below, the point-of-balance. 'Follow the curve of the bridge' is another way of saying the same thing.

Example 1   J. S. Bach: Sonata no. 1 in G minor, BWV1001, *Adagio, b. 1*

- Practise saving bow on the base of the chord by exaggeration: use only five centimetres, arriving at the top of the chord well below the point-of-balance.

- Despite using so little bow on the bottom of the chord, play a long pause. Sustain the bow deeply and evenly in the string and with a pure tone. Play into the elasticity of the wood of the bow, hair, and string.

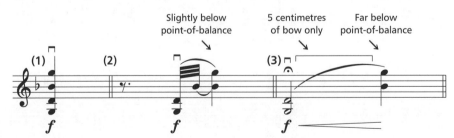

(1) As written

(2) As played

(3) Practice method

If the chord is played instead in a more 'baroque', arpeggiated style, the same bow division and sense of 'following the curve of the bridge' applies.

Example 2 J. S. Bach: Sonata no. 1 in G minor, BWV1001, *Fuga, b. 58*

The same proportions apply to bow division when starting the chord up-bow. Having started near the point, reach the top of the chord midway between the point and the middle.

- Down-bow or up-bow, practise the string crossing in slow motion with 'clicks':[1]

[1] See *'Click' practice*, page 106

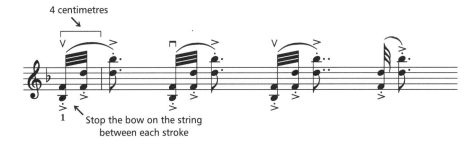

- Follow the curve of the bridge with the bow, measuring the exact distance between the contact point of the hair with one string and the contact point with the next.

- Having arrived at the top of the chord, play the upper two strings with a lot of bow.

Placing the fingers in time before the bow

47

It is always easy for the bow to be ready to play a chord whereas the left-hand fingers may need more time to find their places on the string. The fingers must be placed quickly enough to be ready before the bow moves.

In a rapid series of chords, one way to improve the timing is to think of placing the next chord as the final action of playing the *previous* chord. In other words:

Play the first chord – instantly place the fingers ready for the next chord. (Play–place.)

instead of

Place the fingers – play. Place the next fingers – play, and so on. (Place–play.)

Example 1 J. S. Bach: Sonata no. 1 in G minor, BWV1001, *Fuga, b. 21*

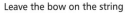

- Play the sixteenth-note (semiquaver) chord with a short stroke that ends with the bow on the string, not in the air.

- At exactly the same moment that the bow stops moving and remains stationary on the string, place the fingers on the double-dotted quarter-note (double-dotted crotchet) chord without playing it (written as x-notes).

- Place the unplayed fingers strictly in time in the rhythm shown.

Example 2   Saint-Saëns: Introduction and Rondo Capriccioso, op. 28, Rondo, *b. 304*

(1) Imagine that you will play each chord twice.

(2) Instead of actually sounding the chord twice, place the fingers for the first chord and play only the second. The silently placed fingers are written as x-notes.

(3) Then instead of equal eighth-notes (quavers), place the silent x-notes as sixteenth-notes (semiquavers), and then as 32nd-notes (demisemiquavers). Place them exactly in time.

48 ## Non-split chords: sustaining

● Practise sustaining three strings together for almost the whole length of bow, down-bow and up. Afterwards the normal length, or the normal splitting of the chord, will seem very easy.

Example 1   Beethoven: Sonata in C minor, op. 30 no. 2, *mov. 1, b. 22*

(1) These chords are often played as 'three–two' chords – three strings played together for about ten centimetres, and then only the upper two strings for the rest of the chord. To the listener this sounds like three strings throughout, but most of the chord is actually only two strings.

(2) Before playing the chords as three–two chords, practise sounding all three strings together.

Build up little by little to the long, sustained chord at the end of the sequence. Start with the shortest possible stroke and gradually add more and more length until using almost the whole length of the bow.

Playing each chord, press the middle of the three strings down until you can see the bow hair contacting the outer strings of the chord. Hold the wood of the bow down towards the hair, without releasing, during the whole length of each stroke.

To gain more power spread the fingers slightly further apart on the bow.[1] Move the first finger (and possibly the second finger) slightly further away from the thumb (i.e. in the direction of the point).

Play as close to the bridge as possible, at least on soundpoint 3.[2] The nearer the bridge the better (so that you can play deeply into the strings without crushing the tone), but the harder it is to catch all three strings at once.

Because the weight of the bow is divided between three strings you need almost triple the weight that you would use for a normal f on one string alone. Remember to keep the left fingers light.[3]

[1] See also *Adjusting the bow hold*, page 88; *Spreading the fingers for leverage*, page 259; *Bow hold*, page 302.

[2] See Fig. 5, page 47

[3] The amount of weight required in the fingers is always the same, i.e. as much as necessary to stop each note cleanly, but as little as possible. It does not make any difference how many fingers you have on the string at the same time. Over-pressing with the left fingers in double stops and chords, as a reaction to the heavier weight required in the bow, is one of the most frequent causes of tension.

Example 2   Vieuxtemps: Concerto no. 5 in A minor, op. 37, *mov. 1, b. 71*

- Practise sustaining all three strings together so that afterwards a three–two chord seems effortless:

Example 3   J. S. Bach: Sonata no. 1 in G minor, BWV1001, *Fuga, b. 3*

- Before playing as three–two or three–two–one chords, sustain all three strings equally with as long and slow a stroke as possible.

Example 4   Tchaikovsky: Concerto in D, op. 35, *mov. 1, cadenza*

The chords marked '+' are played with a medium-speed bow stroke, all three strings equally sustained.

- Practise sustaining the three strings together with a slower and longer bow stroke than in the passage:

Example 5   Bruch: Concerto no. 1 in G minor, op. 26, *mov. 3, b. 189*

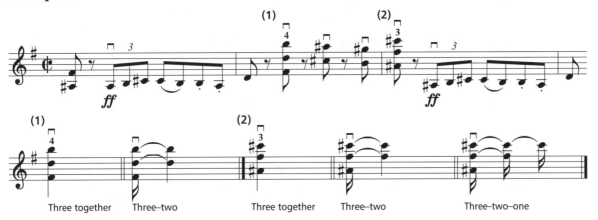

(1) Play all three strings together, sustaining the bottom string equally with the top string.

   Move from three strings to only two, sustaining the top two strings as an ordinary double stop.

(2) Play all three strings together. Move from three strings to two. Move from three strings, to two, to only the top string.

Détaché

Simple *détaché*: the bow speed and pressure stay the same from one end of the stroke to the other. The strokes are connected to each other seamlessly, without a break or alteration in the sound.

Accented *détaché*: the bow speed is fast–slow, and the pressure is heavy–light. There is space between the strokes, ranging from the tiniest gap to a longer silence.

49

[1] The factors that most commonly disturb the bow change are (1) suddenly increasing the bow speed just before changing direction, and (2) at the same time lightening the bow excessively (at the point) or overpressing (at the heel) just before changing direction.

Simple *détaché*: smooth bow changes

To make a smooth bow change: (1) very slightly slow the bow an instant before the bow changes direction, and (2) at the same time very slightly lighten the pressure.[1]

- Practise the bow changes by pausing briefly just before you move the bow the other way. See how slowly you can move the bow, while still sustaining the tone solidly, in the very last centimetre before the bow changes direction.

Example 1 Kreutzer: 42 Etudes ou caprices, No. 2, *b. 1*

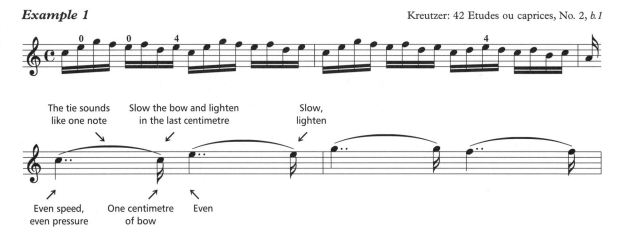

- Begin slowly, playing in the upper half. Imagine that although each note sounds like a half-note (minim), it is actually a double-dotted quarter-note (crotchet) tied to a sixteenth-note (semiquaver).

- At the last moment before finishing the stroke, at the very end of the sixteenth-note, slow and lighten the bow infinitesimally.[2]

[2] The way a playground swing slows to a halt before changing direction provides a useful image for the bow change. The difference is that having changed direction the swing starts off slowly and gathers speed gradually, whereas the bow moves at full speed at the very beginning of moving in the new direction.

The effect to the listener should be of the smoothest, most seamless bow change imaginable, with absolutely no break in the tone between the strokes.

Example 2 Bruch: Concerto no. 1 in G minor, op. 26, *mov. 2, b. 11*

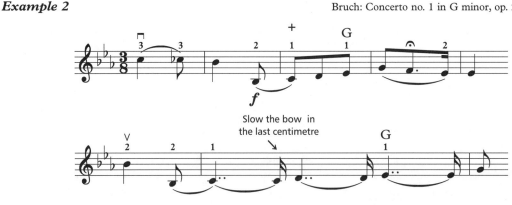

Example 3 Brahms: Sonata no. 1 in G, op. 78, *mov. 3, b. 1*

Simple *détaché*: using slurs as a model

● Use slurs as a model for a perfect legato in separate-bow strokes.

Example 1   Mozart: Sonata in E minor, K304, *mov. 1, b. 103*

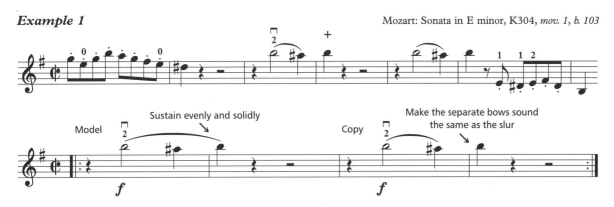

Example 2   Haydn: Concerto no. 2 in G, Hob.VIb, *mov. 1, b. 31*

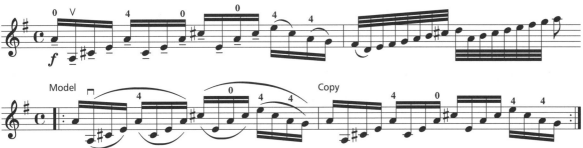

Accented *détaché*: proportions

Each accented *détaché* is the result of certain proportions of speed and pressure. You can create an endless number of different characters of stroke by combining different degrees of 'fast', 'slow', 'heavy' and 'light'.

● Build the stroke gradually by beginning with a smooth, simple *détaché*. Then add the fast–slow and heavy–light stresses, and then add the space between the strokes.

Example   Beethoven: Romanze in G, op. 40, *b. 68*

This passage may be played in the upper half of the bow with a light, slightly detached stroke. The speed pattern of each stroke is fast–slow, and the pressure pattern heavy–light, with a slight gap between each stroke.

(1) Begin with sustained, even strokes (even speed, even pressure). Join each stroke to the next smoothly, without any break between the strokes.

(2) Then add a little accent to the beginning of each stroke (fast–slow, heavy–light), but still with no break between the strokes.

(3) Then add the space between the strokes.

● Also practise the stroke on one note, and then apply the same stroke to the passage:

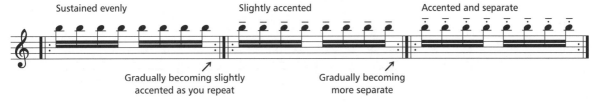

52 *Martelé*

Designing the stroke

Martelé (from the French word for 'hammered') provides a good illustration of proportions. The stroke is made up of fast–slow bow speed, heavy–light pressure, begins with a bite, and often has a space between each stroke.

In searching for an exact variety or shade of *martelé* the questions to ask are: where in the bow does the stroke begin; where does it end; how much bite; how fast is the fast part of the stroke, and how slow is the slow part; how heavy, and then how light; and how much space between the strokes?

- Combine different quantities of these factors to create an infinite number of different characters of *martelé*.

Example   Kayser: Etudes, op. 20, No. 14, *b. 1*

Description: energetic but soft-edged *martelé*, about 5 centimetres of bow for each stroke, in the middle of the upper half; not too heavy a bite. Pressure: very quick release as soon as the bow begins to move after the initial bite. Speed: only very little 'slow' at the end of the stroke. Space between the strokes: small gap.

- Build the stroke on one note, experimenting with soundpoint, place in the bow, length, speed, pressure, and space between the strokes:

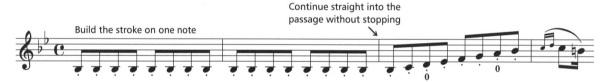

53 ## Adjusting the bow hold

[1] See also *Spreading the fingers for leverage*, page 259; *Bow hold*, page 302.

Because *martelé* is such a powerful stroke, to play without undue effort you have to put together all the factors in the bow hand that give power. Experiment with different bow holds:[1]

1 Move the first finger slightly further away from the thumb (i.e. in the direction of the point), to use the principles of leverage to best effect.

   The bow hold may feel better balanced if you move the second finger one millimetre in the same direction.

2 Bring the knuckles down slightly flatter.

3 Turn the hand slightly more onto the first finger ('pronate').

[2] See Fig. 28, Page 258

4 Raise the elbow slightly more to lever the weight of the arm into the hand and bow.[2]

5 Slightly straighten the fingers more on the down-bow, curve more on the up-bow. (This makes a difference even if the amount the fingers move is almost invisible.)

Example   Brahms: Concerto in D, op. 77, *mov. 1, b. 91*

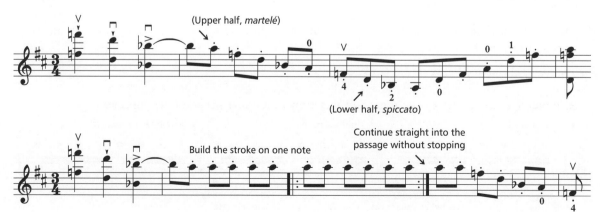

Catching the string

- The bite at the beginning of a *martelé* is an important feature of the stroke. During the silence between the strokes grip the string heavily, ready for the next stroke.[1] Gripping the string, at any part of the bow, is done by pushing the wood at the middle of the bow down towards the hair.

Example   Kreutzer: 42 Etudes ou caprices, No. 6, *b. 1*

[1] 'Catching' the string before playing the *martelé* is an example of *technical timing* as opposed to *musical timing*. Musical timing is *when* you want the note to sound; technical timing is always *before* the sound.

Other important examples of technical timing include pivoting (moving to a new string while playing the old string (page 102)), and finger preparation (page 240).

1   Before playing each *martelé*, stop the bow on the string. Press the bow down heavily to grip the string firmly with the hair (shown as an x-note).

   Use full hair for strength of contact, and to avoid the wood of the bow touching the string. Feel the force of springiness in the wood of the bow, the hair, and the string. They all want to return to a state of relaxation, but hold them still in a state of increased tension.

2   Without releasing the pressure, very slowly pull and push the string from side to side. Do this entirely silently – do not lose hold of the string, letting it snap back.

3   Having moved the string from side to side a few times, stop the bow without releasing the pressure.

4   Then play the *martelé* with a fast–slow bow speed. Release some of the pressure the instant the bow begins to move: the stroke should begin with a single 'click', not a scratch.

5   Stop the bow on the string at the end of the stroke and repeat the process for the next note.

Vibrato accents

In slow to medium *martelé* and at other times when the bow makes an accent, it is usual to mirror this in the left hand with a vibrato that is fast–slow and wide–narrow.[1]

| **Bow** | Fast–slow, heavy–light |
| **Vibrato** | Fast–slow, wide–narrow |

[1] See also *Vibrato accents*, page 138

Apart from the clearly different musical result, this produces a feeling of the hands working together, rather than the unnatural feeling of combining an even-speed vibrato with fast–slow bow speed.

- Practising by exaggeration, make the vibrato accent greater than the bow accent by playing each note with a very fast–slow and wide–narrow vibrato.

Example   Wieniawski: Concerto no. 2 in D minor, op. 22, *mov. 1, b. 188*

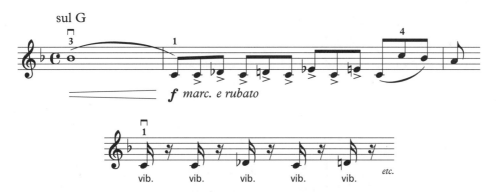

- On each note marked 'vib.', make a fast–slow and wide–narrow vibrato. Keep the bow speed and pressure almost even, creating most of the accent with the vibrato, not the bow.

56 **Releasing between strokes**

Martelé requires a firm bow hold at the beginning of the stroke, but during the *martelé* the hand can release. Tension and awkwardness may result if the hand remains 'fixed' and 'gripping' the bow during and between the strokes. (See margin note 2, page 255.)

Example   Lalo: Symphonie espagnole, op. 21, *mov. 1, b. 66*

- Practise the moments of release into the stroke by pausing between strokes. Completely release the bow, hand and fingers during the pause.

Staccato

Note about rhythm and accent practice
Discussed in full on pages 36–46, practising in rhythms and accents is very helpful for gaining absolute control in staccato.

Example   Sarasate: Zigeunerweisen, op. 20 no. 1, *b. 23*

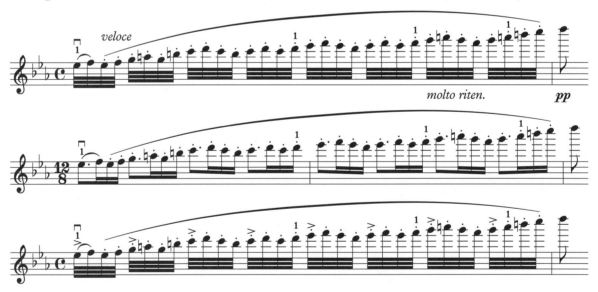

57 **Legato slurs**

For good co-ordination in staccato the left-hand fingers must be very even. At the same time each note should receive an equal amount of bow.

- Before playing a run with staccato, build greater smoothness and evenness into both hands by practising the run with a slurred stroke.

Example   Wieniawski: Polonaise brillante, op. 21, *b. 23*

- Play the slur with the bow unusually solid and deep in the string.
- Use the same amount of bow that you will use in the actual staccato run. (Play nearer the bridge if the sound is scratchy.)

Using *spiccato* as a model

- Play the run with a sparkling and pure *spiccato* to use as a model for the staccato. Even if you cannot make the two strokes exactly the same, just the attempt to do so will improve the staccato dramatically.
- Use short but rounded *spiccato* strokes, with much 'ring' or resonance.

Example   Sarasate: Zapateado, op. 23 no. 2, *b. 114*

- Also practise on one note:

Saving bow

Avoid using too much bow in the beginning of the run and getting to the middle of the bow too soon.

Staccato rarely works comfortably in the lower half of the bow, because the movement of the bow at the point becomes too large to be manageable. The reason for this is a vivid illustration of proportions and of leverage. Play a repeated string-crossing pattern at the extreme heel, and then at the extreme point:

Playing the pattern at the extreme heel, notice how the movement of the bow at the heel is very small, while at the point the movement is very large. Playing it at the extreme point, notice how the movement at the tip of the bow is very small, while the movement at the heel is very large.

- Practise the whole run using only a quarter of the amount of bow you will actually use in the end.
- Then gradually increase the amount of bow.

60

[1] For other examples of curved strokes see *Forearm rotation*, page 95; *Curved Bow Strokes (Sautillé)*, page 98; *Beginning and ending notes*, page 268

Curved bow strokes

Each note in a staccato run is played with a tiny, curved bow stroke. The bow does not go along the string in a straight line.[1] Watch the point of the bow during a staccato to see tiny little 'dipping' movements.

- Exaggerate the curves by playing a double stop for a brief moment at the start of each staccato note.

Example   Wieniawski: Concerto no. 2 in D minor, op. 22, *mov. 1, b. 125*

- Start at a slow tempo and gradually speed up to as fast a tempo as possible:

61

String crossings

Late string crossings in staccato disturb the evenness of the stroke.

- Practise by playing the string crossing too early: play the note before the string crossing, and the note after, as a double stop.[2]

[2] See *Crossing early*, page 102

Example   Kreutzer: 42 Etudes ou caprices, No. 4, *b. 7*

- Use the same amount of bow that you will use in the actual staccato run:

62

Metronome practice

- Play with the metronome, starting at a slow tempo (perhaps two notes to a beat at 60).
- Use a tiny length of bow for each stroke so that the whole run can be played using a normal amount of bow.
- Gradually speed up (63, 66, 72, etc.), to as fast a tempo as possible.

Spiccato

Legato slurs

The left-hand fingers must be even so that they do not disturb the evenness of the bow stroke.

- Practise *spiccato* passages slurred to expose and correct any unevenness in the left hand.

Example   De Falla (arr. Kreisler): Danse espagnole, *b. 163*

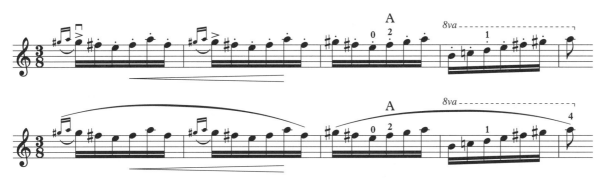

Height and length

In *spiccato* the bow moves in a curved line that ranges from saucer-shaped to U-shaped. The hair touches the string at the very bottom of the curve. The main proportions to consider are height of bounce to length of bow.[1]

The higher the bounce and the less movement along the string, the shorter and crisper the *spiccato*. The lower the bounce and the more movement along the string, the longer and more rounded the *spiccato*.[2]

- Begin with short *détaché* strokes on the string. Gradually let the bow begin to bounce, finally letting the hair leave the string.

- Also do the reverse – begin with a short *spiccato* and gradually play it longer until it remains on the string.

[1] To play a series of completely even *spiccato* strokes, the up-bow must follow in reverse the same path as the down-bow. See also Example 6, page 65.

[2] See also *Lifted strokes*, page 297

Example 1   Beethoven: Sonata in G, op. 30 no. 3, *mov. 1, b. 1*

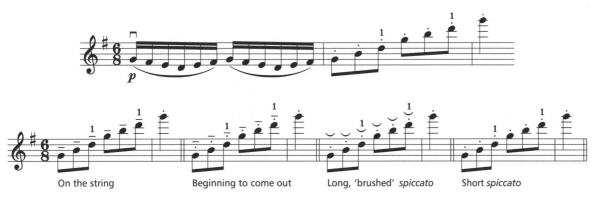

On the string   Beginning to come out   Long, 'brushed' *spiccato*   Short *spiccato*

Example 2   Bartók (arr. Székely): Roumanian Folk Dances, no. 6, *b. 41*

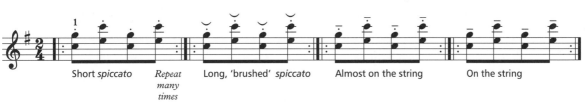

Short *spiccato*   *Repeat many times*   Long, 'brushed' *spiccato*   Almost on the string   On the string

65 **Amount of hair**

The best proportions of height–length–soundpoint, and the best place to play in the bow, and how heavily or lightly you can play, all change according to how much hair is used.

● Playing on one note, experiment with different tilts of the bow.

● Adjust the proportions (height–length–soundpoint–dynamic–tempo–place in the bow–amount of hair) so that the sound is always pure however much hair contacts the string.

● Find the right combination to produce the desired character of *spiccato* for any particular passage.

Example   Vivaldi: Autumn (The Four Seasons), op. 8 no. 3, *mov. 1, b. 1*

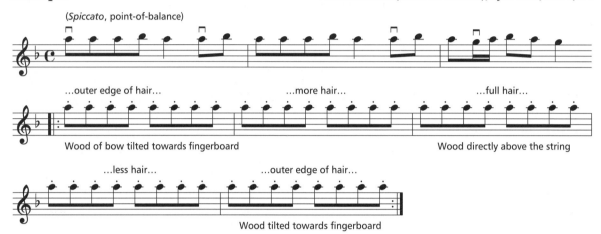

66 **Soundpoint**

Because the string is soft near the fingerboard and hard near the bridge, the best proportions of height–length are different at each distance from the bridge.

Spiccato nearer the **fingerboard**: lower, shorter, lighter, faster
Spiccato nearer the **bridge**:   higher, longer, heavier, slower

● Play a group of notes on soundpoint 5. Experiment with the height, length, pressure, speed, amount of hair, and area of the bow until the tone is pure and ringing.[1]

To adjust the length of bow, make the curve of the total bow stroke flatter or more U-shaped.

[1] See also *Playing a phrase on each soundpoint*, page 48

● Repeat on soundpoint 4. The *spiccato* will now be very slightly higher, longer, heavier and slower.

● Repeat on soundpoints 3 and 2. On soundpoint 2 the *spiccato* will be very much higher, longer, heavier and slower than it was on soundpoint 5. *Spiccato* does not work on soundpoint 1, except in very high positions.

Example   Mozart: Concerto no. 4 in D, K218, *mov. 3, b. 1*

● Play 8 or 16 strokes only on soundpoint 5, then again on soundpoints 4, 3 and 2:

● Another useful approach is to move from soundpoint to soundpoint:

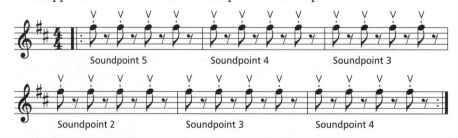

● Continue trying different proportions until finding the purest, most resonant tone in each *spiccato* stroke, entirely free of any scratch or other tonal distortion.

● Then use this same design of stroke in the passage.

Forearm rotation

Forearm rotation in *spiccato* is so slight as to be invisible, yet without it the stroke can easily become heavy and laboured. This is because a tiny amount of forearm rotation takes the place of much larger movements in the forearm and upper arm. It is an essential part of all lifted bowings.[1]

[1] See also *Forearm rotation*, page 265

- Practising by exaggeration, play slowly while making a larger-than-life forearm rotation on each stroke.
- Rotate clockwise a little on each up-bow, anticlockwise on each down-bow (the principal movement still being from the upper arm). The bow makes tiny curves: catch the string at the bottom of the curve.

Examples

Beethoven: Sonata in F, op. 24 ('Spring'), *mov. 1, b. 63*

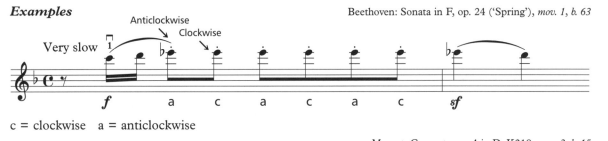

c = clockwise   a = anticlockwise

Mozart: Concerto no. 4 in D, K218, *mov. 3, b. 15*

Co-ordination

68

For *spiccato* to be clean and ringing it is essential that the finger fully stops the string before the bow touches the string. It is easy to blame the bow for a scratchy *spiccato* when the scratch is actually the fault of the finger.

- Exaggerating the timing, place the fingers silently in a syncopated rhythm between the bow strokes (shown as x-notes).

Example 1

Mozart: Sonata in E minor, K304, *mov. 1, b. 8*

- Start at a slow tempo and speed up gradually.

Example 2

Brahms: Scherzo 'Sonatensatz', WoO2, *b. 14*

- Begin at a slow tempo, and gradually speed up until near performance tempo:

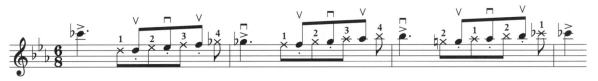

69 **Area of bow**

Spiccato nearer the **middle**:　lower, shorter, lighter, faster
Spiccato nearer the **frog**:　　higher, longer, heavier, slower

- Try different parts of the bow to find the best place for each passage. At each place experiment with the proportions of height and length of bow to find the best quality and character of *spiccato*.

Example 1　　　　　　　　　　　　　　　　　　　Mozart: Concerto no. 3 in G, K216, *mov. 1, b. 64*

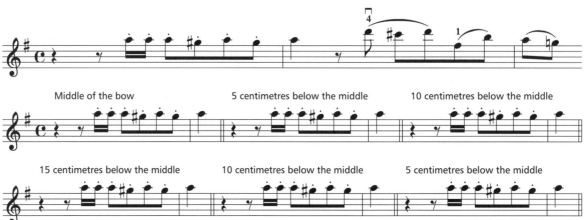

Example 2　　　　　　　　　　　　　　　　　　　Grieg: Sonata in C minor, op. 45, *mov. 3, b. 2*

- Having found exactly the right place in the bow, play straight from the repeated notes into the passage itself:

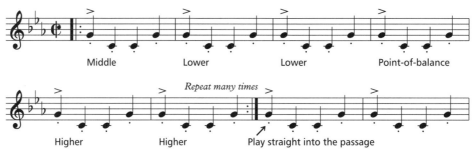

70 ***Collé-spiccato***

In ordinary *spiccato* the speed of bow is the same before, during and after touching the string. In *collé-spiccato* the bow pauses for an instant before playing each note, half a centimetre or so above the string. The bow then moves very quickly in a 'saucer-shape' or 'U-shaped' line, contacting the string with great speed at the bottom of the curve and throwing the *spiccato* note out like a pizzicato.

- Practise by enlarging all the proportions: play at a very slow tempo (wait longer between each stroke), and then move the bow very fast.

Example 1　　　　　　　　　　　　　　　　　　　Mozart: Sonata in B♭, K378, *mov. 1, b. 22*

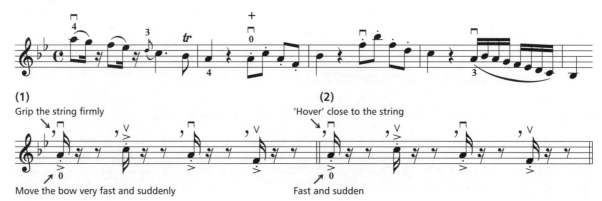

(1) It is often helpful if first you practise the stroke starting with the bow on the string.

The comma represents the bow gripping the string firmly without moving.

(2) Repeat the stroke from the air. The comma represents hovering the bow just above the string. Then move the bow very fast to catch the string with energy.

Example 2   Messiaen: Thème et variations, *Second variation, b. 3*

Avoid tension in the bow arm and hand by releasing during the space between the strokes.

● Exaggerate the moment of release by pausing between the strokes, and then play on into the passage:

| Sautillé | The chief difference between *spiccato* and *sautillé* is that in *spiccato* you are in control of each stroke, whereas in *sautillé* it is more that you *let* the bow spring. Another difference is that whereas in slow |

spiccato the bow hair leaves the string, in faster *spiccato* and *sautillé* the wood of the bow bounces but the hair stays on the string.

Legato slurs

As in staccato and *spiccato*, for good co-ordination in *sautillé* the left-hand fingers must be rhythmically even.

● Practise the passage without *sautillé*, playing long legato slurs.

Example   Saint-Saëns: Concerto no. 3 in B minor, op. 61, *mov. 3, b. 78*

Taking fingers off the bow

● Play a phrase or passage of *sautillé* (or practise on one note) with only the thumb and first finger on the bow (Fig. 9). Feel how the bow is able to move freely, pivoting around the thumb, without being restricted by the other fingers.[1]

● Also do the same with only the thumb, second and third fingers on the bow.

Repeat with a normal bow hold, feeling the same pivoting movement as when holding the bow with only the thumb and first finger.

Fig. 9

[1] See also *Bow hold*, page 302

Practising *sautillé* with only the thumb and first finger

73 **Based on *spiccato***

- Begin a passage of *sautillé* at half speed or less, playing *spiccato*.
- Gradually speed up, while letting the stroke develop into *sautillé*.

Example   Mendelssohn: Concerto in E minor, op. 64, *mov. 3, b. 168*

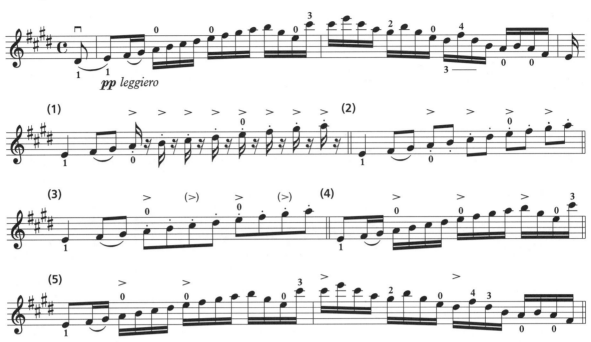

(1) Play slow *spiccato*, feeling how each stroke is an individual action. The hair clears the string completely.

[1] See *Active and passive strokes*, page 260

(2) Playing a little faster begin to group the notes in pairs, almost feeling the strokes as active–passive.[1]

(3) At a moderate tempo let the groups begin to develop into fours. Keep the hair very close to the string.

(4) Faster, feel the groups as one active, three passive. Let the wood bounce with the hair staying on the string.

(5) Very fast, guide the bow in groups of eight.

74 **Curved bow strokes**

[2] See *Curved bow strokes*, page 92

In *sautillé* the bow plays *around* the string in a slightly curved motion. Watch the point of the bow while playing the stroke. Like staccato, it has little 'dipping' movements that move it in a circular line.[2]

Example   Wieniawski: Concerto no. 2 in D minor, op. 22, *mov. 3, b. 137*

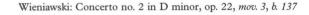

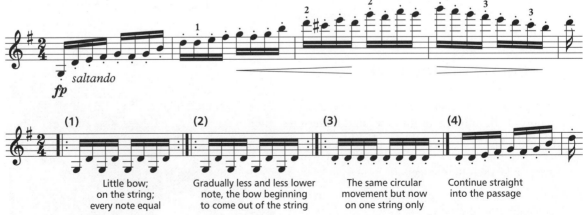

[3] While *spiccato* usually works best with less than full hair (the bow leaning towards the fingerboard), *sautillé* often works best with full hair (the wood of the bow directly above the hair).

(1) Playing at the middle (wherever the bow bounces most easily), repeat this pattern many times. Play firmly on the string with very little bow and full hair.[3] Play each note with equal strength.

(2) Gradually make a smaller and smaller circle so that the bow makes less and less contact with the G string. The lower note gradually becomes quieter until the bow no longer touches the G string at all.

At the same time, gradually let the bow begin to come out of the string.

(3) Finally, make a very small 'circle' on the D string, with the hair staying on the string and the wood of the bow bouncing.

(4) Having found the stroke in **(3)** play straight into the passage without stopping.

Area of bow

Sautillé has to be played in the particular place on the bow where the stick has the greatest natural bounce. The best place varies from bow to bow, but is usually somewhere around the middle of the bow or just above the middle. Just below the middle of the bow is a good place to play a slightly heavier *sautillé*.

Example   Vivaldi: Winter (The Four Seasons), op. 8 no. 4, *mov. 3, b. 120*

- Playing the stroke on one note, move higher and lower in the bow to find the place where the bow has the most immediate and natural bounce. Then use that place in the bow to play the passage:

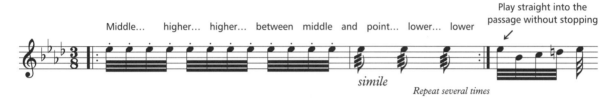

Ricochet

Experimenting with proportions

Ricochet is played in the upper half. Like *spiccato*, the main proportions to consider in ricochet are length of bow to height of bounce.[1] Ricochet nearer the middle: lower bounce, less bow, faster. Ricochet nearer the point: higher bounce, more bow, slower.

Example 1   Paganini: La Campanella, op. 7, *b. 10*

- First practise the stroke on one note. Play a group of ricochet in each area of the upper half. Start in the middle of the bow, work all the way up to the point and back down again to the middle.

- At the middle of the bow use a tiny amount of bow, with a very low, heavy and fast ricochet. As you play the group higher and higher in the bow use more bow and a higher, lighter and slower ricochet. At the point the ricochet will be very high and slow, and will use as much as a quarter of the bow.[2]

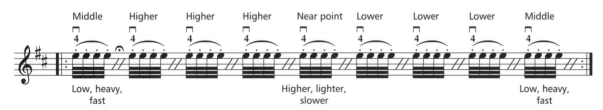

- Then do the same using the actual notes of the passage:

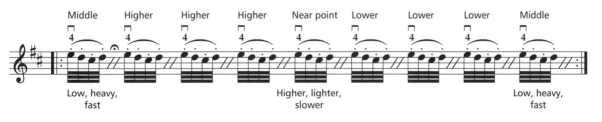

[1] In *spiccato* 'length of bow' means the distance the hair moves along the string during each note (from very short to as long as a centimetre or more). In ricochet 'length of bow' means the distance travelled in the air *between* the bouncing contacts with the string, the length of each note staying more or less the same.

See also *Lifted strokes*, page 297

[2] It is also possible to play a very fast, low ricochet at the extreme point. This will not produce such a ringing tone, but is commonly used in orchestral playing.

Example 2

Tchaikovsky: Three Pieces, op. 42, Scherzo, *b. 56*

- Play in the middle of the bow, keeping the hair very close to the string:

Tiny amount of bow   More bow   More bow   Less bow   Less bow

77 Experimenting with string crossing

- Experiment on open strings to find the best place in the bow, length of bow, and height of bounce for the ricochet to work perfectly across the strings.

Example

Bériot: Scène del Ballet, op. 100, *b. 80*

- As well as practising the specific open-string pattern of the passage, experiment with the other combinations and patterns as well:

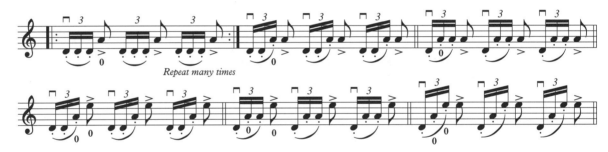

Repeat many times

78 Legato slurs

In ricochet the speed of the bow and pressure must be even, and the left-hand fingers rhythmically even.

- Build greater evenness into both hands by first practising the passage without ricochet, playing normal legato slurs.

Example

Paganini: 24 Caprices, op. 1, No. 9, *b. 61*

- Play ordinary legato slurs in the same part of the bow, and with the same length of bow, as you will use eventually for the bounced stroke.

- Learn how to play the passage with slurs as if you were going to perform it like that. Aim for evenness of bow-speed and pressure, with smooth string crossings that begin to move over to the new string early.

String crossing

String crossings can be smooth or accented. For them to be smooth, the bow should already be near the new string while playing the note or phrase on the previous string; or the bow should start to move towards the new string *while* playing the last note or notes on the previous string. Moving to a new string while playing the old string is called 'pivoting'.[1]

[1] See also *Pivoting*, page 78; *String crossings*, page 92; *'Click' practice*, page 106; *Forearm rotation*, page 265

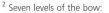

79

Playing close to the new string

In many passages the ideal is to play so close to the next string that it looks almost as if there is no string crossing at all. Bowing close to the next string is one of the most important aspects of bowing.

- The easiest way to practise this is simply to look at the hair of the bow and keep it so close to the next string that you almost touch it.

Example 1   Vivaldi: Concerto in G minor, op. 12 no. 1, *mov. 1, b. 13*

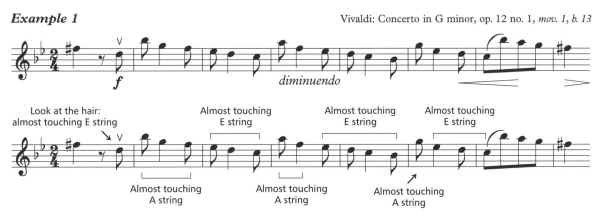

Another way to think of this is that while playing on level 5 (A string) and about to cross to level 7 (E string), the bow should stay closer to level 6 rather than moving all the way between level 5 and level 7.[2]

[2] Seven levels of the bow:

Level 1 G string
Level 2 GD strings
Level 3 D string
Level 4 DA strings
Level 5 A string
Level 6 AE strings
Level 7 E string

Example 2   Mendelssohn: Concerto in E minor, op. 64, *mov. 2, b. 9*

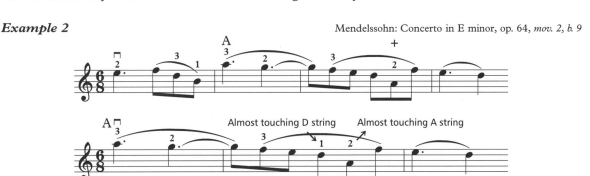

- Exaggerate the feeling of bowing on a flatter plane by playing double stops with the open strings:

Example 3   Moffat: Intrada, *b. 2*

- Exaggerate by playing double stops even if the result is discordant:

Afterwards, watch the bow hair and strings and notice how easy and natural it now seems to bow almost 'flat', close to both strings. The flatter bow produces a more singing and legato musical line, without the disturbance of wide string crossings.

80 Crossing early

The earlier the string crossing begins, the slower the crossing and the more gently the hair contacts the new string; the later it begins, the faster the crossing and the greater the impact of the hair contacting the new string.

- Practising by exaggeration, build smooth string crossings by crossing so early that you play the new string as a double stop with the old string.

Example 1   J. S. Bach: Partita no. 2 in D minor, BWV1004, *Sarabanda, b. 5*

Example 2   Beethoven: Sonata in A, op. 30 no. 1, *mov. 1, b. 3*

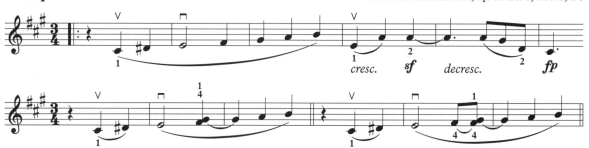

Example 3   Mozart: Concerto no. 5 in A, K219, *mov. 3, b. 16*

Example 4   Beethoven: Sonata in A, op. 47 ('Kreutzer'), *mov. 1, b. 314*

- Start at a slow tempo, keeping the bow deeply sustained in the string. Gradually speed up until near performance tempo:

Afterwards, playing the more hammered stroke that the passage requires, the string crossings will feel much smoother as you play a little more towards levels 2, 4 and 6, rather than purely on 1, 3, 5 and 7.

Example 5

Mozart: Concerto no. 4 in D, K218, *mov. 3, b. 61*

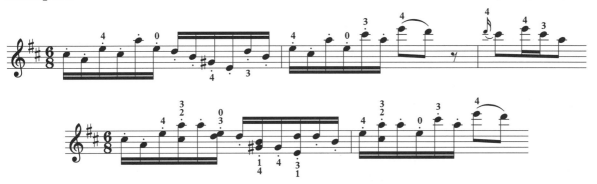

Example 6

Mendelssohn: Concerto in E minor, op. 64, *mov. 1, b. 113*

Example 7

Vieuxtemps: Concerto no. 5 in A minor, op. 37, *mov. 1, b. 113*

- Begin at a slow tempo and gradually speed up:

Example 8

Elgar: Sonata in E minor, op. 82, *mov. 1, b. 68*

In this passage the bow is always pivoting towards another string. The moment it fully arrives on a new string it begins to move towards the next string.

- Begin to move the bow towards another string during the dotted eighth-note (dotted quaver) so that all the string crossings are smooth. Do not wait until the sixteenth-note (semiquaver) to begin the string-crossing movement.

Example 9

Tchaikovsky: Concerto in D, op. 35, *mov. 1, b. 108*

- Watch the bow hair to see that this entire passage is played almost on the A string level rather than the E:

Example 10

Mozart: Sonata in B♭, K454, *mov. 2, b. 50*

Example 11

Brahms: Concerto in D, op. 77, *mov. 1, b. 152*

Example 12

Bruch: Concerto no. 1 in G minor, op. 26, *mov. 1, b. 98*

Staying close to both strings in repeated crossings

During continuous string crossings between adjacent strings the bow often needs to stay as close as possible to both strings.

Example 1   J. S. Bach: Partita no. 3 in E, BWV1006, *Preludio, b. 3*

- First play double stops to gain the feeling of keeping the bow close to both strings:

- Then taking this method further, gradually begin to favour the note in the double stop that is the actual note of the passage.

- Play very slowly at first.

- Begin to move very slightly towards the lower and then the higher string so that the double stops become uneven – one string played louder on the down-bow and the other string played louder on the up-bow:

- Gradually play the other note of the double stop more and more softly:

- Play the extra note more and more softly until playing only single strings, but with the bow so close to the other string that it almost touches it.

After going through this process for only a few moments, the normal bowing strokes will feel very fluid and easy.

Example 2   Ysaÿe: Sonata, op. 27 no. 2, *mov. 1, b. 11*

- Begin with double stops and then begin to favour one string more than the other as in Example 1:

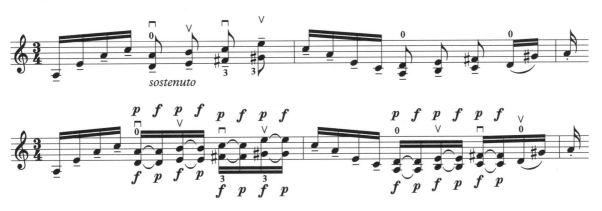

Example 3   Brahms: Sonata no. 3 in D minor, op. 108, *mov. 1, b. 84*

*molto **p** e sotto voce sempre*

82 'Click' practice

After crossing from one string to another the exact part of the hair that contacts the new string is different from the place on the hair that finished playing the previous string.

As the bow moves to a higher string (playing up the strings G–D–A–E), each new contact point of the hair with the new string is lower down the bow, i.e. in the direction of the frog. Moving to a lower string (playing down the strings E–A–D–G), each new contact point is higher up the bow.

- Gain clarity and precision by measuring the changing contact-points consciously, as follows:

  1 Begin each stroke with a 'click'. A click is a sharp, clean attack at the very beginning of the stroke. Sink the bow heavily into the string, and 'bend' the string sideways a little before pulling the bow.[1]

  2 Stop the bow quite suddenly to end the stroke, leaving the bow on the string.

  3 With the bow stationary, not moving along the string, pivot over to the new string. Note the new contact point of the string with the hair.

  4 Begin this new stroke with a 'click', and so on.

[1] See *Catching the string*, page 89

Example 1   J. S. Bach: Partita no. 2 in D minor, BWV1004, *Ciaccona, b. 33*

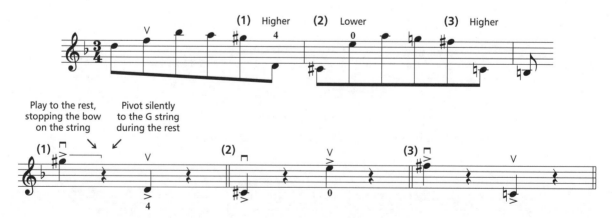

(1) The place on the hair where the up-bow D begins is three centimetres or so higher up the bow than the place on the hair where the G♯ finishes.

(2) The open E begins three centimetres lower down the bow than the place on the hair where the C♯ finishes.

(3) The same as **(1)**.

Example 2

Rode: 24 Caprices, No. 2, *b. 4*

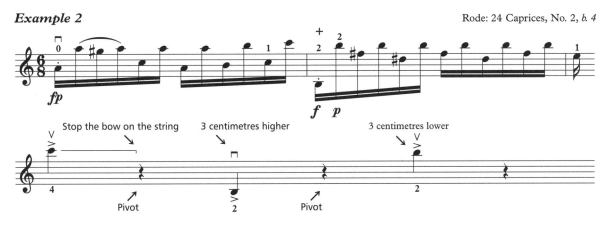

Example 3

Kreutzer: 42 Etudes ou caprices, No. 10, *b. 3*

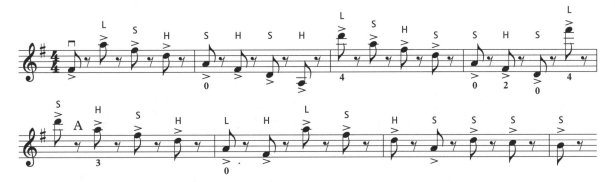

- Practise entire passages with clicks. Play very slowly, measuring the changing contact points as follows:

S = Same
The stroke begins at exactly the same place on the hair as the end of the previous stroke.

L = Lower
The stroke begins lower on the hair (towards the frog) than the end of the previous stroke.

H = Higher
The stroke begins higher on the hair than the end of the previous stroke.

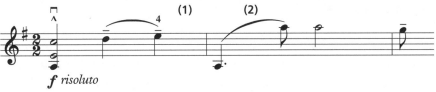

Example 4

Elgar: Sonata in E minor, op. 82, *mov. 1, b. 1*

- Join the two notes of a string crossing by beginning with a space between them, and then reduce the space gradually.

83 One action, not two

Play the stroke that is immediately before a fast string crossing, and the string crossing itself, as one action, not two. In the following example there are three 'actions', not five:

Action 1: Play ⊓ G and in the same movement cross to the E string level
Action 2: Play ∨ E and in the same movement cross to the G string level
Action 3: Play ⊓ G

Not:

Action 1: Play ⊓ G
Action 2: Cross to the E string level
Action 3: Play ∨ E
Action 4: Cross to the G string level
Action 5: Play ⊓ G

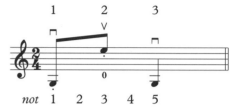

The following examples show various ways to merge the stroke and the string crossing into one action:

- Add extra notes to make the bow begin to move towards the new string earlier.
- Use dotted rhythms to exaggerate the speed of the string crossing.

Example 1

(Upper half, *martelé*) Kreutzer: 42 Etudes ou caprices, No. 17, *b. 1*

Play at the same tempo as the original passage:

Example 2 J. S. Bach: Sonata in G minor, BWV1001, *Presto, b. 12*

- Play the 32nd-notes (demisemiquavers) with a fast, ricochet-like *spiccato*, strictly in time.
- Play in the same part of the bow, with the same amount of bow, as in the passage itself.
- Begin slowly, and gradually speed up to as fast a tempo as possible.

Example 3 Vivaldi: Autumn (The Four Seasons), op. 8 no. 3, *mov. 1, b. 72*

- Play in the same part of the bow as in the passage itself.
- Begin slowly, and gradually speed up to as fast a tempo as possible.

Example 4

- The x-notes = put the finger down on the string, but wait with the bow above the string without playing it.
- Play in the same part of the bow, with the same amount of bow, as in the passage itself.
- Begin slowly, and gradually speed up to as fast a tempo as possible.

Example 5

Kreutzer: 42 Etudes ou caprices, No. 30, *b. 1*

Example 6

Paganini: Concerto no. 1 in D, op. 6, *mov. 1, b. 254*

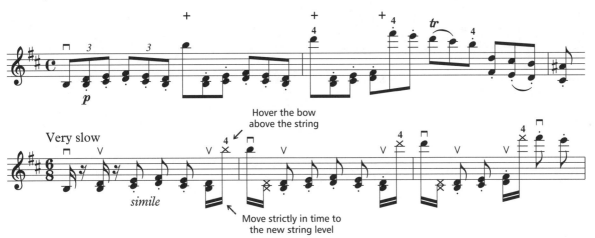

Imagine that each eighth-note (quaver) is a sixteenth-note (semiquaver) followed by a sixteenth-note rest.

- During the rest before the string crossings marked '+' move the bow to the next string level and 'hover' near to the string. This is marked as an x-note.
- Arrive exactly in time on the x-note, feeling the note before the string crossing and the crossing as one single action.
- Begin slowly at about ♪ = 60 and gradually speed up to as fast a tempo as possible.

Bow division

While nothing in playing should be 'fixed', including musical ideas,[1] at the same time every bow stroke needs to be *designed*.[2] Throughout the whole process of building and polishing any passage, at the back of your mind ask yourself a continuous stream of simple questions:

1. Exactly where in the bow does the stroke begin?

2. Where does it end?

3. How close to the bridge (does it stay the same distance away during the whole stroke, or should it move closer to, or further from, the bridge)?

4. How fast is the stroke (is it even, or fast–slow, slow–fast, slow–fast–slow, fast–slow–fast, etc.)?

5. How much pressure (is it even, or heavy–light, light–heavy, light–heavy–light, heavy–light–heavy, etc.)?

6. How much hair?

[1] The great Spanish cellist Pablo Casals would typically learn six or more different ways of playing each phrase, not choosing which 'version' to play (or which variation of a version) until he came to it in the concert. Approached in this way, learning and performing music from the printed score remains natural, spontaneous and improvisatory.

84

[2] The better and more exactly the strokes are designed, the more you build up a repertoire or library of strokes which can be called up and used whenever needed. The standard when first learning a piece then becomes higher, new pieces already sounding good and feeling comfortable right from the start. Sight-reading also improves.

Even, *cantabile* bowing

The bow is to the string player the same as the breath to a singer or wind player. Evenness is everything. Be constantly alert to the beginnings of notes to avoid unintentionally playing a 'slow–fast–slow' bow speed pattern (creating a bulge or 'banana note'), or causing unmusical accents with sudden surges of bow speed.

Example 1   Mozart: Concerto no. 5 in A, K219, *mov. 2, b. 22*

'Banana notes' are created by three factors, usually all three occurring at the same time: (1) bow speed: slow–fast–slow, (2) bow pressure: light–heavy–light, (3) vibrato: none at the beginning of the note.

The passage must not come out sounding as follows:

● Playing at a slow tempo, control the speed of bow by dividing the bow evenly, particularly at the beginning of the stroke where there is the greatest danger of creating a banana note:

Example 2   Raff: Cavatina, op. 85, no. 3, *b. 1*

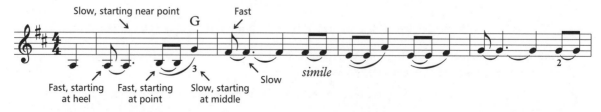

The bow speed must not accidentally surge at the beginning of each stroke:

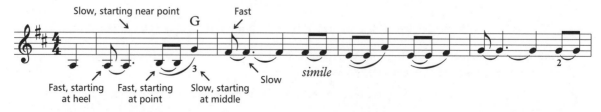

● Practising by exaggeration, hold the bow back at the beginning of each stroke and play 'slow–fast' instead of 'fast–slow'.

- Compensate for the slow speed by playing closer to the bridge, the bow hair deep in the string:

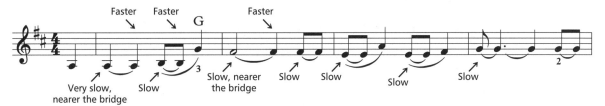

- Change gradually from the exaggerated slow beginning, to the faster speed later in the bow, so that there is no change in tone: throughout make one, rich, sonorous tone, deep in the string and with a feeling of pulling in to the bridge.

Afterwards, playing with an even, singing stroke, the bow will flow very naturally and easily.

Using less bow when a note is important

85

Although more-important notes sometimes need extra bow speed at the beginning of the note, very often there is a feeling of greater stature, as well as deeper expression, when less bow is used. Then the stroke begins with an even bow speed, deep in the string, and usually nearer the bridge.

Afterwards, the bow can move faster and lighter (not with an accent but imperceptibly), using the bow length that was saved at the beginning of the stroke.

- Practising by exaggeration, begin these strokes with such a slow bow speed, and so deep in the string, that the tone feels just on the edge of breaking. Keep the sound pure and evenly sustained nevertheless.

Example 1   Bruch: Concerto No. 1 in G minor, op. 26, *mov. 1, b. 6*

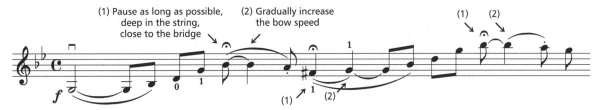

- Play the notes marked by the brackets with a broad stroke. Use as much bow as possible – a third of the bow or more – in the upper half of the bow, about midway between the bridge and the fingerboard.

- Begin the notes marked '+' with a slow, concentrated stroke close to the bridge.

- Then, using the bow that has been saved, develop the note by subtly increasing the bow speed.

Example 2   Beethoven: Romanze in F, op. 50, *b. 24*

The top G could be played with a strong attack. Another approach would be to begin the G with a slow bow deep in the string near the bridge.

- Exaggerate the slow bow at the beginning of the stroke by pausing and sustaining.

- Then, having used little bow during the first half of the G, use the bow that has been saved to keep the note alive and growing with bow speed.

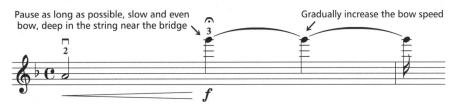

Example 3 Brahms: Sonata no. 2 in A, op. 100, *mov. 1, b. 249*

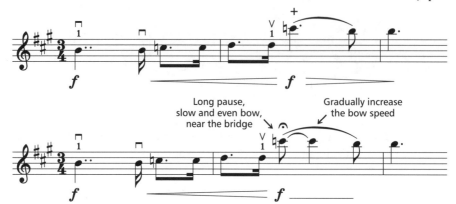

Example 4 Mozart: Adagio in E, K261, *b. 17*

The notes marked '+' are played with a fast–slow bow speed; but then the notes marked '++' are played with a more even bow speed, nearer the bridge.

- Practise with an exaggeratedly long, slow, even-speed stroke, represented by the half-notes (minims) below:

Example 5 Mozart: Sonata in B♭, K454, *mov. 1, b. 50*

The two up-beat C's in each bar are played on the string with a fast–slow bow speed and a slightly heavy–light pressure, and the slurs that follow them are played with a slight stress on the first C. But the C marked '+', and the other notes under that slur, are played with an even bow speed and pressure.

- Practise as in Example 4:

Example 6 Franck: Sonata in A, *mov. 2, b. 95*

- To have enough power in the crescendo to the *ff*, play the eighth-notes (quavers) with strong accents. Pause on the top B (marked '+'), playing deeply into the string, near the bridge, with a very slow bow:

Pause as long as possible, slow and even bow, deep in the string near the bridge

[1] See *Different qualities of the bow at heel and point*, page 69; *The give of the wood of the bow and the hair*, page 297

Feel how the hair of the bow is rigid at the point, at the very beginning of the pause, in contrast to the give of the wood in the middle of the bow.[1]

Two-thirds – one-third – two-thirds

'Two-thirds – one-third – two-thirds', used for groups of three strokes, is a logical method of moving smoothly and evenly to a different part of the bow. It avoids the danger of an unwanted accent caused by suddenly moving the bow faster on one particular note.

- Practising by exaggeration, divide the bow exactly into two-thirds – one-third – two-thirds, even if in performance the bow division may not be as precise as that.

Example 1   Franck: Sonata in A, *mov. 4, b. 162*

The G at the beginning of the second bar, and the B♭ at the beginning of the fourth bar, are whole bows (WB), starting at the heel and finishing at the point.

The first of the three eighth-notes (quavers) marked '+' begins at the point. The question is how to play the three strokes so that you get back to the heel again for the whole bow at the beginning of the third bar.

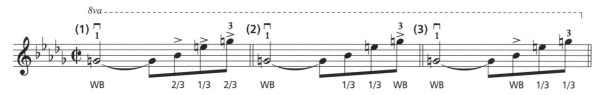

(1) Two-thirds – one-third – two-thirds. With this bow division it is easy to play the strokes evenly, or to crescendo through them evenly.

(2) The note E returns the bow to the point. Using a whole bow on the third stroke could then produce an unwanted accent.

(3) After a whole bow on the B♭ it is difficult to produce enough breadth of tone, in the following two strokes, to equal it.

Example 2   Lalo: Symphonie espagnole, op. 21, *mov. 1, b. 50*

Start at the heel

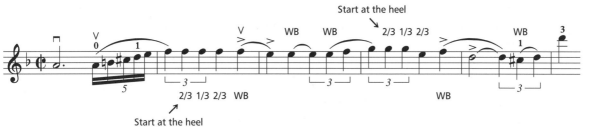

Start at the heel

Example 3

Brahms: Concerto in D, op. 77, *mov. 2, b. 91*

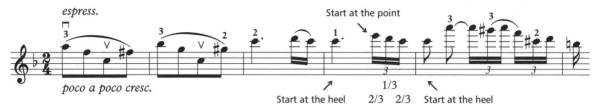

Example 4

Saint-Saëns: Concerto no. 3 in B minor, op. 61, *mov. 1, b. 48*

Example 5

J. S. Bach: Partita no. 1 in B minor, BWV1002, *Corrente, b. 11*

- Practising by exaggeration, enlarge the bow division by using far more bow than necessary to play the slurs, and work back down the bow during the separate bows:

87 Working up or down the bow

Like 'two-thirds–one-third–two-thirds', moving to a different place in the bow by using more bow in one direction than the other is a common feature of bowing.

Example 1

Franck: Sonata in A, *mov. 2, b. 112*

One way to play this phrase is to use as much bow as possible, starting in the middle of the bow and working up in the direction of the heel. To do this, play each up-bow slightly longer than each down-bow.

- Practising by exaggeration, begin at the point and work all the way up the bow so that the top F♯ is played at the extreme heel.

- Connect the strokes to each other without a break in the sound. Make them entirely even, undisturbed by the longer bows on the up-bows, and with the bow remaining deep in the string:

Example 2   Brahms: Sonata no. 3 in D minor, op. 108, *mov. 4, b. 297*

The second bar needs a lot of bow. Rather than saving bow so that the eighth-notes (quavers) marked '+' are played in the upper half, play freely on the up-bow and then work your way back to the upper half again for the A in the fifth bar.

- Exaggerate by using too much bow on the F in the second bar, so that the eighth-notes begin near the heel.

- Making the down- and up-bows sound the same, as if played with an equal amount of bow, use more bow on the down-bows than the up-bows so that the bow ends up in the upper half to begin the fifth bar.

Example 3   Elgar: Sonata in E minor, op. 82, *mov. 1, b. 2*

The eighth-notes in the second bar are played broadly with much bow. They are most comfortable to play in the middle to upper half of the bow, but you need to work up the bow in the direction of the heel for the A♯.

- Exaggerate by saving bow on the half-note (minim) A, so that the eighth-notes begin in the upper half.

- Using broad, sustained strokes, use more bow on the up-bows than on the down-bows so that the bow ends up near the heel to begin the A♯. Make the down- and up-bows sound equal despite the unequal bow lengths.

Long, slow, sustained strokes: practising at a slower tempo

- Exaggerate any difficulty in sustaining by practising the passage at half-tempo.

- Play near the bridge to save bow, always aiming for a good tone.[1]

Example 1   Rode: 24 Caprices, No. 3, *b. 1*

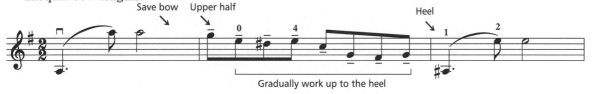

Example 2   Beethoven: Concerto in D, op. 61, *mov. 2, b. 45*

[1] To save bow: play nearer the bridge. This is an example of getting a result by doing something other than the most immediate or obvious thing. Here the obvious way to save bow is to move it more slowly; however, if nothing else changes, the tone may easily become strangled. If instead you move closer to the bridge as an immediate reaction to wanting to save bow, you automatically move the bow more slowly anyway.

String instruments offer many other examples of achieving results by seemingly indirect means, e.g. faster fingers: closer to the string; faster vibrato: narrower movement, or more on the tip of the finger than the pad; faster *détaché* or tremolo: less bow; faster *spiccato*: lower bounce; faster staccato: less bow; faster shift: lighter finger; more *forte*: first finger (right hand) further from the thumb.

88

89 Saving bow: exaggeration

- To practise saving bow on a particular stroke, exaggerate by using a very small amount of bow while still playing with tone and expression. Afterwards, using the right amount of bow feels very easy.

Example 1   Kreutzer: 24 Etudes ou caprices, No. 29, *b. 1*

- Practise playing a whole bar using only the lower half of the bow, playing strictly between the heel and the middle.

- Then use only a quarter of the bow, playing strictly between the heel and point-of-balance.

Afterwards, the whole bow will feel as if it is twice the length that it was before.

Example 2   Brahms: Scherzo (Sonatensatz), WoO2, *b. 8*

If you use too much bow on the phrase in the second bar (marked '+') you end up too high in the bow to play the *ff spiccato* in the next bar; yet having to save bow can make the phrase feel cramped.

- Practise by using only 10 centimetres of bow to play the down-bow – or even less bow if possible.

- Play deep in the string, near the bridge, with as much sonority and expression as possible:

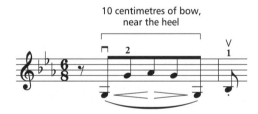

Afterwards, bowing only as far as the point-of-balance, or a little beyond, feels like a generous amount of bow in which to play such a short phrase.

Example 3   Sibelius: Concerto in D minor, op. 47, *mov. 1, b. 222*

Each note in bar 222, the bottom and top B♭, needs about half a bow.

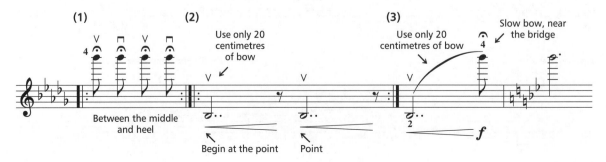

(1) Practise the top B♭ on its own, sustaining it on a long pause in the lower half. Alternate between playing with vibrato, and playing without. Build the most passionate, rich, resonant tone possible on this note.

(2) See how little bow you can use while still making the crescendo. Play very close to the bridge.

(3) Still exaggerating the bow division, join the bottom and the top together. Crescendo on the bottom B♭ using as little bow as possible, and use all the remaining bow for the top B♭, playing a long pause.

Afterwards, when playing the passage normally, there is a feeling of great freedom of expression in the bow.

Using enough bow: exaggeration

90

- For passages that need a lot of bow to bring out the breadth or stature of the music, practise by using an exaggerated amount of bow. Afterwards, the correct amount of bow feels perfectly natural.

For the purposes of the exercise 'whole bow' means from one centimetre above the nut, to one centimetre below the point, even if this is more bow than you will use eventually.

Example 1   Bruch: Concerto no. 1 in G minor, op. 26, *mov. 1, b. 37*

The eighth-notes (quavers) in this passage can be played with half a bow or more each.

- Playing with the metronome, play whole bows on one note.
- Start at ♩ = 40, and gradually increase the speed as indicated.
- Keep the speed and pressure of the bow even, and stay at the same distance from the bridge.

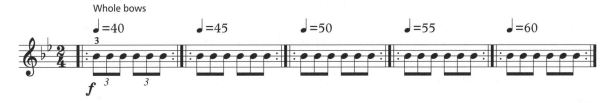

Then play the passage using the correct amount of bow. Even a very broad stroke will now feel effortless.

Example 2   Haydn: Concerto no. 1 in C, *mov. 1, b. 70*

The up-bows in this example can be played with much bow, so that by the end of the crescendo each bar begins near the point and each quarter-note (crotchet) begins near the heel.

- Free the bow arm by practising whole bows in the rhythm of the passage. The up-bows must be played more lightly than the down-bows to avoid an accent.
- Start at ♩ = 60, and gradually increase the speed as indicated. Continue up to about ♩ = 120.

Example 3 Brahms: Sonata no. 2 in A, op. 100, *mov. 1, b. 43*

- Although they must not stand out as an accent, the two quarter-notes (crotchets) marked '+' can be played broadly, almost with whole bows. Practise each of them on its own, and then find the same stroke in the context of the passage:

Whole bows

Example 4 Dvořák: Romance, op. 11, *b. 58*

Whole bows near the bridge

91 Using enough bow: gradually speeding up

Playing separate bows, the faster the stroke the less bow is used – just as the faster the vibrato the narrower it becomes, the faster the trill the closer the trilling finger must stay to the string, and so on.

- To develop a broad, fast stroke, begin at a slow tempo while using much bow (or with exaggerated bow length); then gradually increase the tempo while keeping the bow length the same.

Example 1 Kreutzer: 42 Etudes ou caprices, No. 8, *b. 1*

- Begin slowly at ♪ = 50, using half bows. Keeping the bow length the same with every stroke, gradually increase the metronome through 55, 60, 65, 70, until faster than the tempo of the passage.

- Keep the bow solidly and evenly in the string throughout.

Example 2 Ysaÿe: Sonata, op. 27 no. 2, *mov. 1, b. 3*

- Begin slowly at ♪ = 50, using a whole bow on each note. Gradually increase the metronome through 55, 60, 65, 70, until arriving at the tempo of the passage.

- While always trying to use as much bow as possible, as the speed increases allow yourself to use less and less bow until arriving at the correct tempo with a broad, powerful stroke.

- Keep the bow solidly and evenly in the string throughout.

Left hand

part 4

Isolating the left hand from the bow

One of the most noticeable qualities of a good left-hand technique is the smoothness and evenness of the finger action. The fingers must not be affected by the often energetic and acrobatic movements of the bow. They need always to be ready for the notes that lie just ahead, the whole hand remaining relaxed, light and effortless, the fingers staying close to the strings.

● Work on the left hand on its own in order to see exactly what is happening in the hand and fingers.

Using slurs

One way to focus on the left hand, without the distraction of the bow strokes, is to use long slurs. This removes all factors of the bow or co-ordination, leaving you free to work on left-hand evenness and ease.[1]

● Practise the slurs until the passage is entirely smooth and even, the fingers staying close to the strings and using minimum energy and effort.

● Then keep the same close, relaxed and easy feeling in the left hand when bowing the passage properly.

[1] See *Legato Slurs*, pages 90, 93, 97, 100

Example 1   Smetana: Aus der Heimat, *mov. 2, b. 212*

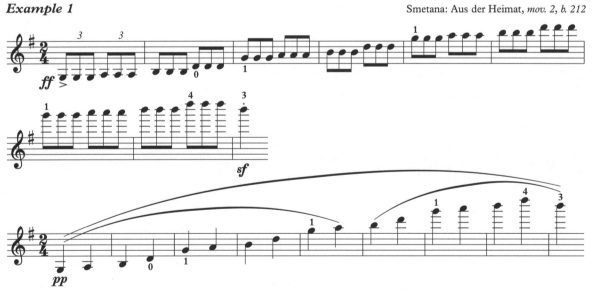

● Vibrate on every note.

Example 2   Mozart: Concerto no. 5 in A, K219, *mov. 3, b. 134*

● Aim for machine-like evenness of rhythm in the fingers.

Left hand   119

Example 3

Prokofiev: Concerto no. 2 in G minor, op. 63, *mov. 2, b. 71*

- Play with the same musical commitment as if the passage were actually written with slurs:

Example 4

Mendelssohn: Concerto in E minor, op. 64, *mov. 1, b. 97*

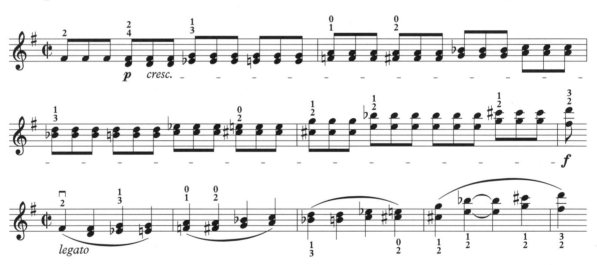

Example 5

Bruch: Concerto no. 1 in G minor, op. 26, *mov. 3, b. 321*

- Play **pp** to encourage the left-hand fingers to be light and effortless.
- Then remember that feeling of effortlessness when playing the correct bowing **ff**.

Example 6

Vivaldi: Winter (The Four Seasons), op. 8 no. 4, *mov. 3, b. 80*

Example 7

Sibelius: Concerto in D minor, op. 47, *mov. 1, b. 234*

- Begin slowly, and gradually speed up. As you get faster play more than one bar to a bow, until finally playing the whole line in one bow.

Example 8

Wieniawski: Polonaise brillante, op. 21, *b. 26*

93 Using double stops

In passages of repeated string crossings it is often helpful to play them as double stops. As well as removing all factors of bowing, the double stops also shine a new light on the placement of the fingers in relation to each other.

Example 1   Mozart: Concerto no. 3 in G, K216, *mov. 3, b. 81*

Example 2   Rode: 24 Caprices, No. 11, *b. 7*

Example 3   Brahms: Sonata no. 3 in D minor, op. 108, *mov. 1, b. 120*

94 Playing without the bow

When playing several notes slurred in one bow, rhythm is entirely controlled by the left-hand fingers.

- Finger a phrase or passage without the bow to check that the fingers are decisive and rhythmically precise. Concentrate on hesitation-free, controlled, rhythmic placement of the fingers.

- Imagine that the fingers themselves are producing the tone and expression, rather than being moved mechanically without musical feeling. Vary the weight of each finger in the string according to the expression. Mentally hear the notes as clearly as if you were actually playing.

[1] See *Co-ordination*, page 14 Since the left-hand fingers always lead the bow,[1] gaining this rhythmic confidence by fingering without the bow also improves co-ordination.

[1] David Blum: *Casals and the Art of Interpretation* (London, 1977), 125.

Trills

The mechanics of playing a trill, like all other matters of technique, work on a much higher technical level when the trill is felt musically and expressively, rather than being merely the result of 'moving your fingers up and down fast'. Pablo Casals described trills as bringing 'exaltation' to a note.[1]

95

Playing without the trill

- Learn the passage without the distraction of trills to find the best rhythm, character and phrasing.

- Then make sure that nothing is disturbed when you put the trills back in.

Example   Haydn: Concerto no. 1 in C, *mov. 1, b. 131*

96

Speed: height of finger

In some ways trills are similar to vibrato. Where vibrato has proportions of speed to width,[2] trills have proportions of speed to height of finger. To vibrate faster it is natural to make the vibrato narrower (unless musically undesirable), to lessen the distance the finger moves. To play more notes in a trill, keep the fingers closer to the strings to lessen the distance they move up and down.

[2] See *Vibrato*, page 298

- Play the trill with such low fingers that they barely clear the string, causing 'fuzz' in the trill. Gradually use a little higher lift-off until the trill is both very fast and very clean.

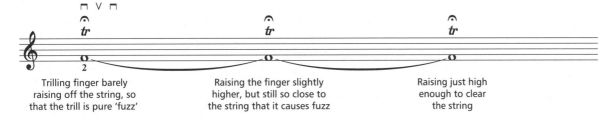

Trilling finger barely raising off the string, so that the trill is pure 'fuzz'   Raising the finger slightly higher, but still so close to the string that it causes fuzz   Raising just high enough to clear the string

97

Speed: direction of movement

Trills and vibrato are also similar in that in vibrato there is only one active movement – forward to the in-tune note (see margin note, page 128). A vibrato with an active forward and active backward movement is difficult to do fast.

In trills there is also only one active movement. The finger moves up–up–up–up, not down–down–down–down or down–up–down–up. Trills with both an active downward and upward movement are difficult to play fast.

Example 1   Beethoven: Concerto in D, op. 61, *mov. 1, b. 209*

- Play trills with these dotted rhythms, lifting the finger quickly as if the string were very hot:

Play   Practise

Example 2

Brahms: Hungarian Dance no. 1, *b. 25*

- Play the grace notes as short as possible.
- Gradually speed up the second bar to as fast a tempo as possible.

98 Clarity: adding notes one at a time in tempo

Rather than leaving the number of notes in a trill to chance, you can gain greater clarity and brilliance by counting the number of notes, and by building up the trill one note at a time. It is often useful to practise more notes than you will eventually use.

- In the following examples play the groups as fast as possible, starting slowly and building up gradually.

Example 1

Mozart: Concerto no. 4 in D, K218, *mov. 1, b. 98*

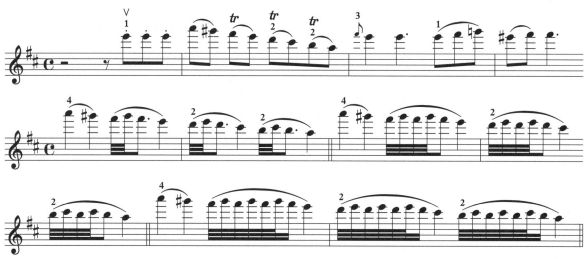

Example 2

Bruch: Scottish Fantasy, op. 46, *mov. 1, b. 21*

Example 3   Prokofiev: Cinq Mélodies, op. 35, No. 2, *b. 49*

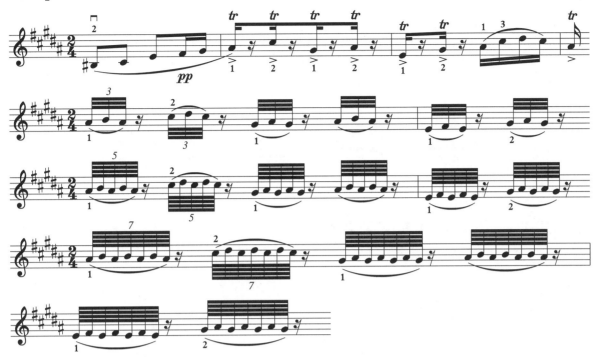

Clarity: adding notes one at a time while pausing

99

One of the aims of this practice method is to make the string vibrate as widely as possible to give the left-hand fingers as big a task as possible.[1] Do this by drawing the bow swiftly with extra bow speed to make the string vibrate the widest, adding the notes of the trill one at a time. Afterwards the normal trill will feel easy to play and each note will speak clearly.

[1] See also *Speed of left hand finger movement*, page 298

- Use many bows during the pauses, sustaining the sound fully and evenly on soundpoint 2 (see Fig. 5, page 47). When you then add the fingers, do not alter the stroke in any way as the fingers lift and fall.

- To isolate the fingers from the bow change, do not change bow and move the fingers at the same time.

Example 1   Schubert: Sonatina in A minor, op. 137 no. 2, *mov. 3, b. 1*

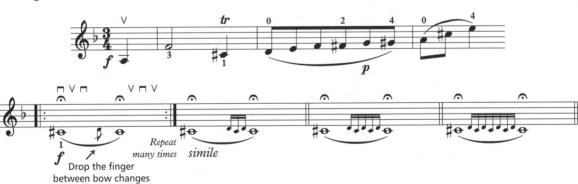

Example 2   Mozart: Concerto no. 3 in G, K216, *mov. 1 cadenza (Sam Franko)*

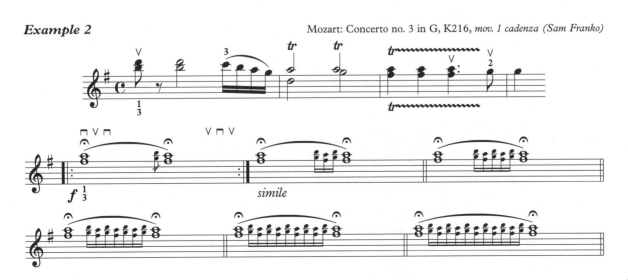

100 Using other fingers as models

- Ideally, any pair of fingers is as good for trilling as any other pair. However, if you find that some fingers trill better than others, use the most comfortable fingers to serve as a model, and then make the correct fingering sound exactly the same.[1]

[1] This is a good example of 'getting the result you hold in your mind'. If you picture the finger trilling slowly and clumsily, the trill will probably come out like that.

The point of using the model is to get a better mental picture very quickly.

Holding an image in your mind of the fingers moving very fast and very easily will improve the trill instantaneously, and often dramatically. See *Mental rehearsal*, page 290

Example 1

Beethoven: Sonata in A, op. 30 no. 1, *mov. 3, b. 67*

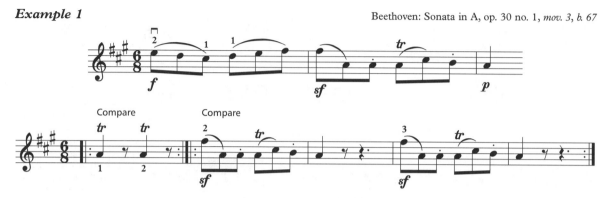

Example 2

Kreutzer: 42 Etudes ou caprices, No. 19, *b. 1*

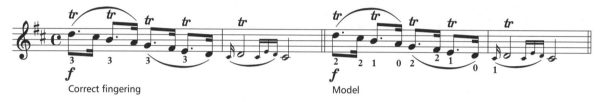

Correct fingering   Model

101 Timing the rhythm of the turn

Build solid, rhythmic pulse and structure into a trill to avoid the common tendency for the turn to be too slow, or to be played after too long a trill. Otherwise the trill as a whole may lose energy, and the first beat of the next bar might be played late.

- Build rhythmic accuracy by adding the trill and the turn separately.

Example 1

Mozart: Concerto no. 3 in G, K216, *mov. 1, b. 79*

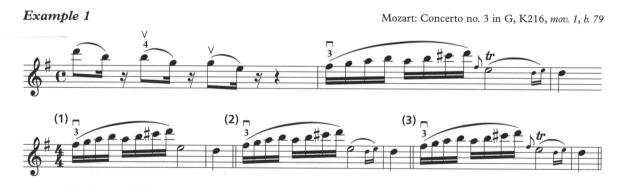

(1) Leave out the trill and the turn. Play exactly in time.

Play with the same musical commitment as if the cadence really was written without a trill.

(2) Still leaving out the trill, play the turn very 'late' and fast, connecting it to the following note (D).[2]

[2] See also *Dotted patterns*, page 287

(3) Play both the trill and the turn.

Example 2

Kreutzer: 42 Etudes ou caprices, No. 31, *b. 1*

No trills, no turns   Only the turns

Example 3   Beethoven: Romanze in F, op. 50, *b. 4*

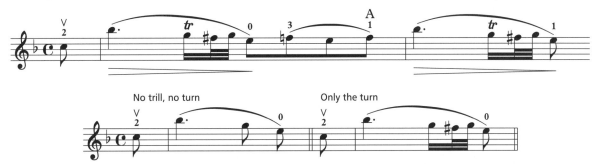

Example 4   Viotti: Concerto no. 22 in A minor, *mov. 1, b. 211*

Inaudible change of bow

102

- To make a change of bow during a trill unnoticeable, change bow on one of the upper notes of the trill.

Example 1   Mozart: Concerto no. 3 in G, K216, *mov. 1, b. 209*

- Practise by playing the trill under tempo, with a very slight accent on the change of bow:

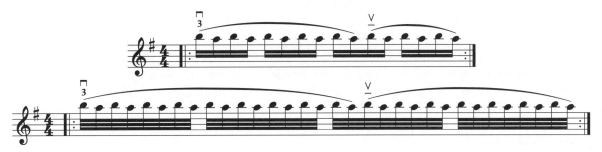

Example 2   Bruch: Concerto no. 1 in G minor, op. 26, *mov. 2, b. 45*

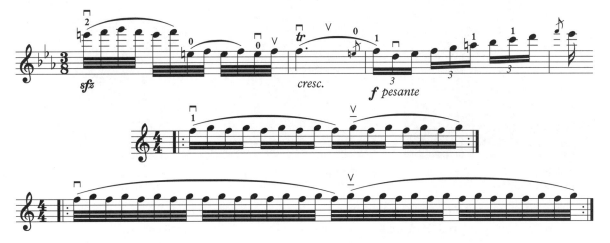

103 **Sustaining trills while playing another line**

- Form repetitive patterns, starting slowly and speeding up gradually. Afterwards, the passage as written will feel much easier.

Example 1   Brahms: Concerto in D, op. 77, *mov. 1 cadenza (Joachim)*

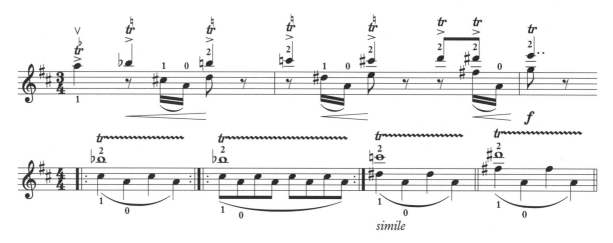

simile

Example 2   Sibelius: Concerto in D minor, op. 47, *mov. 1, b. 119*

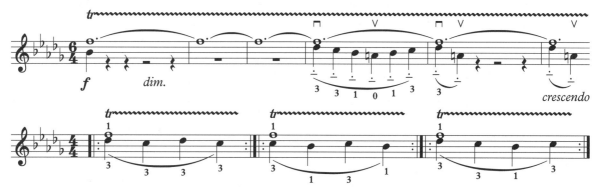

104 Vibrato

The track

The finger rolls backwards and forwards on the 'track'.[1] To see the track, place the second finger on the A string in its normal position to play C.

[1] One complete vibrato cycle:

1 The note in tune
2 The finger rolled back a fraction
3 The note in tune

The finger should never vibrate above the in-tune note. The ear catches the upper pitch of the vibrato as the pitch of the note, so if you vibrate sharp of the note it sounds as though you are playing the note itself sharp.

Slowly roll the finger backwards and forwards as though doing a slowed-down vibrato movement. Roll in both directions as far as you can reasonably go. As you do so press the finger unnaturally hard into the string so that you create a groove (Fig. 10a). The exact position and angle of this line will naturally vary with each individual, and from note to note; but notice how the groove extends to the fingernail at one end, and into the middle of the pad at the other. Using a ballpoint pen, draw a line over the groove before it fades away.

Fig. 10

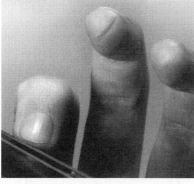

(a) Roll on the string to make a groove

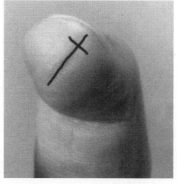

(b) The finger does not roll forward beyond this point

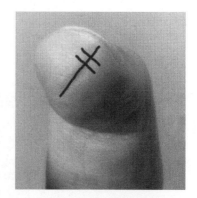

(c) Portion of the track used for 'average' vibrato

The vibrato would be far too wide if it used the whole length of the track, so you have to select a tiny portion of it on which to roll. Find where this is by beginning with the part of the track nearest the nail.

If you roll right to the end of the track near to the fingernail, it causes the entire finger to lean over towards the bridge. Since the finger should always lean the other way, in the direction of the scroll, you have to avoid rolling into the last section of the track nearest to the nail. Mark a new line on the track showing this cut-off point – the furthest point the finger rolls during the forward movement of the vibrato (Fig. 10b).

Find this point by sitting the finger on the string in a comfortable, upright, balanced, natural shape and note how much of the track at the fingertip is not contacting the string.

Now draw a second line a millimetre or two from the first one (Fig. 10c) to find your basic area of the track on which to roll. Sometimes the vibrato will be wider than this, sometimes so narrow that the two lines are almost touching. Sometimes the selected portion of the track is nearer the tip, sometimes nearer the pad – see below.

- During any work on vibrato or intonation, constantly refer back to awareness of the track, in particular asking two questions: (1) how far are you rolling on the track, and (2) where on the track are you rolling?

Area of fingertip: pad or tip

105

The width of vibrato is partly a result of the placement of the fingertip on the string:

- More **tip** of the finger on the string = **narrower** vibrato (Fig. 11a).
- More **pad** of the finger on the string = **wider** vibrato (Fig. 11b).

Fig. 11

(a) Note how the finger contacts the string more on the tip of the finger

(b) Note how the finger contacts the string more on the pad

- Repeat a note or short phrase several times, each time experimenting with a different placement of the fingers. As shown in Fig. 11, move gradually between more on the tip and less on the tip, until finding the desired vibrato colour and expression.

Example 1 Rode: Concerto no. 7 in A minor, op. 9, *mov. 1, b. 83*

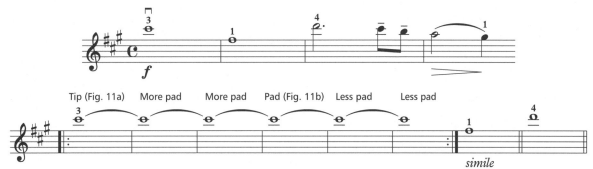

Example 2 Dvořák: Concerto in A minor, op. 53, *mov. 1, b. 22*

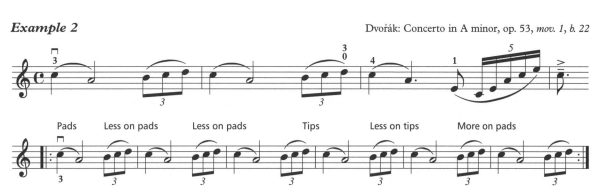

106 ## Correcting over-wide vibrato

If you are used to a wide vibrato, when you make it narrower the vibrato may seem inaudible and expressionless in comparison, and you quickly go back to the wider vibrato that you had before.

- Use non-vibrato as a continual reference point to prevent the vibrato becoming over-wide (and slow).

- After playing non-vibrato, a wide vibrato seems *very* wide in comparison, and much more variety of colour comes into the playing. Apply the process to individual notes in pieces, and to complete phrases.

Example 1   Lalo: Symphonie espagnole, op. 21, *mov. 2, b. 102*

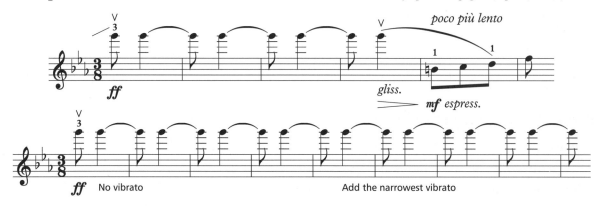

(1) Sustain the G without vibrato near the bridge, looking for the exact proportions of speed and pressure to produce a ringing and even tone, the string vibrating widely.

(2) Add the narrowest vibrato and listen to the tone change from a 'straight', bare sound into one that 'shimmers' or 'throbs'. Notice how the throbbing is part of the tone itself.

This creates a vibrato that sounds like 'G–G–G–G–G–G–G' rather than alternating between G and a lower note somewhere between F♯ and G. Hear the vibrato *in* or as part of the tone itself, rather than something extra put on top of the tone.[1]

[1] The Hungarian violinist and teacher Sándor Végh would often caution against using vibrato 'like putting on thick layers of makeup' – piling it on top of the sound instead of it growing naturally out of the body of the tone itself.

Végh's description of vibrato: 'Two dear friends, who have not seen each other for years, meet by chance at a railway station. The feeling when they meet … *that* is vibrato!'

Example 2   Franck: Sonata in A, *mov. 1, b. 5*

- As well as individual notes, practise whole phrases without vibrato.

- Then add vibrato, and hear it and the tone together as one, pulsating tonal quality rather two combined qualities, i.e. the sound as one thing and the vibrato as another.

107 ## Vibrato pulsing

The vibrato 'pulse' or 'throb' is caused by two factors:

1 When the finger rolls back, flattening the note, it releases the string slightly (written as x-notes below); when it rolls forward to the in-tune note it leans slightly more heavily into the string.

2 The back and forward movement is not even, but moves in a dotted rhythm.

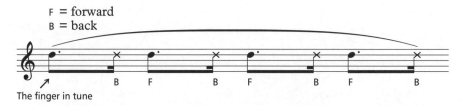

- Make vibrato richer, more expressive and more even, by practising with a slowed-down vibrato that has a specific number of 'pulses' on each note. Practising a phrase or passage like this is also a good way to improve continuous vibrato, and the pitch of the vibrato.

Example 1 Brahms: Sonata no. 2 in A, op. 100, *mov. 1, b. 21*

- Keep the bow strokes smooth, making the 'pulsing' or 'throbbing' with the vibrato only.

  Each sixteenth-note (semiquaver) represents one vibrato pulse (the finger moving forward to the in-tune note).

Smooth bow, 'pulsing' with vibrato only

- Repeat with 32nd-note (demisemiquaver) pulses:

Example 2 Schumann: Sonata in A minor, op. 105, *mov. 1, b. 1*

Each sixteenth-note represents one vibrato pulse:

Example 3 Wieniawski: Concerto no. 2 in D minor, op. 22, *b. 68*

Each 32nd-note (demisemiquaver) represents one vibrato pulse:

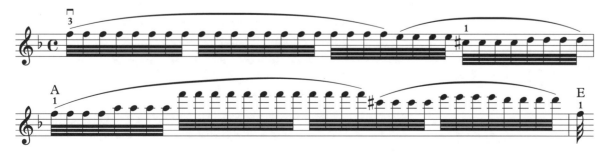

Example 4

Beethoven: Sonata in A, op. 47 ('Kreutzer'), *mov. 1, b. 1*

Each sixteenth-note (semiquaver) represents one vibrato pulse (both fingers moving forward to the in-tune notes):

● Repeat with a 32nd-note pulse:

Example 5

Kreisler: Caprice Viennois, op. 2, *b. 21*

● It is not necessarily important to regulate the pulsing in exact numbers. Simply pause on a note and listen to the pulses:

Example 6

Sarasate: Zigeunerweisen, op. 20 no. 1, *b. 2*

● Select an individual note and develop the vibrato on one long, sustained stroke, down-bow and up.
● Start with a very slow pulse and gradually accelerate.

The following example represents one long, continuous E♭ played on one single bow stroke:

Speeding up with the metronome

- Practise in the following dotted rhythm to develop a free and effortless vibrato.
- Begin slowly with the metronome at ♩ = 60. Then repeat at 66, 72, 80, etc., up to about 108.
- Practise one note or double stop at a time, using long, sustained strokes. Always play four beats on the down-bow and four beats on the up-bow.

Example   Brahms: Sonata no. 3 in D minor, op. 108, *mov. 2, b. 50*

F = move forward to the in-tune note
B = move back, a fraction below the in-tune note

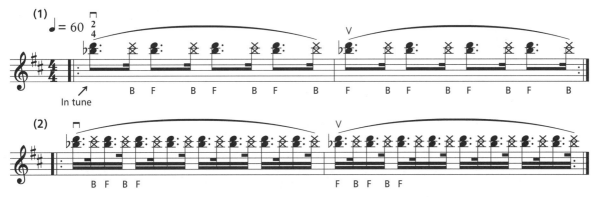

(1) One pulse (forward to the in-tune note) per beat.

(2) Two pulses per beat.

Vibrato not as a substitute for tone

As a normal part of everyday practice, play a phrase or passage completely without vibrato to check that vibrato is not taking the place of musical expressiveness in the bow.

- Play at the normal tempo with projection and communication, as if in performance – but *senza vibrato* and with all the expression coming from the bow.
- Exaggerate the expressiveness in the tone to make up for the lack of vibrato expression.

Example   Sarasate: Zigeunerweisen, op. 20 no. 1, *b. 49*

Tone not as a substitute for vibrato

Play a phrase or passage without any colour or expression in the bow to check that the tone is not taking the place of musical expressiveness in the vibrato.

- Play without any expression in the bow, only in the vibrato.
- Exaggerate the expressiveness in the vibrato to make up for the lack of expression in the bow.

Example   Franck: Sonata in A, *mov. 2, b. 197*

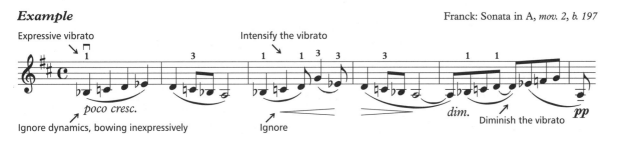

111 Varying speed and width

The two main aspects of vibrato are speed and width. Both vary constantly with the character and expression of each note. It is rare that even two notes in a row have the same proportions of speed to width.[1]

The most natural proportions are wide–and–slow, fast–and–narrow; but like an artist mixing basic colours to obtain an infinite range of different shades, the musician's range of different vibratos extends all the way to wide–and–fast and slow–and–narrow.

- Practising by exaggeration, enlarge the proportions of the vibrato. Make it slightly narrower and wider, faster and slower, than the vibrato you will eventually use.[2]

It goes without saying that there are endless different ways in which vibrato can be used, and the suggestions below serve merely to illustrate the approach.[3]

Example 1   Bruch: Concerto no. 1 in G minor, op. 26, *mov. 2, b. 6*

- Enlarge the proportions. 'Least' = slowest, narrowest vibrato:

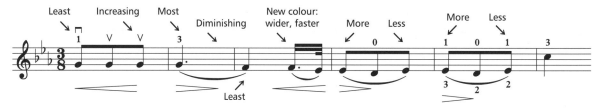

Example 2   Beethoven: Sonata in F, op. 24 ('Spring'), *mov. 1, b. 33*

- Play slowly, enlarging the changes in the vibrato as follows:

Example 3   Saint-Saëns: Introduction and Rondo Capriccioso, op. 28, Rondo, *b. 152*

- Exaggerate the changes in colour:

[1] See also *Vibrato*, page 298

[2] Avoid over-working when playing a fast, narrow vibrato. The faster the vibrato the smaller the part of the left arm required to produce it. Playing a slow vibrato may involve the whole forearm; the fastest vibrato may require only a tiny hand or fingertip movement.

[3] As in every other area of technique, when playing with inspiration vibrato is on a more subconscious level than this, without the player controlling it so directly. However, consciously working out different shades of vibrato during practice means that you can lose yourself all the more in natural expressiveness when in the heat of performance.

Using another finger as a model

Each finger on the same hand may have its own tendency towards one particular vibrato or another, some fingers tending towards a narrower vibrato, others towards a wider vibrato.

- As part of experimenting to find exactly the right quality of expression for a particular note, use other fingers on the same note as a point of comparison. The new finger can serve either as a model, or as an immediate way to get a new musical feeling for the note.

Example 1   Bruch: Concerto no. 1 in G minor, op. 26, *mov. 1, b. 86*

- Use the second finger as a model for the fourth finger Ab and A:

Example 2   Beethoven: Romanze in F, op. 50, *b. 1*

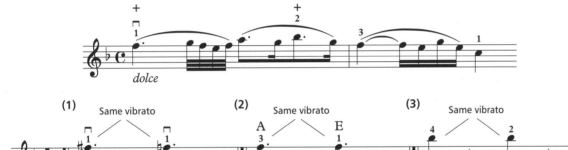

(1) The first finger F, being very 'square' and placed next to the nut, may feel slightly restricted compared with the more extended finger that would play an F♯.[1] Use the first finger F♯ as a model for the vibrato of the F.

(2) Use also the vibrato of the third finger on the A string as a model for the vibrato of the first finger.

(3) The second finger B♭ must not be too 'wobbly', i.e. wide and slow. Use a fourth finger for comparison.

[1] See Figs. 14a and 14b, *Square and extended finger shapes*, page 194

Example 3   Tchaikovsky: Three Pieces, op. 42, *Melody, b. 1*

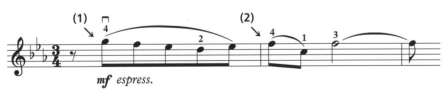

- Make the same vibrato on each pair of fingerings:

113 Continuous vibrato: holding down fingers

When passages seem too fast to allow vibrato on each note, one solution lies in the fact that any fingers that are held down on the string are, in effect, longer-value notes which you can easily vibrate. Then, because these held-down fingers are vibrating, the other fingers vibrate as well.[1]

Such a vibrato must be minimal to avoid the notes becoming unstable, but there is a big difference between fast passages played with a 'background vibrato', and played with no vibrato at all.

- Practise holding fingers down and vibrating them even if in the end you may not hold them down so long. Afterwards, continuous vibrato will feel more automatic.

Example 1   Kayser: Etudes, op. 20, no. 8, *b. 1*

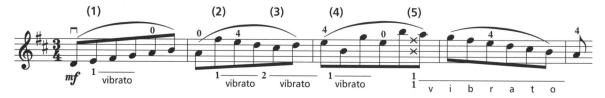

(1) Although the actual notes are eighth-notes (quavers), the first finger is playing a dotted quarter-note (dotted crotchet) because it stays held down on the string for three notes.

(2) The first finger stays on the string for at least a quarter-note while the fourth finger plays the E ('overlapping'), and may stay down into the following third finger D.

(3) Sometime during the D the second finger takes its place on the string, the balance of the hand transfers on to it, and at the same time the vibrato transfers – without stopping – from the first finger to the second finger.

(4) Sometime during the fourth finger E the first finger is prepared and stays for at least a quarter-note.

(5) Sometime during the B or the A the first finger takes its place on the string to give the hand stability. Here, it is as though the first finger is playing a dotted half-note (dotted minim).

Example 2   Beethoven: Romanze in F, op. 50, *b. 29*

Example 3   Viotti: Concerto no. 22 in A minor, *mov. 1, b. 96*

Example 4   Brahms: Sonata no. 2 in A, op. 100, *mov. 3, b. 48*

Example 5   Rode: 24 Caprices, No. 13, *b. 3*

Continuous vibrato: dropping and lifting fingers slowly

Lifting or dropping a finger must not cause the vibrato to stop.[1]

[1] Not allowing finger action to affect the vibrato is a key example of keeping the different elements of playing independent from each other. Other examples include keeping the bow legato while the left fingers lift and drop (page 61); keeping the left fingers light when the bow is heavy (page 235); as well as the whole subject of 'localizing actions' (page 270).

- Drop or lift each finger so slowly that for a moment, between the finger touching or leaving the string, the tone becomes cracked and distorted.

Dropping fingers

Drop the finger very slowly. As the finger slowly approaches the string, keep the vibrato going without allowing it to stop even for a fraction of a second. When the finger gets close enough to the string, each forward movement of the vibrato begins to touch the string. This produces a fuzzy, distorted sound. The sound gradually improves as the finger stops the note more fully, the vibrato continuing all the time, until finally the tone is pure.

Make this stage – between the finger just beginning to touch the string and it fully stopping the string – as long as possible by lowering the finger very, very slowly.

Lifting fingers

Lift the finger very slowly. As the finger begins to release the string each backward movement of the vibrato causes the sound to break, until the vibrating finger is finally completely clear of the string.

Make this stage – between the finger stopping the string and being completely clear of the string – as long as possible by lifting the finger very slowly.

- When descending from an upper finger to a lower finger, make sure that the lower finger is already on the string before lifting the upper finger.[2] Vibrate both fingers together as the upper finger slowly lifts.

[2] See *Placing fingers gently*, page 240

Example 1

Tchaikovsky: Concerto in D, op. 35, *mov. 1, b. 69*

Non-continuous vibrato, the vibrato halting as the fingers drop or lift, could be represented as follows:

- Lift and drop the fingers unnaturally slowly while vibrating without stopping. The jagged line represents the 'fuzz' caused by the finger leaving or approaching the string:

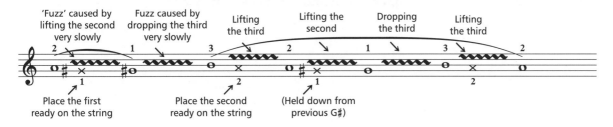

Example 2

Pugnani-Kreisler: Praeludium and Allegro, *Praeludium, b. 23*

First practise slurred, and then with separate bows:

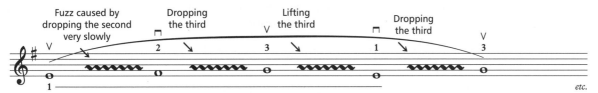

115 ## Vibrato accents

[1] See also *Vibrato accents*, page 89

The following examples contain notes played with an accent or other sort of musical stress. The bow moves fast–slow and heavy–light (more, or less, depending on the example), and the vibrato on each note is fast–slow and wide–narrow.[1]

● Practising by exaggeration, play no accent with the bow at all. Keep a perfectly even bow speed, creating the accent with the vibrato not the bow.

● To create the 'accent' make a separate fast–slow and wide–narrow vibrato on each note.

Examples

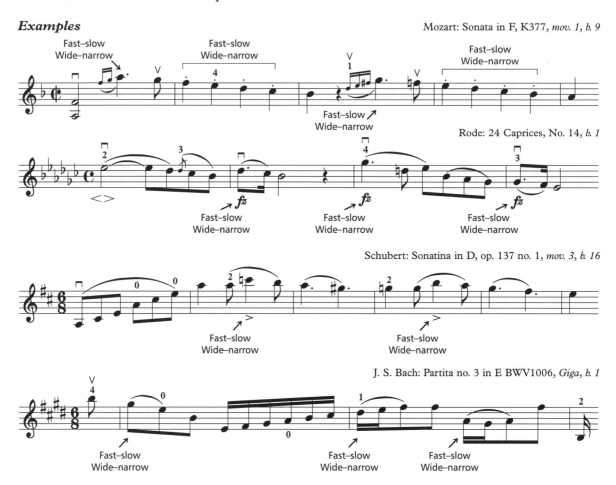

116 ## Double stops: isolating fingers

● Improve the vibrato of double stops by modelling it on single-stop vibrato.

Example Wieniawski: Légende, op. 17, *b. 69*

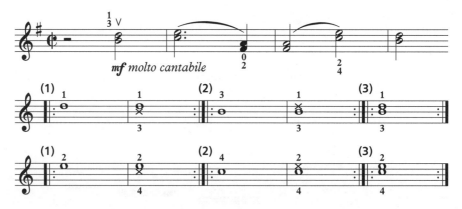

(1) First play just one finger of the double stop, without the other finger on the string. Play a free, loose vibrato.

Then play the same note again on its own, but now with the other finger of the double stop silently placed on the other string (written as an x-note). Find the same free and loose vibrato as before.

(2) Do the same with the other finger: first play it on its own, then on its own with the other finger silently held down on the other string.

(3) Finally, play both together with the same free, loose vibrato on both fingers.

Harmonics

The main factors to consider in harmonics are (1) keeping exactly the right distance between the fingers, and (2) bowing near enough to the bridge. Another factor is the different weight into the string of the lower and the upper finger.[1]

See also *Shifting to a harmonic*, page 188.

Playing fingers separately

117

Example   Bartók (arr. Székely): Roumanian Folk Dances, No. 3, *b. 4*

[1] Although the lower finger in artificial harmonics must stop the string more than the upper finger, the pressure can still be very little – barely enough to 'bend' the string down towards the fingerboard.

Keep the fourth finger straight, hovering just above its note

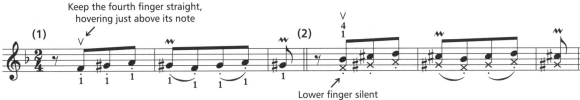

Lower finger silent

(1) First play only the lower finger, with the finger stopping the string just enough to sound the note.

While doing so, keep the upper finger just above its note – a hair's breadth away from the string – so that the hand position is the same as when you play the passage properly (Fig. 12).

(2) Then play only the upper finger, but not as a harmonic: stop the string enough to sound the note properly. Keep the first finger lightly on the string as before.

Only the upper finger will sound. The x-notes represent the silent lower fingers.

Fig. 12

Note how the fourth finger contacts the string on the pad, not the tip

You may find it better if you do this with the fourth finger quite straight (Fig. 12), contacting the string with the pad (as it would be if you were playing an actual harmonic).[2]

[2] This does not apply to the third finger, which in this example should be curved and playing on its tip as usual.

In finding the exact placement of the fourth finger, it is also helpful to alternate between the lower finger alone and the harmonic:

Double stops: practising individual fingers

118

Example   Paganini: Concerto no. 1 in D, op. 6, *mov. 3, b. 95*

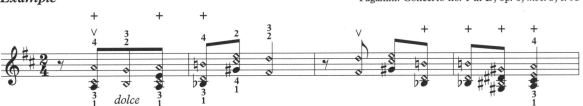

Double stop passages contain frequent examples of harmonics played with the fingering 1–3 (marked '+').

- Make the fingers more familiar with these unusual harmonics by practising scales using 1–3. For example:

Left-hand pizzicato

Two qualities of successful left-hand pizzicato are:

1 Clarity: every note is absolutely clear and equal in strength to the others

2 Machine-like evenness of rhythm

When alternating short bow strokes with left-hand pizzicato, bounce the bow on the string with an almost vertical motion close to the point. The aim is usually to imitate with the bow the sound of the pizzicato.

119 Angle of plucking

On the E string, left-hand pizzicato is easier if you place the elbow more to the left than usual, bringing the base joints down very low.[1]

On the G string, bring the elbow more to the right than usual, so that the plucking fingers lift off at an angle that makes them miss the D string. Do the same for the middle strings.

● Build the elbow movements into the playing.

[1] See Angle and height of knuckles, page 237

Example   Sarasate: Malaguena, op. 21 no. 1, *b. 71*

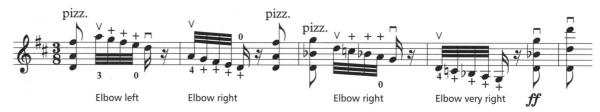

Elbow left   Elbow right   Elbow right   Elbow very right   *ff*

120 Stopping the string

When playing with the bow, the right amount of finger pressure into the string is usually *as little as possible* – just enough to stop the string with a pure tone and no more.

Pizzicato is one of the few areas of playing where the harder the left hand fingers press the string the better.[2]

● Practising by exaggeration, play extremely slowly, using the extra time to stop the string as hard as possible.

[2] A plucked open string rings for longer than a stopped note because the nut stops the open string so precisely, compared with the fleshy pad of the fingertip.

You can get the same ringing effect out of a 'dead' note like B. With the instrument sitting on a flat surface, use something with a solid, precise edge (make sure it will not damage the string) to stop the string instead of your finger. The B will then ring for as long as an open string when plucked.

Example   Paganini: 24 Caprices, op. 1, No. 24, *variation 9*

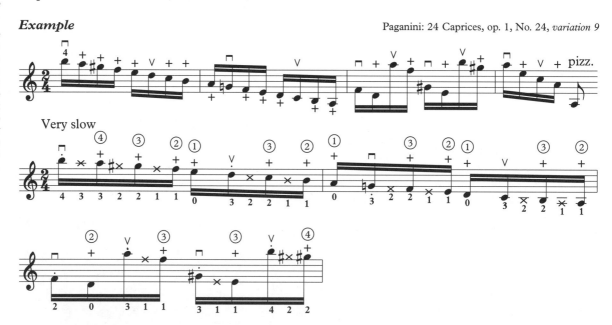

Very slow

The lower fingerings indicate the finger that stops the string; the circled numbers indicate the finger that plucks the string.

● Practise very slowly, at about one note every five seconds.

● After playing the first note (B) with a short *spiccato* stroke near the point, leave the fourth finger down on the string and place the third finger A underneath it. Press both fingers as hard as possible for a few moments, then (without first releasing the fingers) pluck the string with the fourth finger.

● Leave the third finger down on the string and place the second finger G♯ underneath it. Press both fingers as hard as possible, then pluck with the third finger, and so on.

Scales and arpeggios

When a scale is played very well the three main aspects of playing – pitch, sound and rhythm – are all even. Playing scales on a regular basis greatly improves overall playing because the evenness of all the playing increases.[1]

Pitch

Any particular note in the scale or arpeggio must not be sharper in the first octave, flatter in the second octave, sharper in the third octave, and so on.

The intervals between the notes must be even, e.g. the whole-tone between the first and second notes of the major scale must not be wider or narrower than the whole-tone between the second and third notes.[2]

Sound

The sound must be even, so that no note is played louder or softer than another – in particular, before or after a change of string, a change of bow or a change of position.

Rhythm

Each note of the scale must be played evenly, with no disturbance to the rhythm caused by changing string, bow, finger or position.

[1] For other practice methods useful for scale playing see also *Placing fingers gently*, Examples 6–7, page 243; *'Trilling' shifts*, Examples 1, 2, 3, page 183; *Holding fingers down*, Example 1, page 193; *Uniform intonation*, page 207; *ABC practice*, Example 4, page 276

[2] See *Tuning scales: three stages*, page 210

Note about rhythm and accent practice

Discussed in full on pages 36–46, these are two of the most essential practice methods for scales. Every different rhythm or accent pattern is useful. Begin with the basic dotted patterns:

- Note how the following four-note accent pattern does not work out back 'home' onto the tonic, so a different note is highlighted when you go back up again:

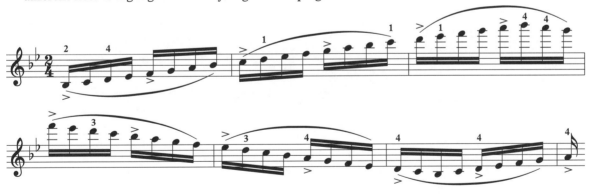

- Combine accent and rhythm patterns:

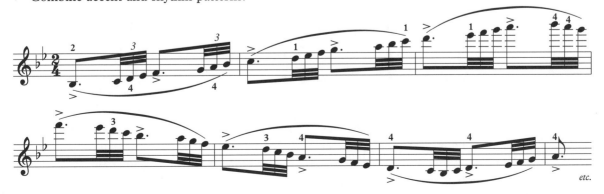

Vibrato

Practise scales with and without vibrato.

- Practise without vibrato, so that the sound is 'bare' and you can hear everything very clearly. Listen closely to the intonation and to the evenness of the bow stroke.
- Practise scales also with a 'background' vibrato, i.e. just enough to warm the tone of each note but without it being particularly noticeable or expressive. This is the vibrato you might use in a scale examination or college audition when you are standing up and performing scales.
- Practise also with an expressive vibrato, as though performing great music. Play scales with the vibrato (and the tone) that you would typically use for Bach, Beethoven, or Brahms.

122 **Playing scales as music**

When we play musically and with inspiration, a better feel comes into the muscles of the arms, hands and fingers, than when we play purely mechanically.

Rather than thinking of the notes in isolation, hear a harmony with each note of the scale and play expressively, bringing out each note's musical importance.

Example 1

Example 2   Sarasate: Zigeunerweisen, op. 20 no. 1, b. 101

Imagine other chords, e.g. the natural harmonies and inner tensions of the scale clashing against the D–F–B chord; but having once thought of the notes with a harmony in mind – rather than consciously trying to move the fingers and bow – there is an immediate new feeling of control and ease when playing the passage up to tempo again.

Bowing patterns

Regularly practise scales with a variety of different bowing patterns. As well as improving the evenness and ease of playing scales, practising bowing patterns improves all-round bowing technique and co-ordination.

Out of the infinite number of possible bowing patterns, a little work on just a few basic patterns is enough to produce dramatic improvement in bow control and tone:

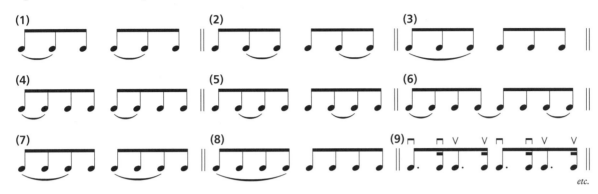

Example 1

- Play at the heel, middle and point.
- Vary the dynamics: play p, f; experiment with crescendos and diminuendos.

Example 2   Rode: 24 Caprices, *No. 1, b. 16*

Another method of using different bowings in scales is to practise a particular bow stroke from a piece.

- The scale does not have to be in the same key as the passage:

Example 3   Sibelius: Concerto in D minor, op. 47, *mov. 3, b. 5*

- Play the scale in the same part of the bow, with the same stroke and in the same tempo, as the passage:

124 Metronome practice

Begin with one note on each metronome beat, then 2, 3, 4, 6 and 8 notes to a beat.

So that there is the right number of notes for all these groups to fit into evenly, add notes at the beginning and end of the scale to make a total of 48.

- Set the metronome according to how fast you want to play the final groups of 8 notes to a beat. A medium tempo is ♩=60.

- Begin with one note to a beat. Play each note with a firm, accented stroke.

- Without stopping (but now playing legato without accents), continue with 2 notes to a beat; then 3, 4, 6 and 8 notes to a beat.

- Always play one bow stroke on each beat, regardless of how many notes you play in each stroke.

- Do not stop between sections. Play straight from one into another.

[1] Which fingerings to use? Learn a system of fingering so that in a scale examination, for example, you have fingerings that you know really well and feel comfortable playing.

As part of your general work on scales, however, practise as many different fingerings as possible – e.g. starting on the first finger, on the second finger, on the third and on the fourth, and shifting up and down on different strings from your normal fingering.

Example 1[1]

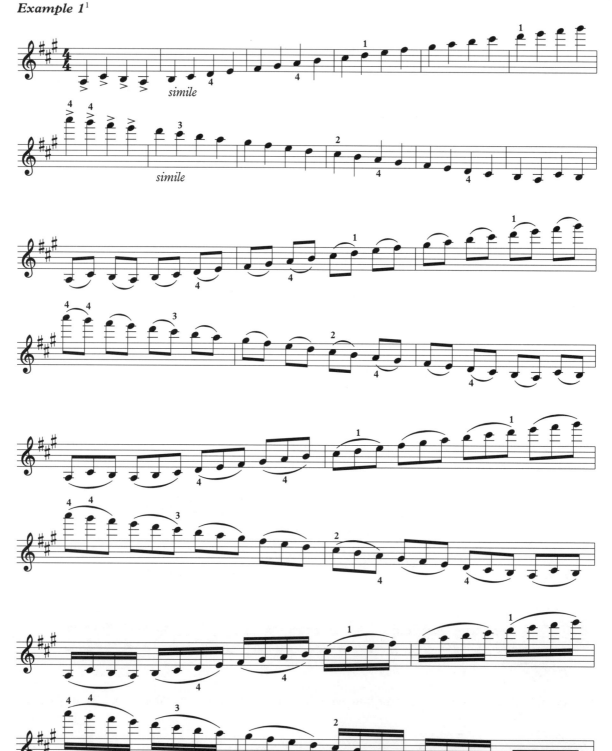

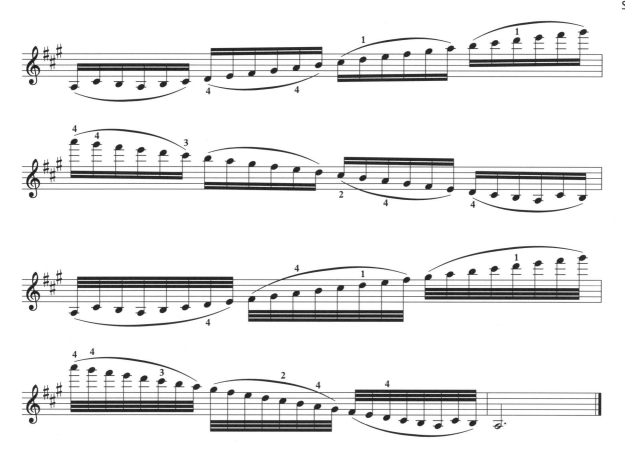

- Play also separate bows, *détaché* or *spiccato*. (*Spiccato* changes into *sautillé* at the faster speeds.)
- Use the ABC method to practise the final groups of 8 notes to a beat (see Example 4, page 276).
- Also begin at the end, playing 8 notes on each metronome beat, then 6, 4, 3, 2 and one note to a beat.

Example 2

In this scale pattern the top note is repeated. Since it goes a semitone below the tonic, the pattern works for all keys except G, for which the following is used instead:

Example 3

There is no need to add extra notes for three-octave chromatic scales. They total 72 notes, so 1, 2, 3, 4, 6 and 8 notes to a beat all work out back onto the tonic on the first beat of a bar.

Example 4

- Set the metronome according to how fast you want to play the final groups of four notes to a beat.
- Play through as a continuous sequence without stopping.
- Play also separate bows, *détaché* and *spiccato*.

Example 5

Example 6

- Instead of adding notes to the arpeggio to make a suitable number for all these groups to fit into evenly, simply repeat the arpeggio until finally it arrives on the tonic on a down-bow.

- Set the metronome according to how fast you want to play the final groups of eight notes to a beat.

- Play through as a continuous sequence without stopping.

- Play also separate bows, *détaché* and *spiccato*.

Three-octave dominant and diminished sevenths do not need to be repeated in order to work out. They total 24 notes, so 1, 2, 3, 4, 6 and 8 notes to a beat all work out back onto the tonic.

125 Improvising

Play the notes of the scale or arpeggio in any consecutive order that you like, making it up as you go along. Run up and down at a slow, medium or fast tempo. Aim for evenness of pitch, sound and rhythm, and a relaxed and easy feel in the hand. Afterwards, the normal scale or arpeggio will feel much more controlled and secure.

Vary the dynamics, sometimes getting louder going up and softer coming down, sometimes the other way round.

There are two ways to finger the improvisations:

1   Keep strictly to the fingerings that you would use for the normal scale or arpeggio.

2   Make the fingerings up as you go along. Do whatever comes naturally, without thinking about your fingers. Listen closely to the sound, and concentrate on the expressiveness and evenness of the scale.

Example 1

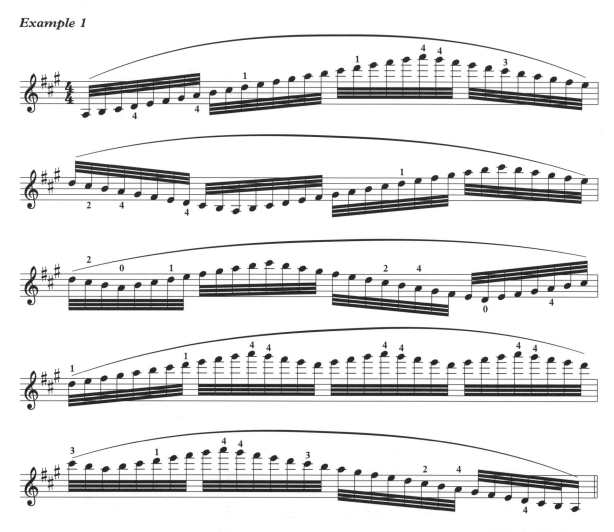

The improvisation does not have to add up to a certain number of notes or bars, or be 'correct' in any way at all. Simply enjoy running up and down the fingerboard as you explore the different octaves.

Example 2

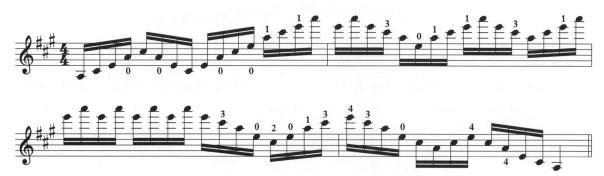

Chromatics: isolating the shift

In the chromatic fingering 3–2–1 the contraction of the hand (a major second between the first and third fingers instead of a minor or major third) may disturb the shifts.

Example 1   Paganini: 24 Caprices, op. 1, No. 17, *b. 18*

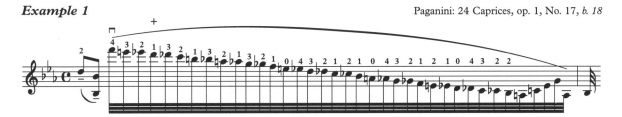

- Clarify the feeling of the distance between the first and third fingers by missing out the second finger:

- Another way to practise this is to play double stops:

- Taking this a step further, practise sixths in scales and broken thirds, up and down the string, with the fingering 3–1. You can even do this with minor sixths, where the fingers are a semitone apart. Afterwards the contracted 3–2–1 fingering in the scale seems very wide in comparison.

Example 2   Grieg: Sonata in C minor, op. 45, *mov. 3, b. 192*

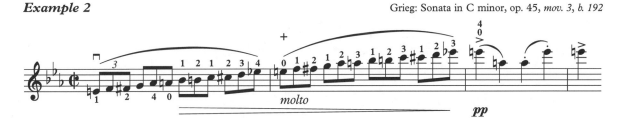

- Miss out the second finger as in Example 1:

Keep the first finger on the string throughout

Example 3   Bruch: Concerto no. 1 in G minor, op. 26, *mov. 1, b. 90*

- Isolate the first finger in the second bar:

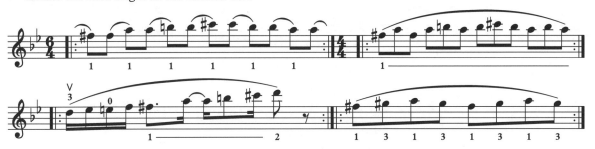

127 **Short-cuts: thirds, sixths and fingered octaves**

[1] See also *Double stops*, pages 218–228; *Thirds and fingered octaves*, page 251

The time spent on preparatory exercises is usually repaid many times over by saving much more time than they take to do. After practising the following exercises, the scale will be more accurate, and feel much easier, than it would have been had you spent the same amount of time practising the scale itself.[1]

Example 1

- Play only the notes that are fingered 1–3 to feel the exact distances of each shift, e.g. in the first shift the first finger moves a major third and the third finger moves a minor third:

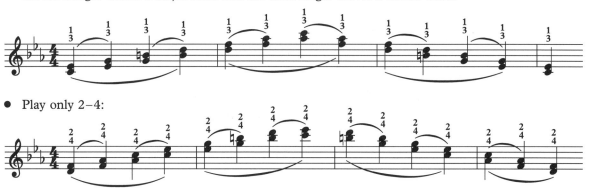

- Play only 2–4:

[2] See *Playing one string at a time while fingering both strings*, page 225

- First, play one string at a time while fingering both strings.[2] Then, place both fingers together but bow only the lower string of the first third, then the upper string of the next third, and so on. The silently placed notes are written as x-notes:

- Do the same the other way round:

- Practise each shift like *'Trilling' shifts* (page 183). Gradually speed up to as fast a tempo as possible:

- Practise each shift using substitutions (see page 159):

Example 2

- Play only 2–1 to feel the exact distances of each shift, e.g. in the first shift the first finger moves a minor third and the second finger moves a major third.

- Play only 3–2:

- Place both fingers together but bow only the lower string of the first sixth, then the upper string of the second sixth, and so on. The silently placed notes are written as x-notes:

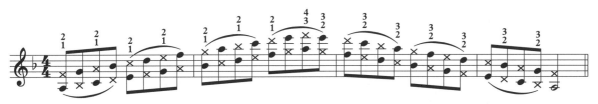

- Do the same the other way round:

- Practise each shift:

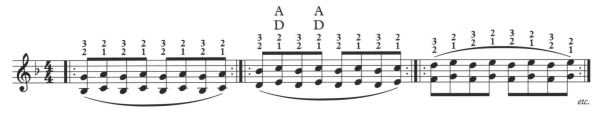

- Practise each shift using substitutions and intermediate notes:

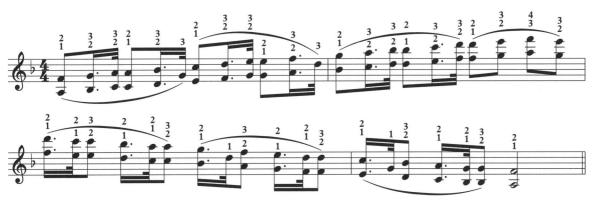

Example 3

- Play only 3–1:

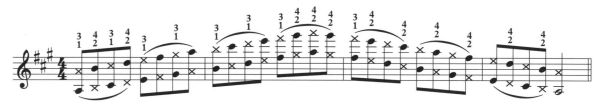

- Play only 4–2:

- Place both fingers together but bow only the lower string of the first octave, then the upper string of the second octave, and so on. The silently placed notes are written as x-notes:

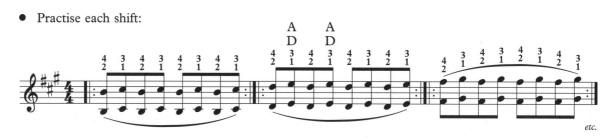

- Do the same the other way round:

- Practise each shift:

- Practise each shift using substitutions and intermediate notes:

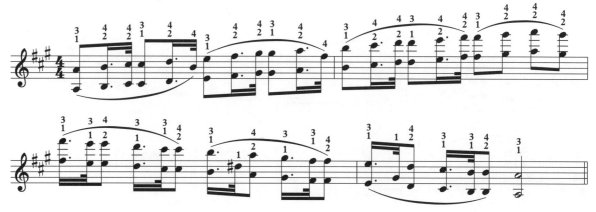

Shifting

part **5**

¹ See also *The feel of the hand and fingers*, page 193

> **The feel of the hand and fingers**

Galamian likened the left hand to blind people feeling their way around an object with super-sensitive touch.¹ This is very obvious in shifting, where the hand orientates itself by the feel of the strings, neck and shoulder of the violin, and all the other physical conditions of playing the arrival note.

Memorizing the feel of the position

128

Learn the feeling of a particular note or position by first taking your hand away from the neck of the violin completely. Then see if you can return straight to the note in tune, without needing to adjust the finger whatsoever.

Example 1   J. S. Bach: Partita no. 2 in D minor, BWV1004, *Allemanda, b. 6*

(1) Learn the feeling of playing first finger D, 3rd position. During each '//' take the hand away from the neck of the violin and turn it to face outwards (Fig. 13). Then return to the violin, finding exactly the same feeling of the hand as before, and play the note in tune.

Each time you play the note feel where the thumb is positioned on the neck; which part of the tip of the first finger contacts the string, and the shape of the finger; the balance of the hand on the finger and at the wrist; any contact of the hand with the body of the violin or the neck; the position of the elbow, and so on.

Fig. 13

Go straight to the note from this position

Take your hand away and return many times in a row, finding the notes in tune every time. 'Hear' each note mentally in advance. Do not tap the string with the finger to test it before playing it with the bow. Do not look at the fingers and string – *feel* where to place the notes.

(2) Now without taking the hand away, check the feeling of the D in relation to the fingers before and after the shift, i.e. second-finger F on the D string and fourth-finger F on the G string. Recall the feeling of the first-finger D.

Example 2

Dvořák: Romance, op. 11, *b. 39*

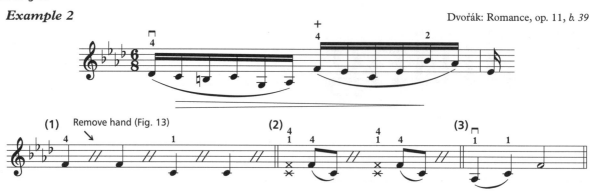

(1) Taking the hand away from the neck of the violin as in Example 1, learn the feeling of playing fourth-finger F, 3rd position, and first-finger C (the first is the finger the position is based on).

(2) Check the feeling of the F in relation to the C by placing both fingers on the string together (shown as x-notes), and then playing them to make sure they are in tune. Take your hand away in between as before.

[1] See *Intermediate notes*, page 160

(3) Practise the shift using first-finger C as an intermediate note.[1] Feel the fourth-finger F based on the first-finger C.

Example 3

Sarasate: Playera, op. 23 no. 1, *b. 20*

To shift from the third-finger harmonic down to the third-finger C♯ (marked '+'):

(1) Learn the feeling of playing first-finger A, third-finger C♯, and the feeling of the first and third fingers together.

(2) Shifting from the harmonic D to the C♯, recall the feel of the hand in 4th position (shown as x-notes) and move the hand straight to that position/feeling.

Example 4

Brahms: Concerto in D, op. 77, *mov. 3, b. 35*

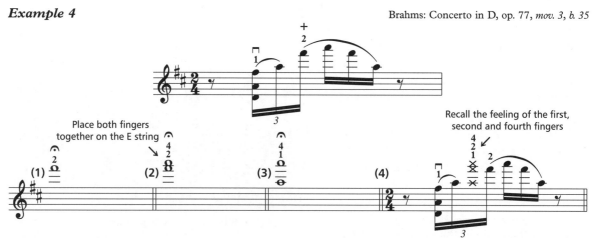

To shift up to the second-finger F♯ (marked '+'):

(1) Learn the feeling of playing F♯, second finger, 7th position.

(2) Learn the feeling of playing the fourth-finger A by placing the second and fourth fingers together on the E string.

(3) Learn the feeling of the octave, first-finger A on the A string with fourth-finger A on the E string.

(4) Shifting from 1st position to the F♯, recall the feeling of the hand in 7th position and move the hand straight to that position/feeling.

Example 5

Using this fingering, the top G is an extension. The shift is to second-finger D in 5th position.

(1) Practise going to the D on its own. Memorize the feel of the hand position.

(2) Practise going to the D in the context of playing an extension fourth-finger G. The hand position may feel slightly different.

(3) Remembering the feeling of the hand position, place the second-finger D on the string without playing it, and continue into the passage.

Example 6

● An easy and natural way to get a feeling for the position is to make up simple note patterns there:

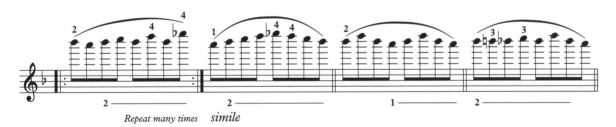

Example 7

(1) Learn the feel of the position. It is especially helpful to use note patterns which include the open string, so that you have to find the note 'from the air'.

(2) The first-finger F is very square; the first-finger E is extended. Practise going from one to the other.[1]

[1] See *Square and extended*, page 194

129 ## Using glissando to measure the shift

- Practise slow, heavy, deliberate slides to make the normal, light shift feel more accurate.

Example 1   Rode: 24 Caprices, No. 11, *b. 1*

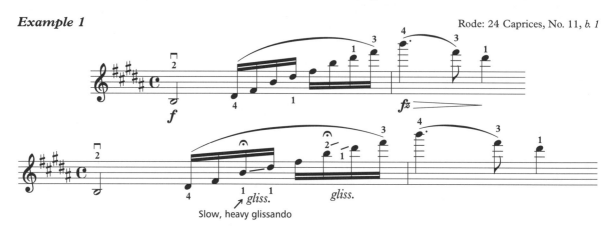

Slow, heavy glissando

Example 2   Sibelius: Concerto in D minor, op. 47, *mov. 1, b. 8*

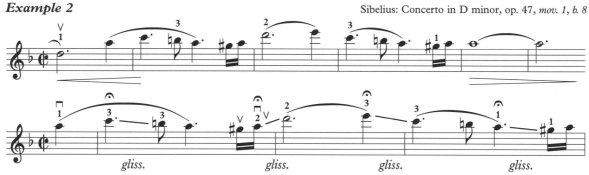

130 ## Comparing shifting to a different finger

- Increase your knowledge of the shift by seeing what other fingers feel like on the same note.
- Use the different feelings in the hand and fingers, in each position, to provide points of comparison with the correct fingering. You then *know* the shift better and it feels more secure.

Example 1   Tchaikovsky: Concerto in D, op. 35, *mov. 1, b. 120*

Example 2   Wieniawski: Polonaise de Concert, op. 4, *b. 92*

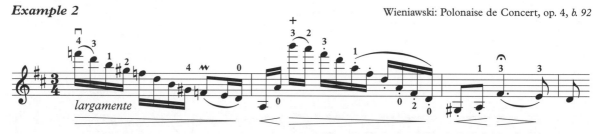

- Shift by dropping the finger directly onto its note, without sliding the finger along the string:

Comparing shifting to adjacent notes

- Clarify and enlarge the mental picture and feel of a note by also learning the feel and exact position of adjacent notes.

Example 1

Brahms: Sonata in D minor, op. 108, *mov. 1, b. 57*

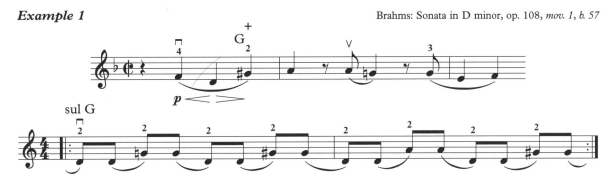

Example 2

Mendelssohn: Concerto in E minor, op. 64, *mov. 1, b. 39*

Make this shift by dropping the finger directly onto its note, without sliding the finger along the string:

- Attack each half-note (minim) with a strong accent, without testing the note first or beginning it hesitatingly:

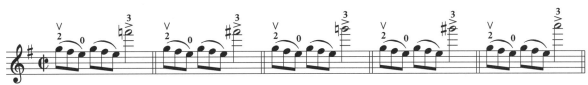

Example 3

Saint-Saëns: Introduction and Rondo Capriccioso, op. 28, *Rondo, b. 11*

- As well as practising shifting to notes above and below the real ending note of the shift, you can also shift from notes above and below the real starting note:

Example 4

Mendelssohn: Concerto in E minor, op. 64, *mov. 3, b. 117*

- Sometimes it is useful to continue for a few notes:

132 Semitone shifts with one finger

[1] See also Example 1, page 212. 'When moving a half step [semitone] with the same finger the distance must be felt larger than anticipated because each half step is equal to the width of the tip of the finger and so must be compensated for.' Raphael Bronstein: *The Science of Violin Playing* (New Jersey, 1977), 5.

When the two notes of a single-finger semitone shift are in tune they may seem surprisingly far apart, particularly in low positions. The tendency is to play the shifts too narrow, almost like a quarter-tone.[1]

● For a simple way to check or discover the correct distance, first play the notes without shifting. Note how far apart the fingers are, then move the same distance using only one finger.

Example 1   J. S. Bach: Sonata no. 1 in G minor, BWV1001, *Siciliana, b.1*

Example 2   Bruch: Concerto no. 1 in G minor, op. 26, *mov. 2, b. 17*

Example 3   Dont: 24 Etudes and Caprices, op. 35, No. 3, *b. 9*

Example 4   Beethoven: Sonata in C minor, op. 30 no. 2, *mov. 4, b. 18*

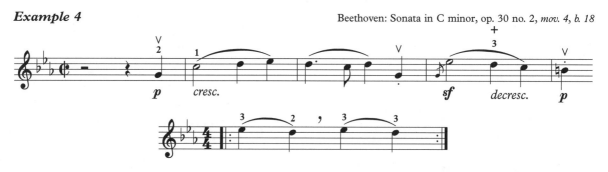

Example 5   Sarasate: Habanera, op. 21 no. 2, *b. 129*

Substitutions

Substitutions are shifts from one finger to another on the same note. They are frequently used as shifts in their own right, and are also part of the mechanism of *Exchange shifts* (see page 166).

Example 1   Mozart: Concerto no. 4 in D, K218, *mov. 1, b. 49*

- To practise the substitution from first- to third-finger A (marked '+'), play from one finger to the other many times, as fast as possible.
- To encourage the fingers to be light on the string, bow very lightly over the fingerboard.

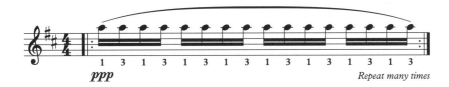

If you are not able to play this very fast, discover where the areas of resistance are. Is either finger pressing too hard, or the thumb pressing too hard against the neck? Is there tension in the base joints of the fingers, or in the wrist or upper arm? Is your neck free? Are you holding your breath?

Example 2   Brahms: Scherzo (Sonatensatz), WoO2, *b. 18*

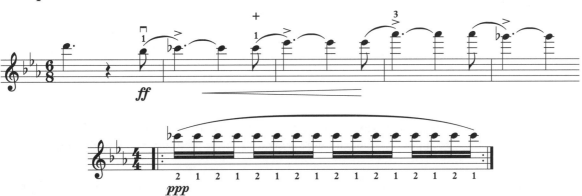

Example 3   Rode: 24 Caprices, No. 11, *b. 84*

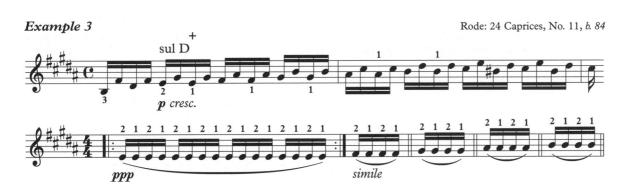

Example 4   Kreutzer: 42 Etudes ou caprices, No. 35, *b. 7*

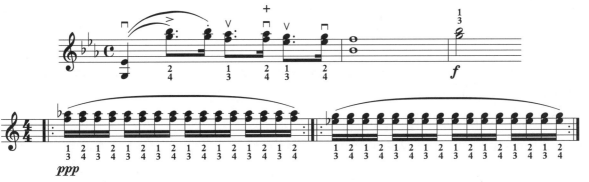

Intermediate notes

Intermediate notes are part of the mechanism of shifting, and help in measuring distances and exact intonation.

How clearly you can hear intermediate notes depends on the type of piece and the context. They can range from inaudible, through to 'ghosting', through to being an expressive element of the shift. 'Ghosting' means to play the intermediate note with as little bow as possible (no more than one centimetre), as little bow pressure as possible (barely touch the string with the bow), and harmonic-like finger pressure.[1]

[1] See also *Ghosting*, page 182

The ideal is that in the end there is no 'shift' at all, i.e. in the following example, play 'note–note–note–note', rather than 'note–note–*shift*–note–note':

However, practising intermediate notes brings great security to each shift by clarifying the positions before and after the shift; the fingers that will actually do the shifting; the exact interval that the shifting fingers must travel.

134 **Classical shifts**

Classical shifts are also known as 'beginning shifts' because you move on the finger that begins the shift.

Ascending Shift up on the lower finger until you are in the right position to place the upper finger directly on its note. The note that you shift to with the lower finger is the intermediate note.

Descending Shift down with the upper finger until you are in the right position to place the lower finger directly on its note. The note the upper finger shifts to is the intermediate note.

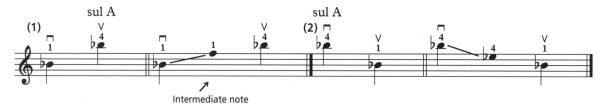

Intermediate note

(1) The note you are shifting to, fourth-finger B♭, is in 5th position. Shift with the first finger to 5th position. This note, F, is the intermediate note. Having arrived there simply drop the fourth finger on B♭.

Although the sound of the shift is an octave, the actual distance of the shift is a perfect fifth, B♭ to F played first finger to first finger.

(2) Shift with the fourth finger to 1st position. E♭ is the intermediate note, and having arrived there simply place the first finger on B♭ and then lift the fourth finger. The actual distance of the octave shift is again a perfect fifth (fourth finger to fourth finger).

Example 1

Mozart: Concerto no. 5 in A, K219, *mov. 3, b. 89*

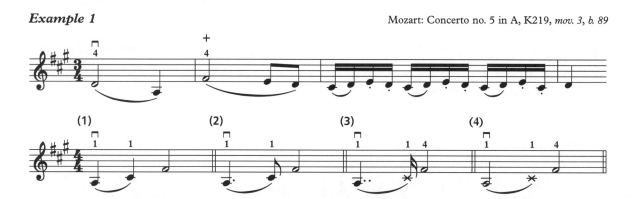

(1) Play the two notes of the shift (A, F♯), and the intermediate note (C♯), with equal length and tone.

(2) Play the intermediate note shorter.

(3) Ghost the intermediate note.

(4) Still thinking of the intermediate note, play A followed by F♯ as if there were no shift – simply two notes one after another.

Example 2   Elgar: Sonata in E minor, op. 82, *mov. 3, b. 40*

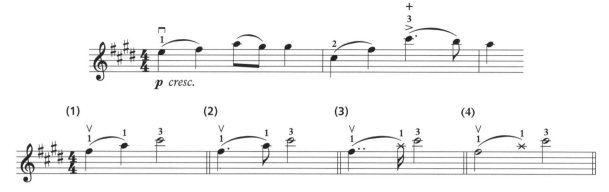

- Practise as in Example 1.

Example 3   J. S. Bach: Concerto no. 1 in A minor, BWV1041, *mov. 2, b. 5*

- Practise as in Example 1.

Example 4   Bruch: Concerto no. 1 in G minor, op. 26, *mov. 2, b. 3*

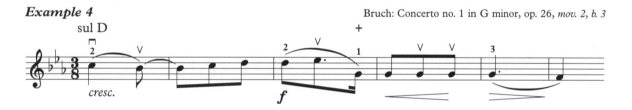

The shift marked '+' can be approached as part-shift part-extension:

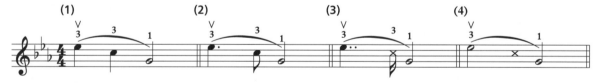

- After reaching the intermediate note (C) with the third finger, extend back with the first finger to G.
- Practise as in Example 1.

Example 5   Beethoven: Romanze in G, op. 40, *b. 20*

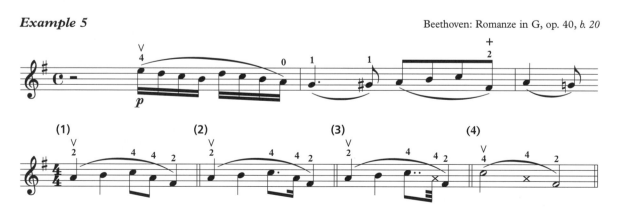

- Practise as in Example 1.

Example 6

Bruch: Concerto no. 1 in G minor, op. 26, *mov. 3, b. 25*

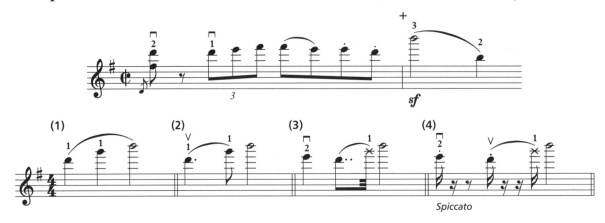

(1) Play the two notes of the shift (D, B), and the intermediate note (G), with equal length and tone.

(2) Play the intermediate note shorter.

(3) Begin to build the shift into the phrase while ghosting the intermediate note.

(4) Play *spiccato*, as in the passage itself. Shift with the first finger to the intermediate note while the bow is in the air after playing D.

Example 7

Paganini: 24 Caprices, op. 1, No. 18, *b. 26*

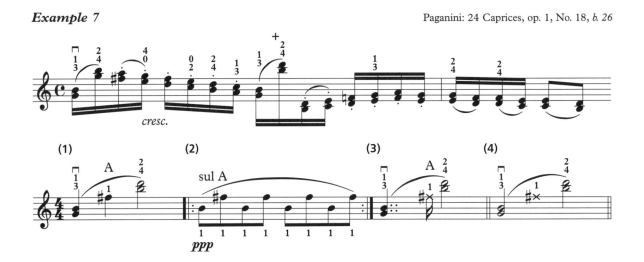

The intermediate note is F♯, making the shift a perfect fifth from B–F♯.

(1) Play the two double stops, and the intermediate note, evenly under one slur.

(2) Learn the distance of the shift. Bow lightly over the fingerboard to encourage the fingers to be light on the string.

(3) Ghost the intermediate note.

(4) Move from one double stop to another as if there were no shift – simply two notes one after another.

Example 8

Beethoven: Concerto in D, op. 61, *mov. 1, b. 335*

The intermediate note does not have to be in the same position as the final note of the shift. Here, the fourth-finger A♭ is an extension. The intermediate note D sets the position for the following notes and should be kept down on the string.

(1) Practise the 1–1 shift on its own, bowing lightly over the fingerboard.

(2) Gradually shorten the intermediate note (D) until playing it as a ghost (written as an x-note).

(3) Play from A♭ to A♭ as if there were no shift.

Example 9 Paganini: 24 Caprices, op. 1, No. 19, *b. 25*

- The two shifts marked '+' can be played as part-shift part-extension. Practise playing the intermediate notes as grace notes:

- Begin slowly, and gradually speed up to as fast a tempo as possible.

Romantic shifts

135

Romantic shifts are also known as 'end shifts' because you move on the finger that ends the shift.

Having played the B♭ with the first finger, place the fourth finger lightly on the string as if to play a harmonic. Shift with this finger on the string, sliding the finger into its note from below.

Although the sound of the shift is an octave, the actual distance of the shift is a perfect fifth, E♭ to B♭ played fourth finger to fourth finger.

How clearly you can hear the slide into the note depends on the type of piece and the context. It can range from inaudible or 'ghosting', through to an expressive *portamento*.

See also *Slow arrival speed*, page 172, for further examples of Romantic shifts.

Example 1 Granados (arr. Kreisler): Danse espagnole, *b. 48*

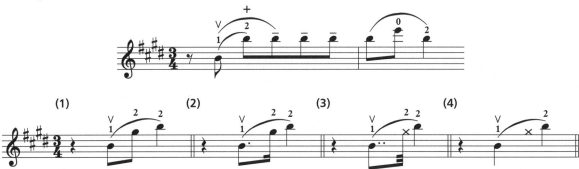

(1) Play the two notes of the shift (B, B), and the intermediate note (G♯), with equal length and tone.

(2) Play the intermediate note shorter.

(3) Ghost the intermediate note.

(4) Still thinking of the intermediate note, play as if there were no shift – just two notes one after another.

Example 2

Viotti: Concerto no. 22 in A minor, *mov. 1, b. 88*

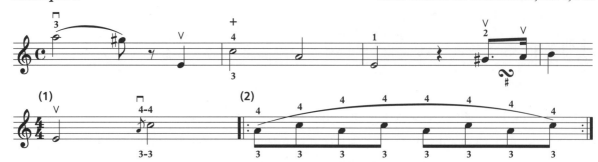

(1) The intermediate note is A whether the shift is with a fourth or a third finger.

(2) Practise the minor third from A to C.

Example 3

Rode: 24 Caprices, No. 13, *b. 1*

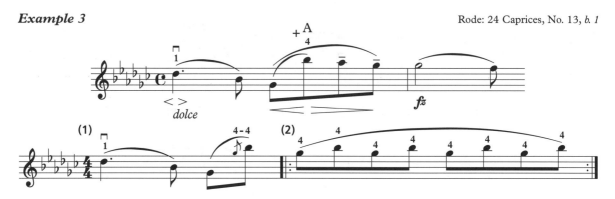

(1) The intermediate note is fourth-finger G♭.

(2) Practise the major third from G♭ to B♭.

Example 4

Brahms: Sonata no. 2 in A, op. 100, *mov. 3, b. 5*

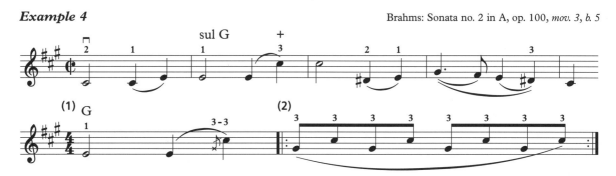

(1) The intermediate note is third-finger G♯.

(2) Practise the perfect fourth from G♯ to C♯.

Like the lower fingering in Example 2, this shift could also be played part-shift part-extension with A as the intermediate note. In **(1)** reach up to A with the third finger. Then in **(2)** shift between A and C♯.

Example 5

Fibich: Poème, *b. 12*

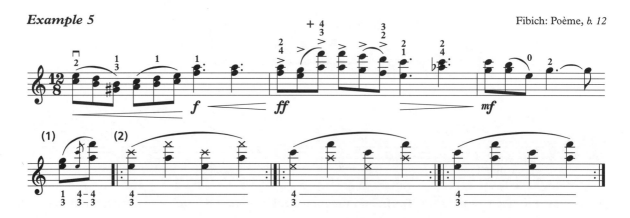

(1) Both fingers shift a perfect fourth.

(2) With both fingers on the string, first play only the lower note, then only the upper, then both notes together.[1]

Combination shifts

Combination shifts are a variation of Romantic shifts. They end and sound like a Romantic shift, but begin (usually inaudibly) like a Classical shift. They are normally used only for ascending shifts, rarely for descending.

Begin the shift with the lower finger on the string and end the shift with the upper finger. Sometime during the shift change over from the lower finger to the upper finger.

Combination shifts make the two notes of the shift seem closer together. In the example (octave B♭ to B♭), shifting a major third with the first finger and a minor third with the fourth finger feels like two very small distances. In comparison the perfect fifth in either a Classical or Romantic octave shift seems much further.

Example 1   Brahms: Sonata no. 2 in A, op. 100, *mov. 1, b. 41*

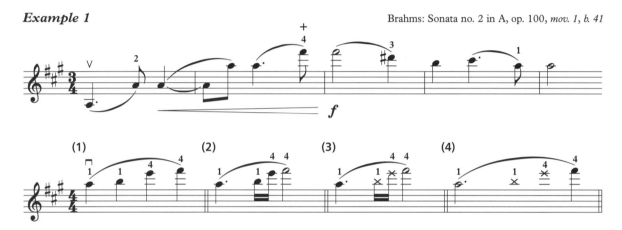

(1) Play the two notes of the shift (A, F♯), and the intermediate notes (B, E), with equal length and tone.

(2) Play the intermediate notes shorter.

(3) Ghost the intermediate notes.

(4) Still thinking of the intermediate notes, play A followed by F♯ as if there were no shift.

Example 2   Schubert: Sonata in A, op. posth. 162, *mov. 1, b. 5*

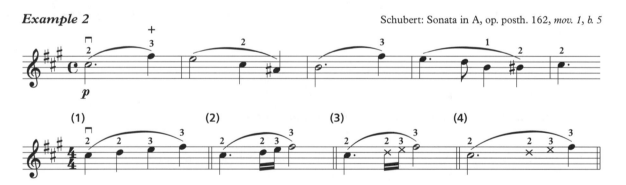

● Practise as in Example 1.

Example 3   Fauré: Sonata in A, op. 13, *mov. 4, b. 47*

● Use an extra intermediate note to emphasize the slow arrival speed, as in a Romantic shift:[1]

● Practise as in Example 1.

[1] See *Slow arrival speed*, page 172

137 Exchange shifts

An exchange shift is one where the fingers 'cross over' each other during the shift:

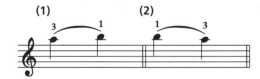

(1) Ascending Begin the shift with the higher finger on the string and end the shift with the lower finger. Sometime during the shift, change from the higher finger to the lower finger.

(2) Descending Begin the shift with the lower finger on the string. When it reaches the destination note, replace it with the upper finger, using a substitution.[1]

At the same time, the lower finger continues down until it reaches whatever its note would be in the new position (either remaining above, or resting on, the string).

[1] See *Substitutions*, page 159

Example 1   Rode: Concerto no. 7 in A minor, op. 9, *mov. 1, b. 44*

p dolce

- Practise the shift to the second finger (marked '+') by shifting the first finger down to its new position:

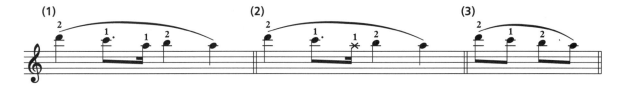

(1) Play the intermediate note (A) distinctly, as an extra note.

(2) Ghost the intermediate note.

(3) Play without the intermediate note as simply one note to another.

- Then repeat the three stages using a substitution, so that now the intermediate note is B:

- Practise the substitution on its own:

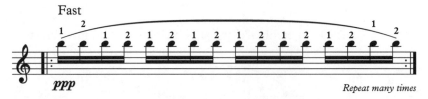

Fast

ppp   *Repeat many times*

Afterwards, playing without the intermediate note as simply one note to another, the shift will feel smooth and easy, and will not disturb the rhythm of the scale.

Example 2

Schubert: Sonatina in A minor, op. 137 no. 2, *mov. 2, b. 25*

- Practise the shift to the third finger ('+') by shifting the second finger down to its new position:

(1) Play the intermediate note (C) as an extra note.

(2) Ghost the intermediate note.

(3) Play the shift in the context of the passage, playing the intermediate note like a grace note.

- Then repeat the three stages using a substitution:

- Practise the substitution on its own:

Example 3

Bruch: Concerto no. 1 in G minor, op. 26, *mov. 1, b. 79*

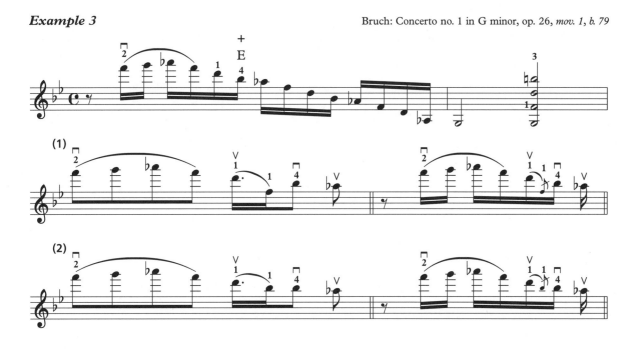

(1) Practise shifting below the note to the new position, first slowly and then at performance tempo.

(2) Practise the shift as a substitution.

Example 4   Beethoven: Sonata in A, op. 30 no. 1, *mov. 3, var. 2, b. 1*

(1) Practise shifting with the first finger to establish the feeling of each new position.

(2) Practise the shifts as substitutions.

Example 5   Arpeggio sequence used by Ševčík and Flesch

While observing the rhythm (which is not precise, but a representation of how the notes might sound) make sure that the movement of the hand is entirely smooth and even, flowing freely from one position to another without stops:

Example 6   Vivaldi: Summer (The Four Seasons), op. 8 no. 2, *mov. 3, b. 40*

● Begin at a slow tempo and gradually increase to as fast a speed as possible:

Example 7   Mozart: Concerto no. 3 in G, K216, *mov. 1, b. 51*

Example 8   Brahms: Sonata no. 2 in A, op. 100, *mov. 1, b. 211*

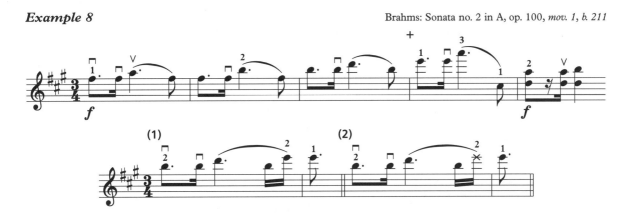

(1) Shift up with the second finger to the intermediate note (E) and then substitute the first finger.

(2) Ghost the intermediate note (written as an x-note).

Ascending shifts: practise three ways

138

- Wherever possible, practise shifts in all three ways using Classical, Romantic and Combination intermediate notes. This improves the feel of the shift regardless of the type you will actually use in the end.

Example 1   Mendelssohn: Concerto in E minor, op. 64, *mov. 1, b. 80*

The shift marked '+' would often be a Classical shift, the first finger shifting to 5th position F♯ – especially since F♯ is the next note after the shift anyway. Nevertheless, practising the shift in all three ways greatly increases security and accuracy:

Example 2 Beethoven: Sonata in D, op. 12 no. 1, *mov. 2, b. 8*

Example 3 Franck: Sonata in A, *mov. 1, b. 57*

139 Position-finding using intermediate notes

Intermediate notes are a secure way to find the correct note or hand position at the beginning of a phrase or after a rest. The fingers are placed silently, often rapidly, in order to move to a different area of the fingerboard.

[1] See *Substitutions*, page 159

Substitutions[1] are often handy for moving quickly from one position to another, but there are always many different ways to reach a particular note, and different players will have their own preferred route.

Example 1 Bruch: Concerto no. 1 in G minor, op. 26, *mov. 1, b. 24*

Suppose that Bruch had written this passage as follows:

Both make it very easy to find the D–B♭ double stop; but it is just as easy to find if you finger the extra notes silently:

(1) Play the intermediate notes as though they were part of the passage.

(2) Place the finger on the first intermediate note without playing it (written as an x-note), and then play on.

(3) Place the first two intermediate notes without playing them, and play on.

(4) Place all the intermediate notes silently, playing the 'destination note' only.

(5) Placing the first and fourth fingers together as a 'block' (as though playing a double stop on one string), put down the silent fingers like fast grace notes, and then begin the passage.

Example 2   Franck: Sonata in A, *mov. 2, b. 153*

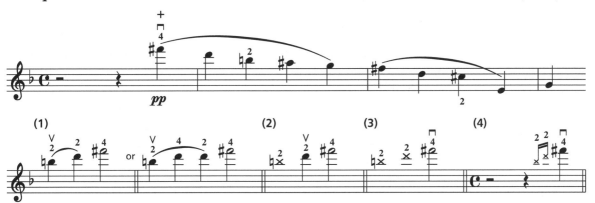

● Practise as in Example 1.

Example 3   Mozart: Concerto no. 3 in G, K216, *mov. 1 cadenza (Sam Franko)*

● Practise as in Example 1.

Example 4   Vivaldi: Autumn (The Four Seasons), op. 8 no. 3, *mov. 1, b. 17*

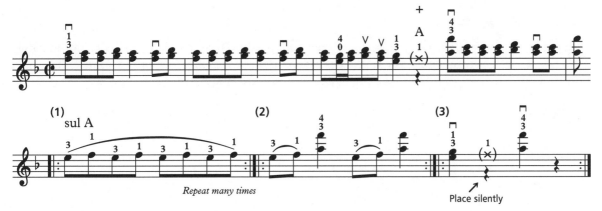

(1) Practise the shift to the intermediate note (F).

　　Begin slowly, and gradually speed up to as fast a tempo as possible. Keep the first finger on the string.

(2) Practise going to the F in the context of playing the double stop.

(3) Play straight from one double stop to another, using the first-finger F as a guide but without playing it.

Timing the shift

140 ## Speed of shift

The speed of the shift is usually in proportion to the speed of the passage:

Slow passages – slower shifts

Fast passages – faster shifts

A slow shift is never good in a fast passage. Sometimes a fast shift in a slow passage helps in sustaining the line or in making a clean, inaudible shift.

● To highlight the right speed for a shift, practise the shift or phrase at all speeds, from very slow to very fast.

● As the tempo increases, speed up the shift proportionately. Afterwards the correct shift speed will feel natural, obvious and reliable.

Example 1   Elgar: Chanson de Matin, *b. 9*

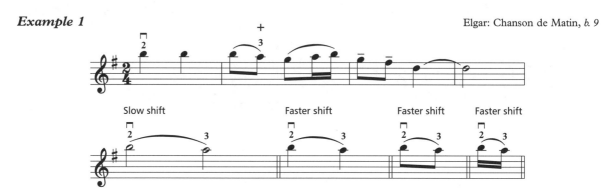

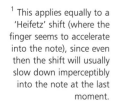

¹ This applies equally to a 'Heifetz' shift (where the finger seems to accelerate into the note), since even then the shift will usually slow down imperceptibly into the note at the last moment.

Example 2   Kreisler: Caprice Viennois, op. 2, *b. 100*

Slow arrival speed applies the least to a Classical shift (see page 160), where the lower finger shifts and the upper finger drops directly down onto its note; however, even here there may be an element of 'fast–slow' in the lower finger.

In separate-bow passages the speed of the shift may be clearer if first you practise with slurs:

141 ## Slow arrival speed

The speed of the shift is often fast–slow rather than one speed from beginning to end. The finger travels fast up or down the string until close to the destination note, and then slows into the note.¹ The single most important thing is to listen to the finger ghosting into the note.²

² Slow arrival does not mean that every shift is a *glissando*. The shift can be completely inaudible and still slow into the arrival note. See *Improving listening*, page 56

Example 1   Bloch: Nigun (no. 2 from 'Baal Shem'), *b. 37*

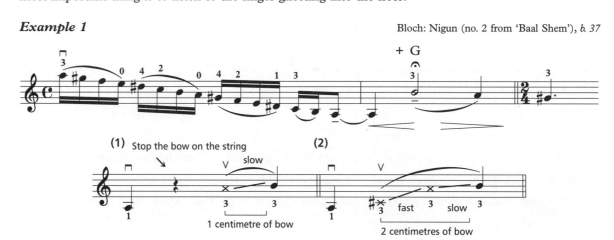

(1) Practise the end of the shift

- After playing the first finger A, stop the bow on the string. With the bow sitting stationary on the string, move the hand quickly to some point just below third finger B (shown as an x-note A).

  In other words, do not slide along the string to move to the higher position, but simply finish in the low position and replace the hand in the higher position, leaving the bow on the string.[1]

- Place the third finger lightly on the string (x-note A). Slowly slide from the x-note into the B using no more than one centimetre of bow and with almost no bow pressure (i.e. ghost the bow). The finger begins very lightly, and gradually settles more heavily into the string as it nears the B.

(2) Join the beginning and end of the shift together

- Having played the first-finger A, begin the up-bow and the shift at exactly the same time. Ghost the bow at the start of the up-bow, moving the finger quickly up to some point just below the arrival note. Arrive with the finger resting on the string as if for a harmonic.

- Continuing to ghost the bow, slowly slide from the x-note into the B, the finger gradually going more heavily into the string until the finger arrives on the B.

[1] One reason why slow arrival speed is so helpful in improving accuracy is that by considering only the very end of the shift you can make long shifts seem like short shifts. Instead of thinking of 'fast–slow' and of the whole length of the shift, think of the shift as 'slow' and very short, and beginning only one centimetre or half a centimetre below the arrival note (ascending), or above the arrival note (descending).

Example 2   Franck: Sonata in A, *mov. 2, b. 134*

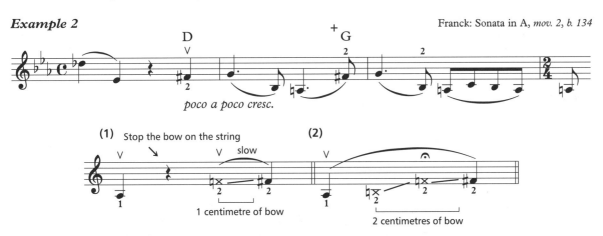

- Practise as in Example 1.

Example 3   Saint-Saëns: Concerto no. 3 in B minor, op. 61, *mov. 1, b. 13*

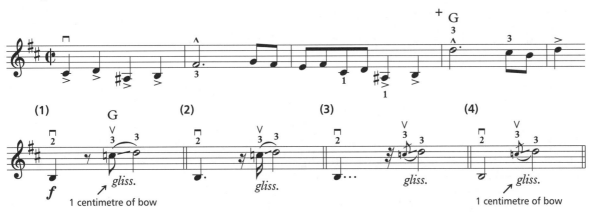

(1) At the end of the B, stop the bow on the string. Reposition the hand in 8th position. Then play from the C into the D with a glissando.

(2) The same as **(1)** but play the B longer, taking less time to move into the higher position.

(3) The same, waiting longer on the B. Do not consider the C an intermediate note any more – simply aim somewhere below the D and slide into it from there.

(4) The same, but now joining the lower and the upper notes together without any break.

Example 4   Bruch: Concerto no. 1 in G minor, op. 26, *mov. 2, b. 1*

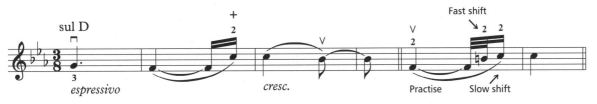

Example 5

Franck: Sonata in A, *mov. 2, b. 14*

Example 6

Saint-Saëns: Havanaise, op. 83, *b. 49*

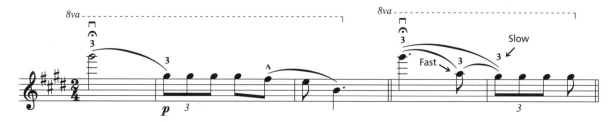

- Descending one-finger shifts work in the same way: shift fast until nearly there, then continue slowly into the destination note.

Example 7

Dvořák: Romance, op. 11, *b. 24*

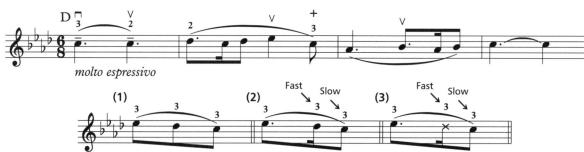

(1) Play the two notes of the shift, and an intermediate note close to the arrival note, equally.

(2) Shift quickly to the D♭, then slowly into the C.

(3) Ghost the intermediate note (written as an x-note), then shift slowly into the C.

Example 8

Brahms: Concerto in D, op. 77, *mov. 1, b. 304*

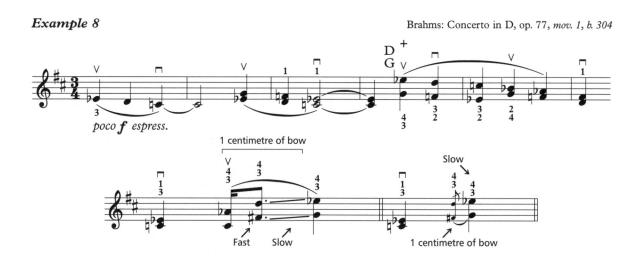

Example 9

Paganini: Concerto no. 1 in D, op. 6, *mov. 1, b. 111*

Taking time from the note before the shift

The short moment that it takes to shift needs to be 'stolen' from the note before the shift. If the note before the shift is played completely full-value, there is no time to shift without arriving late.

The time taken from the note before the shift needs to be so little that the listener would never know that the note was a fraction shorter than it should have been.

- Practise by exaggeration: shorten the note before the shift and shift too early.

Example 1

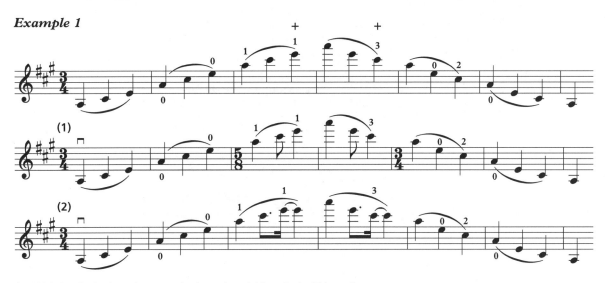

(1) Think of playing the note before the shift only half-length.

(2) Shift a little later, but still getting to the arrival note early.

Example 2   Beethoven: Romanze in F, op. 50, *b. 77*

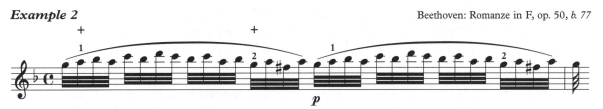

- Begin slowly, and gradually speed up to as fast a tempo as possible:

Example 3   Mendelssohn: Concerto in E minor, op. 64, *mov. 1, b. 25*

- Practise getting to the first finger as fast as possible:

Example 4   Brahms: Sonata no. 2 in A, op. 100, *mov. 2, b. 27*

Think of the note before
the shift as half-length

Example 5   Mendelssohn: Concerto in E minor, op. 64, *mov. 1, b. 174*

- Gradually speed up to performance tempo:

Example 6   Dont: 24 Etudes and Caprices, op. 35, No. 17, *b. 1*

- Gradually speed up to as fast a tempo as possible:

Example 7   Tchaikovsky: Concerto in D, op. 35, *mov. 1, b. 114*

- Gradually speed up to as fast a tempo as possible:

Example 8   Brahms: Concerto in D, op. 77, *mov. 1, b. 116*

Missing out the note before the shift

143

- Miss out the note before the shift to feel the exact moment, within the tempo and rhythmic pulse, when the shifting finger must arrive on its note.

Example 1

- Keep the bow solidly and evenly in the string, completely unaffected by the actions of the left hand.

Example 2

Arpeggio sequence used by Ševčík and Flesch

Example 3

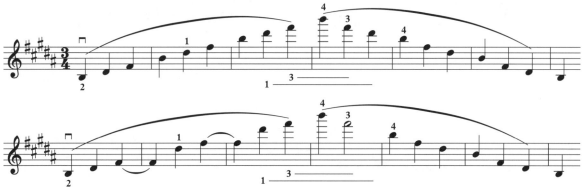

- Begin slowly, and gradually speed up to a fast tempo.

Example 4

Mozart: Concerto no. 5 in A, K219, *mov. 1, b. 74*

Example 5

J. S. Bach: Partita no. 3 in E, BWV1006, *Preludio, b. 7*

- Play the phrase with musical conviction as if it were actually written with the note left out:

Example 6

Beethoven: Romanze in F, op. 50, *b. 2*

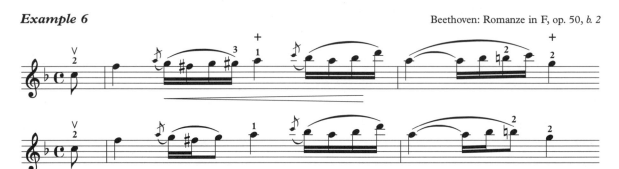

Example 7

Dont: 24 Etudes and Caprices, op. 35, No. 14, *b. 1*

Example 8

Tchaikovsky: Concerto in D, op. 35, *mov. 1, b. 60*

Example 9

Wieniawski: Concerto no. 2 in D minor, op. 22, *mov. 3, b. 55*

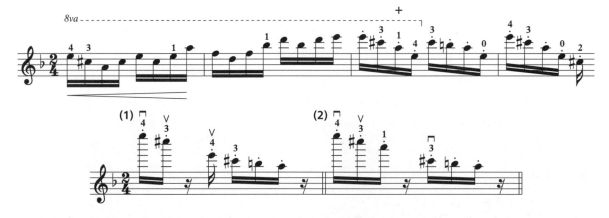

(1) Miss out the first-finger A to find exactly the right timing for the next note, fourth-finger E. Play strictly in time, starting slowly and building up to the correct tempo, or faster if possible.

(2) In this example it would also be helpful to keep the A and miss out the fourth-finger E.

Co-ordination: overlapping with the previous bow

In separate-bow shifts the finger might arrive late (i.e. the bow has already begun to move before the finger has fully stopped the string), because it is much simpler for the bow to change direction than it is for the finger to find the right place on the string.[1]

- To make sure that the finger is in time, practise arriving too early so that the note you shift to is played momentarily by the previous bow stroke.

[1] See also *Co-ordination*, page 14

Example 1

Example 2   Kreutzer: 42 Etudes ou caprices, No. 26, b. 2

- Begin slowly, and gradually speed up to as fast a tempo as possible:

Example 3   Kreutzer: 42 Etudes ou caprices, No. 8, b. 2

Example 4   Vivaldi: Autumn (The Four Seasons), op. 8 no. 3, *mov. 1, b. 39*

Example 5

This practice method works equally well in *spiccato* passages.

- Practise the overlapping with the bow on the string. Afterwards the shift, and the co-ordination of the shift with the *spiccato*, will immediately be greatly improved.

- Begin slowly, and gradually speed up:

Example 6

Example 7

Example 8

- Play the 32nd-notes (demisemiquavers) ricochet.

- Arrive exactly in time at the sixteenth-note (semiquaver) that follows the ricochet.

Playing in one position

The ideal is to play purely musically, with technique always at the service of the music rather than the other way round. The musical line must never be distorted by having to fit itself around technical concerns.

One way to discover the true musical phrase, accent, timing, etc. is to play it on another instrument, or to sing it (or to imagine doing so). Often the phrase appears in a completely new light when freed of the specific violin techniques required to play it.

An easy way to achieve the same effect on the violin is to consider how you might approach the phrase if you played it in a lower position, or without shifting, as though it were meant to be played there. Would you play it faster, or with different accent or rubato?

- Play a phrase or passage in a lower, easier position than the one written, without any problems of shifting, intonation or purity of tone. Work on the phrase to find the ideal direction, shape and basic musical expression.

- Using this as a model, play with the correct fingering and find the same musical idea, and the same timing.

Example 1   Sarasate: Malaguena, op. 21 no. 1, b. 23

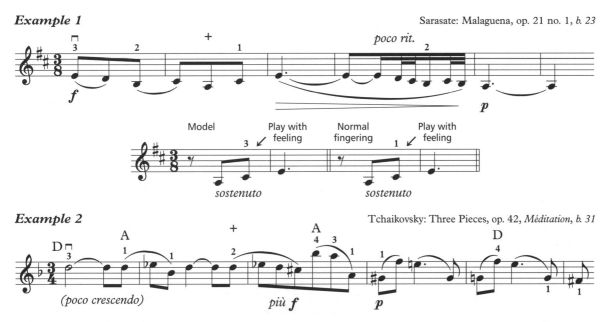

Example 2   Tchaikovsky: Three Pieces, op. 42, *Méditation*, b. 31

Playing from the sustained f in the third bar to the subito p in the fourth bar, with a very slight *ritardando* just before the *subito* p, how would you think of the phrase if you did not shift up on the A string?

- Play several times with a variety of different fingerings, each time searching for the ideal pacing and shaping, the fingering making no difference whatsoever:

Example 3   Chausson: Poème, op. 25, b. 34

(1) Picture playing the phrase on a keyboard. How would you shape it and pace it ideally?

(2) Play it on the violin in 1st position, finding the same ideal shape and pacing.

(3) Find the same approach while playing the whole phrase on the D string.

Example 4   Wieniawski: Polonaise brillante, op. 21, b. 45

Example 5   Tchaikovsky: Concerto in D, op. 35, *mov. 1, b. 30*

Example 6   Wieniawski: Polonaise de Concert, op. 4, *b. 9*

- Alternate between shifting and not shifting, making both fingerings sound identical to each other:

Repeat many times

---

146 **Lightening the shift**   ## Releasing the hand and fingers

Encourage the hand to release during a shift by taking it away from the violin altogether.

1 Play the first note of the shift, then turn the hand outwards (Fig. 13, page 153); or drop your left hand to your side.

2 Allow all the muscles in the arm, hand and fingers to release.

3 Then return the hand to the violin (in the original position) and, keeping the same feeling of lightness and ease in the hand and fingers, shift to the destination note.

147 ## Ghosting

- Practise shifts with harmonic-like finger pressure, the finger lightly touching the string but with no pressure whatsoever.

  Listening to the 'ghost' shift it is impossible to 'over-shoot' and shift too far.[1]

[1] See also *Improving listening*, page 56

Example 1

Ghost

- Practise arpeggios by pausing on the note before the shift and then ghosting slowly into the new note.

Example 2   Mozart: Sonata in B♭, K454, *mov. 3, b. 5*

- Shift the first finger lightly into the new position, ready for the fourth finger to drop on to its note:

Very slow   Ghost

Example 3

Smetana: Aus der Heimat, *mov. 2, b. 43*

- Shift the second finger lightly into the D:

Example 4

Grieg: Sonata in C minor, op. 45, *mov. 1, b. 254*

- Practise speeding up the shift while still listening to the ghost:

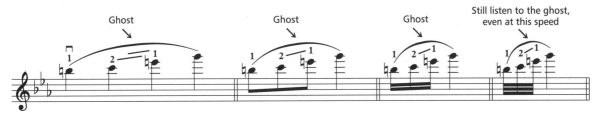

'Trilling' shifts

148

- Make each shift into a sort of 'trill', playing it as fast as possible.
- Encourage the fingers to be very light on the string by bowing lightly over the fingerboard.
- Also practise independence of the hands by bowing heavily near the bridge while keeping the 'trilling' fingers very light.

Example 1

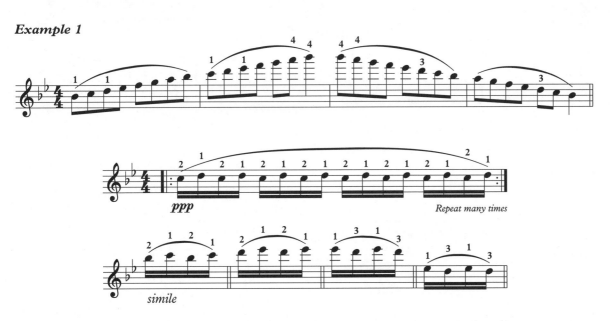

The scroll of the violin should remain still. If it shakes, release the base joint of the left thumb (feel it soften), and the base joint of the first finger;[1] make sure the fingers remain light and buoyant, not *pressing* into the string. Another key area to release is the wrist.

[1] *See Releasing fingers with the base joint of the first finger, page 230*

Example 2

Mozart: Concerto no. 5 in A, K219, *mov. 1, b. 50*

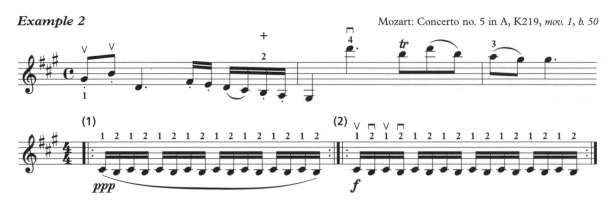

(1) Practise slurred with many shifts in each bow.

(2) It can also be helpful to practise with separate bows, as in the passage.

Example 3

Debussy: Sonata, *mov. 3, b. 106*

● After practising the shift itself, as in Examples 1 and 2, the next step could be to add the note before, and the note after, the two notes of the shift:

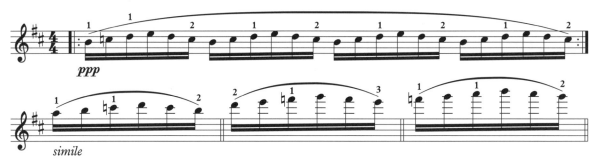

Example 4

Franck: Sonata in A, *mov. 3, b. 48*

Example 5

Lalo: Symphonie espagnole, op. 21, *mov. 1, b. 153*

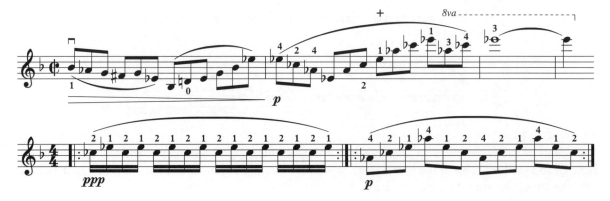

Example 6

Keyser: Etudes, op. 20, no. 32, *b. 1*

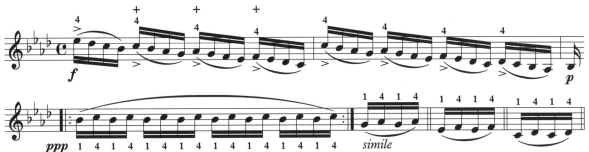

Example 7

Rode: 24 Caprices, No. 1, *b. 3*

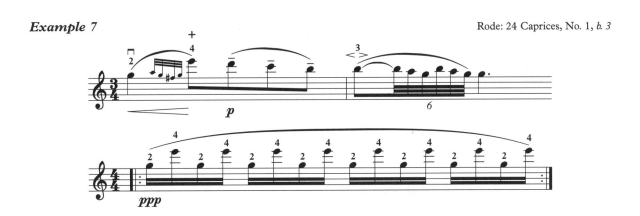

Example 8

Sarasate: Zigeunerweisen, op. 20 no. 1, *b. 98*

- Play with the metronome. Begin slowly, and gradually speed up to as fast a tempo as possible, playing evenly and with a relaxed hand.

- Play slurred and separate bows.

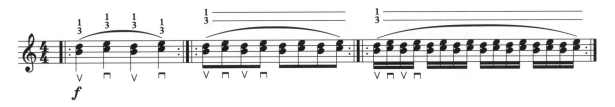

In double-stop shifts where the fingers do not move the same distance, it is often helpful to think only of the finger that moves the bigger distance. In this example think only of the first finger, and let the third finger look after itself.

Example 9

Brahms: Concerto in D, op. 77, *mov. 1, b. 561*

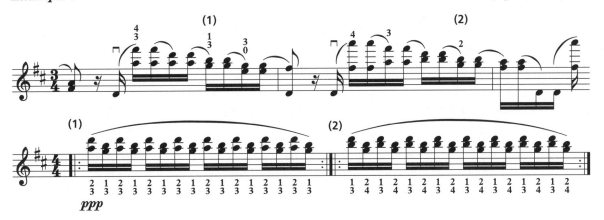

149 Isolating the shift

This section shows a few typical examples of breaking a passage down to find the underlying structure created by the shifts.

Example 1

Lalo: Symphonie espagnole, op. 21, *mov. 1, b. 245*

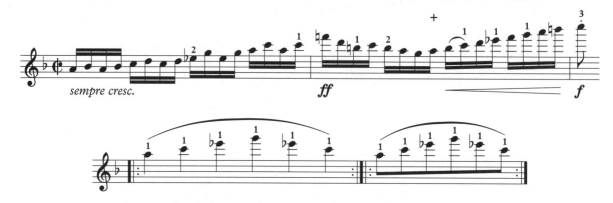

Example 2

Mozart: Concerto no. 5 in A, K219, *mov. 2, b. 107*

(1) Glide smoothly and evenly from note to note, releasing the string slightly during each shift.

(2) Imagine that the phrase is actually written like this. Play evenly, with full expression, as in performance.

Example 3

Beethoven: Concerto in D, op. 61, *mov. 1, b. 128*

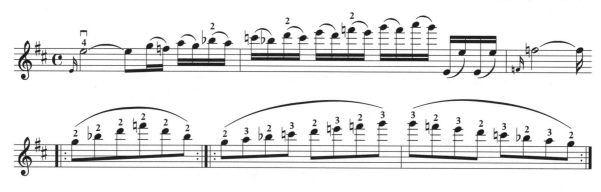

Example 4

Viotti: Concerto no. 23 in G, *mov. 1, b. 135*

The downward shifts in patterns like this can be played either as normal shifts or as 'half-shifts'.[1]

[1] 'The finger is first stretched to a new note outside of the position in which the hand is resting at the moment, and after the stretched finger is placed on the string, the hand follows thereafter into the new position.'
Ivan Galamian: *Principles of Violin Playing and Teaching* (New Jersey, 1962), 25.

186   Shifting

Example 5 Tchaikovsky: Concerto in D, op. 35, *mov. 1, b. 250*

Example 6 Vieuxtemps: Concerto no. 5 in A minor, op. 37, *mov. 1, b. 68*

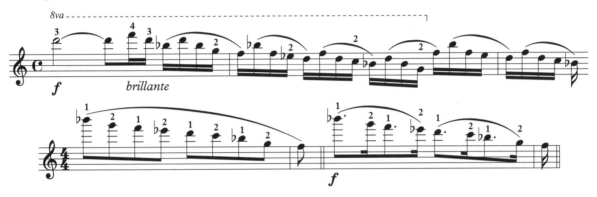

Example 7 Bériot: Concerto no. 9 in A minor, op. 104, *mov. 1, b. 57*

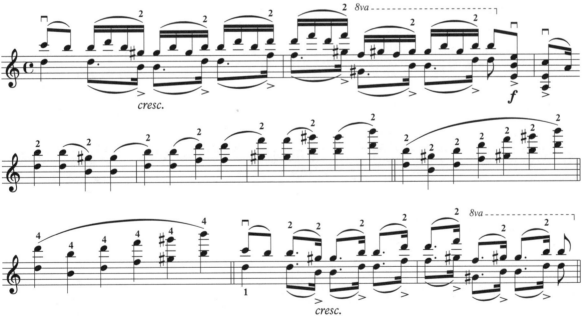

Example 8 Wieniawski: Concerto no. 2 in D minor, op. 22, *mov. 1, b. 127*

150 Shifting to a harmonic

1 The finger must be on the harmonic before the bow moves to play it.

2 The bow should normally move very fast, to throw the harmonic out with power and brilliance.

3 During the harmonic, lift the finger from the string so that the harmonic rings.

Example 1   Mendelssohn: Concerto in E minor, op. 64, *mov. 3, b. 2*

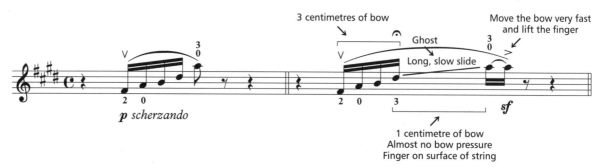

1 Play the first four notes in tempo and pause on the last note, third-finger D♯.

2 Lighten the finger and slide slowly into the harmonic A. Ghost the slide: use the tiniest length of bow and the least bow pressure.[1]

> It is important to change the curve of the finger during the shift, so that you play the harmonic more with the pad of the finger than the tip. See Fig. 12, on page 139.

3 Listen to the ghost, and when you hear that the finger has arrived on the harmonic, move the bow fast.

4 Lift the finger off the harmonic slightly before, or as, the bow leaves the string. (See *Sustaining natural harmonics without the finger*, page 189.)

Gradually speed up, reducing the pause until you can perform the same actions, in the same proportions to each other, without a pause.[2]

[1] Ghost notes: see page 160

[2] Gradually speeding up or slowing down, while keeping the proportions the same, is like reducing or enlarging a photograph. The size of one part of the picture remains the same relative to another part, whatever the change in overall size.

Example 2   Lalo: Symphonie espagnole, op. 21, *mov. 1, b. 9*

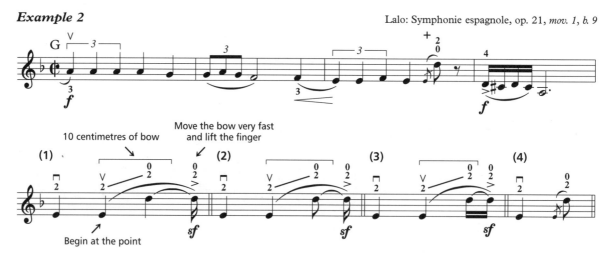

(1) Shift up to the harmonic and hold it for a quarter-note (crotchet). Having used no more than 10 centimetres of bow, suddenly move the bow very fast. Lift the finger off the string as the bow leaves the string, or a little before.

(2) Hold the harmonic for only an eighth-note (quaver), before 'launching' the harmonic with a fast bow speed.

(3) Hold the harmonic for such a short time that the bow has only just begun to move before launching the harmonic.

(4) Tie the different stages together.

Sustaining natural harmonics without the finger

In many cases, you need to take the finger off the string *while* playing a natural harmonic, and continue the harmonic with the bow alone while the hand moves to another position.

To sustain the harmonic without the finger on the string:

1   Accelerate the speed of bow slightly throughout the harmonic. The harmonic will immediately 'break' if the bow speed decreases.

2   Move slightly closer to the bridge throughout the harmonic. The harmonic will break if the bow moves even a fraction away from the bridge.

Example 1   Massenet: Méditation from Thaïs, *b. 28*

● First practise the harmonic on its own:

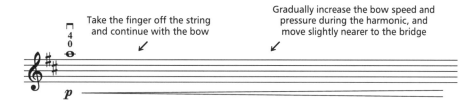

● Then practise the harmonic in the context of the phrase. Pause on the harmonic for as long as possible, having lifted the fourth finger, before playing the G.

● Connect the harmonic to the G smoothly, with no break in the sound whatsoever.

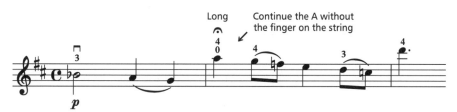

Example 2   Saint-Saëns: Introduction and Rondo Capriccioso, op. 28, *Introduction, b. 8*

● Connect the harmonic to the C smoothly, with no break in the sound:

Example 3   Wieniawski: Concerto in D minor, op. 22, *mov. 1, b. 88*

Chromatic glissando

Also practise the chromatic glissando with rhythms and accents to increase the clarity of each note (*Rhythm practice*, page 36; *Accent practice*, page 43).

152 ### Speed of glissando

The first stage is to find the speed of the glissando. Too fast, and the semitones will be too wide; too slow, they will be too narrow; the transition from slower at the top of the string, where the notes are closer together, to faster lower down the string, must be very smooth and even.

Example 1   Paganini: Concerto no. 1 in D, op. 6, *mov. 1, b. 233*

- Play an ordinary, smooth glissando without individual semitones.
- Play in time, sliding so that you pass, without stopping, the first note of each group of four exactly on each beat. In this example count: 3 – 4 – 1 – 2 – 3 (the first '3' being the A♯ which is the third note of the run).

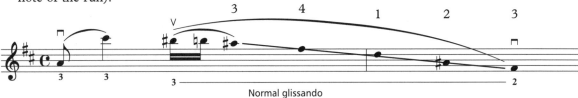

Normal glissando

Example 2   Saint-Saëns: Introduction and Rondo Capriccioso, op. 28, *Rondo, b. 197*

This passage is played *spiccato*, but first play slurred to focus on the exact speed of the descent.

- Play a smooth glissando without individual semitones.
- Slide so that you pass, without stopping, the first note of each group of three exactly on each beat:

Example 3   Saint-Saëns: Havanaise, op. 83, *b. 265*

- Play a smooth glissando without individual semitones:

(1) Practise aiming for the beginning of each beat. Slide strictly in time so that you pass, without stopping, the first note of each group of four exactly on each beat.

(2) Practise aiming for the half-beats. Slide as before without stopping.

Building the run in groups

Having found the speed of the slide as shown on page 190, the next step is to slide in stages – still without the individual semitones – working from the bottom up and the top down. Then add the semitones as the final stage.

Example 1

Sarasate: Carmen Fantasy, op. 25, *Introduction, b. 158*

* Played:

* Working from the bottom up:

* Working in stages from the top down, stopping exactly in tune on the first note of each beat:

* Then play the individual semitones, again working in stages from the bottom up and the top down.

  The accents indicate the vibrato-like movement of the left finger (each forward motion of the 'vibrato' playing a note). The bow should remain even and steady, staying quite near the bridge to save bow:

Example 2   Tchaikovsky: Concerto in D, op. 35, *mov. 1, cadenza*

- Clarify the notes to aim for by accenting the first note of each group:

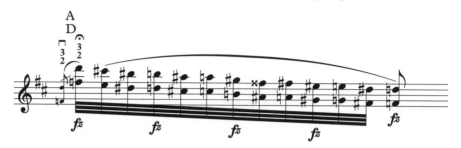

154 ## Using an ordinary fingering as a model

Each note in a chromatic glissando can sound as clear as in a fingered chromatic run.

- To highlight any blurring in the glissando, use an ordinary chromatic fingering as a model.

Example 1   Wieniawski: Concerto no. 2 in D minor, op. 22, *mov. 1, b. 207*

Example 2   Sarasate: Zigeunerweisen, op. 20 no. 1, *b. 19*

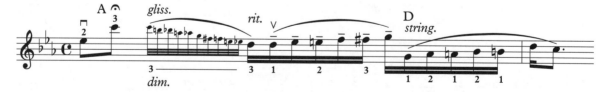

- Alternate between the two fingerings until they sound almost identical:

Intonation

part 6

The feel of the hand and fingers

Thinking of each note or finger in relationship to other notes or fingers is one of the most important aspects of intonation, e.g. tuning notes in relation to each other, thinking in intervals not individual notes, and the feel of the fingers in relation to each other.

Holding down fingers

155

Sometimes the fingers need to stay down on the string after being played, rather than lifting immediately. At other times, the left hand action is more like a pianist's, i.e. as soon as the new finger touches the string, the old finger lifts.

In either case it can strengthen a passage if you practise holding fingers down for an exaggeratedly long time (even to the point of slight awkwardness), and to do so even if you would not usually hold them down in normal playing. Afterwards the normal finger action and intonation will feel much more secure. Holding down fingers also helps in maintaining a good hand shape.

Example 1

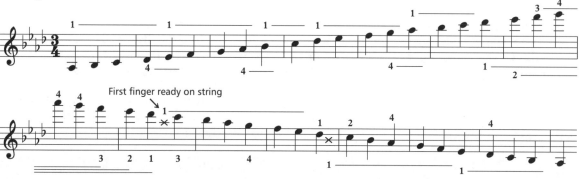

First finger ready on string

Example 2

Kreutzer: 42 Etudes ou caprices, No. 5, *b. 1*

Example 3

Beethoven: Concerto in D, op. 61, *mov. 1, b. 97*

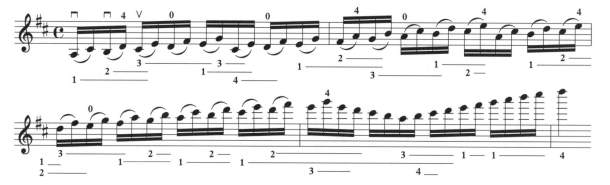

Example 4   J. S. Bach: Partita no. 2 in D minor, BWV1004, *Giga, b. 17*

Example 5   J. S. Bach: Concerto no. 1 in A minor, BWV1041, *mov. 3, b. 44*

Example 6   Tchaikovsky: Concerto in D, op. 35, *mov. 1, b. 28*

156 Square and extended finger shapes

[1] The shape of each finger is always different depending on the build of the hand and the specific pattern of notes. When the finger is square the angle at the nail joint is closer to a right-angle than when the finger is 'extended'. It does not have to be a perfect right-angle but is simply more 'square' than the extended shape. In higher positions the difference between square and extended is much less than in 1st position.

One of the most important requirements for playing in tune is that the left hand and fingers remain free and flexible, the fingers changing shape from note to note. 'Square' and 'extended' refer to the shape of the finger when it is placed on the string (Fig. 14).[1]

Depending on the passage and the individual hand, the normal placements in 1st position (A string), are:

First-finger B♭ – square   **First-finger B** – extended   **First-finger B♯** – very extended
Second-finger C♭ – very square   **Second-finger C** – square   **Second-finger C♯** – extended
Third-finger D♭ – very square   **Third-finger D** – square   **Third-finger D♯** – extended
Fourth-finger E♭ – square   **Fourth-finger E** – extended   **Fourth-finger E♯** – very extended

If the fingers do not change shape enough, or quickly enough, the hand may make a partial 'shift' which can then throw all the following notes out of tune, e.g. the hand should not move up a half position when playing from third-finger C (on the G string) (Fig. 14a) to third-finger C♯ (Fig. 14b).

Fig. 14

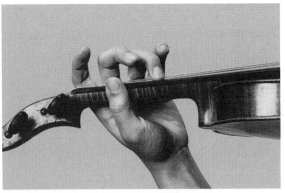

(a) **Third-finger C, G string, square shape**

(b) **Third-finger C♯, extended shape**

● When building or polishing a passage, plan the shape of certain fingers consciously.

□ = square   ◇ = extended

Example 1   Mozart: Concerto no. 3 in G, K216, *mov. 1, b. 124*

Example 2

Kreutzer: 42 Etudes ou caprices, No. 29, *b. 19*

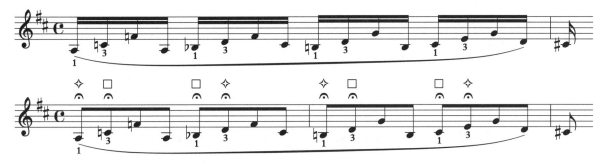

Example 3

Tchaikovsky: Sérénade mélancholique, op. 26, *b. 12*

The third-finger F (marked '+') would be in 4th position if the first finger was on D♭. In that case the third finger would be 'extended' (it would be 'square' on an E). Since here the third-finger F is played with an extension, with the first finger on C and the hand remaining in 3rd position, the third-finger F is 'very extended'. The D♭ it shifts to is 'square'.

- Practise changing the shape of the finger during the shift:

Filling in spaces between notes

When the playing fingers are not consecutive (i.e. 1–3, 1–4, 2–4), the unused fingers in between can help in measuring the exact distance. This is another reason for keeping the fingers close to the string when in the air.[1]

On the A string play second-finger C to fourth-finger E: as well as measuring the fourth finger from the second, picture the feeling of third-finger D, and measure the fourth finger from *the imagined third finger*.

- Play the unused finger to confirm the feeling of its exact placement.

Example 1

Kreutzer: 42 Etudes ou caprices, No. 12, *b. 1*

- Play the passage once or twice with grace notes to focus on the relationship between the fingers.

- Then play without the grace notes. Picture the feeling of placing them on the string and place the actual fingers in relation to the imagined fingers.

[1] See Fig. 1a, page 4

Example 2   Beethoven: Sonata in E♭, op. 12 no. 3, *mov. 1, b. 18*

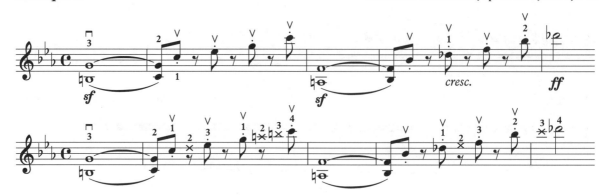

- Place the x-notes silently on the string without playing them, and place the actual notes in relation to them.

158

Practising without rhythm or real tone, learning notes only

- Focus on intonation by ignoring the two other main elements of playing – sound and rhythm. Play each note with equal tone and length, concentrating only on the exact tuning of each note.

- Playing all down-bows can be helpful in separating the notes from each other so that there are no tonal, rhythmic or musical elements.

¹ See *Testing, relating, comparing*, page 207

- Practise phrases, passages or entire pieces in this way, checking and adjusting each note as necessary.[1]

Example 1   Prokofiev: Concerto no. 2 in G minor, op. 63, *mov. 1, b. 1*

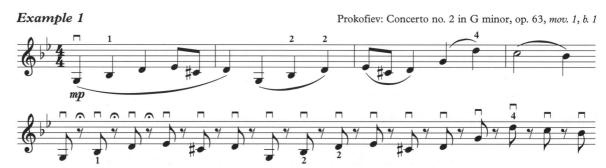

Example 2   J. S. Bach: Partita no. 1 in B minor, BWV1002, *Bourrée, b. 1*

159

Tone–semitone patterns

² See also *Tone–semitone patterns*, page 221

Feel the four fingers in tone–semitone patterns, i.e. tone–tone–semitone, tone–semitone–tone, and so on.[2] Afterwards the passage will feel more secure, the hand and fingers falling immediately into each new tone–semitone 'setting' without hesitation.

Example 1   Mozart: Concerto no. 3 in G, K216, *mov. 1, b. 78*

The tone–semitone patterns of this scale are:

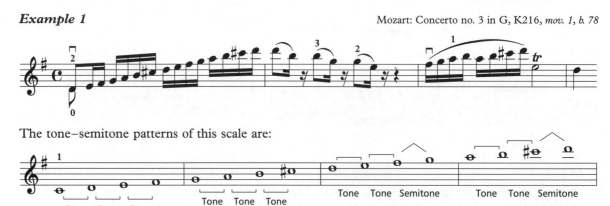

● Focus on the tone–semitone patterns by placing the fingers in 'blocks':

● Play the first finger on its own, and then place the other fingers on the string together, at the same time. (The only fingers that will actually sound are therefore the first and fourth fingers, the second and third being placed silently.)

● Put the fingers down in tune, in their correct tone–semitone patterns.

● Keep the first finger held down on the string as marked.

● Also strengthen the feel of each tone–semitone group by playing quickly and lightly as follows:

Example 2   Mendelssohn: Concerto in E minor, op. 64, *mov. 1, b. 36*

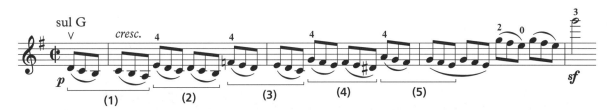

The most obvious passages to practise as tone–semitone patterns are simple scales. When a group of notes is not in consecutive order like a scale, make the tone–semitone pattern clear by rearranging the fingers in the order 1–2–3–4.

Rearranged into ascending finger order, the groups within brackets fall into the following tone–semitone patterns (T=tone; S=semitone):

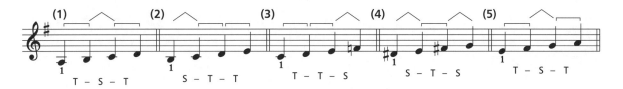

● Place the fingers together in blocks (written as stemless notes, below): having played the first finger, place the second, third and fourth fingers on the string at the same time. Put down the three fingers in tune, in their correct tone–semitone patterns.

● Then play the four notes, descending, to check that they are in tune:

● Also strengthen the feel of each tone–semitone group by playing lightly and quickly as follows:

Example 3   Mozart: Concerto no. 4 in D, K218, *mov. 1, b. 52*

Each group is listed in the order of the fingers (i.e. 1–2–3–4), not in the order of the notes in the actual passage.

- In each position learn the feeling of the tone–semitone pattern in the fingers and hand:

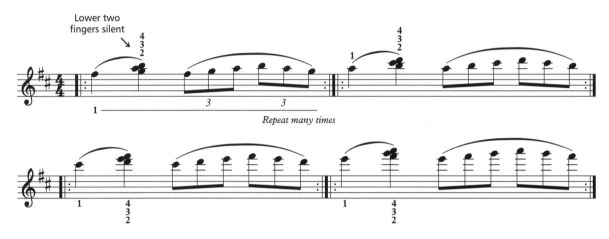

Example 4   Rode: Concerto no. 7 in A minor, op. 9, *mov. 1, b. 63*

The groups of notes in brackets fall into the following tone–semitone patterns:

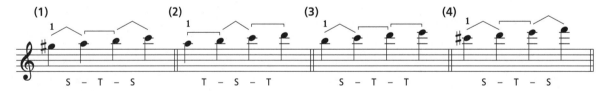

- Place the fingers together in blocks:

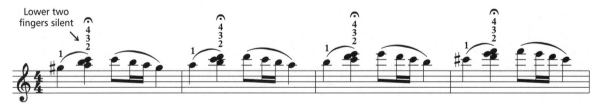

Another way to strengthen this passage would be to place the middle two fingers together as one block, and then the two outer fingers as another (because here the hand is based on the second finger rather than on the first).

- Leave the two middle fingers down as you place the outer fingers around them:

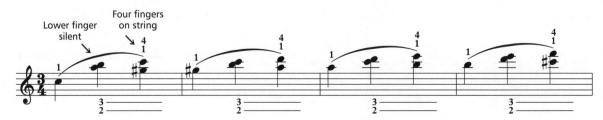

Example 5

Vivaldi: Winter (The Four Seasons), op. 8 no. 4, *mov. 3, b. 12*

Each group is listed in the order of the fingers (i.e. 1–2–3–4), not in the order of the notes in the actual passage.

Repeat many times

- Having played the C, place the notes in brackets silently on the string, in tune. Place 4–3–2 together first, and then place the first finger (so that then all four fingers are on the string).
- Then play the notes fast, like grace notes, stopping on the first finger.
- Keep the first finger down on the string each time until just before it is needed.

Example 6

Vaughan Williams: The Lark Ascending, *b. 148*

Thinking in tone–semitone patterns does not depend on all four fingers being used at once:

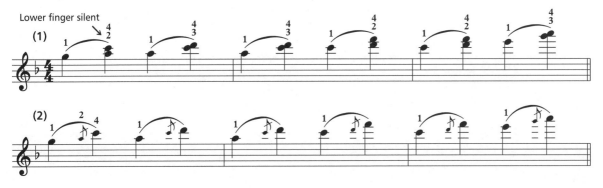

(1) Place the fingers in blocks (sounding only the top note of each).

(2) Play the middle note of each group of three like a very short grace note.

Example 7

Paganini: 24 Caprices, op. 1, No. 19, *b. 27*

The scale in the second bar feels as though it is made up of all whole-tones because the semitones occur only on the shifts.

- Practise in blocks:

160 Playing the same notes in different positions

If we play something out of tune too many times we may get used to it sounding that way. Through repetition it begins to sound normal and we no longer notice it. Because of the different feel in the hand and fingers, playing in a different position quickly shows up any difference between the pitches you may have got used to and the pitches you now find yourself naturally playing in the new position.

● Check the tuning of particular groups of notes by playing in different positions with different fingerings.

Example 1   Granados (arr. Kreisler): Danse espagnole, *b. 32*

Example 2   Dvořák: Romance, op. 11, *b. 31*

Example 3   Franck: Sonata in A, *mov. 2, b. 16*

Example 4   Brahms: Concerto in D, op. 77, *mov. 1, b. 204*

Example 5   Brahms: Sonata no. 3 in D minor, op. 108, *mov. 1, b. 81*

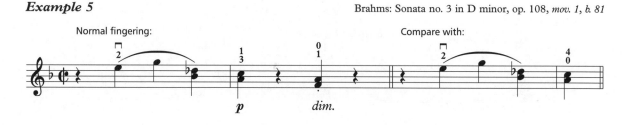

Starting a phrase on different keynotes

Strengthen a specific phrase by practising it starting on different keynotes. Afterwards the phrase on its normal starting note will feel more familiar and more secure.

- Begin below the written pitch of the phrase and work up, semitone by semitone, until above the written pitch; or begin above the written pitch and work down.

- Learn the feeling of the different distances between the intervals (closer together the higher the position), practising the phrase in each position until securely in tune.

Example 1   Beethoven: Sonata in G, op. 30 no. 3, *mov. 1, b. 31*

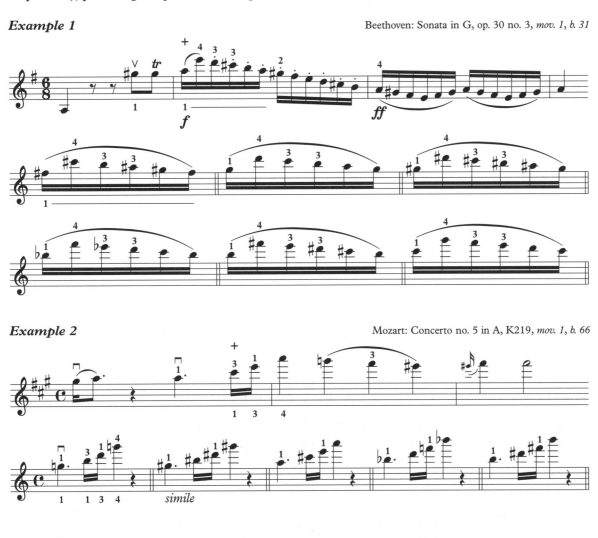

Example 2   Mozart: Concerto no. 5 in A, K219, *mov. 1, b. 66*

Example 3   Paganini: Concerto no. 1 in D, op. 6, *mov. 3, b. 67*

Example 4   Sarasate: Zigeunerweisen, op. 20 no. 1, *b. 21*

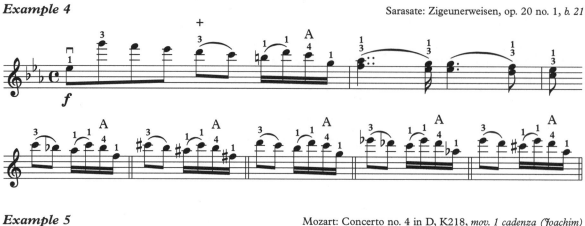

Example 5   Mozart: Concerto no. 4 in D, K218, *mov. 1 cadenza (Joachim)*

- The semitone in the phrase marked '+' feels very close because of the high position. Practise passages like this still higher up the fingerboard so that the correct notes feel quite widely spaced in comparison:

162 Playing the same fingerings on different strings

- Focus on the feel of a phrase or passage by playing the same note patterns and fingerings on another string. This is helpful in high or low positions, and can cast a new light on how to approach playing the passage.

Example 1   Beethoven: Sonata in F, op. 24 ('Spring'), *mov. 1, b. 1*

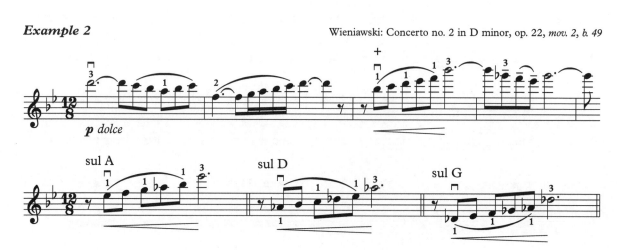

Example 2   Wieniawski: Concerto no. 2 in D minor, op. 22, *mov. 2, b. 49*

Example 3

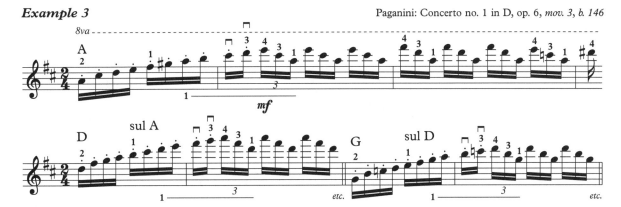

Extensions: dividing the distance

163

Measure extensions by dividing the distance into smaller intervals, rather than measuring only from the note directly before the extension. Each player can choose their own ways of reaching extensions to suit their particular hand, or to go with the harmony in a particular phrase. Some typical examples:

Minor third: major second plus semitone (Examples 2, 3)

Perfect fourth: major third plus semitone (Examples 1, 3, 5)

Augmented fourth/diminished fifth: perfect fourth plus semitone, or three major seconds (Example 4)

Perfect fifth: major second plus semitone plus major third, or major third plus semitone plus major second; or three major seconds plus semitone (Example 7)

Minor sixth: major third plus semitone, then major second plus semitone (Example 8)

Example 1

Mozart: Concerto no. 3 in G, K216, *mov. 2, b. 9*

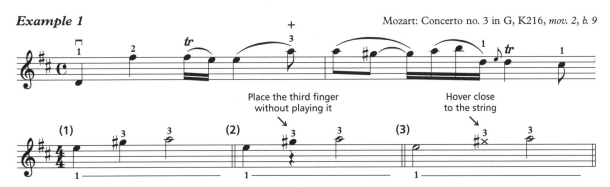

(1) Play G♯ as an intermediate note, and then measure the third-finger A from the G♯. Keep the first finger on the string as marked.

(2) Place the third finger on G♯ without playing it (written as a stemless note), and then measure the A from the G♯.

(3) Remember the feeling of the G♯ without placing the finger (written as an x-note), and measure the A from it as before.

Example 2

Beethoven: Sonata in D, op. 12 no. 1, *mov. 1, b. 1*

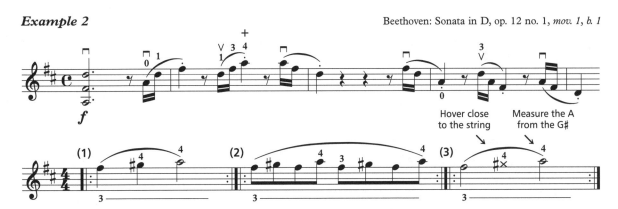

(1) Measure the exact distance and feeling of the A from the G♯. Keep the third finger on the string.

(2) Still relating it to the G♯, place the A from the air rather than sliding along the string.

(3) Do not play the G♯. Hover above the string, remembering the feel of the finger when it plays G♯, and measure the A from it as before.

Example 3 Sibelius: Concerto in D minor, op. 47, *b. 227*

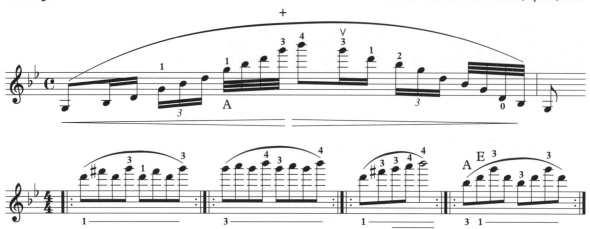

Example 4 Brahms: Sonata no. 2 in A, op. 100, *mov. 1, b. 235*

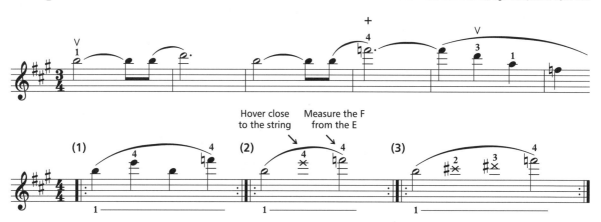

(1) Measure the F from the E. Keep the first finger on the string.

(2) Hover above the string, remembering the feel of the finger when it plays E, and measure the F from it as before.

(3) Feel the equal tone–tone–tone spacing between the fingers. This is a very secure and accurate way to judge any augmented fourth or diminished fifth.

Example 5 Bloch: Nigun (no. 2 from 'Baal Shem'), *b. 5*

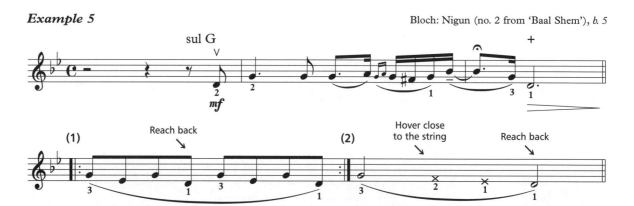

(1) Measure the D from the E♭. Keep the hand balanced on the third finger and reach back with the first finger to the E♭, rather than shifting the whole hand back.

(2) Use the second finger to help measure to the E♭ as you hover the second and first fingers above the string. Then go down a semitone to the D with the first finger, remembering to reach back rather than shift.

Example 6

- Playing slowly, keep the first finger down on the string throughout:

Example 7

- There are three ways to measure a perfect fifth: **(1)** measuring from the second finger, **(2)** from the third finger, or (3) from the fourth finger. Which to use depends on the context and the individual hand.

- In each case first play the intermediate notes, and then hover over them to help measure the interval.

- Practise all three ways to get the feel of the interval, regardless of how you will measure it in the end.

Example 8

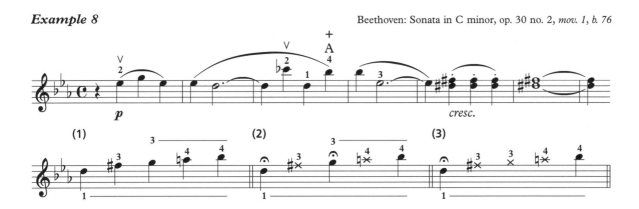

Divide the interval of a minor sixth into a major third plus a semitone (third finger to third finger), and a major second plus a semitone (fourth to fourth).

(1) Play the intermediate notes equally, memorizing the feel of the fingers.

(2) Play only the middle of the three intermediate notes, hovering the fingers above the string for the others (written as x-notes). Remember the feeling of playing the notes so that you hover above them 'in tune'.

(3) Play only the two notes of the interval. Hover above the intermediate notes to measure the extension.

164 Extensions: notes before or after

- The note before or after an extension may easily be pulled out of tune by the extension. Where possible strengthen the feeling of its exact placement by measuring it against the note one semitone lower.

Example 1   Tchaikovsky: Sérénade mélancolique, op. 26, b. 42

The E♭ marked '+' may be played too sharp after the fourth-finger extension A♭:

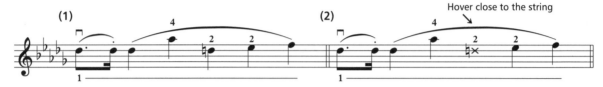

(1) Measure the E♭ from an extended-back D. Hold down the first finger and play the D as a full extra note.

(2) Do not play the extra note. Hover the second finger just above the D (written as an x-note) and measure the E♭ from the memory of the D.

Example 2   Saint-Saëns: Introduction and Rondo Capriccioso, op. 28, *Rondo, b. 69*

The F marked '+' may be played too sharp because of the following fourth-finger extension A.

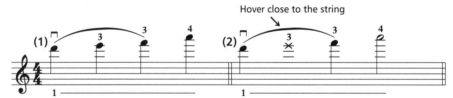

- Practise as in Example 1.

Example 3   Mendelssohn: Concerto in E minor, op. 64, *mov. 1, b. 76*

After the perfect-fifth extension A–E in bar 78 (marked '+'), the perfect fourth A–D (marked '++') may be played too sharp.

- Measure from an extended-back fourth-finger C♯:

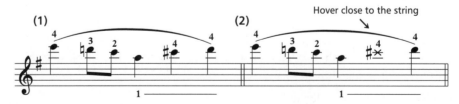

(1) Measure the D from an extended-back C♯. Hold down the first finger and play the C♯ as a full extra note.

(2) Do not play the extra note. Hover the fourth finger just above the C♯ (written as an x-note) and measure the D from the memory of the C♯.

Uniform intonation

There is no one 'system' of tuning which will suit every passage, key, or combination of instruments. The following guide-lines must be subject to constant flexibility and compromise. The ear must always be given priority over any theory of what is 'right' or 'wrong' in tuning.

Intonation is 'uniform' when it has a harmonic and expressive structure, each note tuned in relation to another:

G's, D's, A's and E's are all tuned to the open strings.

Sharps are tuned in relation to the natural above (C♯ is the 'leading note' to D).

Flats are tuned in relation to the natural below (D♭ is the 'leading note' down to C).

C is a perfect fourth above open G. B is the 'leading note' to C. F is the 'leading note' down to E.

The exact tuning of sharps and flats is always relative to the key. B♭ as the tonic in B♭ major will usually be higher than B♭ as a minor third in a dark G minor passage. G♯ as the tonic of G♯ minor will usually be lower than G♯ as the leading note in A major. Playing with the piano, it is often not possible to play 'high' sharps or 'low' flats. Nevertheless, A remains the reference point from which to measure B♭ or G♯, however high or low they are.

- Continuously check that notes are in tune by relating them to the following:

G	Tune to the open G		**C♯**	Tune from D
A♭	Tune from G		**D**	Tune to the open D
G♯	Tune from A		**E♭**	Tune from D
A	Tune to the open A		**D♯**	Tune from E
B♭	Tune from A		**F♭**	Tune from E♭, or same as E
A♯	Tune from B		**E**	Tune to the open E
C♭	Tune from B♭, or same as B		**F**	Tune from E
B	Tune from C		**G♭**	Tune from F
C	Perfect fourth/fifth from G		**E♯**	Tune from F♯
D♭	Tune from C		**F♯**	Tune from G

Testing, relating, comparing

- In the following examples the small notes indicate examples of 'tester' notes used to gauge the pitch and exact positioning of the actual notes of the melody. Play around with them and variations of them, to strengthen your concept of the harmonic and physical relationships of the notes.[1]

Example 1   Vivaldi: Summer (The Four Seasons), op. 8 no. 2, *mov. 1, b. 21*

- **Bar 21:** tune the B♭ as shown in **(1)** below.

  Then tune the D to the open D string.

  Place the C exactly midway between the B♭ and the D.

- **Bar 22:** tune the A♭ as shown in **(2)** below.

  Then place exactly the same B♭ and C as in the previous bar. (The major second between A♭ and B♭ must not be wider or narrower in pitch than the major second between B♭ and C.)

- **Bar 23:** tune the G to the open G.

  Tune the A to the open A.

  Place the B♭ 'close' to the A. (This B♭ should be exactly the same as in the previous bars.)

- **Bar 24:** tune the G and A to the open strings as in the previous bar.

  Place the F♯ 'close' to the G.

[1] The Israeli violinist Itzhak Perlman, when asked to sum up the difference between two of his teachers, Ivan Galamian and Dorothy DeLay, said: 'If Galamian heard a note out of tune he would say so. DeLay might say instead, "Well dear, what is your *concept* of F♯?"' *Keynote Magazine* (New York, June 1979), 12.

Example 2

Wieniawski: Polonaise brillante, op. 21, *b. 110*

Example 3

Bruch: Concerto no. 1 in G minor, op. 26, *mov. 1, b. 76*

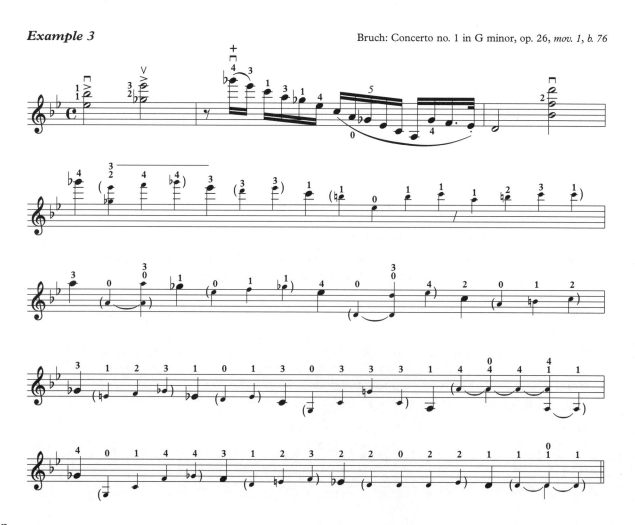

Example 4   J. S. Bach: Concerto no. 2 in E, BWV1042, *mov. 3, b. 1*

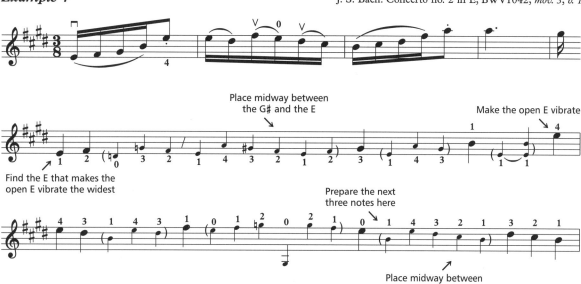

Example 5   Kreisler: Sicilienne and Rigaudon, *Rigaudon, b. 1*

The tuning of the first note, F♯, depends on how you tune the next note, B, which is the tonic of the scale.

If the B is in tune with the open D, it is too flat when played with the open E; if the B is in tune with the open E, it is too sharp when played with the open D:[1]

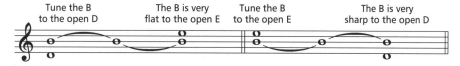

Use a B that is midway between the two extremes, i.e. 'out of tune' with both the D and the E string. The perfect fourth from the B to the E will be slightly wider than a true perfect fourth.[2] Then take the F♯ from that 'middle' B.

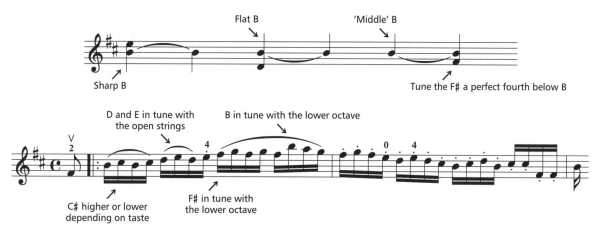

The C♯ can be higher or lower depending on personal preference. It can be tuned a perfect fifth above the initial F♯, making it slightly less bright (because the F♯ is a fraction lower than it could be, having been tuned to the B); or the C♯ can be tuned a fraction closer to the D, making it slightly sharp to the F♯.

The D's and E's should all be in tune with the open strings.

The F♯ on the E string should be in tune with the original F♯ one octave lower, i.e. not too high. In any case, the F♯ in the chord in the piano accompaniment means you cannot play a 'bright' F♯ without it sounding out of tune to the piano. The G should be in tune with the open G, which means that the semitone between the not-high F♯ and the G will be quite wide, i.e. not squeezed together.

[1] One solution which partially solves this problem is to tune in 'narrow fifths': tune the D very slightly sharp to the A; tune the G very slightly sharp to the D; but leave the E as a true perfect fifth with the A. This is particularly helpful in playing unaccompanied Bach, because of all the chords and harmonies built up from the bass, but it is something to consider whatever you are playing. String quartets typically tune in narrow fifths to avoid the C string on the viola and cello being too flat. See also *How to get the third tone in tune*, page 218.

[2] Double-stopped perfect intervals should be exactly in tune. The exact tuning of all the other intervals – major, minor, augmented and diminished – is to a certain extent a matter of taste. One musician prefers a slightly wider major third, another prefers it slightly narrower. Both are 'in tune'; but perfect intervals are either in tune or out of tune.

However, this applies only to double stops. Single-stop perfect fourths and fifths can often be played so that they would be out of tune if played together as a double stop, yet they do not sound out of tune when heard one at a time and in a musical context.

166 Tuning scales: three stages

This method of tuning scales is the quickest way to get scales really in tune. It works by making the *structure* of the scale very clear. Then it becomes obvious exactly where every note is, within that structure, and every note becomes easy to find.

Before playing the complete scale, build the scale up in three separate stages:

1 First tune the notes of the perfect intervals – the 4th, 5th and 8th degrees of the scale – in relation to the tonic. They are the 'skeleton' of the scale.

2 Next add the 3rd and the 7th. Measure the 3rd from the 4th, and feel the 7th leaning up into the octave.

3 The final two notes to add are the 2nd and the 6th. Place these exactly in the middle between the 1st and the 3rd, and between the 5th and the 7th.

Example 1

Stage 1

● Play the 1st, 4th, 5th and 8th degrees of the scale. In this key they are all tuned to the open strings.

Another way to do this is to finger all the notes of the scale but to play only the 1st, 4th, 5th and 8th. Silently finger the left-out notes, written here as x-notes, and bow the rest:

Stage 2

● Add the 3rd and the 7th. It is a matter of taste exactly how high the C♯ and G♯ are; but whether higher or lower, tune or feel them in relation to the 4th and the octave.

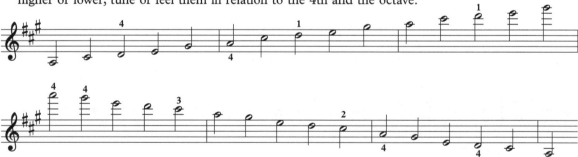

Alternative note order for Stage 2 (ascending)

● The fingering shown here reflects the fingering used in the scale. Use a normal fingering if you prefer.

Stage 3

- Add the 2nd and the 6th (i.e. play the complete scale). If you have chosen a high C♯ very close to the D, the B must be slightly higher. If the C♯ is not so high the B must be slightly lower.

Alternative note order for Stage 3 (ascending)

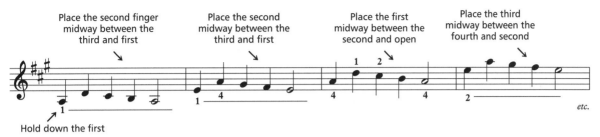

Example 2

Franck: Sonata in A, *mov. 4, b. 2*

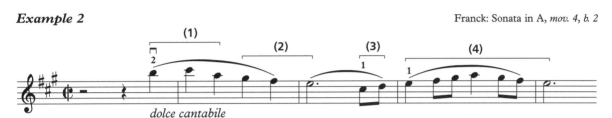

dolce cantabile

(1) The notes in the first group – A, B, C♯ – are the tonic, 2nd and 3rd in the scale of A major. Tune them as follows, using a fourth-finger D to help measure the C♯:

Very slow

- Tune the A to the open A string.
- Tune the D to the open D string. Also hear it as a perfect fourth above the A.
- Tune the C♯ quite high, measuring it close to the D.
- Tune the B midway between the first finger and the third finger.

(2) The notes in the second group – E, F♯, G♯ – are the 5th, 6th and 7th in the scale of A major. Tune them as follows, using a fourth-finger A to help measure the G♯:

Very slow

- Tune the E to the open E string.
- Tune the fourth finger A to the open A string, and as double stops with the open D and E strings. Also compare it with first finger A on the E string.
- Tune the G♯ quite high, measuring it close to the A.
- Tune the F♯ midway between the second finger and the fourth finger.

(3) The notes in the third group – C♯, D – are the 3rd and 4th in the scale of A major. Tune them as follows, using the D to help measure the C♯:

Very slow

- Tune the E to the open E string.
- Tune the D to the open D string.
- Tune the C♯ quite high, measuring it close to the previous note (first finger D).

(4) Tune the notes in the fourth group – E, F♯, G♯, A – the same way as the notes in the second group.

Example 3   Beethoven: Sonata in C minor, op. 30 no. 2, *mov. 1, b. 9*

First phrase:

- Tune the G to the open G string.

- The E♭ may be a little higher or a little lower according to taste. Either way, tune it in relation to a D.

- Place the F exactly midway between the G and the E♭. If the E♭ is a little higher, the F must also be higher. If the E♭ is a little lower, the F must be lower.

- Place the C a perfect fifth below the G.

Second phrase:

- The C should be exactly an octave above the C in the previous bar. Tune it as a perfect fourth above G.

- The A♭ may be higher or lower according to taste. Either way, tune it in relation to a G.

- Place the B♭ exactly midway between the A♭ and the C. If the A♭ is a little higher, the B♭ must also be higher. If the A♭ is a little lower, the B♭ must be lower.

- Place the F a perfect fifth below the C.

Example 4   Mozart: Sonata in G, K301, *mov. 1, b. 128*

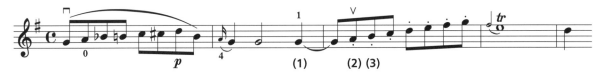

How 'high' to play the 3rd and 7th of the scale, to make the character 'bright', often depends on the open-string notes that are nearby.

In this example **(1)** and **(2)** are 'fixed' notes, i.e. the G must be in tune with the open G, and the A in tune with the open A. **(3)** cannot be played high or else the distance between the A and the B is wider than that between the G and the A. The tonal distance of the two major seconds should be equal.

The second half of this bar is the same as the first half. The D and the E are both 'fixed' notes. The F♯ cannot be too high or else it is too far from the E compared with the distance from the D to the E.

 Same notes, different octaves

Uniform intonation means that in a three-octave arpeggio each major third is the same tonal distance apart, not slightly wider or narrower in different octaves. Or if you play A–B–C on the G string, and then the same letter-names on the E string, each note in one octave will be exactly in tune with the same note in the other octave.

Example 1   J. S. Bach: Partita no. 2 in D minor, BWV1004, *Giga, b. 1*

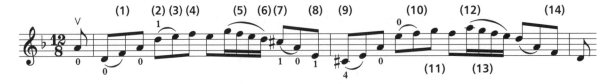

F   Each F should be identical. Place **(1)** close to an imaginary first-finger E, aiming low to bring out the minor character of the music. In the same way place **(4)** close to the preceding E, remembering that the semitone in 3rd position is closer together than in 1st position.

> Care must be taken not to play **(5)** higher than **(4)**. **(5)** may easily have been pulled up slightly by the fourth-finger G that comes before it. Aim the third finger low, close to the second-finger E which follows.
>
> **(10)** should not be squeezed unnaturally close to the nut, otherwise it will be too flat in relation to **(14)**.

D   **(2)** and **(6)** should be identical, in tune with the open D string.

E   **(3)** and **(8)** should be identical, in tune with the open E string.

C♯ (7) and (9) should be identical. You have to be careful not to play a too-narrow semitone[1] from (6) to (7), giving a higher C♯ than when playing from (8) to (9). Measure (9) from an imaginary fourth-finger D.

[1] See *Semitone shifts with one finger,* page 158

G (11) and (13) should be identical, in tune with the open G string. Care must be taken that (11) is not too flat following after the low first-finger F, and (13) not too sharp following after the third-finger A.

Example 2   J. S. Bach: Concerto no. 1 in A minor, BWV1041, *mov. 2, b. 14*

(1) G should be the same as the preceding note.

(2) B could be too sharp because it is the note before an upward extension.[2]

[2] See *Extensions: notes before or after,* page 206

(3) G could be too sharp, having been 'pulled up' by the previous extended fourth finger.

(4) The shifted-to B must be the same as the previous ones.

(5) D should be the same as the previous extended fourth finger. It could be sharp because the previous third finger **(2)** was a major third above the first finger, but **(5)** is a minor third above the first finger.

(6) The shifted-to D must be the same as the previous ones.

Example 3   Lalo: Symphonie espagnole, op. 21, *mov. 1, b. 5*

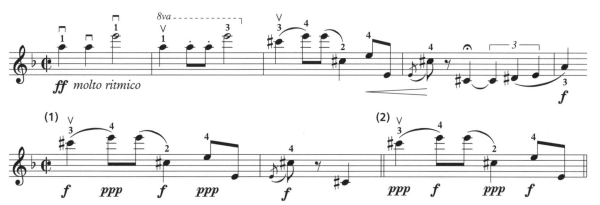

(1) Compare all the C♯'s with each other, playing them *f*. Play the E's *ppp*.

(2) Then compare the E's, playing them *f*. Play the C♯'s *ppp*.

Example 4   Beethoven: Concerto in D, op. 61, *mov. 1, b. 111*

● Finger every note with the left hand but bow only the normal-headed notes. Lift the bow off the string during the x-notes:

Sharps and flats

Sometimes intonation needs to be tempered, like keyboard intonation, which means that C♯ and D♭ are exactly the same. At other times intonation can be 'expressive', so that sharps are sharper ('leading up' to the natural above) and flats are flatter ('leading down' to the natural below). C♯ is then higher than D♭.

168 Wide and narrow semitones

In expressive intonation a semitone is *wider* when the letter names are the same, e.g. C–C♯, A–A♭ ('chromatic' semitone). The semitone is *narrower* when the letter names are different, e.g. C–D♭, A–G♯ ('diatonic' semitone).[1]

[1] Another way to think of this, is that if the heads of the two notes are on the same line or space, it is a wide semitone; if one head is on a line and the other is on a space, it is a narrow semitone.

- Playing at a slow tempo, exaggerate the semitones.

  '∧' = narrow semitone; '⌐' = wide semitone.

Example 1 — Beethoven: Romanze in G, op. 40, *b. 74*

Example 2 — Schubert: Sonata in A, op. posth., *mov. 2, b. 83*

Example 3 — Franck: Sonata in A, *mov. 2, b. 99*

Example 4 — Brahms: Sonata no. 2 in A, op. 100, *mov. 2, b. 121*

Example 5 — Franck: Sonata in A, *mov. 2, b. 20*

Example 6 — Tchaikovsky: Concerto in D, op. 35, *mov. 1, b. 40*

- Treat the fifth note B♯ as a C.

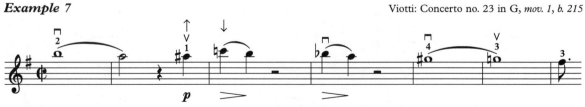

Example 7 — Viotti: Concerto no. 23 in G, *mov. 1, b. 215*

The interval of the diminished third is often narrower than that of a major second. In this typical example tune the A♯ close to a B, giving the A♯ a quality of leaning upwards; tune the C so that it leans towards the B.

'↑' = place higher than usual, closer to the natural a semitone above; '↓' = place lower.

Example 8 Mozart: Concerto no. 4 in D, K218, *mov. 1, b. 71*

- Treat the interval of the diminished seventh the same as that of the diminished third.

Fast intonation

In fast passages, sharps should often be played higher, and flats lower, than in slow passages. Played at a slow tempo 'fast intonation' sounds out of tune, with clearly exaggerated sharps and flats. At a fast tempo, fast intonation sounds in tune and adds energy and colour.

At a fast tempo 'slow intonation' (i.e. more tempered, like a piano, with low sharps and high flats) may sound dull and lack brilliance.

- Playing at a slow tempo, exaggerate the sharps and flats. At speed this will come out sounding in tune.
  '↑' = place higher than usual; '↓' = place lower.

Example 1 Schumann: Sonata in A minor, op. 105, *mov. 3, b. 8*

Example 2 Beethoven: Concerto in D, op. 61, *mov. 3, b. 139*

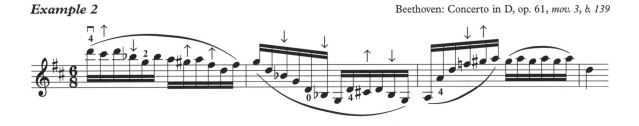

Example 3 Vieuxtemps: Concerto no. 4 in D minor, op. 31, *mov. 3, b. 1*

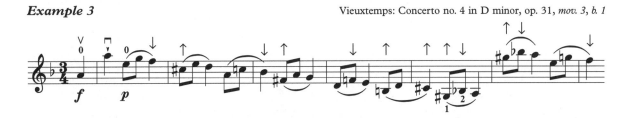

Example 4 Brahms: Concerto in D, op. 77, *mov. 3, b. 55*

- In this example, tune the B's higher so that they are directly in the middle, between the A and the C♯.

Example 5 Paganini: Concerto no. 1 in D, op. 6, *mov. 1, b. 182*

170 Isolating individual notes   **Marking arrows**

- Having identified a note that is consistently too sharp or flat, or which is likely to be so, mark it with a ↑ or ↓.

- Suppose you discover that a note, which you had thought was perfectly in tune, is in fact too sharp. Because you have got used to it, the right pitch sounds too flat and the incorrect pitch sounds in tune. Mark it with a down arrow to remind you to aim lower.

Example 1   Wohlfahrt: Etude, op. 45 no. 34, *b. 4*

(1) The fourth-finger C♯ could easily be too flat after the fourth-finger G at the beginning of the bar.

(2) The first-finger C♯ could easily be too flat after the first-finger G two notes earlier.

(3) The opposite of **(1)**: the fourth-finger G could easily be too sharp after the C♯ two notes earlier.

Example 2   J. S. Bach: Sonata no. 1 in G minor, BWV1001, *Adagio, b. 3*

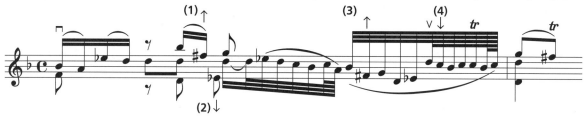

(1) The first-finger F♯ could easily be too flat after the first-finger B♭ at the beginning of the bar.

(2) The first-finger E♭ could easily be too sharp after the preceding F♯.

(3) The second-finger F♯ has to reach up very high after the first-finger B♭.

(4) The second-finger C could easily be too high after the preceding F♯.

171 **Accents**

When a specific finger in a passage tends to be out of tune, play it with an accent and pause on it. The accent and pause create an aiming-point which keeps the unreliable note at the front of your mind while you play the other notes, and create extra time in which to think and listen.

Example 1   Mozart: Concerto no. 3 in G, K216, *mov. 1, b. 60*

[1] See *Tone–semitone patterns*, page 196

In this passage the tone–semitone spacing[1] of the second, third and fourth fingers is the same on both the E string and the A string:

While the second, third and fourth fingers keep the same spacing, the first finger alternates between ♮ and ♯, i.e. lower and higher.

(1) First confirm the tone–semitone spacing of the second, third and fourth fingers.

(2) Then pause on each first finger and play it with an accent. Play the other notes up to tempo.

Example 2   J. S. Bach: Partita no. 1 in B minor, BWV1002, *Allemanda (Double)*, b. 6

- With the hand in half position, the G marked '+' may be too sharp. Playing everything else up to tempo, accent the G and pause on it momentarily before continuing once more in tempo.

Playing intervals not notes

Feel the musical relationships between notes as much as feeling the expression of the notes themselves.[1] Rather than playing one note and then another, e.g. D followed by F, play a **minor third**. Rather than playing C followed by E followed by G, play a **major triad**.

172

[1] Playing intervals rather than notes is also one of the keys to playing from memory. See *Feeling relationships between notes* (Memory), page 294

Example 1   J. S. Bach: Partita no. 2 in D minor, BWV1004, *Allemanda*, b. 14

At the '+' play a **minor seventh** – not an E followed by a D.

- Practise by playing the notes longer, sustaining the bow with a stroke that is deep in the string, even, and not too far from the bridge.

- Make the join between the down-bow E and the up-bow D absolutely seamless and even, with no diminuendo at the end of the down-bow or faster bow speed at the beginning of the up-bow.

Example 2   Mendelssohn: Concerto in E minor, op. 64, *mov. 2, b. 103*

At the notes marked by arrows, play a **diminished third** – not a D♯ followed by an F.

Example 3   Schubert: Sonatina in A minor, op. 137 no. 2, *mov. 2, b. 21*

- Do not play F, B♭, D, A♭, and so on. Instead play a **perfect fourth** (F–B♭), then a **minor sixth** (B♭–D), then a **diminished fifth** (D–A♭) and so on.

- Repeat each pair of notes several times, concentrating on the interval rather than the two notes:

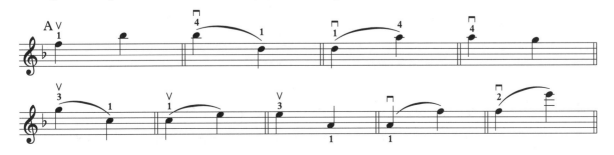

Tuning to a piano, then adjusting sharps and flats

● Settle extremely insecure intonation by tuning each note, one by one, to a piano.

● Leave the finger on the string while you alternate bowing the note on the violin with playing the note on the piano (play the note on the piano with a bow-hand finger while continuing to hold the bow).

● If you wish then to sharpen sharps or flatten flats away from the tempered pitch of the piano, the piano gives you a reference point to measure from.

If an in-tune piano is not available, an electronic Chromatic Tuner is an interesting and helpful alternative.

> ### Double stops

For other double stop practice methods see also *Balancing double stops*, page 72; *Metronome practice*, page 146; *Shortcuts: thirds, sixths and fingered octaves*, page 150; *Thirds and fingered octaves*, page 251.

Using the 'third tone' as a point of reference

When two notes are played together they produce a 'third tone', a low, distant droning in the background which is like a bass note to the two notes of the double stop. It is clearest in high-position thirds and sixths. The third tone is often best ignored, even though when the third tone is exactly in tune with the double stop the notes blend and harmonize with each other, and the interval has a smooth, chord-like quality.

It should often be ignored because the listener's ear catches one or both of the lines as individual notes, *not* as part of a double stop. If you tune first-finger F♯ on the E string with third-finger D on the A string, the F♯ must be played flat if the third tone is to be in tune, and this may sound too flat to the listener who is hearing the F♯ as part of a melody or harmony.

The notes of the double stop then sound more in tune *to the ear* when the third tone is out of tune, as shown in the examples. This is another way of saying that the double stop should deliberately be played *out of tune*. In any case, the third tone is rarely audible to the listener, only to the player.

However, the third tone is a useful point of reference from which to measure the interval:

1 First tune the double stop so that the third tone is in tune.

2 Using that tuning as a reference point, very slightly sharpen or flatten the upper or lower note.

How to get the third tone in tune

The notes of the double stop are either 'fixed' or 'movable'. G's, D's, A's and E's should be in tune with the open strings, and are therefore fixed notes. All other notes are movable, but may also be fixed depending on their place in the melody or harmony.

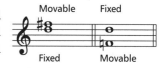

To get the third tone in tune in a major third or sixth:

● If the fixed note is the lower of the two notes, the upper note has to be flattened.

● If the fixed note is the higher of the two notes, the lower note has to be sharpened.[1]

In the first bar the D is fixed because it should be in tune with the open string, so the F♯ must be brought down towards it for the third tone to be in tune.

In the second bar the D is now the upper note. The F should be brought up towards it for the third tone to be in tune.

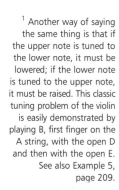

[1] Another way of saying the same thing is that if the upper note is tuned to the lower note, it must be lowered; if the lower note is tuned to the upper note, it must be raised. This classic tuning problem of the violin is easily demonstrated by playing B, first finger on the A string, with the open D and then with the open E. See also Example 5, page 209.

Example 1   Mozart: Sonata in E minor, K304, *mov. 1, b. 170*

(1) For the third tone to be in tune, the G♯ has to be played too flat and no longer feels like a 'leading note' into the following A. The B cannot be moved higher than it was in the previous bar.

First tune the G♯ flat to get the third tone in tune; then move it slightly higher, out of tune with the B.

(2) The A must be in tune with the open A. For the third tone to be in tune, the C has to be too sharp.

First tune the C♮ sharp to get the third tone in tune; then move it slightly lower, out of tune with the A.

Example 2
J. S. Bach: Concerto no. 2 in E, BWV1042, *mov. 1, b. 95*

(1) The E must be in tune with the open E. For the third tone to be in tune, the G♯ has to be played too flat. To maintain the brightness and character of the passage, having got the third tone in tune move the G♯ slightly higher, out of tune with the E.

(2) The D must be in tune with the open D. For the third tone to be in tune, the B has to be too flat. Move it slightly higher, out of tune with the D.

(3) The E–G♯ is the same as **(1)**, but here the G♯ is played on its own one note earlier. This note must be played 'high', being the major third in the scale of E major; and since this pitch and the G♯ in the following double stop must be the same, you are again forced to play the double stop 'out of tune'.

Example 3
Kreutzer: 42 Etudes ou caprices, No. 39, *b. 1*

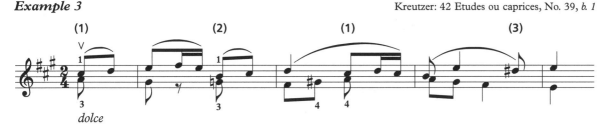

(1) The A must be in tune with the open A. For the third tone to be in tune, the C♯ has to be played too flat. Having got the third tone in tune move the C♯ slightly higher, out of tune with the A.

(2) This works exactly the same as **(1)**. The G must be in tune with the open G; the B sounds dull if it is in tune with the G and should be played slightly higher.

(3) The D♯ 'leans' expressively into the following E. To be in tune with the previous F♯ (in the lower line) the D♯ would need to be played too flat. (Playing the F♯ higher than usual, so that the D♯ can be in tune as well as leading up into the E, does not work since the F♯ then sounds too sharp.)

Example 4
Bruch: Concerto no. 1 in G minor, op. 26, *mov. 3, b. 40*

The A should be in tune with the open A; for the third tone to be in tune, the C has to be too sharp. The passage sounds in tune if a flatter C is used, as an ordinary low minor third in A minor, so then the third tone cannot be in tune.

Example 5
Sibelius: Concerto in D minor, op. 47, *mov. 1, b. 102*

One way to approach double stops is to consider how you would tune them if the passage was played by two violins, each playing one line:

Here, the lower violin would have to play the A♭'s, G♭'s, and E♭'s very sharp to be 'in tune' with the upper line. Instead, the sixths can be played 'wide', the flats remaining low and expressive.

Example 6   Haydn: Concerto no. 1 in C, *mov. 1, b. 53*

The G must be in tune with the open G string, and the E must be in tune with the open E, making it impossible for the third tone to be in tune.

Example 7   Paganini: 24 Caprices, op. 1, No. 18, *b. 17*

(1) The E must be in tune with the open E. For the third tone to be in tune, the C has to be played too sharp. It should be played slightly lower, out of tune with the E.

(2) The G must be in tune with the open G. For the third tone to be in tune, the B has to be played too flat. It should be played slightly sharper, out of tune with the G.

(3) The A must be in tune with the open A. For the third tone to be in tune, the F has to be played too sharp. It should be played slightly lower, out of tune with the A.

(4) For the third tone to be in tune, the C has to be played too sharp. It should be played slightly lower, out of tune with the E.

(5) The same as (4).

175 Using the third tone to tune single stops

It is usually best *not* to check single stops by using double-stopped major thirds or sixths, e.g. do not tune first-finger F♯ on the E string to open A; do not tune second-finger F on the D string to open A. If you tune a single stop by first playing it as part of a double stop with the third tone in tune, and then you play the note by itself, it sounds very out of tune. Single stops must be tuned so that if played as part of a major third or sixth the third tone would be out of tune. Then the single stop sounds correct when played on its own.

However, the third tone is often useful as a reference point from which to measure the placing of a note:

1 First tune the double stop so that the third tone is in tune.

2 Using that tuning as a reference point, very slightly sharpen or flatten the single-stop note.

Example 1   Mozart: Concerto no. 4 in D, K218, *mov. 1, b. 42*

The F♯ marked '+' needs to be played 'high', as a 'leading note' to an imaginary G. If you tune it as a double stop with the open A string (with the third tone in tune) it will sound very flat, and dull the bright, positive character of the major triad.

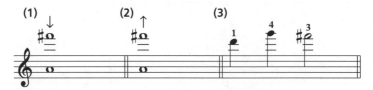

(1) The third tone in tune. The F♯ must be played flat.

(2) The F♯ 'bright', slightly closer to a G, the third tone out of tune. This note sounds correct in the passage.

(3) Tune the F♯ to the G rather than to the open A string.

Example 2   Wieniawski: Scherzo-Tarantelle, op. 16, *b. 4*

The G ('+') should be in tune with the open G. If you tune the B♭ ('++') as a double stop with the G (with the third tone in tune) it will sound very sharp, taking away from the character of the low minor third.

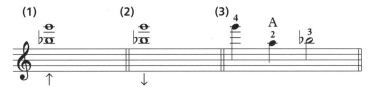

(1) The third tone in tune. The B♭ must be played too sharp.

(2) The B♭ 'dark', slightly closer to an A, the third tone out of tune. This note sounds correct in the passage.

(3) Tune the B♭ to the A rather than to the G.

Thirds: naming intervals and spacing of fingers

176

- While playing one third in a group of thirds, consider three factors before placing the fingers for the next third:

    1 Is the next third major or minor?

    2 What are the intervals between the thirds?

    3 What is the tone–semitone spacing of all four fingers?

1 Major or minor

On the violin fingerboard, a *major* third is a *small* distance because the fingers would be a minor third apart if they were placed on one string.

A *minor* third is a *large* distance because the fingers would be a major third apart if they were on one string.

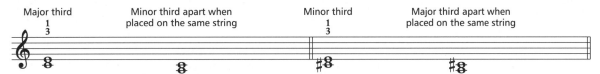

2 Intervals between the thirds

The six most common combinations of thirds:

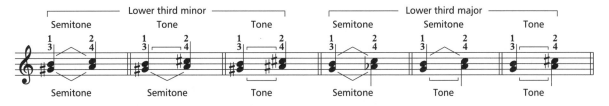

3 Tone–semitone patterns

Find the tone–semitone pattern by imagining placing the fingers together on one string:

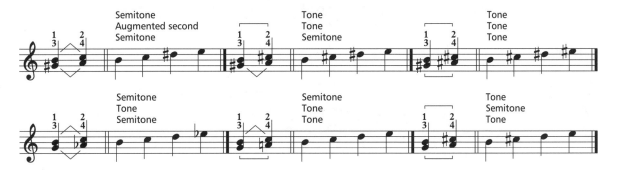

177 Thirds and fingered octaves: placing in blocks

- To clarify the feel of the fingers in relation to each other, practise each pair of thirds (1–3, 2–4) by placing all four fingers on the strings at the same time in a 'block'.

Example 1   Wieniawski: Polonaise de Concert, op. 4, *b. 104*

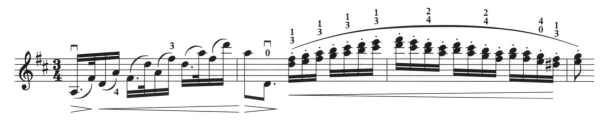

1 Begin with the fingers above but close to the strings (represented below by x-notes). Arrange the fingers, in the air, into their correct tone–semitone pattern (the third and fourth fingers over the A string, the first and second over the E string).

2 Place all four fingers on the strings at exactly the same time.

3 Without first adjusting the placement of the fingers – leave them exactly where they are – check the tuning by playing them. If they were out of tune, repeat until you can drop them exactly in tune, and with a comfortable hand position.

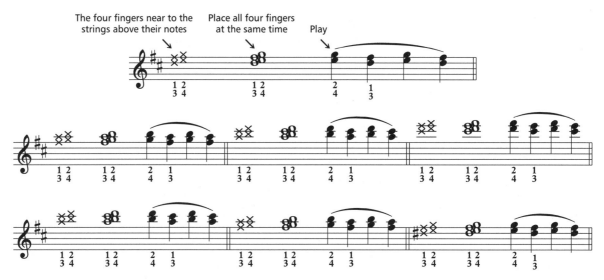

- A further approach is to place the fingers in each tone–semitone pattern without testing with the bow:

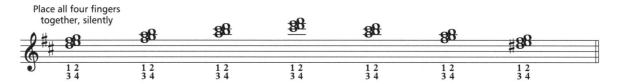

Example 2   Paganini: 24 Caprices, op. 1, *No. 17, b. 24*

- Practise as in Example 1:

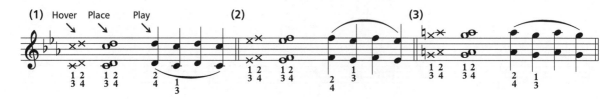

Thirds: using the perfect fourth

178

Adding a perfect fourth in between two thirds is an excellent way to find a balanced intonation and feel in the hand.

Example 1

Example 2

Haydn: Concerto no. 1 in C, *mov. 1, b. 40*

Example 3

Bruch: Concerto no. 1 in G minor, op. 26, *mov. 3, b. 19*

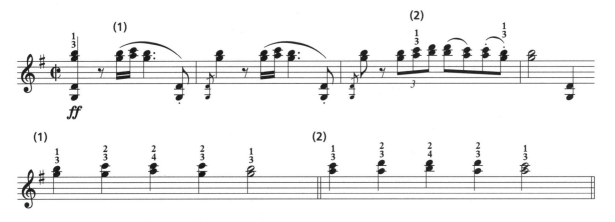

Example 4   Tartini: Sonata in G minor ('Dido abandonata'), *mov. 1, b. 5*

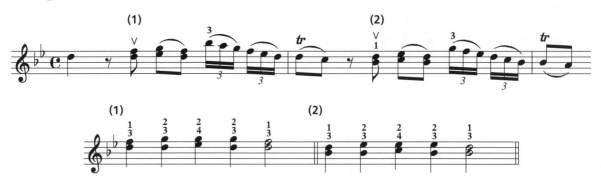

Example 5   Paganini: Concerto no. 1 in D, op. 6, *mov. 1, b. 158*

179

Tuning perfect fifths

- Tune perfect fifths by leaning the finger more onto one string, and then more onto the other.
- Leaning the finger more onto a string sharpens the note; leaning the finger away from a string (towards the other string) flattens the note.
- Find the exact balance of the finger where the fifth is in tune.

Example   Kreutzer: 42 Etudes ou caprices, No. 37, *b. 1*

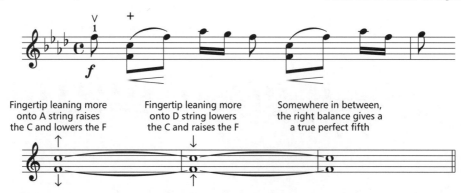

Fingertip leaning more onto A string raises the C and lowers the F

Fingertip leaning more onto D string lowers the C and raises the F

Somewhere in between, the right balance gives a a true perfect fifth

- Memorize the feeling of the finger balanced on the two strings when the fifth is in tune, and then go straight to exactly the same feeling when playing the double stop in context.

Playing one string at a time while fingering both strings

- Finger both notes of each double stop as written, but bow only one string at a time. Practise each line separately until both are comfortably in tune.

Example 1
Kreutzer: 42 Etudes ou caprices, No. 38, *b. 1*

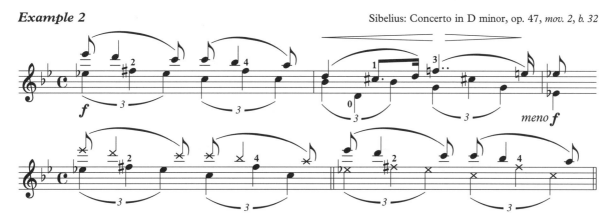

(1) Bow only the lower of the two strings. The x-notes show the notes on the upper string that you finger without playing.

(2) Bow only the upper string while silently fingering the notes on the lower string.

Example 2
Sibelius: Concerto in D minor, op. 47, *mov. 2, b. 32*

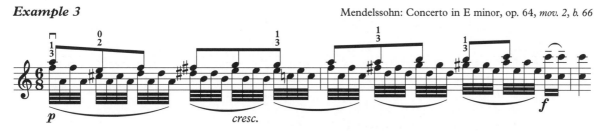

Example 3
Mendelssohn: Concerto in E minor, op. 64, *mov. 2, b. 66*

- Combine other practice methods with playing one line at a time. Examples:

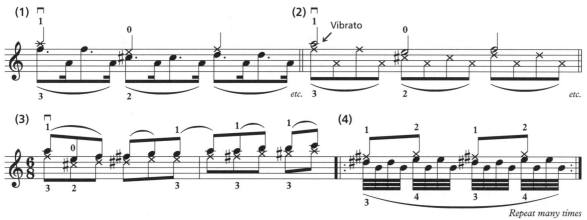

Repeat many times

(1) Rhythm practice (see *Rhythm practice*, page 36).

(2) It is easier to hear what is happening in the vibrato without the lower notes (see *Continuous vibrato*, page 136).

(3) Playing only the 'skeleton' of the passage (see *Isolating the shifts*, page 186).

(4) Repetition practice (see *Repetition practice*, page 280).

Example 4

Bériot: Concerto no. 9 in A minor, op. 104, *mov. 1, b. 67*

- Keeping both fingers down, sound first the lower note, then the upper note, adjusting each as necessary; then play the two notes together perfectly in tune:

Example 5

Bruch: Concerto no. 1 in G minor, op. 26, *mov. 3, b. 193*

- In many passages it is helpful to select certain notes from the upper and lower line. In this example play only the A#'s:

Example 6

Wieniawski: Polonaise brillante, op. 21, *b. 43*

- Play only the G#'s, and then play only the B's and the E:

Example 7

Bruch: Concerto no. 1 in G minor, op. 26, *mov. 3, b. 42*

- Play only the second finger:

Example 8

Bloch: Nigun (no. 2 from 'Baal Shem'), *b. 100*

If there is anything unusual or awkward in the passage – in this example the wide space between Ab and Bb could disturb the intonation – first use an ordinary fingering to find exactly the right tuning:

(1) Play each line separately, using a normal, convenient fingering. Use this as a model for **(2)**.

(2) Finger all the notes with the proper fingering, but bow only one string at a time.

Leaving fingers down to have time to listen

181

Part of playing in tune is the art of instantaneously correcting out-of-tune notes. Ideally a note is corrected so quickly that nobody notices that it was out of tune in the first place.

For practice purposes, however, it is often helpful to leave fingers down exactly where they landed, and to listen to them carefully without adjusting them. This helps to form a clearer picture of where differently to aim next time. It is especially helpful in playing double stops, and produces faster results than simply repeating again and again without knowing exactly what is wrong.

- In the following examples first play the double stop; then stop, leaving the fingers exactly where you placed them (written as x-notes); then play first one note on its own, and then the other.

Example 1

Wieniawski: Polonaise brillante, op. 21, *b. 22*

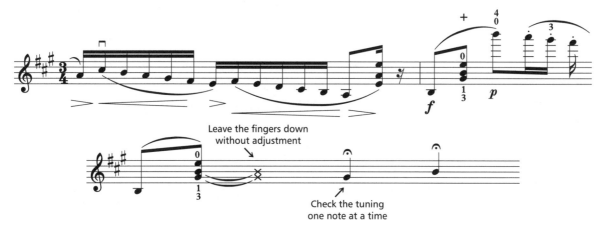

Example 2   J. S. Bach: Partita no. 2 in D minor, BWV1006, *Ciaccona, b. 187*

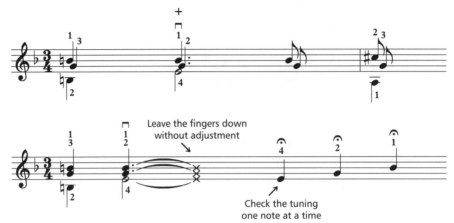

Leave the fingers down
without adjustment

Check the tuning
one note at a time

182 **Tenths: moving from one to another**

Two essential factors in playing tenths are (1) reaching back from the upper finger (see Examples 6–9, page 249), and (2) intonation when moving from a major tenth to a minor tenth, or minor to major.

Example 1   Bruch: Concerto no. 1 in G minor, op. 26, *mov. 3, b. 55*

- The first thing is to be perfectly clear about which finger moves a tone and which finger moves a semitone, or when they move the same distance. T indicates a tone, S indicates a semitone:

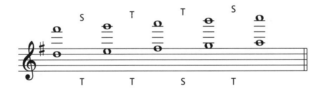

It is often helpful to think only of the finger that moves the bigger distance (see page 185).

- Having tuned each tenth individually, practise moving from one to the next. Then practise groups of three, four, and then all five:[1]

[1] See *ABC practice*, page 275

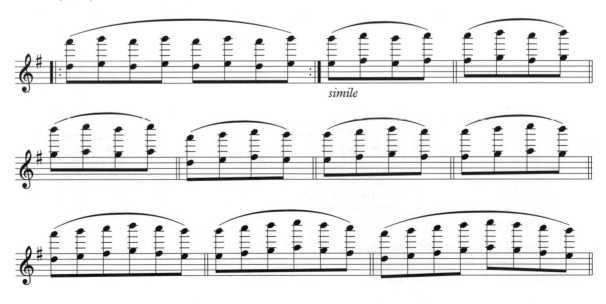

simile

Freedom and ease

Releasing the left hand

Keeping a space between the thumb and first finger

Fig. 15a shows a good, open position of the thumb.[1] Fig. 15b shows the first finger and the thumb squeezing together, a common cause of major tension and one of the most important things to avoid.

- Play phrases or whole passages with the thumb exaggeratedly forward (Fig. 15c). Afterwards the thumb will feel very relaxed, easy and uninvolved.

- If at first it seems impossible to keep the thumb forward, play phrases or, where possible, whole passages with an eraser or other soft object sitting between the base of the first finger and the thumb (Fig. 15d).

[1] See also *Contact point of thumb with neck,* page 301

Fig. 15

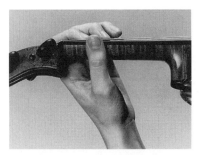

(a) Note the space between the thumb and the first finger

(b) Thumb squeezing

(c) Exaggerated forward position for practice

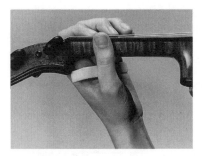

(d) Keeping the space open with an eraser

(e) The thumb rotated clockwise

(f) The thumb rotated anticlockwise

Rotating the thumb

The thumb is able to roll on the neck of the violin, clockwise or anticlockwise, so that more of one side or the other contacts the neck instead of the pad. The positions of the thumb shown in Figs. 15e and 15f are only to illustrate the movement; the thumb will rarely, if ever, be in either of these extreme positions.

A tiny amount of this thumb rotation happens continually throughout the normal course of playing, most of the time so slight as to be invisible. However, there is a big difference between an invisible amount of movement one way or the other (the thumb sitting in a balanced state between the two extremes), and the thumb being *held* rigidly in that middle position.

- Every now and then during any period of playing, regain the elasticity and balance of the thumb by gently rotating it clockwise and anticlockwise, feeling it moving in the base joint.[2] While doing so, keep the thumb very light against the neck of the violin.

[2] One of the most important aspects of the thumb is that, like the other fingers, it has three joints. The base joint is just above the wrist. Having a mental picture of the thumb consisting of only two joints severely restricts the thumb and can lead to tension. Most movements of the thumb should begin at the base joint.

Freedom and ease **229**

Lightening the thumb

The thumb must not press against the neck of the violin. The more the thumb presses, the more the fingers press, and *vice versa*. The ideal is always minimum finger pressure, minimum thumb counter-pressure.

Fig. 16
- Rest the scroll of the violin against the wall. Practise a phrase or passage without the thumb on the neck of the violin (Fig. 16). Keep the thumb well forward, as shown in Fig. 15c.

- Feel how the thumb, without any counter-pressure into the neck of the violin, can remain entirely relaxed.

- Feel how the fingers, without counter-pressure from the thumb, do not press into the strings. Instead of thumb counter-pressure use a little arm weight, 'hanging' the arm from the fingers.

- Playing again with the thumb on the neck, keep the same feeling of non-gripping that you had when playing without the thumb.

Playing without the thumb on the neck of the violin

Releasing fingers with the base joint of the first finger

One secret of playing with a relaxed, strong and easy fourth finger, is to forget about the fourth finger and concentrate on releasing *the base joint of the first finger*.

The same applies to playing any single finger, double stop, shift or chord: release the base joint of the first finger before beginning any action.

Example 1

Mozart: Adagio in E, K261, *b. 10*

- Release the base joint of the first finger before shifting to the G♯.

It is easier to find the feeling of releasing the base joint of the first finger if the fourth finger does not *press* the string down. The fourth finger feels much stronger, and stops the string with far less effort, when there is a feeling of the *weight of the hand* going through the finger and into the string. Lean the finger into the string from the base joint.

Example 2

Vivaldi: Autumn (The Four Seasons), op. 8 no. 3, *mov. 1, b. 36*

- At each '+' (just after each second finger, just before placing each fourth finger), release the base joint of the first finger.

Example 3

Bruch: Scottish Fantasy, op. 46, *mov. 3, b. 44*

- Release the base joint of the first finger before each double stop.

Releasing held-down fingers

187

Fingers that are held down on the string should not continue to be active into the string.

- Exaggerate releasing the held-down fingers by lightening them as if to play a harmonic.

Example 1   Beethoven: Sonata in F, op. 24 ('Spring'), *mov. 1, b. 106*

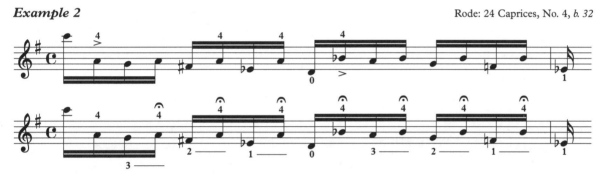

- Play very slowly.

- While playing the second-finger C, lighten the first-finger B so that it rests lightly on the surface of the string (as though playing a harmonic).

- While playing the fourth-finger E♭, lighten the second-finger C in the same way (so that now both the first and second fingers are at 'harmonic' level).

Afterwards, releasing the held-down fingers a normal amount will feel automatic, and bring about a feeling of release throughout the entire hand.

Example 2   Rode: 24 Caprices, No. 4, *b. 32*

- During the pauses, release the held-down fingers as in Example 1.

Releasing between finger actions

188

- Build moments of release into groups of notes, phrases and passages. The more moments of release the better.

- A key area to release is always the base joint of the first finger (see page 230).

Example 1   Vivaldi: Autumn (The Four Seasons), op. 8 no. 3, *mov. 3, b. 53*

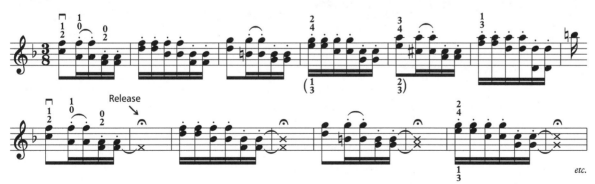

- During the pause, completely relax the hand and fingers, releasing the string as though playing a harmonic (shown as an x-note). Then play on.

- Playing without the pause, make sure that there is a brief moment, between the same two notes, when you feel the same give and relaxation in the hand and fingers.

Example 2   Dont: 24 Etudes and Caprices, op. 35, *No. 5, b. 13*

At the B♭ marked '+', the hand returns to its normal position after a long-held extension down to the first finger and up to the fourth finger.

- Practise releasing the fourth finger:

- During the pause bring the fourth finger back from its extension and 'hover' above the B♭ that it is about to play – the hand and the finger in a completely relaxed state.
- Then play the phrase without the pause but with the same moment of release as the fourth finger returns from its extension.

Example 3   Rode: 24 Caprices, No. 23, *b. 33*

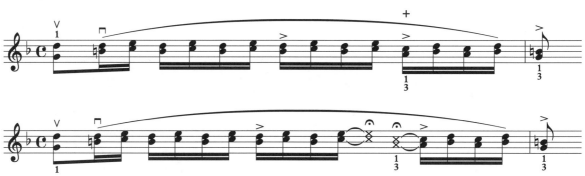

The x-notes = release the string, the fingers resting on the string as if playing harmonics.

- During the pause completely release the hand, particularly the thumb and the base joints of the fingers.
- Then play on, with the same feeling of lightness and release in the hand and fingers.

Example 4   Wieniawski: Concerto no. 2 in D minor, op. 22, *mov. 3, b. 7*

The fingers should release when not in use.

- Pause slightly while playing each open string and release the thumb, the base joints of the fingers, the muscles in the palm of the hand, the wrist, the upper arm, as well as any excess pressure into the chin rest.
- After each pause keep the same feeling of general release while playing the stopped notes.

Stop–release

There should be an immediate give as soon as a finger stops a note on the string.[1] The hand tightens if the finger action is 'stop–press' rather than 'stop–release'.

- Practising by exaggeration, play a phrase very slowly, each note separated by a pause. During the pause release the string and the bow pressure, the finger resting on the surface of the string as if to play a harmonic.

Example 1   Bartók (arr. Székely): Roumanian Folk Dances, No. 4, *b. 3*

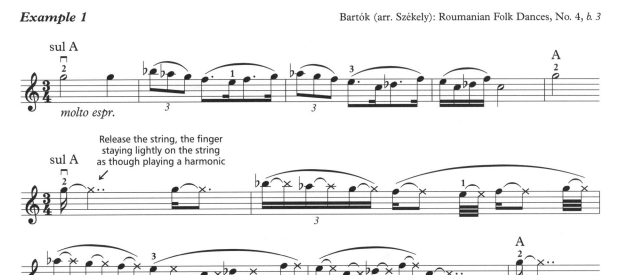

Example 2   Schubert: Sonatina in G minor, op. 137 no. 3, *mov. 4, b. 57*

Example 3   Mozart: Concerto no. 3 in G, K216, *mov. 1, b. 38*

The trill in bar 40 is often played as a turn.

- During the pause completely relax the hand and fingers, releasing the string slightly, and then play on:

[1] A useful analogy is the binary code used in computers, where all information is reduced to numbers made up of ones and zeros – either 'on' or 'off'. The actions of the left hand could be expressed in the same way, '1' representing a muscle in use (i.e. contracted) and '0' representing the same muscle released (even though the finger may still be stopping the string). In some passages the sequence would be '1010 1010', i.e. every action immediately followed by a release before another action. In other passages it would more be a matter of releasing often enough, as in '10111011110'. But if the number reads '1111 1111' for too long, tension may be unavoidable.

Example 4

Mendelssohn: Concerto in E minor, op. 64, *mov. 1, b. 40*

The x-notes = release the string slightly, and at the same time completely release the hand and fingers:

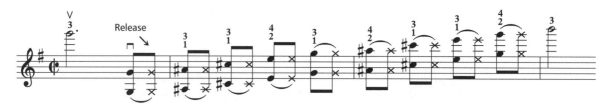

● Start slowly, and gradually speed up.

Example 5

Brahms: Concerto in D, op. 77, *mov. 1, b. 559*

● Playing long slurs, during the second sixteenth-note of each pair lighten the fingers on the strings as though to play harmonics, and completely relax the hand and fingers.

● Begin slowly, and gradually speed up to as fast a tempo as possible.

190 **Building up from *pp***

● Play through a phrase or passage *pp* to encourage the left hand to be soft and relaxed, the fingers light on the string and effortless.

● Repeat *p*, *mp*, *mf*, *f* and *ff*. As the bow weight increases, keep the same feeling of lightness and ease that you had when playing *pp*.

Example

Brahms: Sonata no. 1 in G, op. 78, *mov. 2, b. 66*

Independence: light left hand, heavy right hand

When the bow plays heavily into the string, the left hand finger pressure should remain light, i.e. *as much finger pressure as necessary for a pure tone but as little as possible.*

- Practising by exaggeration, play a phrase or passage very heavily with the bow, but at the same time so lightly with the fingers (as though playing harmonics) that the sound produced is pure scratch.

- Relax the left hand and fingers completely. You need only the slightest muscular activity to place the fingers lightly on the surface of the string. Check the thumb, base joints of the fingers, wrist and upper arm, to make sure that every area is working with minimum effort.

- Repeat several times, playing f with the bow throughout, each time stopping the string slightly more. Continue until the tone is still large but now entirely pure, the fingers stopping the string with the least possible finger pressure throughout.

Example 1   Kayser: Etudes, op. 20, no. 6, *b. 1*

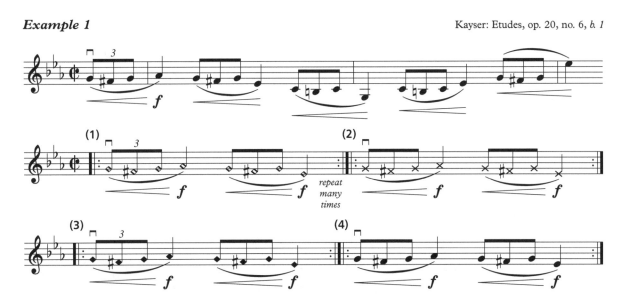

(1) Quarter press the string with the fingers. Playing f with the bow should produce a loud whistling, scratching and scraping sound. Keep the left fingers light on the string, the hand soft and relaxed.

(2) Half press. The tone will still be extremely impure. Keep the feeling in the fingers the same.

(3) Three-quarters press. The tone will be almost pure. Keep the feeling in the fingers the same.

(4) Just enough weight in the fingers for a pure tone, but barely enough to make the strings touch the fingerboard. Notice how soft and easy the left hand feels while the bow plays deeply into the string.

Example 2   Brahms: Concerto in D, op. 77, *mov. 1, b. 90*

- Practise as in Example 1.

Example 3

Mendelssohn: Concerto in E minor, op. 64, *mov. 1, b. 211*

con forza

This method is very useful for lightening the hand and fingers in a passage of shifts:

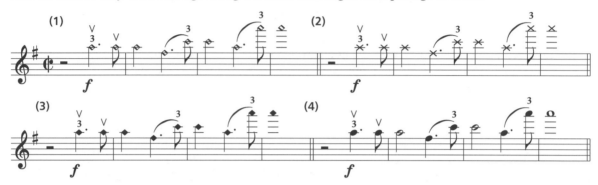

(1)–(4) refer to the numbered list in Example 1 (page 235).

192 Using *spiccato*

- Encourage the left hand to release by playing through phrases, passages or whole pieces using only *spiccato*. The lack of sustaining in the bow encourages the left-hand fingers to release after each note.

Example 1

Bartók (arr. Székely): Roumanian Folk Dances, *No. 1, b. 4*

- Find the same lightness and ease when playing the passage as written, with the bow deeply in the string.

Example 2

Dvořák: Concerto in A minor, op. 53, *mov. 1, b. 5*

- Play every note with a short *spiccato*, so that the half-notes (minims) sound like very short notes followed by rests.

193 Non-vibrato

Playing non-vibrato makes it easier to find out if you really are using the left hand with minimum effort.

- Play phrases, passages or whole movements entirely without vibrato, concentrating on stopping the string with the least finger pressure (just enough to make a proper sound), and with the thumb equally light against the neck. Feel how the forearm and upper arm remain completely relaxed and uninvolved.

- Repeat with vibrato, with the same economy of movement, ease, and lightness of playing as before.

Finger action

This section looks at the basic movement of the fingers, and how the position of the hand and wrist can affect this. For other aspects of effortlessness in the left fingers see also *Low fingers*, page 4; *Fast fingers*, page 7; *Blocks*, page 11; *Defaults*, page 299.

Angle and height of knuckles

Adjust the point of contact of the first finger and the neck of the violin[1] to change the angle of the hand relative to the fingerboard (Fig. 17a). In low positions, on the E string the contact point is nearer the middle joint of the finger; on the G string the contact point is nearer the base joint of the finger. Naturally the exact positions shown in Fig. 17a vary from hand to hand as well as from phrase to phrase.

Finger action feels easier if the angle of the knuckles to the fingerboard is not too steep (i.e. the contact point with the neck is nearer the middle joint than the base joint). The angle shown in Fig. 17b can give each finger a feeling of slight strain. If the knuckles are too low (Fig. 17c) the fingers have too far to reach. Fig. 17d shows a natural angle of the knuckles.

194

[1] In lower positions the side of the first finger should continually brush lightly against the neck of the violin. Awkwardness or tension may be caused by trying to keep a permanent space between the neck and the side of the first finger. Galamian called this 'the principle of the double contact'. See *Contact point of first finger with neck*, page 301.

Fig. 17

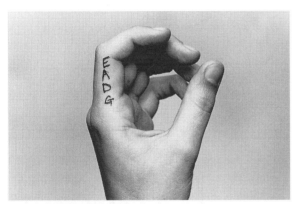

(a) **Contact point of neck with first finger**

(b) **The knuckles are too high and steep**

(c) **The knuckles are too low.**
    The fingers have to stretch to their notes

(d) **Natural angle of the knuckles**

Example 1   Kreutzer: 42 Etudes ou caprices, No. 27, *b. 1*

- Play a phrase or short passage several times, each time experimenting with higher or lower knuckles to find the most comfortable hand position.

- Repeat the phrase several times while moving gradually between too-high, normal and too-low knuckles as shown in Fig. 17.

Example 2   Mozart: Concerto no. 4 in D, K218, *mov. 3, b. 23*

- At each place marked with an arrow, check the contact point between the first finger and the side of the neck (even if the first finger is not playing).

- Experiment with higher and lower settings of the hand, noting the difference in ease of movement between one height and another.

195 Straight wrist

In low positions, the ideal is for the left forearm and the back of the hand to be in a straight line. As the fingers rise and fall the wrist neither collapses in nor pushes out, the hand bending neither to the left nor to the right. (If the arm is very short the wrist may sometimes form a slightly outward-bending shape in 1st position.) The fourth finger in particular may be prone to disturbing the wrist, if there is an association between dropping the fourth finger and pushing the wrist outwards (Fig. 18a).

- Practising by doing the opposite, learn how to drop the fourth finger on to specific notes with the wrist giving, or bending in slightly (Fig. 18b). Afterwards, keeping a straight line will seem much easier.

Fig. 18

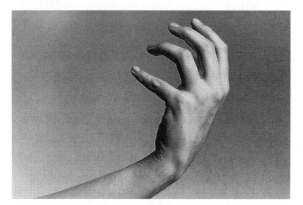
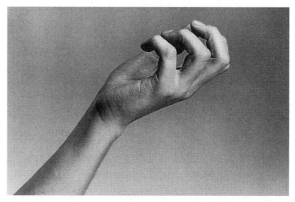

(a) **Pushing the wrist out causes tension**   (b) **Wrist slightly 'giving' for practice purposes**

Example 1   Kreutzer: 42 Etudes ou caprices, No. 9, *b. 1*

Practise the whole passage with the wrist pulled in slightly as shown in Fig. 18b.

Example 2   Mendelssohn: Concerto in E minor, op. 64, *mov. 3, b. 9*

- Practise the extensions (marked '+') with the wrist pulled in slightly (Fig. 18b).

Example 3   Mozart: Sonata in B♭, K454, *mov. 1, b. 19*

- To counteract pushing the wrist out, when playing the fourth fingers (marked '+') pull the wrist in slightly (Fig. 18b).

Moving fingers from the base joints

The most effortless, relaxed and efficient finger action comes from moving the fingers from the base joints.[1] Avoid partly moving the finger with a movement of the whole hand (the finger and hand moving together from the wrist).

Any out-and-in movement of the wrist, as a finger drops or lifts, is a sure sign that the finger is not moving from the base joint. The third and fourth fingers in particular may need occasional attention to ensure that they are moving freely.

Placing the hand flat against the shoulder of the violin is a simple way to remember the feeling of moving the fingers from the base joint.

- Place the palm of the hand flat against the shoulder of the violin so that the base joints are just above the upper rim of the violin (Fig. 19).

- Using the violin to stabilize the hand, tap the finger (without playing it) up and down on the E string. It does not matter exactly where on the string you tap – it is the movement of the finger that matters, not the pitch of the note. Simply make sure that the finger is curved, relaxed and comfortable.

[1] 'When considering technique, it is not so much a question of "good" and "bad", but of "more efficient" and "less efficient" ways of doing things.' – Dorothy DeLay

Fig. 19

Using the shoulder of the violin to stabilize the hand while tapping

Example 1 Mozart: Concerto no. 5 in A, K219, *mov. 2, b. 41*

- To practise the fourth finger marked '+', even though it is in 1st position, place the hand against the shoulder of the violin as shown in Fig. 19.

- Tap the fourth finger up and down on the E string, feeling the finger moving from the base joint, the hand held steady against the shoulder of the violin.

   You may wish to hold down the third finger on the string, as it is in the passage.

- Recapture the same feeling in the finger movement when you then play the passage.

Example 2 Beethoven: Sonata in G, op. 96, *mov. 1, b. 2*

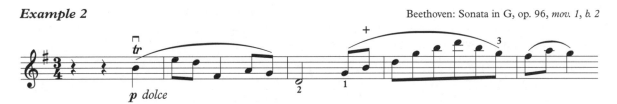

Tapping on the E string is equally helpful when the actual notes are not on the E string.

- Practise the fourth fingers, and the third finger marked '+', with the hand against the shoulder of the violin as shown in Fig. 19.

- Tap the third finger, and then the fourth, up and down on the E string. Feel the fingers moving from the base joint, the hand held steady against the shoulder of the violin.

- Recapture the same feeling in the finger movement when you then play the passage.

Example 3 Paganini: Concerto no. 1 in D, op. 6, *mov. 1, b. 130*

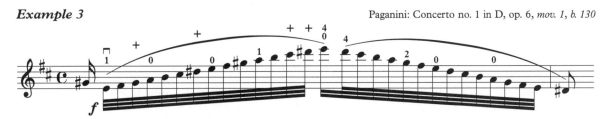

- Tap the third finger, and then the fourth, up and down on the E string as shown in Fig. 19. Feel the fingers moving from the base joint, the hand held steady against the shoulder of the violin.

- Recapture the same feeling in the finger movement when you then play the passage.

197 Placing fingers gently

One of the great secrets of left-hand technique is that there are two ways to stop the string. To play ascending slurred notes, the finger must fall with speed and energy. To play anything else, the finger is placed on the string ahead of the bow.

- Playing ascending slurred notes, the string is already vibrating when you put a finger down. You have to drop the finger fast and decisively so that there is no 'fuzz' at the beginning of the note.

- Playing anything else, the string is motionless at the place where the finger is going to make the stop. The finger has only to create the new string length before the bow arrives. It does not have to force the string to stop vibrating, so the action of placing the finger takes little energy.[1]

[1] Everything feels like hard work if the fingers always drop as if you are playing *f* ascending slurs. Placing the finger takes very little energy in comparison. When all fingers except for ascending slurs are placed, rather than dropped with an impact, the entire hand feels soft, relaxed and completely effortless even in the fastest, most brilliant playing, almost to the extent of feeling as if the fingers are barely doing anything at all.

While bowing the open A string, look at the place on the string where the third finger is going to play the D. Playing *f*, the string visibly swings from side to side. The finger is dropping on to a moving surface. If the finger does not literally 'stop' the string quickly there is a brief moment of 'fuzz' in the sound before the new string length is properly established.

Playing *p*, the finger must also drop fast; but because the sideways vibration of the string is less, the finger can drop slightly more slowly than when playing *f*.

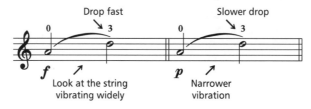

Feel the difference in finger action between ascending slurred and separate. During the slurs, listen to the 'ping' as the finger stops each new note (see *Fast fingers*, page 7):

In faster separate-bow passages, the finger may have to be placed very quickly to get there in time; but placing it very quickly, on a string that is more or less motionless, feels quite different from dropping onto a vibrating string.

Neither of the other possibilities – descending notes either slurred or separate – gains any benefit from being placed with any sort of impact on the string. Everything to do with playing these fingers is a matter of placing, and timing with the bow:

(1) Playing any new finger on a new string, the finger must be placed or 'prepared' before the bow (shown as an x-note). The string is not vibrating, so the finger can be placed gently, simply getting there ready for when the bow arrives. Nothing is gained by creating the new string-length with an impact.

(2) Playing from a higher finger to a lower finger on the same string, the lower finger is prepared before lifting the upper finger. The area of the string on which the finger is placed is not vibrating, so the finger can be placed gently, simply getting there ready for when the higher finger lifts and uncovers it.

(3) Ascending notes with separate bows are the closest to playing slurred ascending notes. In many cases the two may seem the same; but in separate bows, the finger action is more about timing than impact.

The finger must be in place before the bow starts to move. Too early, and the finger will interfere with the previous note; too late, and there will be 'fuzz' because the bow has begun to play a half-stopped string. There is a perfect moment between the bow strokes to place the finger. At that moment the vibration of the string is at its least.

Example 1   J. S. Bach: Sonata no. 1 in G minor, BWV1001, Presto, *b. 4*

It is essential, for musical reasons as well as technical, that fingers do not 'bang' down on the fingerboard. The fingers marked 'place' become like finger accents if they drop with an impact, instead of being gently placed just ahead of the bow. These inevitably break up the phrase or line with wrong groupings of notes or unmusical stresses.

• A simple way to practise any fast, separate-bow passage is to stop before placing the finger: stop the bow on the string; gently place the next finger; play; stop the bow; place; play, and so on:

Example 2   Vivaldi: Concerto in A minor, op. 3 no. 6, mov. 2, *b. 1*

In this *dolce* Largo, the fingers must fall slowly to avoid any hint of articulation. The sideways vibration of the string is less in p, so the finger can drop more slowly than when playing f.

The string vibrates the widest at the middle point between the bridge and the nut or finger. It vibrates the least at the part of the string nearest to the bridge or the stop (in this case first-finger D).

Feel the difference between placing the second finger on an E♭, and placing the fourth finger on a G♯:

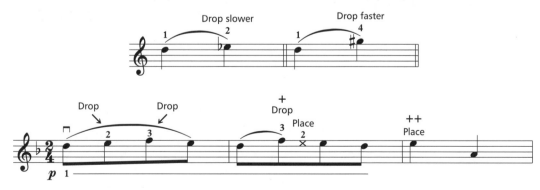

Feel the difference between the third finger dropping to play the F (marked '+'), and placing the second finger ahead of the bow to play the E ('++'). It is difficult to find the legato quality of the E if the second finger makes any sort of vertical impact on the string.

Example 3

Bruch: Concerto no. 1 in G minor, op. 26, *mov. 3, b. 267*

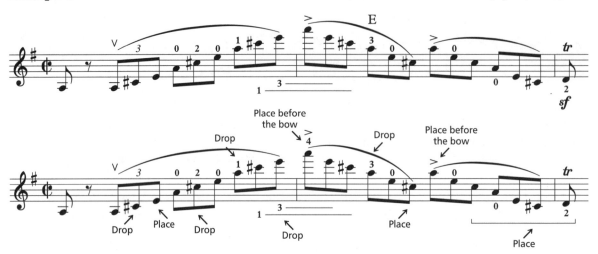

[1]See *Finger accents for rhythmic stability,* page 285

Placing fingers gently, you can still play with rhythmic aiming-points in the left fingers, or give different amounts of emphasis to certain fingers depending on their place in the phrase.[1] Playing the top A at the beginning of the second bar, it is natural to drop the fourth finger with an 'expressive' or rhythmic impact; and to do the same with the third-finger A on the up-bow.

However, the less active, and the quieter and more economical the general action of the fingers, the less has to be done to have an expressive feel in the fingers, or to make musical differences of finger weight or accent.

- Reduce any danger of a too-heavy articulation by first practising a simple co-ordination exercise:

- At the end of each up-bow stop the bow on the string. Place the fourth finger on the string without moving the bow (shown as an x-note). Then bow the note.

- Make the x-note gradually shorter and shorter. As you do so, the speed of placing the finger will have to increase until the finger is dropping onto the string very quickly. However quickly it falls, continue to place the finger gently throughout with no audible sound of the finger hitting the fingerboard.

Afterwards, the smallest amount of rhythmic articulation in the fourth finger will seem sufficient.

Example 4

Tchaikovsky: Three pieces, op. 42, *Meditation, b. 40*

[2] See *Vibrato accents,* page 138

When playing accented notes, ensure that the extra energy for the accent is given to the bow, and to any extra vibrato,[2] rather than to the action of stopping the string.

- Stop the bow before each finger marked '+'; place the finger gently; then play on, making the accent with the bow while the finger remains light and effortless:

Example 5 Mendelssohn: Concerto in E minor, op. 64, *mov. 1, b. 84*

In this passage, only the fingers playing the notes marked '+' are dropped with energy. Place every other finger before the bow plays it. There should not be a 'thud' on the fingerboard as any of these fingers contacts the string.

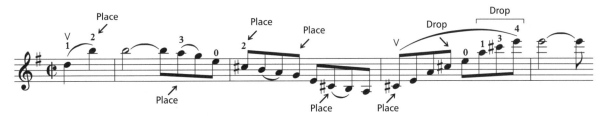

Example 6

In an ascending scale, the only finger to place is the first finger. Getting this finger down on the string before the bow arrives is one of the key elements of smooth scale playing:[1]

[1] See also Example 2, page 102

- Practise preparing and placing fingers exaggeratedly early, like a syncopation:

- The moment when both fingers – in this case the fourth and the first – are down on the strings is called 'overlapping'. Regularly practise scales and scale-like passages holding the fourth finger down longer than usual, until the second finger is on the string.

Example 7

Descending, all the fingers need to be prepared, but a particular one to watch out for is the fourth finger:[2]

[2] See also Example 3, page 102

- The x-note represents placing the fourth finger silently on the string in advance of the bow. Place the finger later and later, but always with the same lightness and lack of impact as in the first bar.

- While playing the F♯ allow the bow to begin to move towards the A string. By the end, feel the movements of the fourth finger and the bow as one combined action, not two actions that need to be co-ordinated with each other.

Example 8

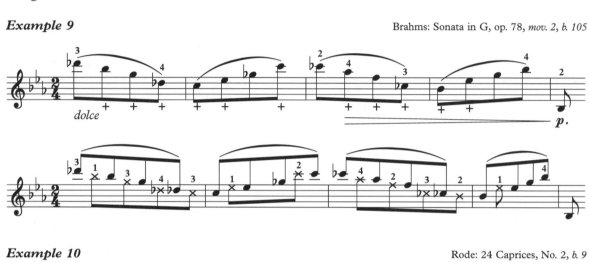

Always having the fingers ready on the string before the bow gets there, is one of the secrets of playing an arpeggio with true *legato* and evenness. Descending, think ahead into the next note in a continuous flow of movement, rather than 'stopping' on each note, so that the lower finger is always ready on the string.

Example 9   Brahms: Sonata in G, op. 78, *mov. 2, b. 105*

Example 10   Rode: 24 Caprices, No. 2, *b. 9*

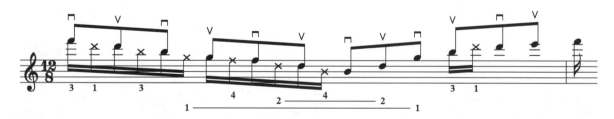

● Feel the fingers 'leading' the bow:

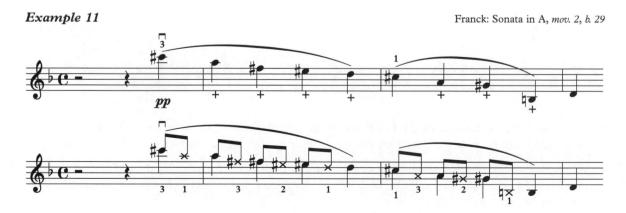

Example 11   Franck: Sonata in A, *mov. 2, b. 29*

Timing the finger and bow for fast playing

The muscular strength, energy or effort of playing need not increase as the tempo of the notes increases. To play two notes faster, or to play them slower, often requires exactly the same finger action. Playing faster is simply a matter of timing the finger with the beginning of the bow stroke, not of working harder.

(1) In the first bar, the third finger drops on to the string long after the bow begins to play the first finger B. In the second bar, the third finger waits only half as long before dropping, and so on. By the fifth bar, the third finger drops an instant after the bow begins to move. In each case the speed and energy of the third finger is exactly the same. The difference in the speed of each pair of notes lies only in *when* the finger drops.

(2) Raising a finger works in the same way. In the first bar the third finger lifts off the string long after the bow begins to play the third finger D. By the fifth bar the third finger lifts off an instant after the bow begins to move, the speed of the finger action remaining the same.

Example 1
Wieniawski: Polonaise-brillante, op. 21, *b. 66*

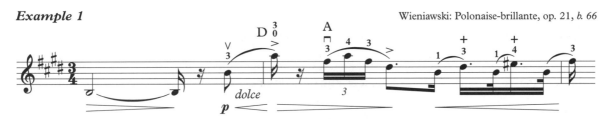

● Exaggerate the timing of the notes marked '+' by dropping or raising the fingers almost at the same moment as the beginning of the bow stroke.

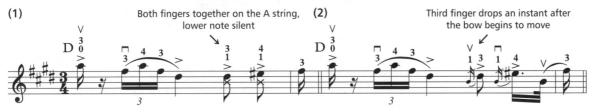

(1) Place the fingers at the same time, as though playing a double stop on one string.

(2) Drop the finger so soon after the beginning of the bow stroke that the grace note is only just audible.

Example 2
Mendelssohn: Concerto in E minor, op. 64, *mov. 3, b. 37*

● Playing very short grace notes, begin slowly. Gradually speed up to as fast a tempo as possible:

Widening the hand at the base joints

Shifting the balance of the hand a little onto the upper fingers, with the lower fingers reaching back a little to their notes, is one of the great 'secrets' of playing with a comfortable and efficient left hand. The smaller the hand the more, or the more often, it needs to be based on the upper fingers, but large hands benefit from this as well.

The idea of widening the hand at the base joints is most obvious when playing wide intervals like tenths. In the beginning, tenths feel easier if you place the fourth finger on its own and then reach back with the first finger, rather than beginning on the first finger and stretching up to the fourth. When you reach back, the hand automatically widens at the base joints (the space between the knuckles increases), particularly between the first and second fingers (Fig. 20a). If the hand does not widen (Fig. 20b), starting on the first finger and reaching up to the fourth is too far to stretch.[1]

[1] When it is part of your playing to widen at the base joints it does not matter whether you begin on the fourth finger and reach back, or begin on the first finger and reach forwards.

The key to making extensions feel easy is to *lead with the base joint*. Leading the movement from the fingertip can make the extension feel constricted. The order is always base joint first, finger second; not finger first, base joint second.

Fig. 20

 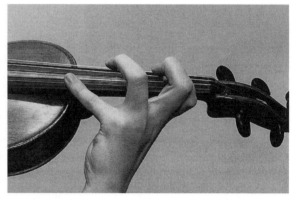

(a) Note the space between the first and second fingers

(b) Note how the first and second fingers have not opened

199 ## Basing the hand position on the upper finger

- Large hands or small, from time to time practise basing the hand on the upper fingers and reaching back to the lower notes. There will be a feeling of great openness and effortlessness when you return to normal playing.

Example 1

Mozart: Concerto no. 3 in G, K216, *mov. 2, b. 8*

Fig. 21a shows the hand after the fourth finger A (marked '+' in the Example above) has been placed on the string. While keeping the second finger placed more on the left side of the fingertip, the fourth has been placed more on the right side of the fingertip. Note the 'V' shape made by the second and fourth fingers, and by the first and second fingers. There is a feeling of the hand position balanced on the fourth finger.

In Fig. 21b the hand is balanced on the second finger, and shows the strained position of the fingers caused by the fourth finger having to stretch forwards. Note how the second and fourth fingers are now parallel, and the second and first fingers are squeezing together.

Fig. 21

(a) Note the wide space between the fingers

(b) The fourth finger is straining to reach the A

(c) After reaching back, one finger at a time, from the fourth finger

- Find the hand position by first balancing the hand on the fourth finger, and then reaching back with the other fingers one by one:

  1 Place the fourth finger without playing it (written as an x-note, below). Contact the string more on the right side of the fingertip. Leaving the fourth finger on the string, place the third underneath it without affecting the fourth, or affecting it as little as possible. Keeping the fingers down on the string, place the second finger, and then the first. See Fig. 21c.

  2 Then, playing the passage as written, find the same feeling of openness in the hand.

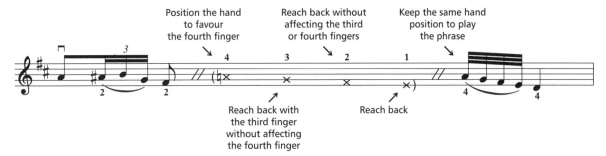

Example 2   Kayser: Etudes, op. 20, *No. 1, b. 3*

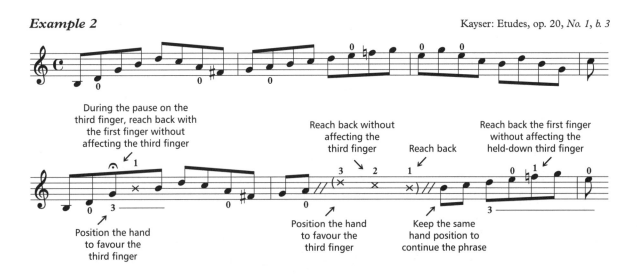

Example 3   Beethoven: Sonata in A ('Kreutzer'), op. 47, *mov. 1, b. 61*

Many chords feel more comfortable when the hand is positioned to favour the upper fingers, with the lower fingers reaching back. If the hand is based on the lower fingers, the upper fingers may have to strain to reach their notes.

- Establish the hand position for each chord by silently placing the fingers in the order 4–3–2–1.

- Position the hand to favour the upper finger, and then reach back with the other fingers. While reaching back, change the balance of the hand as little as possible.

- Keep a space between the base of the thumb and the first finger.[1]

[1] See Fig. 15a, page 229

Example 4   Tchaikovsky: Three Pieces, op. 42, *Melody, b. 6*

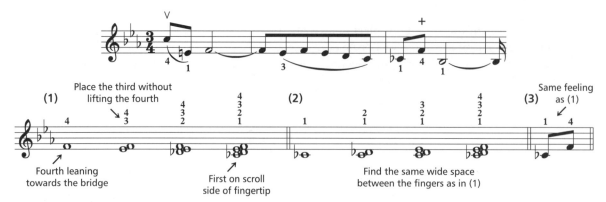

(1) Without the bow, place the fingers on the string in the order 4–3–2–1. Use different areas of the fingertip to open the hand at the base joints: lean the fourth finger towards the bridge and the first finger towards the scroll (creating the fan-like shape of the fingers shown in Fig. 21a, page 246). It does not matter if you cannot actually lean towards the bridge – just go as far as you can.[1]

[1] See *Space between fingers*, page 300

(2) Find the same angle of the fingers, and the same wide space between them, ascending 1–2–3–4.

(3) Find the same feeling of opening the hand when playing first to fourth finger in the context of the phrase.

Example 5   Beethoven: Sonata in A minor, op. 23, *mov. 1, b. 84*

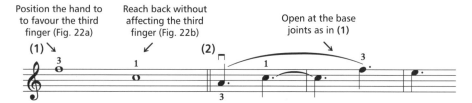

The third-finger F (marked '+') is often reached with an extension to avoid any sound of shifting (to save any 'expressive' shifting for the shift to the fourth-finger A four bars later).

(1) Play the F by itself, positioning the hand to favour the third finger, and making sure the finger is curved, relaxed and comfortable (Fig. 22a).

Reach the first finger back to the C without affecting the shape of the third finger, or affecting it as little as possible. Feel the space opening at the base joints between the first and second fingers (Fig. 22b).

(2) During the tied first-finger C remember the feeling of opening the hand. Then widen at the base joints as you reach the third finger up to the F, arriving again in a shape similar to Fig. 22b.

Fig. 22c shows the strained position of the fingers if the hand is based on the first-finger C, and the third finger has to stretch up to the F. Note the tension in the wrist.

Fig. 22

(a) Position the hand to favour the third finger

(b) Note the wide space between the fingers

(c) The third finger has had to stretch up to the F

Example 6   Kreutzer: 42 Etudes ou caprices, No. 26, *b. 34*

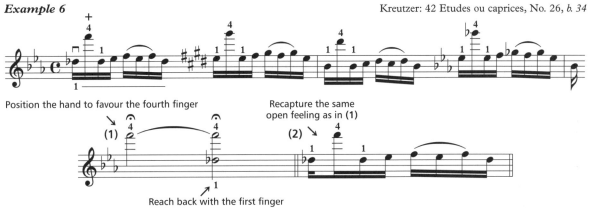

Position the hand to favour the fourth finger   Recapture the same
                                                              open feeling as in **(1)**

Reach back with the first finger

Example 7   Brahms: Concerto in D, op. 77, *mov. 1, b. 217*

- First play the upper note to establish the hand position, and then reach back with the first finger.

- Hold down fingers as marked.

Example 8   Ysaÿe: Sonata, op. 27 no. 2, *mov. 1, b. 11*

- Feel the hand position favouring the fourth finger. Alter the shape of the fourth finger as little as possible as you reach back with the first finger to the tenths:

Balance the hand on the fourth finger

Reach back with the first finger

- Afterwards, find the same feeling of basing the hand on the upper finger, and reaching back, when you play the tenths in the passage.

Example 9   Paganini: Concerto no. 1 in D, op. 6, *mov. 1, b. 265*

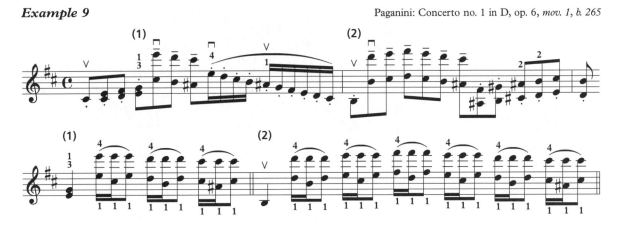

200 Extending the reach of the fourth finger

Widening the hand at the base joints applies to any sort of fourth-finger extension, even simply playing down from first-finger F on the E string to fourth-finger E on the A string (or the equivalent on the other strings).

- Extend the reach of the fourth finger by finding the note one semitone higher than written. When you have learnt how to release and widen the hand to play this higher note, the correct note feels much easier.

- Play in reverse: begin on the fourth finger and reach back, then find the same opening and widening in the hand while starting on the lower finger and reaching forwards.

Example 1   Kreutzer: 42 Etudes ou caprices, No. 32, *b. 1*

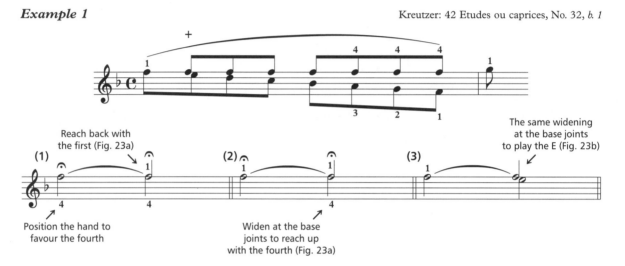

(1) Begin by practising an F instead of an E. Start in reverse: place the fourth-finger F, and then reach back with the first finger (Fig. 23a).

Open the space between the first and second fingers. Keep a space between the base of the thumb and the first finger.[1]

_{1 See Fig. 15a, page 229}

(2) Then play the same thing but the right way round: play the first finger F and then reach up to the fourth finger F, the hand and fingers arriving again in a shape similar to Fig. 23a.

Reach up partly by bringing the base joint of the fourth finger closer to the neck of the violin.

(3) Then return to playing the correct note, E (Fig. 23b). Reach the E, which now feels like a very small distance away, with the same opening and widening at the base joints as when reaching up to the F.

Fig. 23b shows the first finger continuing to stop F on the E string while the fourth finger easily reaches the E on the A string. Notice the curve of the fourth finger and the space between the first and second fingers.

Fig. 23c shows the first and second fingers squeezing together. This reduces the reach of the fourth finger, which is now forced to straighten. Notice in Fig. 23a and Fig. 23b how the first and second fingers widen at the base joints to form a 'V', whereas in Fig. 23c they are parallel.

Fig. 23

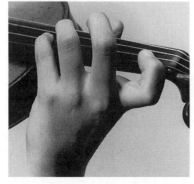  

(a) **Reaching back from F to F**

(b) **Opening between the first and second fingers helps the fourth finger reach the E**

(c) **Squeezing the first and second fingers together forces the fourth finger to straighten**

Example 2 Dont: 24 Etudes and Caprices, op. 35, No. 3, *b. 4*

Reach back with
the second finger

(1)   (2)

+

4 2 4

Position the hand to
favour the fourth finger

(1) Begin by practising an E instead of a D♯. Start in reverse: place the fourth-finger E, and then reach back with the second-finger F♯.

(2) Practise the E in the context of the passage. If your hand is small you may not be able to reach it, but just from trying to play an E the D♯ will feel much nearer and easier to reach afterwards.

Thirds and fingered octaves

In playing thirds and fingered octaves it is essential that the hand position is based on the third and fourth fingers, the lower fingers reaching back (Figs. 24a, 24c). If the hand position is based on the lower finger the upper fingers cannot reach their notes without straightening, and the hand becomes tense (Figs. 24b, 24d).

Fig. 24

(a) Basing the hand on the curved fourth finger, the second finger reaches back easily

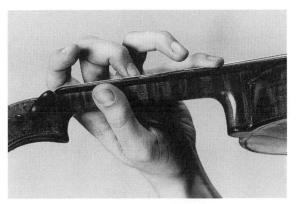

(b) Basing the hand on the second finger, the fourth finger strains to reach up far enough

(c) Reaching back from the upper finger

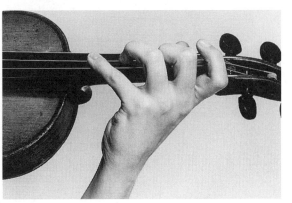

(d) Stretching up from the lower finger

Use the following method to build the correct hand position:[1]

● Set the hand position for each third or fingered octave individually.

● Place the upper finger first, positioning the hand so that the finger is curved, relaxed and comfortable.

● Then place the lower finger by extending back.

● While placing the lower finger, as far as possible do not alter the shape of the upper finger, or change the way the hand is balanced on the upper finger.

[1] Apart from being helpful for specific thirds or fingered octaves, used as a daily warm-up exercise this is also one of the quickest ways to build a good hand shape in general, i.e. whatever the left hand is doing, the fingers remain curved, staying close to the strings without pulling excessively sideways or upwards, and with the hand balanced to give every finger maximum ease and reach.

Example 1

- Play slowly, without keeping to any particular pulse:

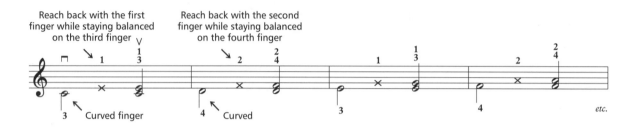

Reach back with the first finger while staying balanced on the third finger

Reach back with the second finger while staying balanced on the fourth finger

Curved finger   Curved

etc.

Example 2

Brahms: Concerto in D, op. 77, *mov. 3, b. 1*

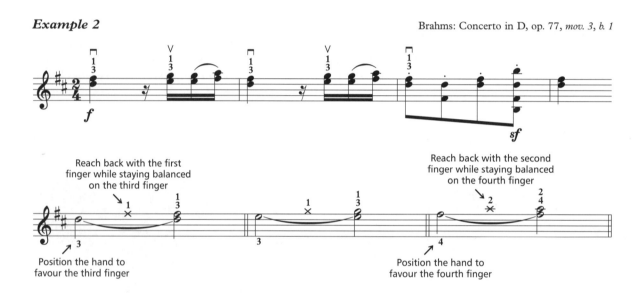

Reach back with the first finger while staying balanced on the third finger

Reach back with the second finger while staying balanced on the fourth finger

Position the hand to favour the third finger

Position the hand to favour the fourth finger

Example 3

Hand positioned to favour the third finger so that it is curved, relaxed, comfortable

Hand positioned to favour the fourth finger so that it is curved, relaxed, comfortable

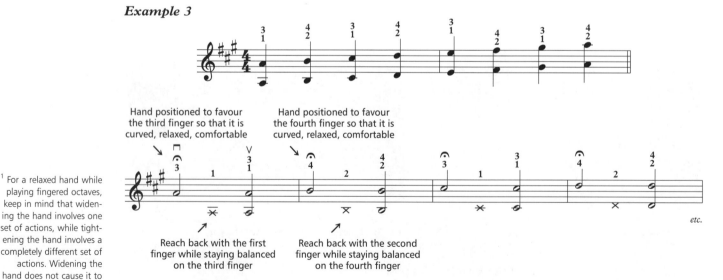

Reach back with the first finger while staying balanced on the third finger

Reach back with the second finger while staying balanced on the fourth finger

etc.

[1] For a relaxed hand while playing fingered octaves, keep in mind that widening the hand involves one set of actions, while tightening the hand involves a completely different set of actions. Widening the hand does not cause it to tense – contracting the muscles in the hand does. The two are not related or connected in any way. Doing one does not mean that you have to do the other.

[2] See Fig. 15c, page 229

- If you have small hands it may not be possible to keep the fourth finger rounded, but keep it as rounded as possible.[1]

- Keep a space between the base of the thumb and the first finger. For practice purposes position the thumb well forward.[2]

Releasing the right hand

Bow-hold flexibility

Flexibility and give are an essential element of bowing technique. Galamian likened the right hand to a system of springs which, although sometimes looser and sometimes tighter, must never be locked and tight.

Sometimes the fingers, thumb and knuckles in the bow hand seem not to move at all. At other times the movements are visible and obvious. How much movement there should be depends on each stroke and the individual hand.[1]

- To make sure that there is a give in every joint in the bow hand, with no resistance or tension anywhere, exaggerate the natural movements of the fingers and knuckles by making them conscious and larger-than-life.[2]

- Just before each up-bow, straighten the fingers and raise the knuckles (Fig. 25a).

- Just before each down-bow, curve the fingers and lower the knuckles (Fig. 25b).

- If necessary, play much more slowly than normal, using the time to feel the give in every joint.

(a) **Straighten the fingers at the end of the down-bow**

(b) **Curve the fingers at the end of the up-bow**

Example 1   Beethoven: Concerto in D, op. 61, *mov. 1, b. 134*

S = Straighten the fingers   C = Curve the fingers

Afterwards, playing without any visible movement in the fingers, find the same feeling of flexibility and smoothness in each stroke.

Example 2   Lalo: Symphonie espagnole, op. 21, *mov. 3, b. 81*

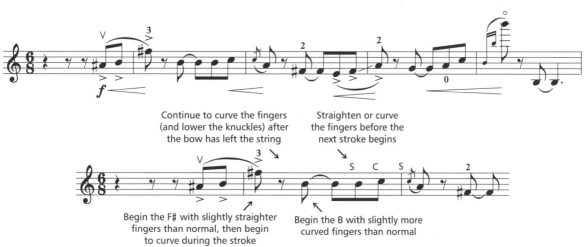

[1] In one player, no visible flexibility in a particular bowing action could mean stiffness, while in another player the same apparent lack of movement might be entirely natural and in fact contain plenty of invisible give.

The Greek philosopher Aristotle taught that every virtue lies on the Golden Mean between two vices. Accordingly, both a stiff bowing hand and one that is too floppy are 'vices'; a natural give in the hand is the virtue that lies in between.

Fig. 25

[2] 'I introduced the finger-stroke into violin peda-gogics in my Urstudien (Basic Studies) in 1910. Intended as a purely help-ful gymnastic exercise, I had not imagined what damage it would come to…at the hands of other theoreticians by making it the crucial point of bow technic [sic]. I had already warned…that this bowing was not to be used inde-pendently for practical playing. If assigning the change of bow to the fingers as their exclusive privilege, one will achieve exactly the opposite of an inaudible change. The finger stroke must only be used…in conjunction with the wrist movement and even then only in minimal doses, because – if the change of bow is seen, it will also be heard!' Carl Flesch: *Problems of Tone Production in Violin Playing* (Baden-Baden, 1931), 14.

203

Playing without the first finger in f passages

[1] The feeling of pulling sound out of the string should always be one of 'sinking the weight of the bow into the string', rather than one of 'pressing'; of sharing the job of tone production between all the fingers, the hand, and the arm, rather than giving it just to the first finger; and of more often using extra bow speed, rather than weight, to equalize the lower (heavier) and the upper (lighter) parts of the bow.

Over-using the first finger to press the bow into the string can cause tight, pressed tone production.[1] This is less likely to occur in the lower half, but when playing f in the upper half it is sometimes helpful to practise passages without the first finger on the bow.

- Position the fingers on the bow so that the second finger is able to exert a little leverage (very slightly to the left of the thumb rather than opposite it). See Fig. 26a.
- Notice how you can produce a good tone without needing the first finger at all.
- Then play the same passage with the first finger sitting lightly on the bow. You will find that much of the feeling of playing without the first finger remains.

Fig. 26

(a) Tone production without the first finger

(b) Feel the weight balanced by the fourth finger

(c) 'Pull in' with the third finger, the 'tone finger' of the bow

204

Playing without the first finger: lifted strokes

During any lifted strokes – *spiccato*, *sautillé*, ricochet and so on – the bow makes an almost invisible see-saw movement, pivoting around the thumb.

The first finger must remain entirely loose and 'giving' at its base joint. If it is tight at the base joint it will restrict this natural see-sawing of the bow.

1 To make sure that the bow hand allows these tiny, natural movements to happen, practise a phrase of lifted strokes without the first finger on the bow (Fig. 26a). Feel how the bow has a natural 'swing' within the hand.

2 Then play the phrase with a normal bow hold, feeling the same almost invisible movements of the bow within the hand.

Examples

Mozart: Concerto no. 5 in A, K219, *mov. 1, b. 84*

Wieniawski: Concerto no. 2 in D minor, op. 22, *mov. 3, b. 39*

Mendelssohn: Concerto in E minor, op. 64, *mov. 1, b. 336*

Paganini: Concerto no. 1 in D, op. 6, *mov. 3, b. 2*

Balancing with the fourth finger

The fourth finger balances the weight of the bow whenever the bow is lifted from the string. Playing on the string, particularly in the lower half but also in the upper half, the fourth finger acts as a counterbalance to the first and second fingers, helping to avoid squashing the tone with too much downward pressure into the string.

Example 1   J. S. Bach: Partita no. 3 in E, BWV1006, *Gavotte en Rondeau, b. 6*

- Take the second and third fingers off the bow to highlight the feeling of balancing with the fourth finger (Fig. 26b). Make sure you have the tip, not the pad, of the fourth finger on the bow so that the finger naturally curves.[1]

- At each '+', where the bow is momentarily in the air, feel all the weight balanced by the fourth finger.

- Afterwards, playing with a normal bow hold, feel the same amount of weight going into the fourth finger.

Example 2   Wieniawski: Polonaise de Concert, op. 4, *b. 5*

- Play the first bar without the second or third fingers on the bow (Fig. 26b).

Pulling in with the third finger

In many strokes, particularly when a deep or firm tone is required, pull the third finger in against the side of the bow. This helps maintain a feeling of balance in the hand, and avoids over-pressing with the first finger. Sandor Vegh referred to the third finger as the 'tone finger of the bow'.

Notice the thumb, and the first and third fingers on either side of the thumb, opposing each other so that you very slightly squeeze the bow between them.[2]

In the lower half feel the *pad* of the third finger firmly contacting the frog of the bow. Near the point, the pad of the third finger may need to come off the bow, but the part of the third finger just below the crease of the nail joint maintains the same strong contact with the bow.[3]

- Practise phrases or passages without the second or fourth fingers on the bow (Fig. 26c). Feel the third finger pulling in firmly against the bow.

Examples   Kreutzer: 42 Etudes ou caprices, No. 36, *b. 1*

Tchaikovsky: Concerto in D, op. 35, *mov. 1, b. 23*

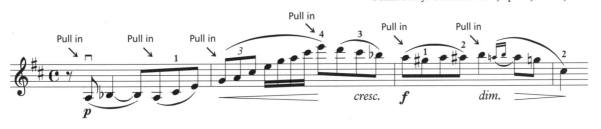

[1] If the tip of the fourth finger sits on the bow, the finger is more curved; if the pad sits on the bow, the finger is straighter.

The same applies to the right thumb. The ideal is for the thumb to bend outwards, so that it has flexibility and give (Fig. 42a, page 303). This is difficult to achieve if the pad of the thumb contacts the bow instead of the tip, since then the thumb automatically straightens.

The same applies also to the left hand: place the fourth finger more on the tip if it has a tendency to straighten as it stops the string.

206

[2] At times the bow is held firmly, at times quite loosely. 'Gripping' the bow is not in itself bad so long as it is not a fixed state, and is always followed by release when no longer required.

[3] See *Bow hold*, page 302

Releasing the right arm

207 Supporting the wrist in the upper half

Fig. 27

'Supporting the wrist' means to resist the natural slight downward curve of the wrist in the upper half. The movement of the hand is the same as the movement that produces the 'high wrist' shown in Fig. 31c, page 267. There are two reasons for supporting the wrist in the upper half:

1 To produce expressive, deep bow contact directly from the hand (the hand moving from the wrist), rather than from the upper arm.[1]

2 To channel power from the arm or hand directly into the string. If the right wrist collapses in the upper half, power may be lost because

(a) Natural slight downward curve

(b) Supporting the wrist to channel power into the string

the energy does not get as far as the bow – it 'leaks out' at the wrist. Then it is natural to 'try harder' because of the lost power, and the playing becomes full of effort.

At the point, a slight downward curve at the wrist (Fig. 27a) is often more natural than a straight line. However, by playing into the string with the hand – which has the effect of raising the wrist – it is possible to inject tone directly into the string without the need for weight from the upper arm.

- To practise producing expression from the hand, or to practise supporting the wrist when playing f in the upper half, play from the hand more than usual, i.e. go to the other extreme and raise the wrist slightly.

- Lever the bow into the string with the hand moving from the wrist.

Fig. 27b shows the wrist when it is 'supported' in the upper half, channelling the power directly into the string. The amount shown is slightly exaggerated for the purposes of the illustration: if you can see the wrist raised, it is probably too much.

[1] The more delicate the action in the bow arm, the closer to the hand or fingers the action originates; the bigger, the more powerful the action, the closer to the upper arm the action originates. The softest, most subtle changes of tone may require only a slight change of contact of the fingers on the bow; whereas playing heavy three-string chords may require a large and powerful movement of the upper arm. In between these two extremes, many bow strokes use some degree of 'playing into the string from the hand'. The same principle of 'the more subtle, the closer' applies equally to the left arm, e.g. shifting is 'led' by the fingertip, rather than originating higher up the arm, and the same applies to vibrato.

Examples

Wieniawski: Légende, op. 17, *b. 8*

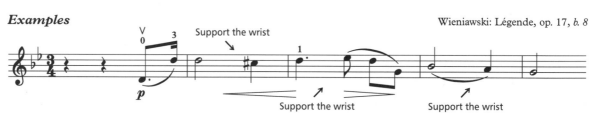

Beethoven: Sonata in D, op. 12 no. 1, *mov. 1, b. 32*

Brahms: Sonata no. 3 in D minor, op. 108, *mov. 3, b. 1*

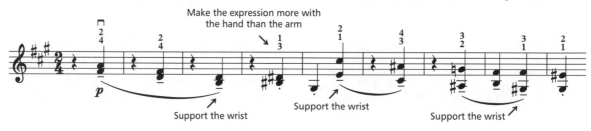

Bowing from the elbow

In the **lower half of the bow** you can gain great stability and control by feeling the elbow[1] *moving at the same speed* as the frog of the bow.[2]

In the **upper half**, many bow strokes appear to consist only of the forearm movement when in fact they are being powered from the upper arm. Sometimes the upper arm does remain 'quiet', while all the movement takes place only in the forearm; but just as often the forearm movement actually originates in the upper arm. The upper-arm movement in turn originates in the back.

Example 1   Wieniawski: Polonaise brillante, op. 21, *b. 150*

At the extreme heel (i.e. in the lowest three or four centimetres of the bow), there is no opening-and-closing movement of the forearm at the elbow. All the movement of the bow comes from the upper arm only (which is called the elbow movement here). Feel the elbow leading that upper-arm movement.

- Exaggerate the movement of the upper arm by playing these down-bows without any forearm movement at all.

  Before playing each stroke, note the angle formed at the elbow between the upper arm and the forearm. Do not alter this angle as you play the stroke. It does not matter if, for now, the bow goes slightly crooked to the bridge.

- Control the movement of the bow not from the hand and fingers but from the elbow, feeling it and the frog of the bow moving together as one unit.

- Repeat, adding all other forearm, hand and finger movements as required, but still feeling the elbow moving at the same speed as the frog.

Example 2   Bruch: Concerto no. 1 in G minor, op. 26, *mov. 3, b. 94*

Playing at the point-of-balance there is some opening and closing of the forearm, and near the middle of the bow there is much more. Nevertheless, in many passages you can still have a perception of the elbow and the frog moving together as one unit, and of directing the bow from the elbow, almost up to the middle of the bow.

- Playing at the point-of-balance, exaggerate the movement of the upper arm by playing without any forearm movement.

- 'Kick' each separate-bow note, powering the stroke from the elbow.

- Repeat, adding all the other forearm, hand and finger movements, but still feeling the elbow moving at the same speed as the frog.

Example 3   Mozart: Concerto no. 3 in G, K216, *mov. 1, b. 68*

These sixteenth-notes (semiquavers) are played off the string, or partly off, slightly below the middle of the bow.

- Exaggerate the movement of the upper arm by playing without any forearm movement. Play very slowly, moving the upper arm back on each down-bow, forwards on each up-bow.

Afterwards, playing normally, find the same feeling of bowing from the upper arm even if the amount the upper arm moves is invisible.

[1] Using the word 'elbow' is not strictly correct since it is the upper arm that moves the elbow, not the other way round. However, it is convenient shorthand for this aspect of bowing.

Similarly, 'wrist vibrato' is an inaccurate term which has largely been replaced by 'hand vibrato'. There may be a movement of the hand *at* the wrist, but the wrist itself cannot move.

[2] Feeling the elbow and the frog moving at the same speed does not apply if there is a lot of vertical upper arm movement in the lower half of the bow, i.e. gradually raising the elbow on the up-bow when approaching the heel, lowering the elbow just before or at the bow change.

This vertical movement of the elbow causes the elbow and the frog of the bow to move at different speeds from each other.

Raising the wrist above the level of the elbow as you approach the heel has the same effect as raising the elbow, i.e. it also interrupts the connection between the elbow and the frog.

Example 4   Kayser: Etudes, op. 20, No. 9, *b. 1*

[1] Sometimes the movement of the right upper arm in the upper half is the exact opposite: towards the end of the down-bow in the upper half the upper arm pushes *forward*, at the beginning of the up-bow the upper arm moves *back*. See also *Angle of the bow to the bridge*, page 76.

Galamian called these movements 'out' (down-bow) and 'in' (up-bow): '...as the bow-hand moves outward to the right, it must also push very gradually forward in approaching the tip of the stick in order to preserve the bow's parallel relationship with the bridge ...unless the upper arm purposely pushes forward, the lower arm will *naturally* describe a backward-moving arc as it opens up on the down-bow.'

Ivan Galamian: *Principles of Violin Playing and Teaching* (New Jersey, 1962), 53.

Playing in the upper half, as the forearm opens on the down-bow the elbow invisibly moves back, and on the up-bow the elbow moves forwards.[1] If you can see the upper arm moving it is probably too much; yet the difference between an invisible 'push' from the upper arm, and bowing only from the forearm, is striking. Powering the strokes from the upper arm in the upper half produces a feeling of exceptional freedom and effortless power.

● As in the lower half, a simple way to get the feel of the upper arm is to use no forearm whatsoever.

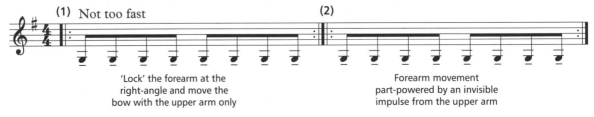

(1) 'Lock' the forearm at the right-angle and move the bow with the upper arm only

(2) Forearm movement part-powered by an invisible impulse from the upper arm

(1) Note the angle at the elbow when playing just above the middle of the bow: probably around 90°. Keep that angle the same – i.e. do not move the forearm, only the upper arm – as you play a few strokes down-bow and up. Naturally the bow will go crooked to the bridge on each stroke but this does not matter.

(2) Then reduce the backwards-and-forwards movement of the upper arm to an invisible amount and add to it the normal opening and closing of the forearm at the elbow.

Feel the slight, invisible motion of the upper arm sending an impulse up into the forearm, injecting extra power and momentum into the stroke.

 Levering into the string with the elbow

For extra power in the upper half, raise the right elbow slightly above the level of the hand (Fig. 28a). Feel the elbow levering weight directly into the hand and from there into the string.

The correct amount of raising the elbow is usually so slight as to be unnoticeable. If you can see it, it is probably too much; but without it there may be a feeling of unnecessary effort as you try to find the power by other means (e.g. over-pressing with the first finger on the bow).

Fig. 28

(a) **The elbow 'leaning' into the string**

(b) **The elbow is too low to exert leverage**

(c) **Exaggerating raising the elbow for practice**

● Fig. 28b shows a too-low elbow, lacking the power of leverage. To practise a specific phrase or passage, exaggerate raising the elbow as shown in Fig. 28c. Feel the arm leaning naturally into the string.

Example   Saint-Saëns: Concerto no. 3 in B minor, op. 61, *mov. 1, b. 5*

Spreading the fingers for leverage

The principles of leverage dictate that the further the first finger is placed from the thumb the less downward pressure is required.[1] The louder the playing = the further the first finger from the thumb = the most leverage.

Playing with the first finger too close to the thumb can cause the entire bow arm to lose power and gain effort. The tiniest adjustment of the position of the first finger, moving it further away from the thumb, gives a very large increase in power and ease.

- Playing powerful, accented or sustained passages, experiment with different positions of the first and second fingers, positioning them a little further up the bow than usual (Fig. 28b).

- Move the fingers slightly further away from the thumb, and slightly closer to the thumb, until finding the place that gives the greatest power with the least effort.

[1] Similarly, the handle of a door is usually placed on the opposite side of the door to the hinges. If the handle were to be positioned close to the hinges, much extra effort would be required to pull the door open.

See also *Adjusting the bow hold*, page 88; *Bow hold*, page 302

Example Brahms: Concerto in D, op. 77, *mov. 1, b. 495*

Fig. 29

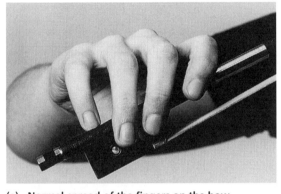

(a) **Normal spread of the fingers on the bow**

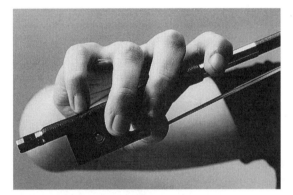

(b) **The fingers more spread for extra leverage**

Flat or tilted hair

Playing f with only half the hair (the wood of the bow tilted too much towards the fingerboard) takes double the effort for half the result. Even if you work hard to make up for it, the tone may remain thin, with the added danger of the wood of the bow scraping against the string.

Playing with full hair, or nearly full hair, produces a fatter tone as well as a feeling of effortless power.

When the bow is too tilted in the upper half there is the added problem of the fingertips losing contact with the bow.

- Play a phrase or passage several times, each time experimenting with a different tilt of the bow.[2] Find the tilt which gives the maximum power for the minimum effort. Feel the fingers firmly contacting the bow.

[2] 'Quarter', 'half' and 'three-quarters' are loose terms since more hair than that may contact the string, depending on how strongly you play; but because of the tilt of the bow the weight is not spread evenly across the whole width of the hair. 'Full hair' means that the wood of the bow is directly above the hair.

Example Schumann: Sonata in A minor, op. 105, *mov. 3, b. 62*

- Begin on one note:

- Then do the same using the notes in the passage:

Active and passive strokes

In these examples feel how each pair of notes, or group of three notes, feels as though it is played with one action, not two or three. Feel the first of each group as an *active* bow stroke, and the others as *passive* strokes, like a rebound. In other words, in a two-note pattern play:

Action–rebound, action–rebound, action–rebound

not

Action–action, action–action, action–action

Example 1   Bruch: Concerto no. 1 in G minor, op. 26, *mov. 3, b. 44*

- Use accents and rhythms to exaggerate the difference between active and passive:

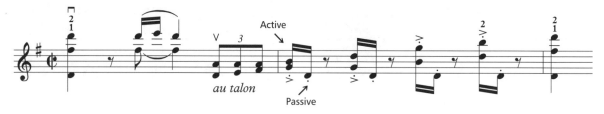

Example 2   Mozart: Concerto no. 3 in G, K216, *mov. 1, b. 90*

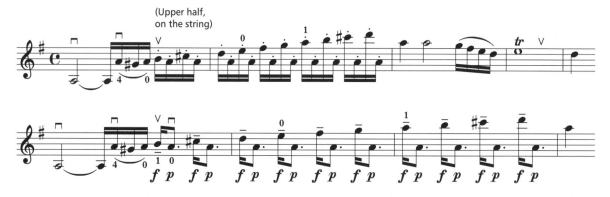

- Begin at a slow tempo, feeling the up-bows active and the down-bows passive, and gradually speed up to near performance tempo.

Example 3   Chausson: Poème, op. 25, *b. 121*

- Practise as in Example 2.

Example 4
Kayser: Etudes, op. 20, No. 3, *b. 1*

In this typical rhythm pattern, the eighth-notes (quavers) are active, the sixteenth-notes (semiquavers) are passive. The feeling of playing each group of three notes is very similar to the feeling of playing single down- and up-bows.

(1) Practise the stroke on one note using an accented *détaché*. Feel each stroke as a firm, individual action.

(2) Add the two sixteenth-notes without changing the feeling of playing the principal down- and up-bows. Play the sixteenth-notes *p* to exaggerate the feeling of rebound.

Example 5
Tchaikovsky: Concerto in D, op. 35, *mov. 3, b. 368*

- Practise the passage *pp*, with *f* accents, feeling the unaccented notes as passive strokes that 'play themselves':

Example 6
Mozart: Sonata in F, K377, *mov. 1, b. 1*

Triplet patterns are often the same as the long–short–short rhythm pattern in Example 4. The first note is active, the second and third notes passive.

(1) Practise only the first note of each group. Use an accented *détaché* as in Example 4.

(2) Add the passive second and third notes, playing a dotted pattern to exaggerate the feeling of active and passive.

213 Arm or hand leading string crossing

The upper arm does not always move at exactly the same time as the hand when crossing from one string level to another:

Crossing from a lower string to a higher string (G–E): the hand leads, the elbow follows.

Crossing from a higher string to a lower string (E–G): the elbow leads, the hand follows.

Even if they do move at exactly the same time, the impulse of the movement, i.e. the feeling of where the arm movement starts from, is different depending on whether you are moving up or down the strings (whether it is a down- or an up-bow makes no difference). The following passage shows the order of the movements:

J. S. Bach: Sonata no. 1 in G minor, BWV1001, *Adagio, b. 6*

The right amount of these movements, even in the widest string crossings, may be so small as to be almost invisible. Yet without them there may be a feeling of awkwardness and lack of precision when the arm moves all in one piece, or if the opposite movements are made (leading with the elbow crossing lower to higher, leading with the hand crossing higher to lower).

● Practise the leading and following by dividing the arm movement into two, exaggerated steps:

Crossing from a lower string to a higher string

Having played the note on the lower string, stop the bow on the string (Fig. 30a).

(1) Move the bow to the higher string using only the hand (and forearm), leaving the elbow more or less on the lower-string level. Having arrived on the higher string, stop the bow on the string without playing the new note (Fig. 30b).

(2) Move the elbow to the higher-string level (Fig. 30c). Then play the new note.

Crossing from a higher string to a lower string

Having played the note on the higher string, stop the bow on the string (Fig. 30d).

(1) Keeping the bow on the higher string, move the elbow towards the lower-string level (Fig. 30e).

(2) Move the bow to the lower string (Fig. 30f). Then play the new note.

Fig. 30

(a) **Having played down-bow on the G string**

(b) **Elbow on G-string level, bow on E string**

(c) **Having moved elbow to E string**

(d) **Having played up-bow on E string**

(e) **Bow on E string, elbow on G-string level**

(f) **Having moved bow to G string**

Example 1

Schubert: Sonatina in A minor, op. 137 no. 2, *mov. 1, b. 15*

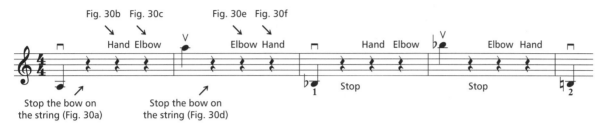

- Play in time at a slow tempo (♩ = 60):

  First bar

  Beat 1 – Play the down-bow A with the whole arm on the G-string level.

  Beat 2 – Stop the bow on the string (Fig. 30a).

  Beat 3 – Move the bow to the E string with the hand only, keeping the elbow on the G-string level (Fig. 30b).

  Beat 4 – Move the elbow to the E-string level (Fig. 30c).

  Second bar

  Beat 1 – Play the up-bow A with the whole arm on the E-string level.

  Beat 2 – Stop the bow on the string (Fig. 30d).

  Beat 3 – Move the elbow to the G-string level, keeping the bow on the E string (Fig. 30e).

  Beat 4 – Move the bow to the G string (Fig. 30f).

- First, playing at a very slow tempo, stop between each movement.

- Then gradually increase the tempo. As you do so, the separate movements begin to blend into each other until they finally become continuous.

Example 2

Viotti: Concerto no. 22 in A minor, *mov. 1, bar 132*

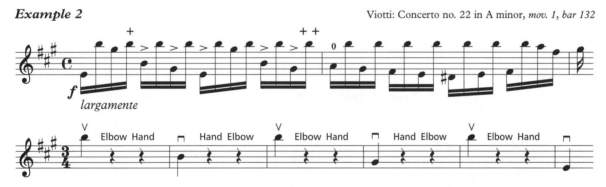

- Practise as in Example 1, in the rhythm play–move–move, play–move–move.

Example 3

Vivaldi: Autumn (The Four Seasons), op. 8 no. 3, *mov. 1, b. 75*

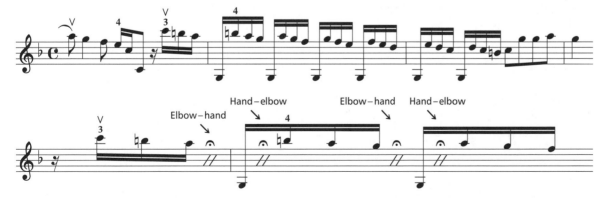

- During the pauses, stop the bow on the string and move the elbow and hand separately.

(214) Returning for the next stroke as part of the last

In a rapid series of down-bows, each stroke needs to finish up where it started. After each stroke the bow continues in a circular movement, in the air, back to the heel.

Example 1   De Falla (arr. Kreisler): Danse espagnole, *b. 118*

- Having played the E at the beginning of the example, return as part of the same motion, in the air, to the heel; place the bow on the string (shown as an x-note) ready for the next stroke.

  In other words, the stroke is *circular*, the lower line of the circle playing the down-bow E, the bow stroke curving up to lift the bow from the string, and the upper line of the circle being the journey in the air back to a lower place in the bow.

- Practise by making a point of putting the bow back on the string as part of the previous stroke. Begin slowly, and gradually speed up, playing and placing the bow on the string strictly in time:

Example 2   Pugnani-Kreisler: Praeludium and Allegro, *Allegro, b. 84*

Play the first chord and in the same motion return in the air to the starting place. Wait.

Play the next chord and return, and so on. (Play-return – wait – play-return – wait.)

Instead of:

Play the first chord. Wait at the end of the down-bow with the bow on the string (or just above it).

Return in the air to the starting place and play the next chord. (Play – wait – return-and-play – wait.)

- Do not play the x-notes: they represent positioning the bow *above* the string at the heel.

- Perform the actions exactly in the rhythm shown: be ready, above the string near the heel, for the second chord at the beginning of the second sixteenth-note (semiquaver) beat.

- Start slowly, and gradually speed up to performance tempo.

Example 3   Brahms: Sonata no. 3 in D minor, op. 108, *mov. 1, b. 162*

- At the places marked '+', position the bow (just above the string) lower down in the bow than where the last stroke ended.

- Exaggerate the coming-back by returning faster:

Example 4   Bruch: Concerto no. 1 in G minor, op. 26, *mov. 3, b. 32*

- Begin both down-bows at the same place near the heel.

- Play the first of each pair with a long stroke, f; return to the heel in the same motion, moving in a curve.

- Play the second of each pair with a very short stroke, p.

Forearm rotation

Forearm rotation is the same movement as turning a key. Although the upper arm is the main part of the arm used to cross from one string to another, a small amount of forearm rotation replaces a large amount of vertical upper-arm movement. String crossing is then a much smaller operation than when using the upper arm alone. Forearm rotation is also a part of beginning and ending strokes, of lifted strokes like *spiccato*,[1] and even of playing just one note on one string from heel to point.

[1] See also *Forearm rotation*, page 95

Repeating the movement

- To avoid moments of over-working caused by using more upper arm than necessary, build forearm rotation into a phrase by repeating the movement on its own many times.

- Exaggerate the forearm rotation by using almost no upper-arm movement.

Example 1   Mozart: Concerto no. 2 in D, K211, *mov. 1, b. 26*

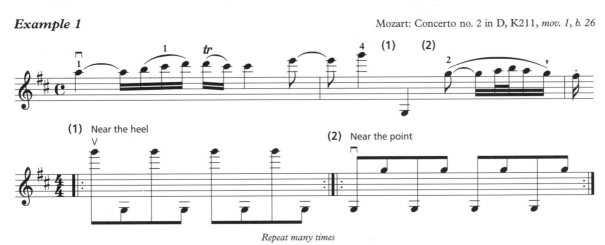

- For practice purposes, to maximise the forearm rotation play the upper G on the outer edge of the hair (the edge nearest the fingerboard), and the lower G on the inner edge of the hair.

Example 2   J. S. Bach: Partita no. 1 in B minor, BWV1002, *Allemanda, b. 1*

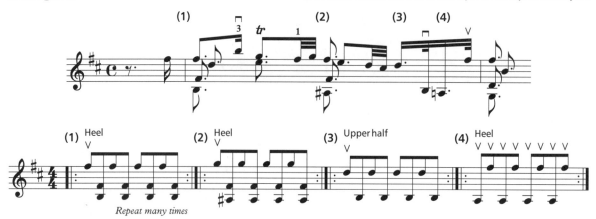

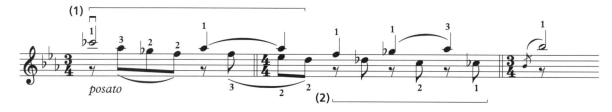

Repeat many times

Example 3   Chausson: Poème, op. 25, *b. 69*

posato

- Practise on open strings, using only the forearm to change from the E string to the E–A double stops:

216 Hand movements in forearm rotation

Forearm rotation is often used not on its own, but in conjunction with hand movements. The hand moves up and down from the wrist. When the hand moves down, the wrist is 'high' (Fig. 31c). When the hand moves up, the wrist is 'low' (Fig. 31b). Hand movements may be obvious, or so slight as to be almost invisible.

Crossing to a higher string: higher wrist, and clockwise forearm rotation

Crossing to a lower string: lower wrist, and anticlockwise forearm rotation

- To build these forearm-and-hand movements into a passage, exaggerate them by using almost no upper-arm movement to cross strings.

Example 1   J. S. Bach: Partita no. 3 in E, BWV1006, *Preludio, b. 38*

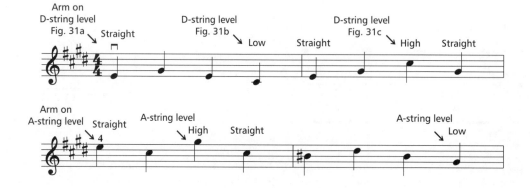

'High', 'low' and 'straight' refer to the wrist as described above and shown in Fig. 31.

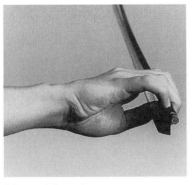 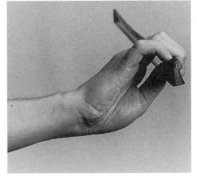 

(a) **Straight wrist** (b) **Low wrist** (c) **High wrist**

Example 2 Kreutzer: 42 Etudes ou caprices, No. 14, *b. 1*

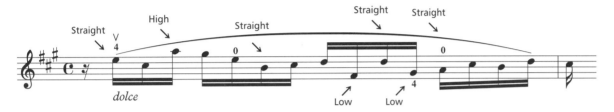

Proportions of forearm and upper arm

217

How much hand and forearm movement there is in crossing strings, in proportion to how much upper-arm movement, depends on the passage. The more weight and attack, the more the whole arm moves in one piece, with every movement powered from the upper arm; the less weight and attack, the more movement there is in the hand and forearm.

To find the best proportions of upper-arm movement to hand/forearm movement, play a phrase or passage using only the upper arm; then play it without using the upper arm at all; then combine the movements.

1 Change string using only the upper arm. Without actually locking the arm tight, do not allow much or any movement in the forearm or hand.

2 Then change string using no upper arm whatsoever. Use only forearm rotation, and any other forearm or hand movements you need.

3 Then find the right combination of upper and lower arm to produce the most comfortable and least effortful bow stroke.

Examples Rode: 24 Caprices, No. 2, *b. 1*

Beethoven: Sonata in F, op. 24 ('Spring'), *mov. 1, b. 11*

Sarasate: Carmen Fantasy, op. 25, *Introduction, b. 77*

218 Beginning and ending notes

Forearm rotation is an essential part of putting the bow on the string and of taking it off. It produces rounded, natural gestures that add greater stature and musicianship to the whole performance. Lack of forearm rotation can be a direct cause of stiffness and lack of ease.

- Practising by exaggeration, make the path of the bow larger-than-life as it approaches or leaves the string. Afterwards, a much smaller amount will feel completely natural.

Example 1   Brahms: Sonata no. 3 in D minor, op. 108, *mov. 1, b. 151*

For a clean beginning to each f down-bow, the path of the bow needs to curve into the string like a plane approaching a runway.

In a forceful attack on the E string the bow can start (in the air) almost on the level of an imaginary 'B string'. As the arm brings the bow down towards the string the forearm rotates anticlockwise a little. (The more gentle the attack the less forearm rotation.)

The same angle is needed to attack the string up-bow, from the air, at the point. If the contact with the string comes at too vertical an angle, the bow bounces on impact.

Example 2   Ravel: Tzigane, *b. 1*

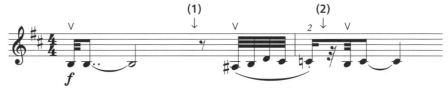

If there is no rotation as it leaves the string, the bow arm can feel tight and off-balance. Exaggerate the rotation movements:

(1) At the end of the B, the bow leaves the string partly with the same arm movement that had been playing the note, partly with clockwise forearm rotation.

(2) At the end of the C, the bow again leaves the string partly with a continuation of the arm movement, partly with clockwise forearm rotation.

219 Rapid string-crossing passages: leaning the elbow against the wall

Fig. 32

Passages of continual, rapid string crossings are often best played with little upper-arm movement. You then use much more forearm movement, even though you still power and direct the strokes from the upper arm.

- To get the feeling of using only the forearm and hand, with no upper-arm movement whatsoever, practise the passage with the elbow resting against the wall (Fig. 32).

- Afterwards, keeping the same movement in the forearm and hand, add a small amount of upper-arm movement to the forearm stroke.

- Despite using only a small upper-arm movement, continue to power the strokes from the upper arm.

Resting elbow against wall

Example   J. S. Bach: Concerto no. 2 in E, BWV1042, *mov. 1, b. 57*

Forearm rotation on one string

There is a small amount of forearm rotation during the journey from heel to point even when the bow is playing on one string only. Playing on the A string at the heel, the forearm is more parallel with the floor (more or less, depending on the tilt of the violin). At the point, it is more at an angle to the floor, in some cases as much as 45°.

(There must not be too much forearm rotation when moving towards the point, or the wrist is forced into an awkward shape.[1])

- Practise strokes very slowly, feeling the turning of the forearm as the bow travels up or down the string.

Example 1   Viotti: Concerto no. 22 in A minor, *mov. 1, b. 102*

- Practising by exaggeration, begin the down-bow with the hand more upright on the bow than usual. (This is called supination, the opposite of pronation.) Feel the weight of the bow balanced by the fourth finger (Fig. 33a). Note the angle of the forearm to the floor.

- During the down-bow feel the forearm turning anticlockwise, arriving at the position shown in Fig. 33b. Note the new angle of the forearm to the floor.

- Returning on the up-bow to the heel, feel the forearm turning clockwise until, by the end of the D, you arrive back at the position shown in Fig. 33a.

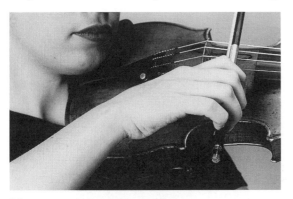

(a) Exaggerated starting position for practice

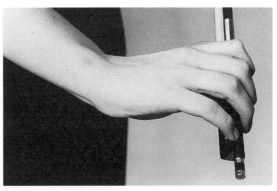

(b) Note the different angle of the wrist to the floor

Fig. 33

Example 2   Kreutzer: 42 Etudes ou caprices, *No. 28, b. 1*

Watch the point of the bow while playing the first two notes: it does not move in a straight line. During the up-bow the forearm rotates clockwise very slightly, so the bow is a fraction more vertical at the start of the down-bow than at the start of the up-bow.[2]

The actual difference in the angle of the bow may be so slight as to be barely visible; but without it tension may arise in the hand and arm.

- To build it into the playing, enlarge the movement as follows:

- Use forearm rotation to move from the double stop to the E string.
- Join the two B's without any gap in the sound.

[1] A key issue which affects forearm rotation is whether or not the fourth finger should stay in contact with the bow at the point.

One advantage of not allowing it to come off the bow is that even in the upper half, the fourth finger can continue to counterbalance the weight of the first finger.

You have to let it come off the bow in the upper half if your arm is too short to allow you to reach the end of the bow comfortably with the fourth finger staying in place.

[2] This is similar to the movement of the point of the bow during staccato. See *Curved bow strokes*, page 92.

221

Localizing actions

One of the keys to technical mastery lies not only in knowing what to do, but equally in knowing what *not* to do, or what to *stop* doing. 'Localizing' actions means that you do as little as possible to play each note, the absolute minimum that is required to perform the specific left- or right-hand action, and nothing else. The action takes place in one locality, without all sorts of unnecessary simultaneous actions happening elsewhere.[1]

Of course, eliminating unnecessary movement does not mean standing or sitting stiffly, blocking the sympathetic movements that happen naturally throughout all playing. The bow arm in particular sends a flow of movement down the back and legs and into the feet that is an essential element of playing.

To play the first three notes of the Tartini Sonata shown below, all that needs to happen in the left hand is that the second finger lowers onto the string from the base joint. It then lifts again from the base joint. The shape of the finger stays basically the same before, during and after playing the note.

Tartini: Sonata in G minor ('Dido abandonata'), *mov. 1, b. 1*

Nothing else needs to happen while the second finger drops onto the string and rises again:

All four fingers should remain relaxed, particularly at the base joints.

They should not squeeze together sideways.

The first finger should not press harder into the string.

The thumb should remain relaxed, not pressing harder or squeezing back.

The wrist should move neither in nor out.

The upper arm should move neither to the left nor to the right.

The head and shoulders should not clamp the violin tighter.

The left hand/arm should not move the scroll of the violin.

The face, tongue, lower jaw and throat should remain relaxed, completely unaffected by the second-finger action.

The muscles in the back or front of the body should not contract, causing the spine to bend forwards or backwards, to the left or to the right.

It is especially important not to 'pull down' (i.e. the chest is brought down and the scroll of the violin visibly lowers). Lengthen the back when playing the fourth-finger G (marked '+' in the Tartini Sonata above). Rather than pulling down, raise the scroll an invisible amount to get a feeling of the string coming to meet the bow hair.

Pulling down often happens during string crossings. In the Tartini, the fourth-finger C (marked '++') is a typical example: it is common to see players bend forwards slightly as the fourth finger reaches over and the bow arm makes the string crossing. Instead, great stature and control instantly comes into the playing when only the finger moves, as described above; and when the movement of the right arm is independent of the shoulder and back.

Pulling down is also common in 'big' actions like a long shift or powerful accent:

Beethoven: Sonata in D, op. 12 no. 1, *mov. 3, b. 10*

At each *sf* in the above example there may be a tendency to pull down: instead, lengthen the back, and watch the scroll to see that it does not move down.

● Playing at a slow tempo – or examining your playing of just one note at a time – be acutely aware of the physical movements you are making. Stop any movement that is not directly related to whatever note you are playing or action you are performing.

● It may be revealing if you practise phrases, passages or whole movements with the scroll of the violin resting against the wall to fix it in one place. (Make sure the strings are level with the floor.[2])

When all actions are performed in this way, the greatest economy of movement and energy comes into the playing.

[1] Suppose you habitually tense the left upper arm every time you use your fourth finger. It is as though there were two 'wires' in the brain running parallel to each other and very close together. One wire carries the command to place the fourth finger; the other wire carries the command to contract the muscles in the left upper arm. The two wires have somehow got fused together so that the command to place the fourth finger also commands the upper arm to pull in to the side. The wires must be pulled apart to repair the 'short circuit'.

Very often the extra movements are related to musical expression. It is crucial that these movements do not take the place of expression in the actual sound. For example, shifting the balance of your body at an expressive moment is fine so long as you do not *only* shift your balance, meanwhile doing nothing with the bow or vibrato to make the expression.

Most damaging of all is when the extraneous movements not only take the place of musical expression, but also get in the way of good playing, with the result that sound or intonation suffers. For example, 'expressive' tension in the left upper arm can easily disturb intonation, shifting or vibrato.

[2] See *Angle of strings to the floor*, page 57

Back and neck

Playing without the chin on the chin rest

Habitually pressing the chin down hard into the chin rest can lead to severe, all-over tension, spreading down from the neck and shoulders into the arms and back. Except for isolated moments, for example during certain descending shifts, the weight of the head resting into the chin rest is normally enough to hold the violin in place.

- Play a passage without the chin on the chin rest. Phrases or short passages that stay in one position, or which have ascending shifts only, can easily be played while holding the violin as shown in Fig. 34.

- Learn how to play the phrase without any reaction whatsoever in your head, neck and shoulders.

- Then play the phrase with the violin in its normal position, resting the weight of the head lightly into the chin rest. Keep the same feeling of release as you had before.

Placing the chin on the chin rest

Playing without the chin on the chin rest

Be continually on the lookout for any tightening in the neck and shoulders caused by clamping the violin between the chin and the shoulder, or excessive pressing into the chin rest. Every time you raise the violin into playing position, re-establish the best balance of the head and neck with the following four-step sequence:

1 Place the violin on the collar-bone/shoulder without yet dropping the head onto the chin rest.

2 'Lengthen' your neck: feel the back of the top of your head seeming to rise (Fig. 35a). Feel your back lengthening at the same time. Check that your left shoulder is not raised.

3 Rotate your head sideways until your chin is above the chin rest (Fig. 35b).

4 Drop the head, without pressing, on to the chin rest (Fig. 35c).

This produces exceptional benefits of ease and freedom. The way *not* to place the chin on the chin rest, which can easily produce immediate and on-going tension, is as follows:

1 Place the violin on the shoulder.

2 Rotate and drop the head at the same time, moving 'diagonally' into the chin rest (Fig. 35d).

Fig. 35

(a) 'Lengthening' the back and neck

(b) Having rotated the head

(c) Having dropped the chin on to the chin rest.

(d) Note the unnatural angle of the head and the obvious tension in the neck

224 **Counter-exercising**

Counter-exercising means to move in different directions from those you habitually move in – e.g. the left arm must rotate clockwise so that the fingers can reach the strings: counter-exercising means to rotate the arm anticlockwise.

The exercises featured here, though only a small sample of this huge field, are important ones which may become a part of everyday practice.

- Constantly widen between the shoulders, at the same time lengthening the neck (making sure that the head is *balanced* on top of the spine, not *held* in place), and lengthening the back, particularly between the shoulder blades.

Example 1

Fig. 36a shows the typical posture that violinists must avoid, and Fig. 36b the same posture with the violin removed. Note how the muscles across the top of the chest and shoulders have contracted to pull the shoulders closer in together; note how the muscles down the front of the body and around the stomach have contracted to make the back hunch forward. Note also the tension in the neck.

- At regular intervals counter-exercise by putting the violin onto the shoulder from the position shown in Fig. 36c. This is similar to the backmost position of the arms when yawning and stretching.

  Feel a releasing and widening across the shoulders. At the same time feel the spine lengthening as you bend backwards slightly. Do not try to squeeze the shoulder blades closer together.

- Slowly move from that position into playing position.

  As you do so, continue to widen across the shoulders and lengthen the back. Note the wider shoulders and more balanced, upright posture shown in Fig. 36d.

Fig. 36

(a) Pulling 'in' and 'down', twisting the back, raising the shoulders

(b) The same posture as (a) with the violin removed

(c) Starting from this position, widen the shoulders while reaching back, as though stretching

(d) Note the openness of the playing position

The crucial thing is for nothing ever to be 'fixed' in one position. Every physical action is most comfortable and efficient when starting from, passing through, and returning to, a state of balance. The posture shown in Fig. 36a would not in itself be harmful if it occurred only for a brief moment in the natural course of playing, followed immediately by release and a return to a state of balance. It is when you hold yourself 'fixed' for long periods in that or any other position that overall tension can develop.

Example 2

- Place both hands in the small of your back, palms facing the floor and the tips of the middle fingers touching (Fig. 37).

- Gently move both elbows back as far as you can without straining.

- While moving the elbows, keep the whole length of each little finger touching the back.

  Feel both shoulders releasing and widening. Do not try to squeeze the shoulder blades together as you pull the elbows back. Lengthen the back, and feel the space between the shoulder blades widening. At the same time feel the top of the chest lengthening and widening.

Example 3

- Hold both arms outstretched at a comfortable angle (Fig. 38a). Before beginning the exercise, lengthen the back, and widen across the top of the chest and at each shoulder. Lengthen the neck, feeling the head balanced on top of the spine rather than holding it in place.

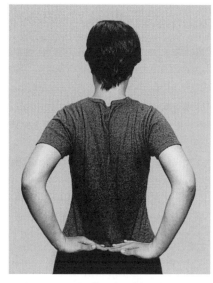

Fig. 37

Widening across the shoulders by bringing the elbows back

- Gently rotate the upper arms outwards (left arm anticlockwise, right arm clockwise) as far as you can go without straining (Fig. 38a); rotate in the opposite direction as far as you can go (Fig. 38b). It is essential that you do not move the shoulders with the arms as they rotate.

The ideal is to be able to do this exercise with the arms horizontal, the hands level with the shoulders, rotating freely in either direction until the palm of the hand faces the ceiling. Work up to this level gradually. Meanwhile the exercise is still very effective whatever the angle of the arms.

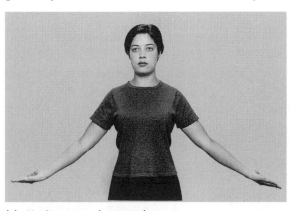

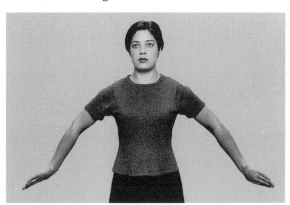

Fig. 38

(a) **Having rotated outwards**

(b) **Having rotated inwards**

Example 4

- To counter-exercise the muscles in the left upper arm – especially if you tend to pull the arm in too far to the right (Fig. 39a) – hold the violin backwards, with the scroll pointing over your left shoulder (Fig. 39b).

- Finger a phrase silently with the left hand, raising and dropping the fingers normally, and with a free vibrato. Relax all the muscles in the upper arm.

Then play the phrase with the violin in its normal position. You will feel a great ease throughout the entire left arm, hand and fingers.

Fig. 39

(a) **Pulling the upper arm in too far to the right**

(b) **Counter-exercising the left upper arm**

225 Hip joint

¹ Should you sit or stand
to practise?

It makes sense to practise
orchestral or chamber
music sitting down, and
solo pieces standing.

However, standing up to
practise orchestral or
chamber music can
encourage greater freedom
which then feeds through
into the performance when
you play sitting down.

Practising a solo piece sitting down may encourage
greater economy of effort
which then feeds through
into the performance when
you are standing up. It can
also be less tiring so that you
are able to practise for longer.

Many types of practice, e.g.
slow intonation work or
long sessions of accent or
rhythm practice, are just as
effective standing or sitting.

Playing sitting down, the line of the centre of balance extends from the top of the head all the way down to the 'sitting bones' (Fig. 40a).¹ The hip joint must neither press forwards (Fig. 40b) nor collapse back-wards (Fig. 40c).

Playing when standing, the hip joint must not collapse forwards (Fig. 40d). Make sure also that the knees do not lock backwards (locked knees go together with the hip joint collapsing forwards). Fig. 40e shows a good standing posture.

● From time to time stand for a few moments, in playing position, with your spine against an edge such as the corner of a cupboard, a jutting-out corner of a room, or the edge of an open door (Fig. 40f).

Position your feet far enough back that you can stand perfectly upright while contacting the edge. The spine is naturally curved, so only two small areas near the bottom and top of the spine will touch the edge, with a space between the two contact points large enough to slide a hand into. Touch the back of the head against the edge in such a way that your head is in a normal position.

● Rotate your hip joint backwards as if trying to contact the edge at a point slightly higher up the spine.

● Similarly, raise your chest as if trying to move the upper point of contact slightly higher up the spine.

Do not 'raise the chest' by trying to squeeze the shoulder blades closer together. Raise the chest by 'lengthening' the back. At the same time *widen* across the back at the shoulder blades.

Fig. 40

(a) **Good posture, upright hip joint** (b) **Hip joint pressing forwards** (c) **Hip joint collapsed backwards**

(d) **Hip joint collapsed forwards** (e) **Good posture, upright hip joint** (f) **Touch the edge of the door as high up the spine as possible at both contact points**

Further essentials

part 8

ABC practice

ABC practice is like making a patchwork quilt, where you join small squares together to make larger squares, which in turn are joined together to make even larger ones.

226

First decide what is 'A', 'B', 'C' and so on. Practising short phrases and passages, each letter might represent only one note at a time; or it may represent a group of notes, or a short phrase.

- First practise A on its own, B on its own, C, D and E.

- Then practise A followed by B, B followed by C, C followed by D, D followed by E.

- Then practise ABC, BCD and so on.

A – B – C – D – E
AB – BC – CD – DE
ABC – BCD – CDE
ABCD – BCDE
ABCDE

After you have done the beat-by-beat or phrase-by-phrase work, each letter can then represent a larger unit. One letter may stand for 4, then 8, then 16 bars; or half a page; or it may stand for the whole exposition of a sonata-form movement.

Example 1

Kayser: Etudes, op. 20, No. 13, *b. 1*

A_ _ _ B_ _ _ C_ _ _ A_ _ _ B_ _ _ C_ _ _ A_ _ _ B_ _ _ C_ _ _ A_ _ _ B_ _ _ C_ _ _

- In this example first give a letter to each beat group: A, B, C. Practise each group on its own, repeating until achieving the four basic factors of **pitch**, **sound**, **rhythm** and **ease**, i.e. every note is in tune, the tone is completely pure, the rhythm is even and precise, and the playing is easy and free of excess effort.

- Then play two groups together – AB, BC – and practise them in the same way. Then practise ABC together.

- Once you have practised ABC together, begin to work in larger units of whole bars, sewing them together in the same way.

Example 2

Schubert: Sonatina in A minor, op. 137 no. 2, *mov. 1, b. 31*

- The groups do not have to be of equal length. Here, you may not need to split 'C' into 'C' and 'D':

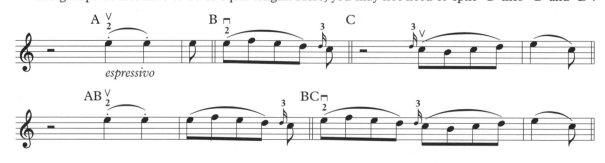

Example 3

Mozart: Concerto no. 5 in A, K219, *mov. 1, b. 213*

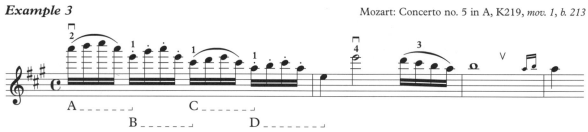

- Carrying on over to the first note of the next group helps build continuity:

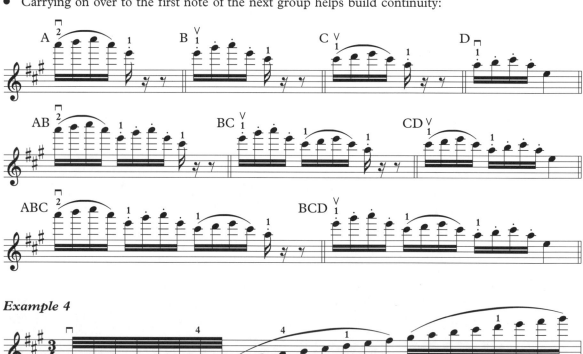

Example 4

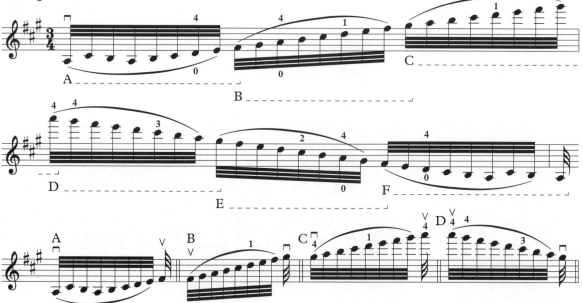

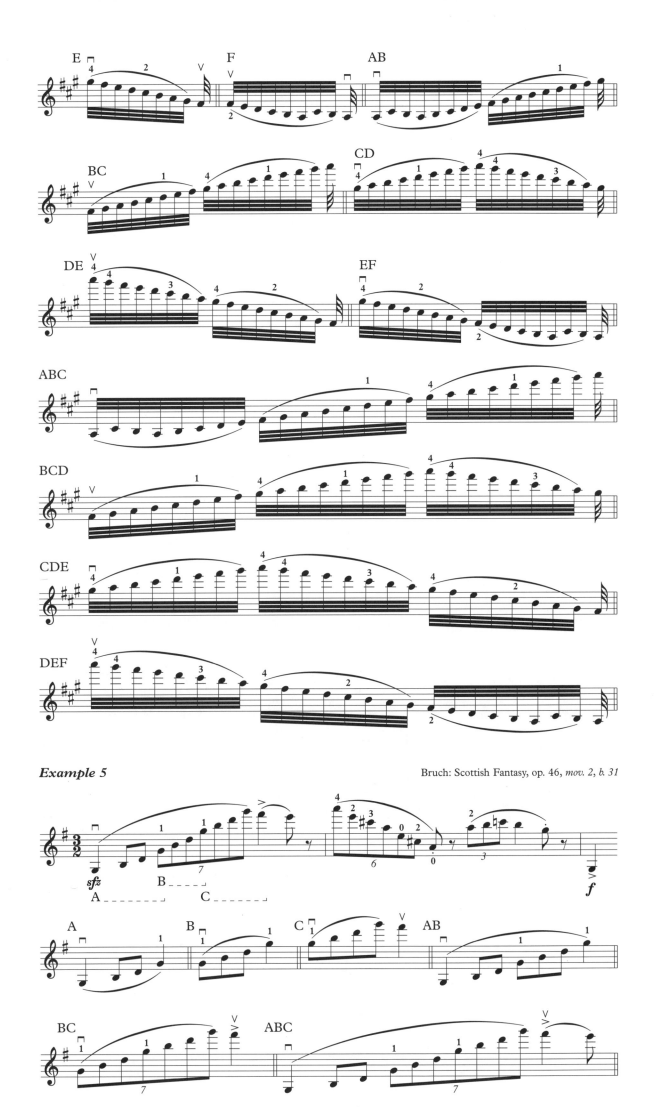

Example 5

Bruch: Scottish Fantasy, op. 46, *mov. 2, b. 31*

Example 6

Bruch: Concerto no. 1 in G minor, op. 26, *mov. 1, b. 89*

Example 7

Pugnani-Kreisler: Praeludium and Allegro, *Allegro, b. 25*

It is very helpful when it is possible to repeat groups continuously in a 'loop':

Repeat many times

● Repeat each group many times until it is fluent, working up to as fast a speed as possible.

Example 8

Vivaldi: Spring (The Four Seasons), op. 8 no. 1, *mov. 1, b. 51*

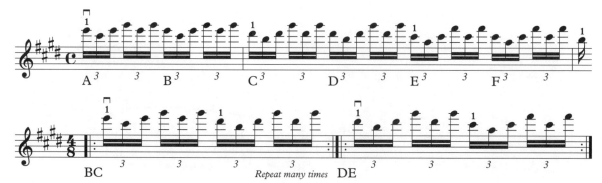

Repeat many times

● In this passage it would also be helpful to practise as follows:

Example 9

Dont: 24 Etudes and Caprices, op. 35, No. 4, *b. 1*

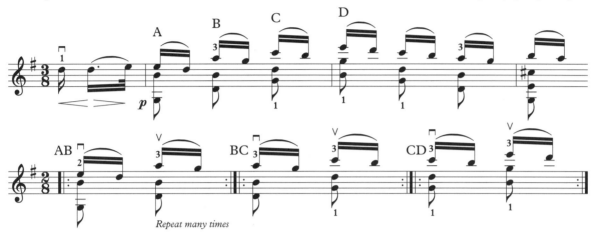

Repeat many times

Example 10

J. S. Bach: Partita no. 2 in D minor, BWV1004, *Ciaccona, b. 13*

The chord marked '+' can be divided into four stages:

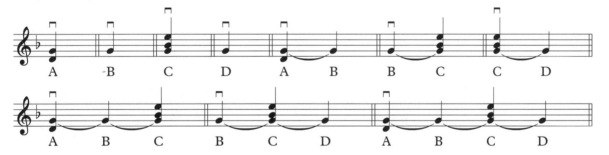

Note that the D string has been played without a break throughout the sequence.

Example 11

Paganini: 24 Caprices, op. 1, No. 9, *b. 17*

The groups could also be arranged like this:

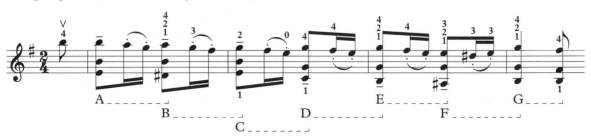

227 Repetition practice

Repeating something enough times is an important element of most practice methods. As a method of practice in its own right, repetition is one of the very best.

Muscle memory is quickly ingrained when you are focusing on a very small area, often more so than when spreading attention over a larger section or movement.[1]

- Repeat a note or phrase many times, up to tempo, so that both the left hand and the bow arm have time to learn the feel of the notes.

- Listen carefully so that with each repetition you get nearer and nearer to the goals of **pitch–sound–rhythm–ease**, i.e. every note in tune, every note expressively and tonally as desired, every note exactly and musically in time, and every note played without tension or effort.[2]

[1] There is really no such thing as 'muscle memory' (the technical term is 'motor memory'). Playing the violin is a matter of 'command–response', as described on page 36. Nevertheless, when we can play something easily it does feel as if our fingers know where to go on their own.

The four stages of learning are:
(1) unconscious incompetence;
(2) conscious incompetence;
(3) conscious competence;
(4) unconscious competence.

Reaching only stage 3 can lead to things unexpectedly going wrong in performance simply because when we are under pressure it can be difficult to think fast enough.

In sports training the term 'grooving' is used to describe the process of repetition where a new action is repeated again and again, like wearing a groove into a surface by constant rubbing, until it becomes an unconscious habit.

[2] Because repetition practice is so effective it can also be the most dangerous. You have to be very aware of what you want and what to avoid – and listen very carefully – to avoid strengthening mistakes.

It is said that the old adage 'Practice makes perfect' should really be: 'Only perfect practice makes perfect – bad practice makes worse'.

Example 1
Viotti: Concerto no. 23 in G, *mov. 1, b. 84*

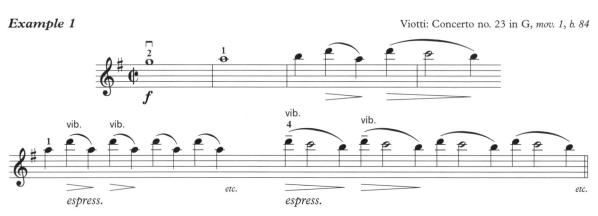

Example 2
Vivaldi: Concerto in G minor, op. 12, no. 1, *mov. 1, b. 161*

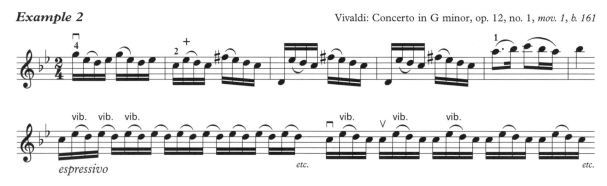

Example 3
Vaughan Williams: The Lark Ascending, *b. 79*

Example 4
Schubert: Sonatina in D, op. 137 no. 1, *mov. 1, b. 17*

Example 5 Mozart: Concerto no. 4 in D, K218, *mov. 1, b. 173*

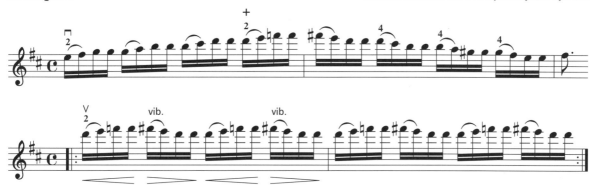

Example 6 Dont: 24 Etudes and Caprices, op. 35, *No. 13, b. 19*

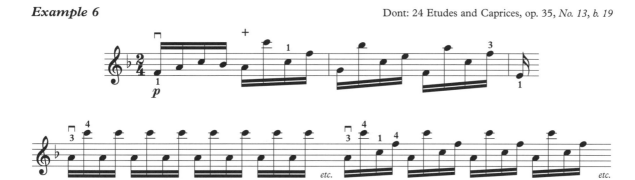

Example 7 Kreisler: Variations on a Theme of Corelli, *Theme, b. 1*

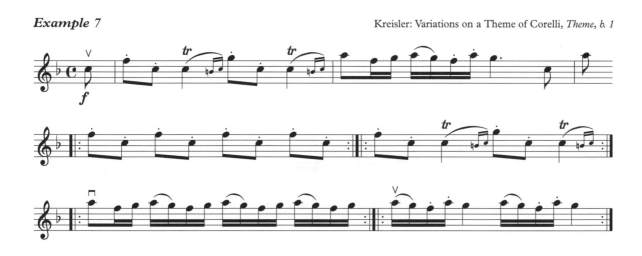

Example 8 Wieniawski: Légende, op. 17, *b. 25*

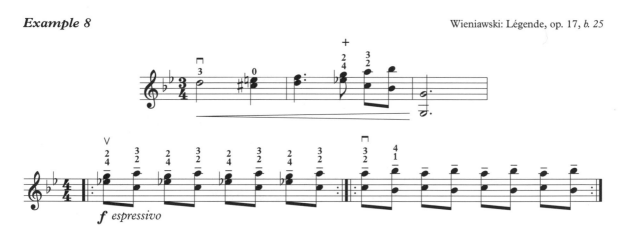

228 **Rhythm**   **Singing and tapping subdivided pulse while playing**

There is a difference between playing the right rhythms, and playing with *underlying rhythmic pulse*.

- Sing a regular pulse, or tap your foot, or sing and tap at the same time, while playing a phrase or a passage.[1]

Practising only a few passages in this way greatly improves rhythmic pulse in general as well as in the passages themselves.

[1] Walking on the spot while playing the violin (for example a waltz step when there are three beats in a bar) involves the whole body. Doing this from time to time, for a few moments, can help children find the rhythmic basis of the music, and can also help them to free up physically.

Example 1   Handel: Sonata in D, op. 1 no. 13, *mov. 1, b. 1*

Example 2   Prokofiev: Sonata in D, op. 94 bis, *mov. 4, b. 1*

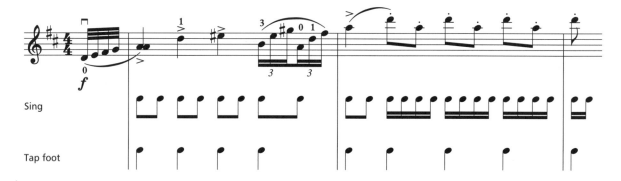

Example 3   Mozart: Concerto no. 5 in A, K219, *mov. 3, b. 1*

229 **Subdividing**

Subdividing is one of the keys to playing rhythmically. It ensures that full value is given to every note, and helps to maintain musical direction and flow. All notes, except those that are very fast, are subdivided in the player's mind.

Example 1   Beethoven: Romanze in F, op. 50, *b. 58*

- First 'pulse' the subdivisions with the bow:

- Afterwards, play without pulsing, but hear and feel the pulses in your mind.

Example 2 Brahms: Sonata in G, op. 78, *mov. 1, b. 11*

Example 3 Franck: Sonata in A, *mov. 1, b. 28*

- Subdividing is essential for feeling the logic of a ritardando, like a revolving wheel gradually slowing to a stop:

Example 4 Mozart: Sonata in B♭, K454, *mov. 1 (Largo), b. 3*

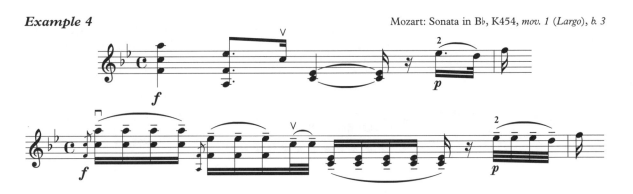

Example 5 Mozart: Concerto no. 4 in D, K218, *mov. 1, b. 86*

- Feel the second of each pair of tied notes as an up-beat to the next pair:[1]

[1] Raphael Bronstein, a pupil of Leopold Auer, called these subdivisions 'psychological up-beats': 'In a sustained melody where a feeling of intensity and of moving forward is needed, the mind supplies an up-beat before each note change and bow change. This gives a feeling of conducting your own performance.' Raphael Bronstein: *The Science of Violin Playing* (New Jersey, 1977), 34.

Example 6   Beethoven: Sonata in A, op. 30 no. 1, *mov. 3*, var. 1, *b. 1*

Even quite fast notes can be subdivided in the player's mind to ensure that they are given full musical and rhythmic value.

● Practise subdividing fast notes a little under tempo.

Example 7   Mendelssohn: Concerto in E minor, op. 64, *mov. 1*, *b. 420*

● Play subdivisions to lock them firmly into your feeling for the phrase:

230   Bow accents to mark rhythmic groups

Although a run should end up sounding even, in the player's mind it needs to be subdivided into groups with rhythmic aiming-points.

● Establish aiming-points by playing an accent. Afterwards, with the accent removed, the run will retain structure and control.

Examples   Vivaldi: Summer (The Four Seasons), op. 8 no. 2, *mov. 3, b. 10*

Rode: Concerto no. 7 in A minor, op. 9, *mov. 1, b. 152*

Bériot: Concerto no. 9 in A minor, op. 104, *mov. 1, b. 38*

Granados (arr. Kreisler): *Danse espagnole, b. 55*

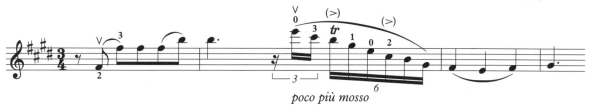

poco più mosso

Bruch: Concerto no. 1 in G minor, op. 26, *mov. 1, b. 18*

Finger accents as rhythmic aiming-points

231

- To strengthen exactness of rhythm, establish rhythmic aiming-points by using finger accents, lifting or dropping the fingers extra-fast. Afterwards, playing without the finger accents, the same rhythmic structure will remain.

Example 1   Mendelssohn: Concerto in E minor, op. 64, *mov. 3, b. 12*

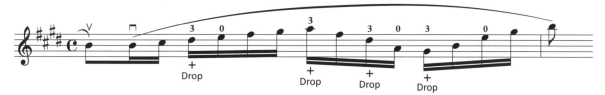

- For practice purposes, drop each third finger with a little extra speed and impact (marked '+'). The underlying rhythm created by these finger accents is:

- Play the passage without the bow, 'tapping' the notes out with the fingers. Feel the rhythmic aiming-points.

Example 2   Bruch: Concerto no. 1 in G minor, op. 26, *mov. 1, b. 88*

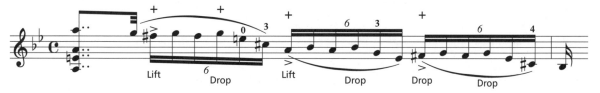

- Lift and drop the fingers marked '+' with extra speed and suddenness. The '+' notes give the following rhythmic structure to the phrase:

Example 3   Beethoven: Sonata in E♭, op. 12 no. 3, *mov. 1, b. 8*

cresc.

- Drop the fourth finger (marked '+') with extra speed and impact. Afterwards, without the finger accent, the rhythmic stability will remain.

Example 4   Mozart: Concerto no. 3 in G, K216, *mov. 1 cadenza (Sam Franko)*

Drop the second fingers (marked '+') with extra speed and impact.

Example 5   Vivaldi: Autumn (The Four Seasons), op. 8 no. 3, *mov. 3, b. 86*

- To maintain rhythmic stability, play the two third-finger notes marked '+' by lifting the preceding fourth finger very fast, at the last possible moment:

Lifting off at the last possible moment

232

[1] See also Examples 11, 12, page 31

Rhythm is all too easily disturbed by fingers lifting off fractionally too early.[1]

The timing of lifting fingers is different from that of dropping fingers. The finger begins to drop *before* the new note is to sound and lifts *when* it is to sound. For perfect accuracy of rhythm, the feeling of raising fingers should be one of lifting off *at the last possible moment*, at the precise instant that you want the new note to sound.

- Practising by exaggeration, play the lift-off fingers extra-long and then lift off extra-fast.

Example 1   Schubert: Sonatina in A minor, op. 137 no. 2, *mov. 4, b. 1*

At the bar marked '+' the finger action must be very disciplined to avoid any hint of the following:

[2] See *Placing fingers gently*, page 240

- When you raise a finger, the new finger must be ready on the string before the lift-off.[2] Lift off late and fast:

Example 2   J. S. Bach: Sonata no. 1 in G minor, BWV1001, *Presto, b. 75*

Lift off late and fast

Avoid   3   Practise

Example 3   Mozart: Concerto no. 5 in A, K219, *mov. 1, b. 137*

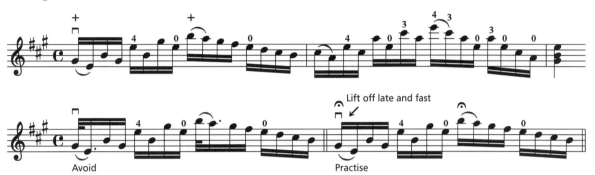

Lift off late and fast

Avoid   Practise

Dotted patterns

233

In dotted patterns the short note usually belongs to the following note, not to the previous one.[1]

The dotted pattern must not come out sounding like a triplet:

[1] See also *Timing the rhythm of the turn*, page 126

Correct   Incorrect

Example 1   Schubert: Sonatina in G minor, op. 137 no. 3, *mov. 1, b. 1*

- Exaggerate by pausing slightly before each sixteenth-note (semiquaver). Then feel the connection between the sixteenth-note and the following note.

Example 2   Brahms: Sonata no. 2 in A major, op. 100, *mov. 2, b. 8*

- Pause slightly on each dotted sixteenth-note and then play the 64th-notes a little faster (marked '→'), feeling them connected to the following sixteenth-note:

234 Sound + silence = note value

When a note is played shorter than its full written value, e.g. when there is a dot marked above it, the silence that follows must be given its full value. Care must be taken not to shorten the space between the notes, leading to a feeling of hurry or instability.

- Exaggerate by very slightly lengthening the silence between the notes.

Example 1   J. S. Bach: Concerto no. 2 in E, BWV1042, *mov. 1, b. 1*

Example 2   Mozart: Concerto no. 3 in G, K216, *mov. 1, b. 86*

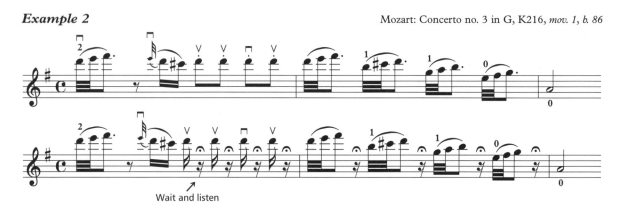

Example 3   Brahms: Sonata no. 2 in A, op. 100, *mov. 2, b. 56*

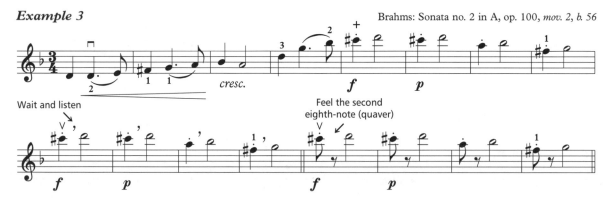

235 Playing the rest

In off-the-beat passages like the following, it is important not to play late after the rest.

Example 1   Mozart: Concerto no. 4 in D, K218, *mov. 1, b. 70*

- Play an extra note in the rest to check that you are not extending it and coming in fractionally late.

Example 2   Beethoven: Concerto in D, op. 61, *mov. 1, b. 176*

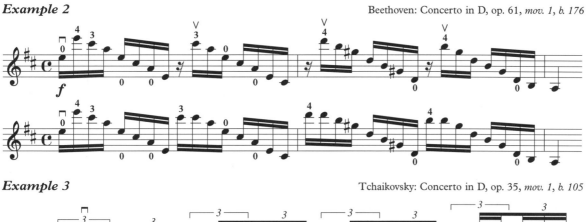

Example 3   Tchaikovsky: Concerto in D, op. 35, *mov. 1, b. 105*

- Another way to practise not coming in late after the rest is to play the rest shorter than written:

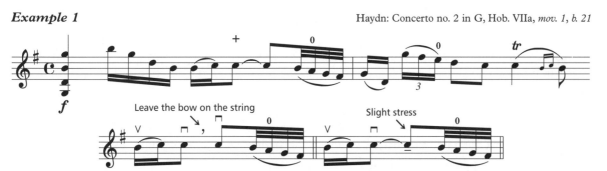

Playing the dot or tie

Playing a dot or tie first as a separate note on its own has been practised since at least the eighteenth century.[1]

- Establish the pulse and exact note length by playing a dot or tie as a separate note. Then tie the separate note back in, connecting it to the main note with a slight emphasis.

Example 1   Haydn: Concerto no. 2 in G, Hob. VIIa, *mov. 1, b. 21*

Example 2   Mozart: Adagio in E, K261, *b. 25*

Example 3   Kreisler: Sicilienne and Rigaudon, *Sicilienne, b. 1*

This rhythm may be played with a slight lilt, so that the sixteenth-note (semiquaver) is played a little later and shorter. However, it is still useful to practise first as follows:

236

[1] '...the dot is at first to be made noticeable by an after-pressure of the bow, in order to play strictly in time. When, however, one has established oneself firmly in the time, the dot must be joined on to the note...'

Leopold Mozart: *A Treatise On The Fundamental Principles Of Violin Playing* (Augsburg, 1756; Eng. trans. Editha Knocker, Oxford, 1948), 41.

237 Mental rehearsal

Mental rehearsal – picturing the ideal outcome or result – is probably the single most powerful accelerated-learning technique there is. Mental rehearsal techniques have been employed in sport for decades. Coaches in international football, tennis, athletics or any other sport emphasize the importance of building the mental pictures just as much as any physical training. All the most successful performers in any field rehearse mentally, whether or not they do it knowingly and deliberately.

Mental rehearsal is the simplest and the most natural activity possible. All it means is that you go off into an ordinary daydream, the difference being that you actively choose the images that you hold in your mind and actively screen out images that you do not want to include.

Each session of mental rehearsal may last for a fraction of a second, or several seconds, or sometimes a few minutes. Even just the odd brief moment of really seeing the perfect result can be enough to make a vast difference. As the performance date approaches, top athletes or musicians may spend every possible moment building, sculpting, refining and polishing their mental picture of the perfect performance.

Mental rehearsal means to visualise exactly how you want to play the beginning, middle, and end of each note, phrase, passage, movement, and entire work, musically and technically, as clearly as if you were watching yourself on film. The pictures need to be in great detail and include the musical drama and expression, tonal colours, precise physical motions, general ease of playing and physical calmness, a calm mental and emotional state, and so on. Since there are no limits to what you can imagine, you are free to 'design' images of yourself playing in any way you like.

The following example of mental rehearsal is concerned with technique, but the same process of building pictures of the ideal result can be applied to every aspect of a performer's work.[1]

Bruch: Concerto no. 1 in G minor, op. 26. *mov. 1, b. 8*

Suppose that when you play the fourth-finger D (marked '+') five things happen: (1) the finger feels tense, (2) vibrato feels tense and tight, (3) the scroll of the violin shakes, disturbing the bow, (4) the bow arm feels awkward, (5) the stroke is uneven.

[1] Many performers find that building vivid images of themselves relaxed and calm during the concert ensures a performance undisturbed by nerves.

The key point is that it is not enough simply *not* to think about, say, the bow shaking, with an approach of 'I am worried that my bow may shake, so I will try not to think about it at all'. Rather than not thinking about it, the answer is to build clear pictures of the result that you *would* like – the bow arm easy, responsive and calm; every bow stroke completely smooth and even, the bow carried by its own momentum, and so on.

Without the instrument, picture yourself playing the up-bow D. Picture the fourth finger curved, relaxed, loose, light, contacting the string near the tip of the finger (see margin note 1 on page 255). The finger is vibrating freely, evenly and expressively; it is relaxed and beautifully in tune, making the note ring. The left thumb is loose and free, the muscle of the base joint of the thumb soft to the touch, providing 'shock absorbers' which prevent the vibrato from shaking the scroll. The bow is perfectly smooth and even, the bow arm free and effortless, the shoulders relaxed and uninvolved, all the energy directed powerfully into the string.

Use size and colour: visualize the results you want in large images, in three dimensions, in colour, including as much detail as possible. If this process is interrupted by images of what you do *not* want (e.g. the finger being tense), shrink them into tiny, flat, two-dimensional images, in black-and-white, and in blurred detail.

At first it may take some time to assemble the picture. You may need to return to it on several occasions, building more and more detail and clarity into it each time. The more times you run the picture through your mind, the easier and quicker the process becomes. Carry on until you can summon up the complete picture instantaneously. When you next come to play the note, you will find that it has improved dramatically, and often far more than it might have improved had you actually practised it.

Negative images must be completely eliminated by putting a positive picture in their place. Since you cannot think two thoughts at the same time, holding the image of what you want (e.g. the finger relaxed) automatically gets rid of the image of the undesired result (the finger tense). The same works in reverse: if you allow into your mind a picture of the undesired result (e.g. a picture of yourself being very nervous) it means that you cannot at that moment hold in your mind a picture of the desired result (a picture of yourself being very calm).

In mental rehearsal you tend to see in your mind's eye exactly the same strengths and weaknesses as exist in your actual playing. If everything feels fine as you play a particular phrase, when you picture yourself playing the phrase you will picture it that way too. You may even find your hand and fingers making almost invisible playing movements, although you are not even holding the instrument. This is because by picturing yourself playing you are directly accessing the very same 'computer program' that 'runs' your playing. By changing the pictures in the 'computer program', you change the actual, physical playing.

If you habitually play a wrong note, you will see yourself going for that wrong note when you imagine playing the phrase. Play through the phrase in your mind quite slowly, over and over again, hearing, feeling and seeing yourself playing the right note. When you next play the passage on the violin, it will feel strong and secure. Changing the pictures in our mind is all that we are doing when we are practising with the instrument anyway.[1]

Always work on the picture before you work on the note or phrase. If you think you cannot stop gripping the neck of the violin too hard with your left thumb, then 'picture it perfect': see yourself playing with a relaxed thumb. If you want a faster and more relaxed trill; or a stronger fourth finger; or a fatter but sweeter tone; or a more relaxed left upper arm – first you must run the images of these things clearly through your mind, and then keep coming back to them. These images directly affect your performance.[2]

Negative images often go back to first experiences of playing – the first time in your life you shift from one position to another, or play in a high position, or trill with the fourth finger, or begin to use vibrato, or play a run of fast staccato, and so on. If any difficulties are encountered in these first experiences, memories of tension, precariousness or unreliability inevitably become associated with that particular aspect of technique. Years later the same player may still be filling their mind with the same images of tension and difficulty every time they approach a passage of, say, double stops, and for that reason never be able to play them easily and confidently.

One way to achieve the picture is to imagine perfect playing in the future, and then to *do it now*. For example, you play a scale: it feels a little effortful, the left hand is not quite relaxed and the fingers are a little uneven; some of the shifts are inaccurate and bumpy, the tone weakens as you reach the top of the scale; and so on. Ask yourself this question: suppose over the next year you practised scales for at least an hour every day; and that you always practised them intelligently and musically; always listening well; practising slow, medium and fast; in rhythms and accents; speeding up with the metronome; and so on. In addition, during the year you play many pieces that contain scale-like passages, e.g. the Beethoven Concerto, so you are used to playing scales very musically and expressively. The question is: at the end of the year what would your scale playing be like?

Assemble a detailed, vivid, colourful, three-dimensional picture of yourself playing the scale one year from now, i.e. smooth, even, effortless; the hand and fingers relaxed and easy; every note in tune; a glowing, even tone that crescendos up to the top of the scale; the posture upright and confident. See a picture of yourself standing perfectly relaxed and calm, playing the scales easily and nonchalantly; see close-ups of your left hand moving effortlessly from position to position, the fingers so light that they are almost without sensation, and so on.

The point is that if you can see it, you can do it. Having visualized yourself playing a scale excellently, when you then play it the instantaneous improvement can be as great as if you had practised for hours, yet the whole process can take just a minute or two. The reason why this is so effective is that if you did practise scales for a year, most of what you would be doing in all that time is simply shaping, reshaping and clarifying over and over again your mental pictures of what to do and what not to do, of what works and what does not work. If you can arrive at the same mental pictures right now, you can expect the same result and literally save yourself years. It is like leaping ahead through the months, thought by thought.

It is important to note that answering the question with 'great' or 'brilliant' or 'much better' is no good at all if the words do not contain within them the detailed vision of the final result in all its perfection. Mental rehearsal depends entirely on knowledge. That is why it is not possible for an elementary player simply to visualize playing the Brahms Concerto and then be able to play it: an elementary player would not be able to visualize it in the first place. To say 'picture every note in tune' is not enough in itself unless the player has a vivid concept of the tuning and of the relationships of each note to others (as described in *Uniform intonation* pages 197–204, or according to whatever other organization or concept of tuning that the player has).

Continually add to the mental 'bank' from which your images come. Attend as many concerts as possible, hearing 'everybody who's anybody'; listen to recordings, if possible several different performances of the pieces you are studying; watch videos of great players and teachers; read about music, players and teachers; study technique books by great teachers such as Flesch and Galamian, violin in hand; work together with a teacher; attend and participate in masterclasses; discuss music and technique with friends and colleagues; study other activities and disciplines, like sport or yoga, to find principles which apply equally to playing the violin, and so on.

Two essential aspects of mental rehearsal are (1) assemble sufficient detail in the visualization, (2) repeat the process enough times for it to become easy, quick and automatic for you to summon up the picture. With practice at building such detailed images they can be called up instantaneously, and in the end become so habitual that you forget that you are holding them naturally, easily and unknowingly in your mind. The process of mental rehearsal, applied to any activity or field, has been humorously summed up as a simple three-step process:

(1) Picture the ideal result
(2) Make it happen
(3) If there is any problem with Step 2, repeat Step 1.

[1] Most of the time that we are practising we are training the mind, not the muscles. Suppose you sight-read through a piece, making many mistakes of intonation, sound, rhythm, and excess effort. Then you practise it for two hours, after which you can play it fluently and with half the effort. What has changed? Physically you have not changed at all. It is not like working out in a gym for three months, after which the muscles you have trained are now physically different. All that has changed is that your mental picture, of what and how to play, has now taken shape.

[2] The great thing to avoid is that you continually picture what you want to change, instead of what you want to change to, i.e. you want a faster vibrato, but instead of seeing yourself vibrating faster, you see instead a picture of yourself with a slow vibrato that you need to practise to improve. Instead, focus on a clear image of an already improved fast and free vibrato.

Memory

Playing from memory is all to do with *knowing* the piece well. If there are any problems playing a passage from memory there is usually no need to look further than simply getting to know it better.

One of the main aspects of memorization is *association*. To remember something you create a 'peg' or 'hook' on which to hang it. Playing music from memory involves criss-crossing associations between all the aspects of playing, i.e. aural, visual, tactile and intellectual. The musical character and expression is the ultimate 'hook' from which to hang everything else.

238 Practising from memory

From the very beginning of learning a piece for the first time, practise it from memory immediately, even if you have never heard it before.

Having first played it through from beginning to end to get the overall feel of it (playing up to tempo where you can and as slowly as you need to elsewhere), suppose you then begin to practise in detail:

- Play the first short phrase while looking at the music and noticing every detail on the printed page – notes, rhythms, bowings, fingerings, articulation marks, dynamics, etc.

- Having formed a clear picture of the phrase, move your eyes away from the music and practise the phrase from memory. Work on the four main factors of intonation, sound, rhythm and ease, while getting used to the bowings, fingerings, shifts, string crosssings, etc.

- The moment your memory fades in any way and you are no longer entirely sure what you are playing, return to the printed music and play the phrase several times until you are clear again. Then look away again and practise from memory.

If you cannot grasp the entire phrase, it may mean you are attempting too long a phrase all in one go, and you should learn it in smaller units. If necessary, practise only two notes from memory at a time, joining them together like ABC practice.[1]

[1] See *ABC practice*, page 275

Work through the whole piece like this, phrase by phrase or bar by bar. Then apply the same process to longer phrases or passages. When you come to play the whole piece from memory it will feel entirely normal because you will never have got used to playing from the music anyway.

239 Aural

Strengthen the memory of what the notes, phrases and passages sound like:

- Sing the piece through in your mind, hearing the pitch of every note very clearly.

- Sing passages aloud.

- Play short phrases or passages from memory, repeating many times over and over again until entirely fluent and without hesitation.[2]

[2] See *Repetition practice*, page 280; *Performing a short phrase*, page 305

- Listen to recordings and live performances.

240 Visual

Playing from memory does not mean that you have to play without the music – it is just that you read from your inner 'photograph' of the music instead of from the printed page. During the process of practising a piece you automatically become familiar with all the 'landmarks' on the page: you soon know that such-and-such a passage is at the bottom of the page, that the top of the next page is 'black' with sixteenth-notes (semiquavers) and then in the next line 'white' with many half-notes (minims).

You get used to the shape of the phrases: some notes sitting on ledger lines above or below the stave; some phrases looking like scales, arpeggios, broken thirds; rows of repeated notes; notes in regular patterns or sequences; passages that are very irregular; the look of double-stop passages or chords, and so on.

You get used to the dynamic markings and other articulations: the '*f*' marked at the beginning of a passage soon becomes part of that passage in your mind's eye, or the accents or dots over each note of a particular phrase; the appearance of hairpins and printed markings like *cresc.* or *dolce* become familiar, and so on.

- Study the printed music away from the instrument. Reading through, note all of the details and landmarks which make up the inner music from which you 'read' when playing from memory.

- Mental rehearsal: play through mentally to discover exactly which notes or phrases are strong, vague or blank.[3] Play through phrases, passages or whole sections in your mind, visualizing the printed music in detail, bar by bar, seeing all the bowings, fingerings and other markings. 'Hear' the violin tone; 'feel' the instrument and bow in your hands and under your chin. If you get lost or cannot remember a note, look at the music or play the phrase on the violin, and then go back over it again mentally. Continue until you can play fluently in your mind's eye without hesitation.

[3] See *Mental rehearsal*, page 290

Tactile

It is impossible to 'forget' whether the opening solo of the Brahms Concerto begins on a down-bow or an up-bow. The physical feel of the down-bow attack, and the tone and character of the note, are inextricably linked.

The same applies to every other note. Each movement of the bow or the left hand has a particular physical feel: the feeling of a finger on a particular note, and the overall feeling of a group of notes; the feeling of a shift when the timing and distance are exactly right; the feeling of the bow in the string when a particular note sounds just right, and so on.

Obviously, it is by repeating that feeling that you can repeat the same sound over and over again. You bring the bow down onto the string and get a certain tone. Then you bring the bow down on to the string again, with exactly the same feeling of the bow in the string, and you get the same tone. Therefore, you can think in terms of 'the feeling of the sound' and 'the sound of the feeling'. Experimenting during practice is literally a matter of asking 'What does this sound *feel* like?' and 'What does this feeling *sound* like?'

- Practise phrases, passages or whole movements with your head turned away from the instrument, or with your eyes shut, or practise in the dark, concentrating entirely on the feel of each note or action.[1]

- Practise groups of notes and phrases until you can play each group under one mental command, instead of one command per note. A major part of playing by 'feel', this was looked at earlier in *Groups*, page 24.

Intellectual

Knowing all kinds of details about a piece is an essential factor in memorizing. Each detail acts as a 'hook' from which other aspects of the piece can hang:

- knowing that the first time a certain phrase comes it is loud, the next time soft, the next time loud again.

- knowing that the first time a certain phrase comes it is slurred in one bow, the next time slurred in two bows, and the last time played with separate bows.

- knowing that a particular important note is going to be on a third finger in one bar, while in the next bar the same phrase recurs but this time requiring a fourth finger on that note.

- knowing the orchestral score or piano part, knowing the structure and form, the harmonic structure, and how different phrases are derived from or related to other phrases.[2]

- Throughout the whole process of working on a piece, constantly be on the lookout for facts, ideas and features which can help to anchor the memory.

- If you continually stumble over a particular phrase because it is complex, confusing or deceptive in some way, describe each note of the phrase in terms of the following:

1 String   **2** Interval   **3** Finger   **4** Position   **5** Bow   **6** Note

Example   Mendelssohn: Concerto in E minor, op. 64, *mov. 1, b. 363*

- Describe each note one by one:

A string, first finger, 1st position, up-bow, B; up an octave to fourth finger, 5th position, up-bow, B; down a minor third to second finger, 5th position, down-bow, G♯; up a semitone to third finger, 5th position, down-bow, A, and so on.

- Describe groups and sequences:

Every rising pair of quarter-notes (crotchets) in the sequence rises by a semitone.

The first and third beats of the notes marked '+' (G♯, F♯, E♯) share the same pattern of tones and semitones as the notes marked '++' (E♯, D♯, D). Both are a tone followed by a semitone.

- Describe exceptions, e.g. the second and third notes of bars 364 and 366 are a minor third apart, but in 368 they are a major third apart.

You can do all this with or without the instrument. After fully describing just a few passages in this way, the process soon becomes automatic and unconscious. Thereafter, only the most complex passages will require conscious description again.

[1] Playing without looking is also important in another sense: too much *looking* at the fingers or the bow, either directly or in a mirror, can be counter-productive if it encourages a feeling of 'I, who reside somewhere behind my eyes and between my ears, *have* a hand and fingers and I must move them like this or like that'. There should instead be a feeling of 'I *am* my hand and my fingers'.

Similarly, players and teachers throughout the ages have emphasized the need for the violin to feel as though it is a part of the body, and the bow an extension of the arm, rather than being objects which we hold and manipulate.

[2] A classic analogy is that learning only the violin line on its own, without getting to know the piano part or orchestral score, would be like an actor learning a play from a script that showed only their own lines. It would be impossible to understand the play if you did not know what anyone else was saying or doing.

243

Looking and thinking ahead

When you are driving a car very slowly, you do not need to look very far ahead. Driving at high speeds, you may need to be aware of what could happen a great distance away down the road.

Playing a piece at a slow tempo, you may need to think (and hear the notes in your mind, like a singer) only one or two notes ahead. Playing at high speeds, you may need to be thinking one or two whole bars ahead.[1]

Memory often seems insecure when the cause is actually that you are not thinking ahead sufficiently. Every note and phrase, every shift or string crossing, seems to come upon you too suddenly and feels too last-minute, just as though you did not remember what to play.

- Using the music, play through passages, sections or whole movements while focusing your eyes on the bars ahead of the actual notes you are playing. At moderate speeds look at the notes in the next bar, and at faster speeds look two or more bars ahead.

- Do the same playing from memory, picturing and singing in your mind the bars ahead of where you are playing.

Having consciously gone through this process just once or twice, you soon start thinking ahead all the time without being aware of it anymore. Playing from memory immediately feels much easier and more secure.

244

Feeling relationships between notes

- Strengthen memory by feeling the relationships between notes, rather than the notes in isolation. Looked at earlier in the context of intonation (see *Playing intervals not notes*, page 217), this could also be thought of as 'emotional' memory: the musical character or expression in the intervals acts as memory 'pegs' on which to 'hang' the notes.

The suggestions that follow are naturally intended to serve only as examples. Any number of other musical views is possible, especially if the orchestral harmonies, colours and textures are included in the picture.

Example   Prokofiev: Concerto no. 2 in G minor, op. 63, *mov. 1, b. 52*

Bar 52   Part of the character of this phrase is in the expression of the **minor second** between the first two notes, followed by a **major second** between the second and third notes. Playing a **minor third** from the F to the D increases the feeling of momentum in the descent. This D has a feeling of leading forward because the line immediately rises a **minor second** before settling again on the more-definite D at the beginning of bar 53.

Bar 53   Play a **major sixth** from the D to the F, and again from the C♯ to the E. Play an **augmented fifth** from the F to the C♯. Feel also the **minor second** between the D and the C♯, and the F and the E.

Bar 54   Feel the **minor third** carrying into this bar from the E in the bar before. In the first two bars the phrases have mainly been descending. Here, there is a feeling of expansion and opening out created by playing a rising **major second** followed by a **minor third** followed by a **perfect fourth**.

After these expanding intervals, the semitones cause a momentary contraction and holding back, as well as creating a build-up of tension. Play a **minor second** from the B into the A♯, but then an **augmented unison** from the A♯ to the A. In other words, play a narrow semitone and then a wide semitone.[1]

Bar 55   After holding back in bar 54 there is a feeling of release? confidence? optimism? in leaping up a **major ninth** from the A in bar 54 to the B here. The music continues to gather and lead towards the first note of bar 56, which is the peak of the passage. Feel the E, D♯ and D the same as the last three notes of bar 54 (except that being higher, being the second occurrence, and being just before the peak, they have more energy than their counterparts in the previous bar).

Bar 56   First practise going to the E♭ an octave lower: feel how the D seems to want to move up into the E♭, and the intensity of the close **minor second**. Then feel the same quali- ties in going up to the E♭ as written, feeling also the serenity? satisfaction? of the **minor ninth** after the less settled but more energetic character of the **major ninth** into bar 55.

---

[1] 'When asked if I ever allowed myself to think ahead while actually playing in public, I explained I never played *without* thinking a measure or two ahead. I always had a mental impression of the next measures. For me there was always a key note in each passage around which I would plan my fingerings and shifts. And then set the passage. In my mind, as I played, I mentally had a picture of the way my left hand would set and where the fingers should be before and after this key note.'

Isaac Stern: *My First 79 Years* (New York, 1999), 217.

[1] See *Wide and narrow semitones*, page 214

This bar could have followed the same intervals as the first bar and still have arrived on the G in bar 57. The openness of the **perfect fifth** from D♭ to G♭ throws off the squeezed feeling of the semitones at the beginning of the bar. Play a narrow **minor second** from the E♭ to the D, and then a wide **augmented unison** from the D to the D♭. Play a wide **augmented unison** from the G♭ to the G, and then a narrow **minor second** from the G to the A♭.

Bars 57–60 Bar 57 is like bar 53. Also feel the descending line G–F♯–E–E♭ (ignoring the second and fourth notes in bar 57). Play a wide **augmented unison** from bar 58 to bar 59. The E♭ in bar 59 is the resolution of the E in bar 58, but it then begins to grow as it prepares to hand the phrase back over to the orchestra.

Accenting weak-memory notes

It can easily happen that we think we do not know something from memory, when actually we know nearly all of it very well; however, because we are unclear about the odd note here and there, these notes become like a weak link in a chain and the chain breaks. Then, if the passage breaks down as a result, we think we do not know any of it from memory, when in fact it was only that one note that was not secure.

Example 1   Mozart: Concerto no. 4 in D, K218, *mov. 1 cadenza (Joachim)*

Suppose, in this example, you continually play D instead of D♯ in the second bar (marked '+'). Perhaps this happens because in bar 60 of the first movement the note is D.

- Play all the other notes at performance tempo but play the D♯ with an accent and a pause. Repeat several times until the image of the note, as well as the physical feel of it, is solidly formed in your mind:

Example 2   J. S. Bach: Partita no. 2 in D minor, BWV1004, *Giga, b. 37*

In the first bar, playing E instead of E♭ (marked '+'), or in the second bar playing B♭ instead of B, are frequently-heard errors. It is easy to confuse the two notes because of their similar position in the sequence.

- Pause on the E♭ and B♮ and play them with an accent. Play everything else up to tempo:

Example 3   Vivaldi: Winter (The Four Seasons), op. 8 no. 4, *mov. 1, b. 28*

It may be tempting to play D♮ instead of D♭ (marked '+') because the tone–semitone pattern of the scale is tone–semitone–tone in the lower half of the scale, but semitone–tone–tone in the upper half.

- Pause on each second finger and play it with an accent. Play everything else up to tempo:

Example 4   Brahms: Concerto in D, op. 77, *mov. 1 cadenza (Joachim)*

At the double stops marked '+' the feeling is of placing the first finger a semitone *behind* second-finger E on the D string, or behind second-finger D on the G string.

At '++' the feeling is of placing the first finger a semitone *in front of* the first-finger C. Following the pattern of the previous double stops, you may mistakenly aim for D♯–F♯ instead of E♯–G♯.

● Pause briefly on the two double stops marked '+' and play them with an accent. Pause longer on the double stop marked '++'. Play everything else up to tempo:

(246) ## Playing under tempo, exaggerating expression

Playing under tempo with exaggerated expression is a simple way to discover musical 'blind-spots', since you have to know what you want before you can magnify it.

● Play through under tempo. The speed can range from very slow to only a little slower than normal.

● Using the extra time that the slower tempo gives you, enlarge every detail of the musical design to larger-than-life proportions. Imagine that you are playing to someone who has never heard classical violin music before, and you are playing everything very slowly, deliberately and obviously, to try to make it as clear and easy to understand as possible.

● Practise short phrases, passages, and entire pieces in this way.[1]

[1] See also *Some other ways to use playing-through practice*, no. 5, page 305

Example 1   Pugnanin-Kreisler: Praeludium and Allegro, *Allegro, b. 41*

Example 2   Mozart: Concerto no. 3 in G, K216, *mov. 3, b. 141*

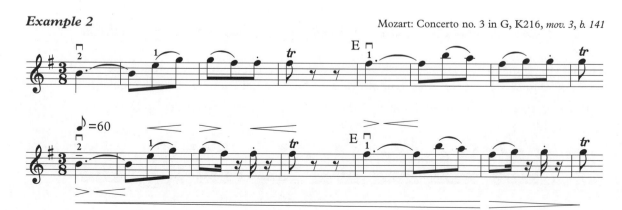

Experimenting with proportions

Leonardo da Vinci was once asked to give his opinion of an ancient statue that had recently been discovered.[1] When he arrived at the statue he found it surrounded by people admiring and describing it in terms like 'the radiance of the expression' or 'the openness of the gesture', 'the serenity of the line', or whatever.

Leonardo looked at the statue in silence and then took out measuring tools with which he measured the statue in every possible way – the widths, lengths, diameters, angles, etc. He wrote everything down and, without a word, went home.

Like anyone else, he too could see the 'radiance', the 'openness', or the 'serenity' in the statue – but as an artist he knew that everything about the statue was the result of certain *proportions*.

Looking at everything in terms of proportions is the key that opens the door to every aspect of technique on a string instrument. It is also fundamental to every musical consideration, for example dynamics, intonation, tempo, attack, etc.

[1] The Florentine artist Leonardo da Vinci (1452–1519), painter of the *Mona Lisa*, was also a sculptor, architect, engineer and scientist. Always fascinated by the subject of proportions, he assisted the Italian mathematician Luca Pacioli in the celebrated work *Divina Proportione* (1509).

Some key examples of proportions

The violin and bow

The shapeliness of the violin itself, the thinness of the plates, the spiralling lines of the scroll, the design of the bridge, the properties and exact position of the soundpost, the weight, thickness and balance of the bow, are key examples of proportionality.

Tone production See *Describing the sound*, page 48; *Playing a phrase on each soundpoint*, page 48

Every sound the bow makes is the result of certain proportions of speed of bow to pressure to soundpoint.

The tension of the string See *Quality*, page 47

Greater, the nearer the bridge. The difference, in speed or weight, between playing on soundpoint 5 and playing on soundpoint 4 is much less than the difference between soundpoint 2 and soundpoint 1. When you are playing on soundpoint 2, it can make a big difference if you move just a millimetre closer to the bridge. If you are on soundpoint 5 and you change it by a millimetre, it barely makes any difference at all.

The give of the wood of the bow and the hair See *Different qualities of the bow at heel and point*, page 69.

At the heel, the hair gives, and the wood of the bow is rigid; at the point, the wood gives (in the middle of the bow), and the hair is rigid.

To illustrate the proportions, number the different tensions in the wood and the hair on a scale from zero to ten: 10 = much give in the wood or hair, 0 = no give. At the heel (all hair, no wood), the balance would be 10:0. At the point (all wood, no hair), the balance would be 0:10. The middle of the bow is therefore 5:5, where, as you would expect, both the wood and the hair give equally. The entire range from the heel to the point:

10:0 (heel), 9:1, 8:2, 7:3, 6:4, 5:5 (middle), 4:6, 3:7, 2:8, 1:9, 0:10 (point).

Leverage in the bow hold See *Spreading the fingers for leverage*, page 259; *Bow hold*, page 302

The closer the first finger is to the pivot (i.e. the thumb), the harder the first finger has to work to apply weight into the bow. The closer the fourth finger is to the pivot, the harder it has to work to balance the weight of the bow.

Pressure of the thumb into the bow

At the heel, the thumb supports and helps balance the bow in the hand, but even in f it barely needs to exert counter-pressure. At the point, the thumb must exert counter-pressure, especially when playing f.

On a scale from 1 to 10, thumb counter-pressure can be expressed as follows:

1 (extreme heel), 2, 3, 4, 5 (middle), 6, 7, 8, 9, 10 (point).

The amount of counter-pressure should always be *as much as necessary but as little as possible*.[2]

[2] A common mistake: start at the heel with minimum thumb counter-pressure; play f to the point, by which time the counter-pressure has gradually increased to, say, '8'; return on the up-bow to the heel *without releasing the thumb* (keeping it at '8'). This immediately creates tension in the thumb. The increase in counter-pressure when playing to the point does not matter; what is important is to release the thumb back to zero when returning to the heel.

Length of string and soundpoint See *Moving in to the bridge*, page 59

The higher up the string the finger, the nearer to the bridge the bow. Playing top E, two octaves up on the E string, with the bow midway between the bridge and the fingerboard, is proportionately the same as playing the open string with the bow several centimetres over the fingerboard.

Lifted strokes

All lifted strokes are the result of the proportions of height of bounce to length of bow. The faster the stroke the lower the bounce, the less bow, the higher up the bow, the nearer the fingerboard. These proportions of length to height change depending on the tilt of the bow (how much hair), as well as on the place in the bow.

Attacks See *Beginning and ending notes*, page 268

When attacking the string from the air at the heel or the point, the beginning of the note will be clean if the angle at which the bow approaches and touches the string is neither too steep nor too flat. The angle has to be gauged in proportion to the speed of descent: the faster the flatter.

Intonation See *Uniform intonation*, page 207; *Tuning scales: three stages*, page 210

Everything about intonation is a question of proportions, since each note is placed in relation to another note, e.g. tuning any stopped A to the open string, or placing C♯ or E♭ as a 'leading note' to D.

The shorter the string, i.e. the higher up the string you play, the closer together the notes:

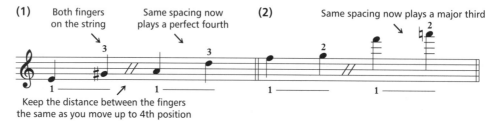

(1) Play a major third in 1st position. Keep both fingers on the string. Move up to 4th position, keeping the fingers exactly the same distance apart. Now the same spacing plays a perfect fourth.

(2) The same spacing that plays a major second in 1st position plays a major third in 8th position.

Left hand and arm placement See *Angle and height of knuckles*, page 237

Longer arms: scroll of the violin pointing more to the left.

Shorter arms: scroll of the violin pointing more in front.

Larger hands: knuckles lower; in 1st position, first finger positioned closer to (or behind) the nut.

Smaller hands: knuckles higher; in 1st position, first finger positioned in front of the nut.

Vibrato See *Varying speed and width*, page 134

Each different type or quality of vibrato is the result of certain proportions of width to speed. These proportions are affected by the amount of finger pressure (e.g. heavier finger pressure may necessitate a narrower vibrato).

Leaving aside musical considerations, vibrato must be narrower the higher up the fingerboard it is, in proportion to the length of string: a note high on the G string is played with much narrower vibrato than a note in first position.

Vibrato is also narrower the higher in pitch the note, so that first finger F♯ on the E string will generally be played with a narrower vibrato than first-finger A on the G string.

Speed of shift See *Speed of shift*, page 172

The speed of the shift often reflects the speed of the passage.

Slow passages: slower shifts

Fast passages: faster shifts

Sometimes a fast shift in a slow passage helps to achieve a clean, inaudible shift.

Long shifts: when you slow into the arrival note (see *Slow arrival speed*, page 172), the speed pattern of the shift is 'fast–slow'. How fast, how slow, and how much of the shift is fast before it is slow, is proportionate to the speed of the passage and the distance of the shift.

Speed of left hand finger movement See *Fast fingers*, page 7; *Placing fingers gently*, page 240

The louder the volume, the wider the string vibrates (i.e. swings from side to side); the wider the string vibrates, the faster the fingers must lift and drop. There is a sound of 'fuzz' at the beginning of notes if the speed of stopping or unstopping the string is too slow in proportion to the sideways movement of the string. The trill exercise on page 125 provides a good example.

Height of fingers See *Low fingers*, page 4

The faster the passage, the nearer the fingers must stay to the strings. High-lifted fingers are rarely good in fast passages (up to a certain speed limit they are sometimes used for greater articulation). However, low fingers are often used in slow passages for greater legato and *cantabile*.

Defaults: building good habits

'Default' is a term used in computer science, meaning a setting or mode of operation that is put into effect automatically, without you having to think about it. You have a default size of print for the words you type, the one the program automatically selects when it starts; the margins are already set to the right width, and so on. You can change these settings whenever you want to, but if you do nothing then they are the ones that will be used.

The settings of the controls on a television are defaults, so that when you press button 4 you get Channel 4, the picture is a certain brightness, the volume is at a certain level, and so on. We employ thousands of defaults in the day-to-day running of our lives.

In most music you do not have to decide how to tune the open strings because tuning in fifths, up from G below middle C, is the default tuning. Sometimes this default is changed, as in Paganini's 'Moses' variations in which the G string is tuned up to a B♭. The clef at the beginning of a stave of music, and the key and time signatures, are default settings.

Each bow has its own default tension to which you always adjust it before playing. This default is sometimes changed to suit a particular piece or passage in a piece – the tension may be relaxed a little to give the bow more spring for a piece full of *spiccato*, perhaps. Even the exact place you position a shoulder rest on the instrument, or the height of the rest, becomes a default, one that you change if you wear unusually thick or thin clothing.[1]

Defaults can be likened to habits. Anything that is a habit in playing, and therefore happens continually and automatically without conscious thought, could be called a default. The complete collection of defaults that you use is called your 'technique'. 'Good' technique is a collection of defaults that work well. 'Improving' technique means building up an ever larger collection of automatic, unthinking actions that have a desired, not an undesired, effect, and means replacing the less helpful defaults with more helpful ones.[2]

For example, placing the bow on the string without thinking about it: if the bow is not parallel to the bridge, or too near the fingerboard or bridge, or too pressed, or too light, or not angled correctly to touch only the intended string, the default needs to be redesigned. Finger pressure provides another key example. The default amount of finger pressure for any note should be as little as possible, i.e. just as much as necessary to stop the note well. The wrong default here, where you habitually press your fingers hard into the string, can make the left fingers feel heavy and laboured.

The defaults of technique should be attended to before all else, so that you are left free to concentrate on the music without having to think too much about *how* to play.

Some key examples of technical defaults

Height of scroll See *Angle of strings to the floor*, page 57

> The scroll should ideally be slightly higher than the chin rest so that the strings are parallel to the floor. A further benefit is that this throws the weight of the violin towards the body, which helps to maintain an upright and balanced posture.

Angle of violin

> Slightly tilted. If the violin is too tilted, the E string does not give enough support to the bow, causing weak tone production on that string. If the violin is too flat, playing on the G string becomes effortful: the fourth finger has to reach further to the G string, and you also have to raise the right, upper arm much higher.

> The best default tilt is one where the E string gives sufficient support to the bow, while at the same time the right arm and fourth finger can reach the G string easily enough. Like most defaults, this can be changed while playing, sometimes tilting the violin less when playing on the E string, and tilting it more when playing on the G string.

Left upper arm (elbow position)

> The elbow is mobile underneath the violin, not fixed in one position.

> **E string**: elbow positioned more to the left

> **G string**: elbow positioned more to the right

> The default position of the elbow is *only as far to the right as necessary (for the fingers to reach the strings), and no further.*

> The left upper-arm position is also affected by which part of the fingertip contacts the string. The more the finger is placed on the left side of the fingertip, the more the elbow moves to the right; the more the finger is placed on the right side of the fingertip, the more the elbow moves to the left.

[1] Carl Flesch advised his students to practise in their concert clothes for a day or so before the concert. Putting on unfamiliar clothes at the very last moment before walking out on stage can cause an otherwise well-prepared performance to feel awkward or uncomfortable, e.g. new shoes that force the body into an unfamiliar state of balance, neck ties that force the violin into an unfamiliar playing position, materials that make the actions of the bow arm feel different, etc. At the very least such new sensations can be distracting just at the moment when you need the greatest concentration.

[2] The well-known saying tells us that 'Habits are easy to make and hard to break'. If that is so, then do not try to break old habits – just form new ones!

Angle of base joints to fingerboard See *Angle and height of knuckles*, page 237

This is largely determined by which part of the fingertip contacts the string. The more the finger is placed on the left side of the fingertip, the more angled up are the knuckles; the more the finger is placed on the right side of the fingertip, the more parallel are the knuckles with the fingerboard.

The placement of the hand varies according to the specific notes. The default should set the knuckles neither at too much of an angle in relation to the fingerboard, nor too parallel to the fingerboard, but at some natural point in between.

Space between fingers

How much space there is between the fingers is partly determined by which part of the fingertip stops the string. If you place the first-finger B (on the A string) slightly more on the left side of the fingertip (from your point of view), and place the second-finger C next to it more on the right side of the fingertip, the fingers will open sideways at the base joints (Fig. 41a). If you place both fingers on the left side of the fingertip, the fingers remain parallel to each other with a tendency to squeeze together (Fig. 41b).

The amount of space between the fingers naturally varies from player to player and from one group of notes to another, ranging from a real gap to no space at all. What is important is that there is never any *sideways* *pressing* between two fingers, for example always squeezing the fourth finger against the third finger when playing the third finger.

Fig. 41

(a) Note the space between the fingers

(b) The fingertip placement is causing the fingers to squeeze together

Finger action See *Moving fingers from the base joints*, page 239

The fingers lift and drop from the base joints, the rest of the hand remaining entirely uninvolved. At times, this default is changed and the hand itself moves as well, bringing the base joint towards the string at the same time as the finger moves from the base joint.

Great tension may result if it is the other way round, the hand and fingers generally moving together, with only occasional finger movements that are independent of the hand. This is true even when the amount the hand moves is so slight as to be almost invisible.

In general, the fingers are not *lifted up* from the string so much as pulled back from the base joints. Lifting changes the shape of the finger, which means that there is too much activity in the middle joint of the finger; pulling back keeps the curve of the finger more as it was when the finger was on the string, and the finger naturally moves more from the base joint.

Speed of finger movement See *Fast fingers*, pages 9–10; *Lifting off at the last possible moment*, page 286

The default should be fast, the fingers lifting and dropping 'at the last possible moment'. This changes to earlier and slower actions for more *dolce* or *piano* passages.

If it is the other way round, with slow fingers the default and fast fingers the exception, there may be many moments of 'fuzz' in the sound caused by the finger stopping or un-stopping the string too slowly; or caused by poor co-ordination, the bow beginning to play the note before the finger is ready on the string.

Finger pressure See *Releasing the left hand*, pages 233–6

Dropping the finger in a passage of ascending slurs, after the initial impact the finger releases the string slightly. The default should be 'stop–release' rather than 'stop–press'.

The general rule is always 'as much as necessary but as little as possible'. This default may be changed for pizzicato when a very ringing tone is required, or for certain tone colours that you can get from too-heavy or too-light finger pressure.

Contact point of first finger with neck See Fig. 17a, page 237

E string: nearer the middle joint

G string: nearer the base joint

Large hands: lower placement

Small hands: higher placement

In lower positions, the side of the first finger lightly contacts the neck to give the hand orientation and stability. Galamian called this 'the principle of the double contact'.[1]

Contact point of thumb with neck See *Keeping a space between the thumb and first finger*, page 229

The thumb is mobile and active on the neck of the violin, never remaining 'fixed' in one position. The default position that it moves from, and returns to, is opposite the first or second finger, or between them (Fig. 15a, page 229).

If the default position of the thumb is too near the nut, it throws the balance of the hand too much onto the first finger. It also increases the likelihood of squeezing between the base joint of the first finger and the thumb (Fig. 15b). Nor should the default thumb position be too close to the third finger, which can cause tension in the base of the thumb.

The thumb is sometimes higher (sticking above the fingerboard); sometimes lower (almost underneath the neck).

The left fingers 'lead' the bow; the bow 'leads' the right hand and arm
See *Co-ordination*, page 14

1 The finger must establish the string length before the bow can set the string into vibration, so the impulse is always one of the fingers 'leading' and the bow 'following'. If the bow leads and the fingers follow, there may be many impure sounds caused by the finger not being ready before the bow moves.

2 Although the physical fact is that the hand pulls the bow, feel the bow's own momentum 'leading' the hand. The difference between a feeling of the hand trying to do things with the bow, as opposed to the hand following the bow, can be dramatic.

Finger preparation See *Placing fingers gently*, page 240

Moving from a higher to a lower finger on the same string, every lower finger is placed on the string ('prepared') before lifting the upper finger. This default is changed when playing fast *spiccato* or *sautillé*, where the left-hand finger action is more like that of a pianist (the lower finger dropping while the upper finger lifts). Finger preparation is indispensable for producing a legato, singing tone.

Separate-bow shifts

Shifting on the old finger: shift on the old bow.

Shifting on the new finger: shift on the new bow.

Left wrist See *Wrist*, page 238

In 1st position, unless the arms are very short in proportion to the size of the instrument, the usual default is a straight line from the elbow to the base joints of the fingers.

Double stops and chords often require a natural alteration of this straight line. Players with shorter arms or fingers may need a default in which the wrist curves out slightly.

Tilt of bow See *Flat or tilted hair*, page 259

Full or three-quarters hair, playing on the side of the hair when required.

not

Playing on the side of the hair, playing full hair when required.

Speed not pressure See *Quality*, page 47

To produce a large, free, sweet and singing tone, tone production is based on speed of bow, not pressure. More pressure is used for darker, denser or more depressed colours, but even then the speed of bow is the controlling factor, not the pressure.

Soundpoint See Fig. 5, page 47

A logical default would be soundpoint 3, or 2½ – a normal speaking voice is neither a whisper nor a shout.

[1] 'The term [double contact] signifies that the left hand has to have two points of contact with the instrument in order to orient itself properly and securely. In the lower positions, the double contact is provided by the thumb and the side of the first finger…The contact need not be permanent or continuous…It must be very slight, since the more gentle it is, the more sensitive becomes the feeling of touching…An exception [applies] in the playing of expressive passages. In order to facilitate the vibrato action, the hand can release the double contact, retaining only that of the thumb.

From the fourth position upward, the hand itself contacts the body of the violin and replaces the index finger in forming the second point of contact. From the fifth position on, the thumb and hand contact various parts of the instrument, but the principle of double contact is still maintained.'

Ivan Galamian: Principles of Violin Playing and Teaching (New Jersey, 1962), 21.

Pivoting See *Crossing early*, page 102

The default should be smooth string crossings – the bow moving early towards the new string before the new string needs to be played – with later, more sudden and accented string crossings when required. If it is the other way round, with accented string crossings the default and smooth crossings the exception, it may be difficult to create long lines and to play with a naturally singing and sustaining tone.

Angle of the bow to the bridge See *Angle of the bow to the bridge*, page 76

When the bow is angled 'out', so that the frog is slightly further forwards than the point (Fig. 8a, page 76), on the down-bow the bow automatically drifts towards the bridge; on the up-bow it automatically drifts towards the fingerboard.

When the bow is angled 'in', so that the point is slightly further forwards than the frog (Fig. 8b), on the down-bow it drifts towards the fingerboard, and on the up-bow it drifts towards the bridge.

The default is the bow parallel to the bridge. Angled bowing is used to move closer to, or further from, the bridge. It is also used for tonal reasons. When the bow speed is not too fast, you can get a different kind of resonance by deliberately drawing the bow at the slightest angle to the bridge (point nearer fingerboard than frog) while forcing it to stay on one soundpoint.

Bow hold

How to hold the bow depends on where in the bow you are playing and the type of stroke.

At the heel, the hand is more upright (supinated), balancing the bow with the little finger (Fig. 42d). At the point, the hand is leaning (pronated) in the direction of the first finger (Fig. 42e). Since the change from more upright at the heel to leaning at the point is gradual rather than sudden, during one whole bow the angle of the hand – and therefore the exact finger placement – is slightly different at every place in the bow.[1]

Spiccato requires a different kind of supination to allow the bow to 'swing' slightly within the hand (see *Playing without the first finger: lifted strokes*, page 254), as does ricochet. *Sautillé* requires a different kind of pronation, allowing the fourth finger (and even the third finger at times) to leave the stick (*Taking fingers off the bow*, page 97). Playing *pianissimo* requires a looser, often feather-like contact with the bow, whereas full-bodied playing requires a much firmer hold, with the first finger moved further away from the thumb (*Spreading the fingers for leverage*, page 259), the third finger solidly on the frog (*Pulling in with the third finger*, page 255), and lower knuckles.

Basic functions and positions of the fingers are as follows:

- **Thumb**. The tip of the thumb, not the pad, contacts the bow (Fig. 42a), so that the thumb bends outwards (see margin note 1, page 255). It contacts the bow partly on the thumb-piece and partly on the actual stick (or thumb leather, if the leather extends all the way to the thumb-piece without leaving a gap). Therefore the thumb sits diagonally on the bow. Note how the thumb wants to straighten if the pad is placed on the bow (Fig. 42b).

- **First finger**. The part of the first finger on top of the stick helps to produce tone.[2] The default position is neither too close to the second finger (leading to loss of leverage) nor too far from it (leading to tension in the base joints). The louder the playing = the further the first finger from the thumb = the most leverage (Fig. 42g).

  Fig. 42c shows how the contact point of the first finger changes between the heel and the point. At the heel the contact point with the stick is nearer the crease at the first joint of the finger (Fig. 42d); this gradually moves during the down-bow so that at the point it is nearer the crease at the middle joint of the finger (Fig. 42e). During the up-bow the contact point gradually moves back closer to the crease at the first joint of the finger.[3]

  The pad of the first finger, on the side of the stick, helps steady the bow so that it can be drawn parallel to the bridge. This contact point barely changes between the heel and the point, so any change in the contact point on top of the bow is barely noticeable.

- **Second finger**. The contact point of the second finger with the bow is around the crease at the first joint of the finger, higher or lower depending on the length of the finger (Figs. 42d, 42g). The second finger sits opposite the thumb slightly to the left of centre (from the player's viewpoint). The pad and tip of the second finger should not curl in towards the thumb, and are entirely redundant in holding and using the bow (Fig. 42f).

- **Third finger**. In the lower half, the pad of the third finger contacts the bow between the pearl eye and the rounded edge of the frog (Figs. 42d, 42g). In the upper half, depending on the length of arm, it may feel awkward to keep the pad of the finger on the frog. Then the contact point of

[1] Many bows seem to have a built-in tremble just after the middle during the down-bow. The cause is often found in the hand resisting the gradual leaning into the bow. If the hand remains in the 'heel position' for too long, and then suddenly leans into the bow somewhere around the middle, the wood shakes. Instead, lean gradually into the bow as the down-bow progresses, with a feeling of 'following the curve of the stick'.

[2] Some of the job of contacting the string can be given to the second finger (see *Playing without the first finger in f passages*, page 254); some can be given to leaning into the string with the hand (see *Supporting the wrist*, page 256); some can be given to forearm rotation (see *Forearm rotation*, page 265) and arm weight, with a feeling of relaxing the whole arm into the bow and the string.

[3] Note that this change of the first-finger contact point is never made deliberately but happens naturally and subconsciously. In some schools of violin playing, the contact point of the first finger with the bow is the same at the heel and the point.

the finger is around the crease at the first joint of the finger, contacting the bow on the upper, outside edge of the bow (Fig. 42h).

- **Fourth finger**. The fourth finger balances the weight of the bow. This is particularly so in the lower half, where it sits on the bow as on a see-saw, but also in the upper half where it can counterbalance the first finger. Sometimes it sits directly on top of the stick, sometimes on the upper, inside edge. (See margin note 1, page 255.) Playing in the lower half the finger is more rounded and flatter at the knuckle (Fig. 42d); at the point the finger is extended (Fig. 42h).

Fig. 42

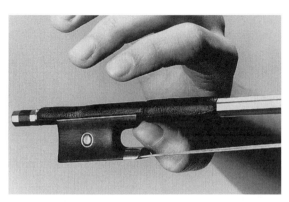

(a) The thumb sits on its tip and bends outwards

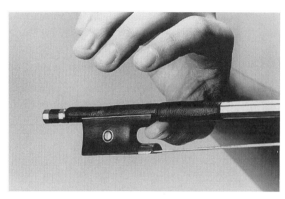

(b) The thumb should not contact the bow on the pad

(c) The contact point of the first finger is different at the heel and at the point

(d) Playing at the heel

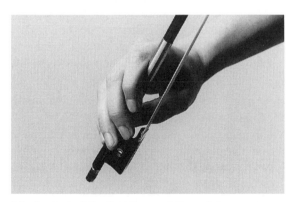

(e) Contact of the first finger at the point

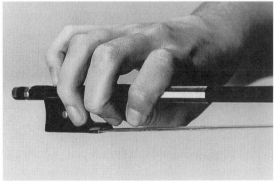

(f) The second finger should not curl in to the thumb

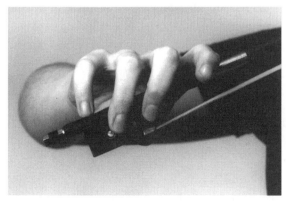

(g) The fingers are spread to give more leverage

(h) At the point, the third finger pad may leave the bow

Practising performing

To be practising always from a technical point of view – breaking passages down into their technical components, practising in rhythms, practising slowly, practising for intonation, and so on – can be counter-productive. It must not turn out that the one thing you do not practise is your actual performance. This essential element of practice is often missed out because of the constant feeling that you should practise the piece a little bit more first.

The closer the performance date, the more practice time should be given to playing *as if in the heat of performance*. Make music with intensity and communication for a long enough period, before standing on the stage, for the performance simply to be a natural continuation. Whenever possible, performing with the piano should obviously be a major part of this, but it is not essential.

249 Playing-through practice

In 1983 at the Aspen Music Festival in Colorado, USA, Itzhak Perlman gave a talk about making music and playing the violin. The session included questions from the audience. He was asked how he goes about learning a piece for the first time, starting from the very beginning. His answer went something like this:

> The first thing I always do, before anything else, is play through from beginning to end. Then I play through a few times from beginning to end, and then finish off by playing through from beginning to end.

> I have a wonderful way of continuing to work on the piece on the second day. What I do is this: I always begin by playing through from beginning to end, and then I find that the best thing to do is to play through from beginning to end a few times. I'll probably finish off by playing through from beginning to end.

> The next day I play through a few times from beginning to end...

> After a few days like this, I have to admit to myself that this or that phrase is still not in tune; such and such a passage is still not sounding good; I still need to find the best fingering for various phrases; I am still not happy with this or that passage of double stops, and so on.

> So I do the equivalent of spot-cleaning clothes before taking them to the laundry: I practise those particular bars or passages that need attention.

> Immediately after that, I play through from beginning to end. Then I play through from beginning to end a few times, and then finish off by playing through from beginning to end.

'Playing-through practice' can be one of the quickest ways to learn a new piece. Two essential points are:

1 Listen so attentively that you hear every sound that comes out of the instrument.

2 Keep a clear musical conception of each phrase, and a clear picture of technical ease and comfort, at the front of your mind.

Play as if in a real performance with full expression, dynamics and pacing (wherever possible). Do not stop whatever happens. As you play through, simply notice what is happening: 'That was OK – oh, completely missed all of that – good – that's difficult – great, that was fine – I hope nobody else heard that – where *is* that note? – no problem – etc.'

Play through again and again. Simply notice what happens and continue without stopping. Many times you will find something like this: 'Here comes that shift I missed last time I played through – yes, missed again; here is the bit that gets all uncoordinated – yes, it really is uncoordinated; here is that passage which was all out of tune – yes, the intonation is all over the place'; and so on. However, even in the second play-through you will find that passages which were unsuccessful last time are now working better this time.

Gradually the piece will begin to settle into shape, and the happy moments of – 'Oh, that was the bit I used to miss all the time, but I've just played it and it was fine' – will start to occur more and more often. After some days you will arrive at the same point as Perlman: you will find that while much of the music is now lying naturally under the fingers, certain phrases or passages are still not working. Then is the time to take those passages apart to work on them in detail.

Some other ways to use playing-through practice

1 End each day's practice with a full-performance play-through of whatever you were working on earlier.

2 Begin each day's practice with a full-performance play-through. Playing when you are not warmed-up exposes the weakest areas that can then be given priority in the detailed practice that follows.[1]

3 In the same practice session, alternate playing-through practice with other types of practice so that all of the building work is always directly relevant: play through – decide which passages need remedial work and apply a variety of different practice methods to them – play through – do remedial work, and so on.

[1] When playing without warming up, take great care not to force or strain. The great Canadian pianist Glenn Gould would often warm up by going for a brisk walk, or by soaking his hands in hot water.

4   If you are studying more than one piece at a time, one approach is to practise one or two of them only by playing through a few times each day, meanwhile concentrating all the detailed work on the other pieces. After a few days swap them around: play through the pieces you were practising in detail, and do detailed work on the ones you were playing through.

5   Play through under tempo, exaggerating expression.[1] Playing under tempo with enlarged musical drama and expression brings great life, colour and variety into the playing which remains when you return to a faster tempo. This is as helpful as playing a passage slowly for technical reasons. One way to think of it is to imagine that you are playing to somebody who has never heard 'classical' music before, and you are helping them understand the music by making everything very, very obvious.

[1] See *Playing under tempo, exaggerating expression*, page 296

6   Play through many times coolly and calmly, from beginning to end, at 10 or 20 per cent under tempo.

7   Add a new piece to your repertoire with playing-through practice. Set aside just half-an-hour each week to play through a solo piece, a sonata or a concerto. Play through all the movements, playing up to tempo where you can and as slowly as you wish elsewhere.

Having played through only once, from beginning to end, leave it for a week and then play through it again. You may wish to work briefly on the odd passage or phrase, but basically just give the best performance you can and leave it at that.

Continue like this for a month or two and you will find that you already know the piece and can play it quite well. Later, when you begin to study it in depth, it will take much less time to learn than it would otherwise have taken. Also there will be the feeling of it having deep roots that go back over an extensive period, giving far greater confidence and sense of security than a piece which feels completely new.

8   Relearning old repertoire is an important element of daily practice. To avoid having a list of pieces that you once played, though you can't exactly remember what or when, continually relearn everything on a rotating basis: piece number one in week number one, piece number two in week number two, and so on until covering all of them. Then go back to the first piece and cycle through again.

Practise one or two passages for a few minutes if you like, but basically just play through from beginning to end and enjoy the music and the playing. Play through concertos, sonatas, short pieces, everything important that you have learnt.

You may be able to rotate your whole repertoire several times over just a couple of months. The feeling of being at home with a whole repertoire as opposed to just one piece gives you tremendous confidence; and regular practice of a wide variety of already familiar music adds to your overall command as a musician and instrumentalist.

Performing a short phrase

Performing a short phrase over and over again is one of the very best ways of practising. Once you can already play something, repeating it many times as if in the full heat of performance is where a different level of practice begins. It is then that you gain real musical command, polish and security.

- Play a short phrase over and over again many times with the same inspiration, intensity, commitment, involvement, passion, drama and expression as if you were in the middle of a performance.

- Each time, ask yourself if this is exactly how you want the phrase (or group of notes, or short passage) to sound. Is this exactly the expression, colour or atmosphere that you want to create?

  If you were in the middle of a concert performance, is this exactly what you would want the audience to hear and feel when you play this phrase? If your playing were to be recorded, and later somebody were to switch the recording on at this precise point, is this exactly what you would want them to hear?

- Continue sculpting and polishing the phrase until there is no difference between your inner vision of the music (which includes freedom, balance and lack of effort) and your actual playing.

- Begin by practising every phrase or other small group of notes in this way. Later, perform larger passages over and over again in exactly the same way; then whole sections; then whole movements; then whole works.

Index *of music examples*

Movement 1, bar 111   213

Movement 1, bar 128   186

Movement 1, bar 134   253

Movement 1, bar 139   40

Movement 1, bar 174   67

Movement 1, bar 176   289

Movement 1, bar 209   123

Movement 1, bar 335   162

Movement 2 [Larghetto], bar 45   115

Movement 3 [Rondo], bar 75   34

Movement 3, bar 137   19

Movement 3, bar 139   215

Romanze in G, op. 40

[Andante], bar 20   161

bar 56   76

bar 68   87

bar 74   214

Romanze in F, op. 50

[Adagio cantabile], bar 1   135

bar 2   178

bar 4   127

bar 24   111

bar 28   22

bar 29   136

bar 58   282

bar 77   175

Sonata in D, op. 12 no. 1

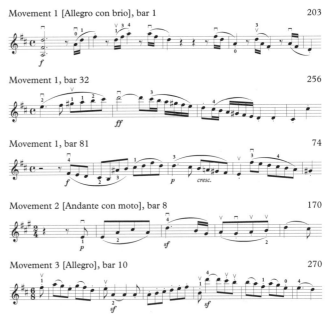

Movement 1 [Allegro con brio], bar 1   203

Movement 1, bar 32   256

Movement 1, bar 81   74

Movement 2 [Andante con moto], bar 8   170

Movement 3 [Allegro], bar 10   270

Sonata in E♭, op. 12 no. 3

Movement 1 [Allegro con spirito], bar 8   285

Movement 1, bar 18   196

Sonata in A minor, op. 23

Movement 1 [Presto], bar 84   248

Sonata in F, op. 24 ('Spring')

Movement 1 [Allegro], bar 1 — 202

Movement 1, bar 11 — 267

Movement 1, bar 33 — 134

Movement 1, bar 63 — 95

Movement 1, bar 106 — 231

Movement 3 [Allegro molto], bar 18 — 1

Sonata in A, op. 30 no. 1

Movement 1 [Allegro], bar 3 — 102

Movement 3 [Allegretto], bar 1 — 284

Movement 3, var. 2, bar 1 — 168

Movement 3, var. 6, bar 67 — 126

Sonata in C minor, op. 30 no. 2

Movement 1 [Allegro con brio], bar 9 — 212

Movement 1, bar 22 — 84

Movement 1, bar 55 — 34

Movement 1, bar 76 — 205

Movement 4 [Allegro], bar 18 — 158

Sonata in G, op. 30 no. 3

Movement 1 [Allegro assai], bar 1 — 93

Movement 1, bar 31 — 201

Sonata in A, op. 47 ('Kreutzer')

Movement 1 [Adagio sostenuto], bar 1 — 132

Movement 1 [Presto], bar 61 — 247

Movement 1, bar 314 — 102

Sonata in G, op. 96

Movement 1 [Allegro moderato], bar 2 — 239

Bériot, Charles Auguste de

Concerto no. 9 in A minor, op. 104

Movement 1 [Allegro maestoso], bar 38 — 284

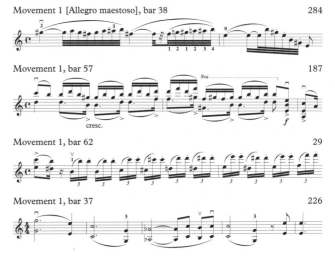

Movement 1, bar 57 — 187

Movement 1, bar 62 — 29

Movement 1, bar 37 — 226

Scène de Ballet, op. 100

[Tempo di Bolero] bar 70 — 4

bar 80 — 100

Bloch, Ernst

Nigun (no. 2 from 'Baal Shem')

[Adagio non troppo] bar 5 — 204

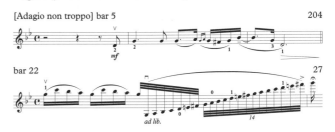

bar 22 — 27

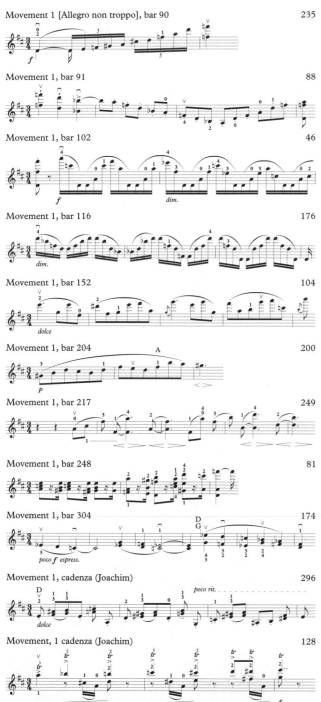

Movement 1, bar 24   75

Movement 2 [Adagio], bar 66   234

Movement 2, bar 105   244

Movement 3 [Allegro molto moderato], bar 1   86

Movement 3, bar 101   33

Sonata no. 2 in A, op. 100

Movement 1 [Allegro amabile], bar 3   61

Movement 1, bar 21   131

Movement 1, bar 31   64

Movement 1, bar 41   165

Movement 1, bar 43   118

Movement 1, bar 211   169

Movement 1, bar 235   204

Movement 1, bar 249   112

Movement 2 [Andante tranquillo], bar 8   287

Movement 2 [Vivace], bar 27   175

Movement 2, bar 56   288

Movement 2, bar 121   214

Movement 3 [Allegretto grazioso, quasi Andante], bar 5   164

Movement 3, bar 48   136

Sonata no. 3 in D minor, op. 108

Movement 1 [Allegro], bar 1   51

Movement 1, bar 57   157

Movement 1, bar 61   68

Movement 1, bar 81   200

Movement 1, bar 84   106

Movement 1, bar 120   122

Movement 1, bar 151   268

Movement 1, bar 162   264

Movement 2 [Adagio], bar 1   55

Movement 2, bar 50   133

Movement 3 [Un poco presto e con sentimento], bar 1   256

Movement 4 [Presto agitato], bar 9   28

Movement 4, bar 107   38

Movement 4, bar 297   115

Scherzo (Sonatensatz), WoO2

[Allegro] bar 1   53

bar 8   116

bar 14   95

bar 18   159

bar 28   74

Bruch, Max

Concerto no. 1 in G minor, op. 26

Movement 1 [Allegro moderato], bar 6   111

Movement 1, bar 10   3

Movement 1, bar 16   64

Movement 1, bar 18   285

Movement 1, bar 24   170

Movement 1, bar 34   79

Movement 1, bar 37   117

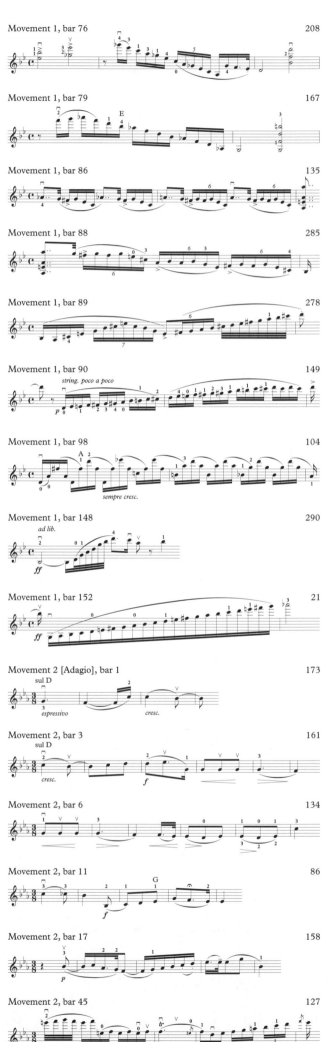

Movement 1, bar 76   208

Movement 1, bar 79   167

Movement 1, bar 86   135

Movement 1, bar 88   285

Movement 1, bar 89   278

Movement 1, bar 90   149

Movement 1, bar 98   104

Movement 1, bar 148   290

Movement 1, bar 152   21

Movement 2 [Adagio], bar 1   173

Movement 2, bar 3   161

Movement 2, bar 6   134

Movement 2, bar 11   86

Movement 2, bar 17   158

Movement 2, bar 45   127

Movement 2, bar 52   32

Movement 3 [Allegro energico], bar 19   223

Movement 3, bar 25   162

Movement 3, bar 27   27

Movement 3, bar 32   265

Movement 3, bar 40   219

Movement 3, bar 42   226

Movement 3, bar 44   260

Movement 3, bar 55   228

Movement 3, bar 94   257

Movement 3, bar 115   61

Movement 3, bar 189   85

Movement 3, bar 193   226

Movement 3, bar 237   51

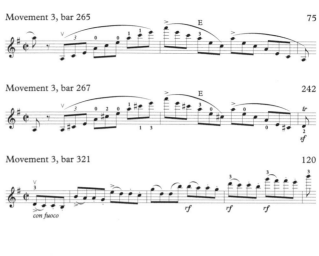

Movement 3, bar 265   75

Movement 3, bar 267   242

Movement 3, bar 321   120

Scottish Fantasy, op. 46

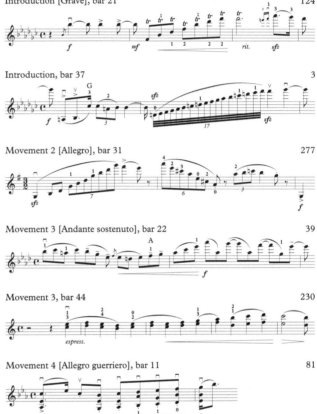

Introduction [Grave], bar 21   124

Introduction, bar 37   3

Movement 2 [Allegro], bar 31   277

Movement 3 [Andante sostenuto], bar 22   39

Movement 3, bar 44   230

Movement 4 [Allegro guerriero], bar 11   81

Chausson, Ernest

Poème, op. 25

bar 34 [Lento e misterioso]   181

bar 65   76

bar 69   266

bar 73   73

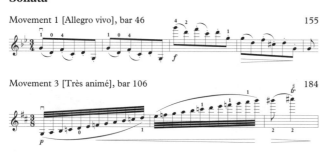

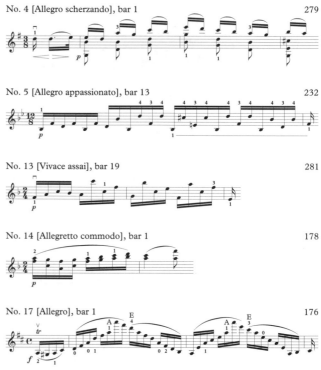

Elgar, Edward

Chanson de Matin

bar 9 [Allegretto]   172

bar 30   50

Sonata in E minor, op. 82

Movement 1 [Allegro], bar 1   107

Movement 1, bar 2   115

Movement 1, bar 9   66

Movement 1, bar 68   103

Movement 2 [Andante], bar 31   41

Movement 3 [Allegro, non troppo], bar 40   161

Falla, Manuel de

Danse espagnole (arr. Kreisler)

[Molto ritmico] bar 118   264

bar 163   93

Sonata in A, op. 13

Movement 3 [Allegro vivo], bar 4   10

Movement 4 [Allegro quasi presto], bar 47   165

Movement 4, bar 205   42

Fibich, Zdeněk

Poème

[Andante], bar 12   164

Franck, César

Sonata in A

Movement 1 [Allegretto ben moderato], bar 5   130

Movement 1, bar 28   283

Movement 1, bar 57   170

Movement 2 [Allegro], bar 14   174

Movement 2, bar 16   200

Movement 2, bar 20   214

Movement 2, bar 29   244

Movement 2, bar 32   64

Movement 2, bar 95   112

Movement 2, bar 99   214

Movement 2, bar 112   114

Movement 2, bar 134   173

Movement 2, bar 153   171

Movement 2, bar 172   62

Movement 2, bar 197   133

Movement 2, bar 225   72

Movement 3 [Ben moderato], bar 4   77

Movement 3, bar 48   184

Movement 3, bar 59   205

Movement 4 [Allegretto poco mosso], bar 2   211

Movement 4, bar 162   113

Glazunov, Alexander

Concerto in A minor, op. 82

bar 32 [Andante]   55

Granados, Enrique

Danse espagnole (arr. Kreisler)

bar 32 [Andante]   200

bar 48   163

bar 55   285

Grieg, Edvard

Sonata in C minor, op. 45

Movement 1 [Allegro molto e appassionata], bar 1   68

Movement 1, bar 254   183

Movement 3 [Allegro animato], bar 2   96

Movement 3, bar 192   149

Handel, George Frideric

Sonata in D, op. 1 no. 13

Movement 1 [Affettuoso], bar 1   282

Movement 2 [Allegro], bar 24   37

Movement 2, bar 30   8

Haydn, Joseph

Concerto no. 1 in C

Movement 1 [Allegro moderato], bar 40   223

Movement 1, bar 53   220

Movement 1, bar 70   117

Movement 1, bar 131   123

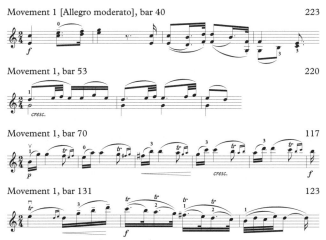

Concerto no. 2 in G

Movement 1 [Allegro moderato], bar 21   289

Movement 1, bar 31   87

Hubay, Jenö

Bolero, op. 51 no. 3

[Allegro molto], bar 49   31

Kayser, Heinrich Ernst

Etudes, op. 20

No. 1 [Allegro moderato], bar 3   247

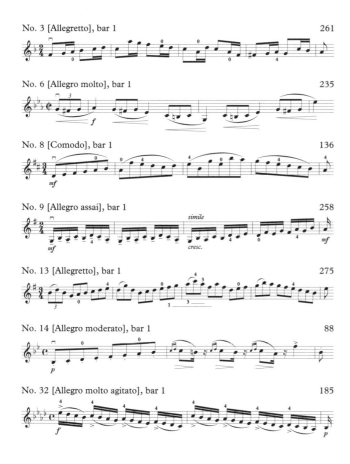

Kreisler, Fritz

Caprice Viennois, op. 2

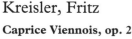

Praeludium and Allegro

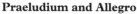

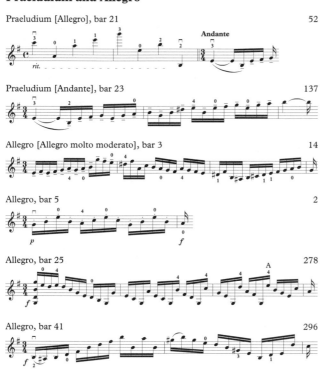

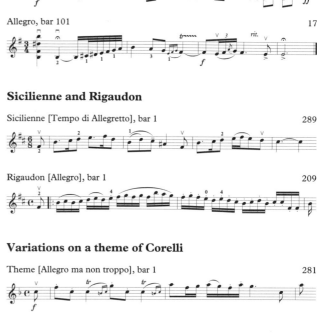

Sicilienne and Rigaudon

Variations on a theme of Corelli

Kreutzer, Rodolphe

42 Etudes ou caprices

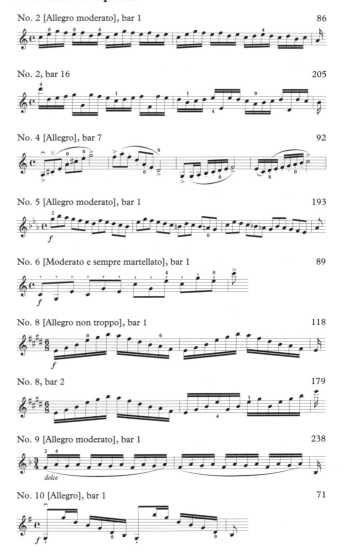

Lalo, Edouard

Symphonie espagnole, op. 21

Movement 3, [Allegro non troppo], bar 81   253

Massenet, Jules

Méditation from Thaïs

Mendelssohn, Felix

Concerto in E minor, op. 64

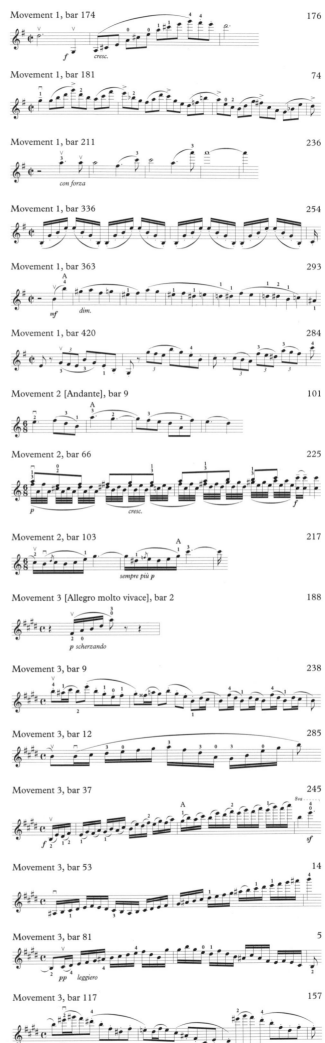

Movement 3, bar 168   98

pp leggiero

Messiaen, Olivier

Thème et variations

Variation 2 [Un peu moins modéré], bar 3   97

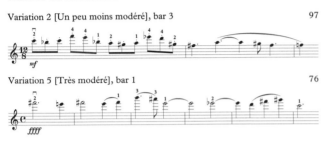

Variation 5 [Très modéré], bar 1   76

Moffat, Alfred

Intrada

bar 2 [Allegro]   101

Mozart, Wolfgang Amadeus

Adagio in E, K261

bar 10 [Adagio]   230

bar 17   112

bar 25   289

Concerto no. 2 in D, K211

Movement 1 [Allegro moderato], bar 22   49

Movement 1, bar 26   265

Movement 2 [Andante], bar 9   67

Concerto no. 3 in G, K216

Movement 1 [Allegro], bar 38   233

Movement 1, bar 51   169

Movement 1, bar 60   216

Movement 1, bar 64   96

Movement 1, bar 68   257

Movement 1, bar 78   196

Movement 1, bar 79   126

Movement 1, bar 86   288

Movement 1, bar 90   260

Movement 1, bar 106   14

Movement 1, bar 124   194

Movement 1, bar 209   127

Movement 1, cadenza (Sam Franko)   286

Movement 1, cadenza (Sam Franko)   82

Movement 1, cadenza (Sam Franko)   171

Movement 1, cadenza (Sam Franko)   125

Movement 2 [Adagio], bar 8   246

Movement 2, bar 9   203

Movement 3 [Allegro], bar 81   122

Movement 3, bar 141   296

Concerto no. 4 in D, K218

Movement 1 [Allegro], bar 42 — 220

Movement 1, bar 47 — 7

Movement 1, bar 49 — 159

Movement 1, bar 52 — 198

Movement 1, bar 53 — 180

Movement 1, bar 59 — 31

Movement 1, bar 68 — 62

Movement 1, bar 70 — 288

Movement 1, bar 71 — 215

Movement 1, bar 78 — 25

Movement 1, bar 86 — 283

Movement 1, bar 98 — 124

Movement 1, bar 104 — 65

Movement 1, bar 166 — 43

Movement 1, bar 173 — 281

Movement 1, cadenza (Joachim) — 202

Movement 1, cadenza (Joachim) — 295

Movement 1, cadenza (Joachim) — 63

Movement 3 [Andante grazioso], bar 1 — 94

Movement 3, bar 15 — 95

Movement 3, bar 23 — 238

Movement 3, bar 61 — 103

Concerto no. 5 in A, K219

Movement 1 [Adagio], bar 44 — 58

Movement 1 [Allegro], bar 46 — 55

Movement 1, bar 49 — 5

Movement 1, bar 50 — 184

Movement 1, bar 66 — 201

Movement 1, bar 74 — 177

Movement 1, bar 84 — 254

Movement 1, bar 108 — 26

Movement 1, bar 137 — 287

Movement 1, bar 213 — 276

Movement 2 [Adagio], bar 22   110

Movement 2, bar 41   239

Movement 2, bar 107   186

Movement 3 [Tempo di menuetto], bar 1   282

Movement 3, bar 16   102

Movement 3, bar 89   160

Movement 3, bar 134   119

Sonata in G, K301

Movement 1 [Allegro con spirito], bar 128   212

Sonata in E minor, K304

Movement 1 [Allegro], bar 1   35

Movement 1, bar 8   95

Movement 1, bar 103   87

Movement 1, bar 170   218

Movement 2 [Tempo di Menuetto], bar 101   53

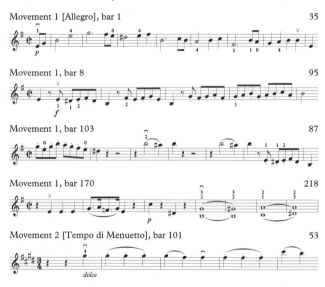

Sonata in F, K377

Movement 1 [Allegro], bar 1   261

Movement 1, bar 9   138

Sonata in B♭, K378

Movement 1 [Allegro moderato], bar 22   96

Sonata in B♭, K454

Movement 1 [Largo], bar 3   283

Movement 1 [Allegro], bar 19   238

Movement 1, bar 50   112

Movement 2 [Andante], bar 50   104

Movement 3 [Allegretto], bar 5   182

Paganini, Niccolò

24 Caprices, op. 1

No. 9 [Allegretto], bar 17   279

No. 9, bar 61   100

No. 17 [Andante], bar 9   62

No. 17, bar 18   149

No. 17, bar 24   222

No. 18 [Allegro], bar 17   220

No. 18, bar 26   162

No. 19 [Allegro assai], bar 25   163

No. 19, bar 27   199

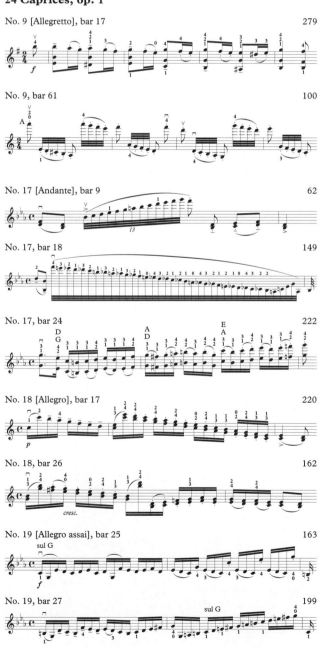

No. 24 [Quasi presto], var. 9, bar 9   140

Concerto no. 1 in D, op. 6

Movement 1 [Allegro maestoso], bar 111   174

Movement 1, bar 113   180

Movement 1, bar 130   239

Movement 1, bar 131   79

Movement 1, bar 158   224

Movement 1, bar 182   215

Movement 1, bar 233   190

Movement 1, bar 254   109

Movement 1, bar 265   249

Movement 1, bar 298   11

Movement 3 [Allegro spirituoso], bar 2   254

Movement 3, bar 67   201

Movement 3, bar 95   139

Movement 3, bar 146   203

La Campanella, op. 7

[Allegro grazioso] bar 10   99

bar 105   30

Moto perpetuo, op. 11

[Allegro vivace] bar 1   25

Prokofiev, Serge
Cinq Mélodies, op. 35

No. 2 [Lento, ma non troppo], bar 49   125

Concerto no. 2 in G minor, op. 63

Movement 1 [Allegro moderato], bar 1   196

Movement 1, bar 28   34

Movement 1, bar 52   294

Movement 1, bar 241   33

Movement 2 [Andante assai], bar 71   120

Sonata in D, op. 94 bis

Movement 1 [Moderato], bar 42   65

Movement 4 [Allegro con brio], bar 1   282

Raff, Joachim
Cavatina

bar 1 [Larghetto quasi andantino]   110

Ravel, Maurice

Tzigane

Rode, Pierre

24 Caprices

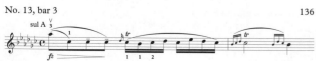

Concerto no. 7 in A minor, op. 9

Saint-Saëns, Camille

Concerto no. 3 in B minor, op. 61

Havanaise, op. 83

bar 49 [Allegretto lusinghíero]   174

bar 265 [Allegro non troppo]   190

Introduction and Rondo Capriccioso, op. 28

Introduction [Andante malinconico], bar 8   189

Rondo [Allegro ma non troppo], bar 11   157

Rondo, bar 69   206

Rondo, bar 152   134

Rondo, bar 197   190

Rondo, bar 304   84

Sarasate, Pablo de

Carmen Fantasy, op. 25

Introduction [Allegro moderato], bar 49   6

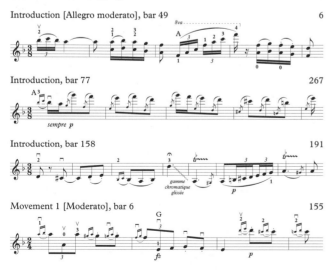

Introduction, bar 77   267

Introduction, bar 158   191

Movement 1 [Moderato], bar 6   155

Habanera, op. 21 no. 2

bar 1 [Allegretto]   158

Malaguena, op. 21 no. 2

bar 23 [Andantino]   181

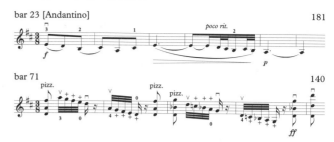

bar 71   140

Playera, op. 23 no. 1

bar 4 [Lento]   52

bar 20   154

Zapateado, op. 23 no. 2

bar 114 [Allegro]   91

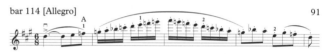

Zigeunerweisen, op. 20 no. 1

bar 2 [Moderato]   132

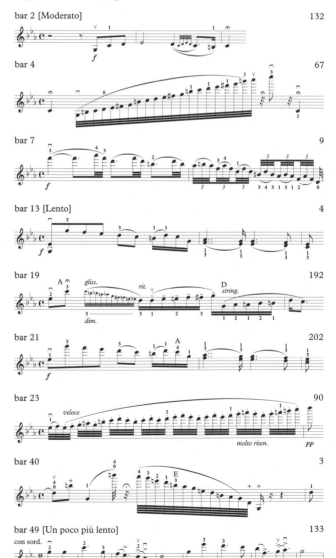

bar 4   67

bar 7   9

bar 13 [Lento]   4

bar 19   192

bar 21   202

bar 23   90

bar 40   3

bar 49 [Un poco più lento]   133

bar 72 [Allegro molto vivace]   24

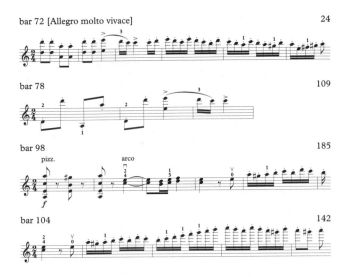

bar 78   109

bar 98   185

pizz.   arco

bar 104   142

Schubert, Franz

Sonata in A, op. posth. 162

Movement 1 [Allegro moderato], bar 5   165

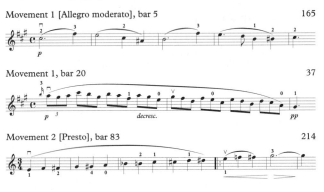

Movement 1, bar 20   37

Movement 2 [Presto], bar 83   214

Sonata in D, op. 137 no. 1

Movement 1 [Allegro molto], bar 16   280

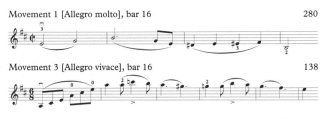

Movement 3 [Allegro vivace], bar 16   138

Sonata in A minor, op. 137 no. 2

Movement 1 [Allegro moderato], bar 15   263

Movement 1, bar 31   276

Movement 2 [Andante], bar 21   217

sul A

Movement 2, bar 25   167

Movement 3 [Allegro], bar 1   125

Movement 4 [Allegro], bar 1   286

Movement 4, bar 63   50

Sonata in G minor, op. 137 no. 3

Movement 1 [Allegro giusto], bar 1   287

Movement 4 [Allegro moderato], bar 57   233

Schumann, Robert

Sonata in A minor, op. 105

Movement 1 [Mit leidenschaftlichem Ausdruck], bar 1   131

sul G

Movement 2 [Allegretto], bar 8   4

Movement 3 [Lebhaft], bar 8   215

Movement 3, bar 62   259

Sibelius, Jean

Concerto in D minor, op. 47

Movement 1 [Allegro moderato], bar 8   156

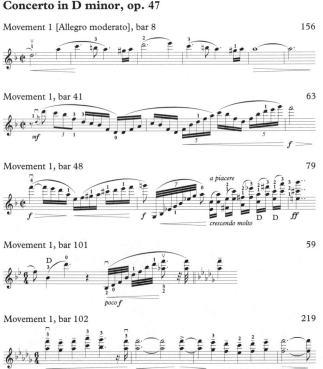

Movement 1, bar 41   63

Movement 1, bar 48   79

a piacere

Movement 1, bar 101   59

poco f

Movement 1, bar 102   219

espress.

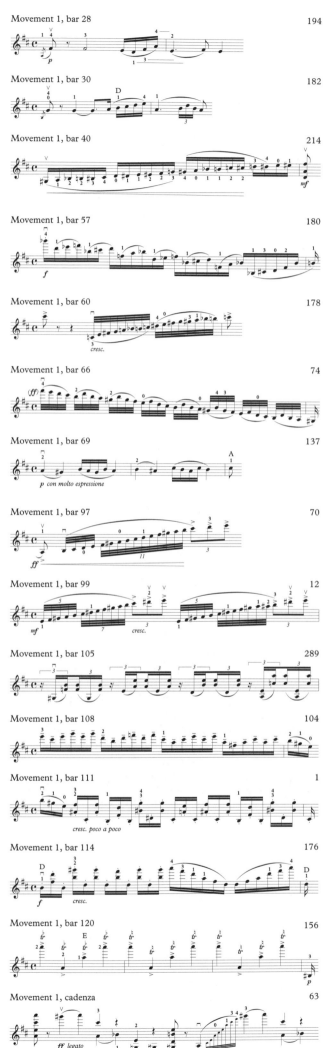

Movement 1, cadenza   85

Movement 1, cadenza   192

Movement 1, bar 250   186

Movement 3 [Allegro vivacissimo], bar 53   38

Movement 3, bar 114   20

Movement 3, bar 368   261

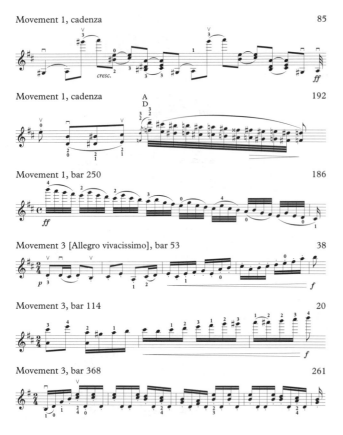

Sérénade mélancolique, op. 26

[Andante] bar 12   195

bar 42   206

Méditation, op. 42 no. 1

[Andante molto cantabile] bar 31   181

bar 40   242

bar 53   16

bar 77   59

bar 154   155

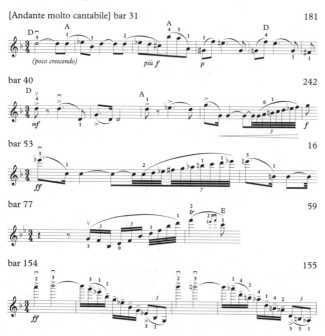

Scherzo, op. 42 no. 2

[Presto giocoso] bar 56   100

Melody, op. 42 no. 3

bar 1 [Moderato con moto]   135

bar 6   248

Vaughan Williams, Ralph

The Lark Ascending

bar 3 [Andante sostenuto]   46

bar 79 [Allegretto tranquillo]   280

bar 148   199

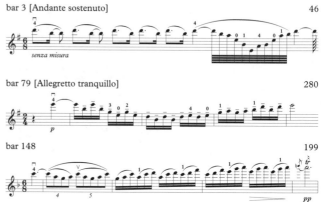

Vieuxtemps, Henri

Concerto no. 4 in D minor, op. 31

Movement 3 [Vivace], bar 1   215

Concerto no. 5 in A minor, op. 37

Movement 1 [Allegro non troppo], bar 68   187

Movement 1, bar 71   85

Movement 1, bar 87   59

Movement 1, bar 109   2

Movement 1, bar 111   26

Movement 1, bar 113   103

Viotti, Giovanni Battista

Concerto no. 22 in A minor

Concerto no. 23 in G

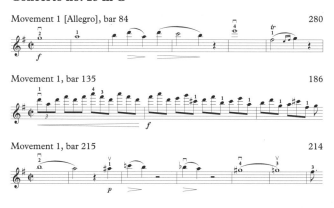

Vivaldi, Antonio

Concerto in A minor, op. 3 no. 6

Concerto in G minor, op. 12 no. 1

Spring (The Four Seasons), op. 8 no. 1

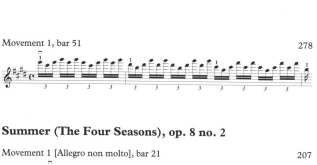

Summer (The Four Seasons), op. 8 no. 2

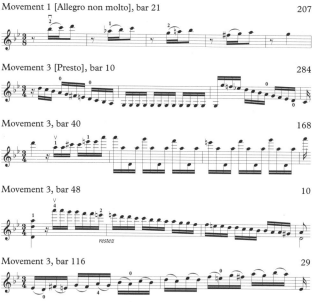

Autumn (The Four Seasons), op. 8 no. 3

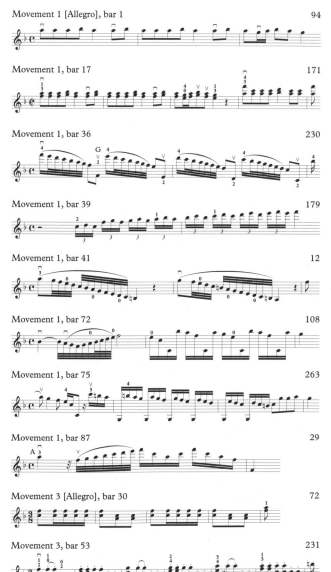

Movement 3, bar 86   286

Winter (The Four Seasons), op. 8 no. 4

Movement 1 [Allegro non molto], bar 26   24

Movement 1, bar 28   295

Movement 3 [Allegro], bar 12   199

Movement 3, bar 80   121

Movement 3, bar 120   99

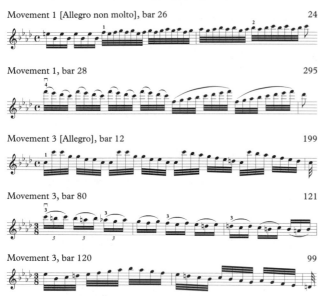

Wieniawski, Henryk

Concerto no. 2 in D minor, op. 22

Movement 1 [Allegro moderato], bar 68   131

Movement 1, bar 86   15

Movement 1, bar 88   189

Movement 1, bar 108   66

Movement 1, bar 115   33

Movement 1, bar 125   92

Movement 1, bar 127   187

Movement 1, bar 188   89

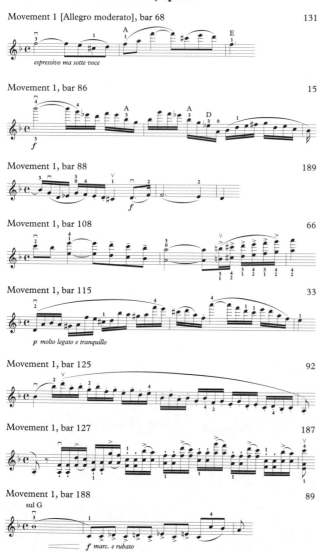

Movement 2, bar 207   192

Movement 2 [Andante non troppo], bar 1   55

Movement 2, bar 49   202

Movement 3 [Allegro con fuoco], bar 7   232

Movement 3 [Allegro moderato], bar 39   254

Movement 3, bar 55   178

Movement 3, bar 137   98

Légende, op. 17

bar 8 [Andante]   256

bar 25   281

bar 69 [Allegro moderato]   138

bar 144 [Moderato maestoso]   59

Polonaise brillante, op. 21

bar 21 [Allegro moderato]   13

bar 22   227

bar 23   90

bar 26   121

bar 43   226

bar 45   181

bar 66   245

bar 76   75

bar 110   208

bar 150   257

bar 155   9

Polonaise de Concert, op. 4

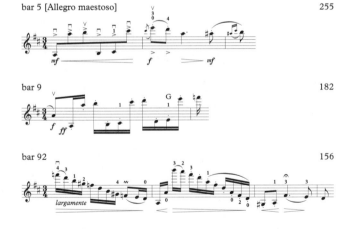

bar 5 [Allegro maestoso]   255

bar 9   182

bar 92   156

bar 104   222

Scherzo-Tarantelle, op. 16

bar 4 [Presto]   221

bar 12   25

bar 40   13

Wohlfahrt, Franz

Etude, op. 45 no. 34

bar 4   216

Ysaÿe, Eugène

Sonata, op. 27 no. 2

Movement 1 [Poco vivace], bar 3   118

Movement 1, bar 11   105

Movement 1, bar 39   249

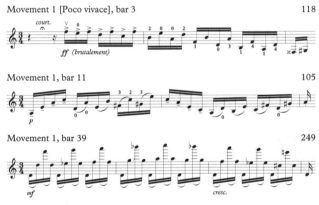

Sonata, op. 27 no. 4

Movement 1 [Lento maestoso] bar 1   53

General index

335